Also published in *The People's Bible* series:

Genesis

The Conquest of Canaan
The Books of Joshua and Judges

The Books of Samuel

Song of Songs
With the Books of Ruth, Lamentations, Ecclesiastes
and the Book of Esther

St. Luke & The Apostles
The Gospel of St. Luke and The Acts of the Apostles

The Genius of Paul
The Apostle's Letters

The People's Bible

Moses

Book 1 · Moses, Man of God
Exodus, Numbers and Deuteronomy

Book 2 · The Laws of Moses
Exodus, Leviticus, Numbers and Deuteronomy

newly translated and edited by
Sidney Brichto

Sinclair-Stevenson

First published in Great Britain by
Sinclair-Stevenson
3 South Terrace, London SW7 2TB

British Library Cataloguing in Publication Data
A CIP catalogue record for this book is available from The British Library.

ISBN 0 9540476 8 0

Typeset by Rowland Phototypesetting Ltd. Bury St Edmunds, Suffolk.
Printed and bound by Bookmarque Ltd. Croydon, Surrey.

Dedicated to
SILAS KRENDEL
a gentleman and a scholar

This series of new interpretative translations has been made in memory of my brother, Chanan Herbert Brichto. He loved the Bible with enormous passion not for its historical veracity but for its moral and literary genius. His seminal books Towards a Grammar of Biblical Poetics *and* The Names of God *will, I am convinced, in time revolutionize biblical scholarship. His respect, bordering on worship, of those geniuses who were the vehicles of the 'Still Small Voice of God', is what inspired me to make this attempt to give the Bible back to the people of great, little, or no faith.*

I want to thank Christopher Sinclair-Stevenson whose faith in this project has never wavered since it began. He has been the source of enormous encouragement to me when the task began to feel very heavy. I thank Rabbi Rachel Benjamin for her painstaking work in checking the draft of the double-volume against the original to make certain that in the process of editing nothing was omitted; also for her queries, which led me to rethink certain translations of mine. Her involvement has given me greater confidence in the final result; to Beverley Taylor, my devoted secretary for her continued support of my literary efforts; to Peter Bate for his labours beyond the call of duty in designing this book so that its contents can be more easily appreciated; finally to my wife and family for their patience in my obsessive interest in persuading more people that the Bible is not only for owning but also for reading.

SIDNEY BRICHTO

Preface

As explained in the preface to the previous books in this edition of the Bible, its 'objective was to recast it in such a manner as to make it readable'. No biblical books are in greater need of such treatment than those that are subsumed under the various titles: The Pentateuch[1], The Five Books of Moses, and the Torah.[2] The five books: *Genesis, Exodus, Leviticus, Numbers* and *Deuteronomy* – were according to rabbinic tradition dictated by God to Moses.

Genesis stands on its own as the epic description of the creation of the world and the history of the Hebrew Patriarchs, chosen by Yahweh to be the founders of his people. By my decision to move the irrelevant genealogies and other matter to the appendix and to make occasional interventions, *Genesis* is capable of being read continuously as one story.

This is far from the case with the other four books. *Exodus, Numbers,* and *Deuteronomy* tell and retell the story of the liberation of the household of Israel from Egypt until their arrival at the Jordan River to enter the Promised Land. On numerous occasions, however, the narrative is interrupted for no apparent reason, at least to the unscholarly modern reader, with blocks of chapters concerned with ritual, civil and criminal law in addition to building instructions for the paraphernalia of the sacrificial cult, and censuses of the tribes and their ancestral genealogies. If truth were told, it is in the traditional format an impossible read. Anyone undertaking it does so not as a labour of love but as an act of pious self-affliction. While *Leviticus*, with its description of the sacrificial cult and the rites for dealing with leprosy, wood rot, etc., is not compelling reading, at least it is a book which, with few exceptions, is a ritual and civil code.

Reshaping these four books into a double volume – ***Moses, Man***

---

[1] Greek for 'the five books,' the equivalent of *Humash*, meaning five in Hebrew, and used by Jews to describe the Pentateuch in its printed form, and not as the Torah, handwritten on a scroll of parchment.

[2] Hebrew: usually translated as the Law, but more recently as the Teaching.

of God, containing only the narratives and the orations of Moses, and *The Laws of Moses* containing all of God's instructions to his Prophet – has a double advantage. It gives the reader not only a continuous tale, without the need to turn pages to see where the narrative picks up again, but also all the biblical laws in one volume which can be cross-referenced and indexed. The latter can be owned as a reference book, readily accessible should a question arise, as it often does: "Is this a biblical law?" Also, to my knowledge, this is the first time it has been done in this way. I can only explain the lack of such a compendium of biblical laws until now because the biblical text was considered as sacrosanct and the laws as primitive and irrelevant. My Introduction to *The Laws of Moses* will show the latter reason to be without foundation.

The use of bold font in the text
Words and sentences in **bold font** are interventions from the translator to provide an interpretive interaction with the narrative to encourage the reader to do the same; also to provide continuity and explanations that would not have been required by those who heard or read these texts in antiquity.

Origins, meanings and names

THE ORIGINS OF THE FOUR BOOK TITLES

The Hebrew titles derive from a substantive word in the first sentence:
Sh'mot: 'These are the *Names* of the sons of Israel who went down to Egypt.'
Vayikra: 'The LORD *Summoned* Moses from the Tent of Meeting.'
Bamidbar: 'The LORD spoke to Moses in the *Wilderness* of Sinai.'
D'varim: 'These are the *Words* that Moses spoke to the Israelites:'

The English titles originate from the Septuagint, the earliest Greek translation, or the Vulgate, the Latin translation:
Exodus: from the Greek, *Departure* of the Israelites from Egypt.
Leviticus: from the Latin, the *Book of the Levites*. In Jewish tradition, this book was also called *The Laws of the Priests*, who are descendants of the tribe of Levi.
Numbers: based on the Septuagint's translation of another Jewish title for it, *The Book of Numberings* (of the Israelites).
Deuteronomy: from the Greek, *The Second Law*. In Jewish tradition, the book was also called *The Repetition of the Torah*, as Moses retells the story of the wanderings in the wilderness for the benefit of those who were too young to remember or had not yet been born at the time of the Exodus.

THE MEANING OF TORAH

The Hebrew word *torah* is rooted in the verb *ya-rah* meaning: to teach. The first five books of the Bible became known in Jewish tradition as the *Torah*, the teaching. When these books became known as *The Laws of Moses*, it became also known as the *Law*. This is not surprising as so many of the teachings take the form of laws and commandments that are the basis of Judaism. The tendency to refer to it as the *Law* was reinforced by the development of commentaries based on a tradition that God gave laws to Moses which he did not write down. These new laws, formulated over six hundred years, were ultimately collated in the *Talmud*, which was also known as the *Oral Law*; and the *Torah* was often referred to as the *Written Law*. In this translation, *Torah* is sometimes left un-translated and sometimes as teaching or law, as the translator felt appropriate to its meaning.

THE NAME OF GOD

The name of God as it appears in the Bible is YHVH (Hebrew script has no vowels). This is the ineffable name which was always read as Adonai, meaning 'my Lord'. The traditional translation of YHVH is therefore Lord. The Jerusalem Bible translation refers to God as Yahweh which most scholars believe was the pronunciation of the four consonants. I was tempted to follow this example, because the name makes God into a vital personality – the real hero of *Genesis*: creator, monitor and judge of humanity – rather than an abstract force. Cautious respect for tradition made me hold to 'the LORD', but I hope that the reader will remember that the LORD, the God of Israel, is portrayed as a personality revealing the full range of emotions; paternal justice, maternal compassion, love and reason, regret and anger, punishing and forgiving.

NAMES

Biblical narratives usually name individuals by their own name with those of their fathers linked by the Hebrew word *ben*, son of. In order to avoid constant repetition, the Hebrew ben has been retained except when the importance of the relationship between child and parent is significant in the context of the narrative.

List of contents

Book 1 · *Moses, Man of God*

Book 2 · *The Laws of Moses*

Although published together in one volume, MOSES, MAN OF GOD *and* THE LAWS OF MOSES *are two distinct and separate texts.*
As will be apparent from the list of contents above, these texts appear as two distinct books – each with its own separate sequence of page numbering.

1 Moses, Man of God

Introduction

The place of Moses in Jewish theology presents us with a paradox. He is the first prophet of Israel but also its greatest, because the concluding words of the Torah preclude the possibility of any greater human being ever walking on the face of the earth:

> No prophet has ever arisen in Israel like unto Moses
> Whom the LORD knew face to face,
> In all the wonders the LORD sent him to do
> In the land of Egypt to Pharaoh, to all his ministers
> And to all his country; for all the power of his hand
> And to the great dread that Moses wielded
> In the sight of all Israel.

It has never been properly appreciated that one important reason for St. Paul declaring the divinity of Jesus was that Scriptures had already dictated that no human could ever excel Moses. The paradox is that Moses, the liberator, the lawgiver, the prophet and priest is deemed unworthy to enter the Promised Land and is not mentioned once in the retelling of the Exodus in Jewish homes on the eve of Passover. The theological resolution of the paradox: As Moses is human, even in his perfection, he is imperfect; though acting as his most trusted agent, his splendour cannot put the LORD, the true Redeemer, into the shade. Tradition has it that the burial place of Moses is unknown so that it would not become a centre for worship.

A careful and unprejudiced reading of the narrative indicates that the man Moses has been so intoxicated by God that he begins to partake in his divinity. His face becomes so radiant that he must cover it to avoid blinding the Israelites. When Moses complains that he cannot alone bear the burden of leading Israel into its new historic destiny, God promises to send him a *malach Adonai*, a Messenger of the LORD. While he never appears to keep the promise, he does, because he gives Moses a portion of his own divine spirit and so transforms him into the 'angel' he failed to deliver; that is when his forehead emits the rays of light which Michaelangelo converts into horns in his majestic statue of the Lawgiver.

Unless one is a fundamentalist, it is hard to treat the description of Moses except as a literary and theological invention. The existence of a historical Moses is interesting but not relevant to the significance of his portrayal as the leading human player in the deliverance and creation of the nation of Israel. The essence of the faith, priorities and values of Judaism were all projected into the life of Moses. He is the Lawgiver because the essence of Judaism is the belief that the relationship to God is based on obedience to his commandments – the condition for the Israelites to enjoy God's love and protection. He is the Prophet because it is the role of the prophets to monitor Israel's morality, to exhort her to repent and to give warnings of the catastrophic consequences of disloyalty to the God who chose her to be his treasured people. In Jewish tradition Moses is known primarily as *Moshe rabbeinu*, Moses our teacher; it is because he explains the basic motives of the place of Commandment in the God-Israel partnership, that Jews to this very day believe that only through the study of the Law can God be understood.

This then is the substance of the Jewish faith, but what of the emotional relationship between Moses and God, which will become the pattern of how Jews will live with their God during their future victories and defeats. Their relationship is remarkably human, dynamic and confrontational. Indeed there are times in the story that one feels that it is Moses who is exhorting God to repent of his intentions and to understand their awful consequences, were they implemented. It is clear that God needs Moses for the accomplishment of his objectives as much as Moses needs God to achieve his own goals. Yahweh (the LORD) requires a people to make his own, and the enslaved tribes of Jacob require a deliverer to make them into a nation with a territorial home. It is Moses who makes the partnership happen and sustains it. The ditty: 'How odd of God to choose the Jews; not so odd – the Jews chose God,' reveals much of the truth, except that it was

Moses who must be credited with choosing both and putting them into each other's company.

Moses and God seem to be struggling together, pulling and pushing, sometimes together and sometimes in different directions to mould this slave people into 'a kingdom of priests, a holy nation.' When the Israelites by their impatience and ingratitude, bring both God and Moses to the end of their tether, like troubled parents, they turn on each other because with whom else can they safely vent their spleen! But as Israel, because of his promise to Abraham, is the chosen vessel to carry God into human history, Moses has no choice but to persevere until he brings her to the gates of the Promised Land.

Moses, as the paradigmatic prophet, must reveal all the prophetic qualities: the righteous indignation of an Amos, the tenderness of a Hosea and the lofty moral eloquence of a Jeremiah. He is described as the humblest man on all the earth. How can this be so when he is the most powerful of all men? How can this not be so when he constantly is in the presence of God? He is God's vessel and whatever strength and eloquence he possesses is that which God pours into him. The divine spirit may be like wine, which can be head-spinning and make the prophet in his anger become as terrifying as the god who sent him. But when the seizure is over, he is once again a man emptied of everything but the desire to serve his God and his people. Prophecy is a gift, which the prophet is reluctant to accept but cannot refuse because the very offer of it becomes like a fire burning in his belly.

But Moses is different. He is not even eloquent but no matter: as the LORD reassures him, he will be like God; Aaron, his brother, will be his prophetic spokesman. So long as the spirit of God is in him, what can he not achieve! One cannot help but feel as one turns the pages that it was Moses who invented the God of Israel so that he could find a vehicle for redeeming his enslaved brethren, rather than the other way around. To change the characters in a popular saying: Moses ran after God until God caught him. The first encounter of Moses and God is spectacular and lays the foundations of a tumultuous relationship in which

Moses moves from challenging God to advising and placating him.

*   *   *

There is no extra-biblical evidence that the entire nation of Israel was in Egypt; and the indications are, even in the book of Joshua, that the establishment of the tribes of Israel in Canaan was a long and tortuous process, and archaeologists are now casting doubts on whether even King David achieved the conquests attributed to him. This should not worry us, because it gives an even greater moral significance to the perceived origins of Judaism and Christianity. I remember a moving moment when I was discussing the story of Joseph in Egypt with my brother while he was fighting his last round with cancer. We spoke about the inconsistencies of Joseph's descent into Egypt. I asked him, "Why did they tell such an unbelievable tale?" He replied that it was important that the Israelites be enslaved in Egypt and the story of Joseph was the way of getting them there. When I then asked him why it was necessary for the Israelites to become slaves, he said, with a sadness that seemed to reflect his own personal hopeless situation, "Because God had to redeem them from slavery."

The significance of Israel's history is that her God is a redeeming god, who can cross all borders, who is not tied to space but reveals his power in time. While the Exodus is the tale of the deliverance from a house of bondage to a Promised Land flowing with milk and honey, its eternal message is that God is the source of freedom and human dignity. The passage: 'You shall be holy for I the LORD your God am holy' is not about spirituality. It is about human integrity based on the concept that every one of us is created in the image of God and the divine breath that gave life to Adam is still within all of us. Moses says to Pharaoh on God's behalf, "Send forth my people, so that they may serve me." The service of God is more than sacrifices. It is the obedience to a code whose objective, at least for those who chose him as their God, is the freedom of each individual to achieve security and prosperity.

When one reads the lofty oratory of Moses, it is difficult not to see the eloquence of Jeremiah, who, interestingly enough, began his prophetic mission in 622 BCE, the same year that the Scroll of the Covenant, (also called the Scroll of the Torah) was found in the Temple during the reign of King Josiah. Does this mean that the real Moses never said the words attributed to him? Yes. Does this mean that what follows is at worst a pack of lies or at best a pious fraud? No. If the eternal God put such moral exhortations into the mouth of Jeremiah, could this prophet not assume that he spoke the same words through Moses? Was Jeremiah seeking to give greater authority to his own convictions? What was wrong with that if these utterances were divinely inspired? If God's moral will does not change, why should not the message he grants his prophets be the same?

The realization that the Books of Moses were not historically true made their translation for me both intellectually and morally liberating. God need no longer be on the firing line for his injunctions to wipe out the enemies of his chosen people, or, for that matter, for his merciless punishment of the Israelites whenever they thwart his will. The stories need no longer be interpreted as battles between peoples but rather as the conflicts between human desires and values. We should be looking for meaning rather than factual veracity. Our questioning the reporting of events need no longer divert us from the exploration of the portrayal of human nature and the moral truths being revealed. Happenings are accidents over which we may have had little control while they were occurring and none once they occurred. Ideas, however, are totally under our control so long as we are autonomous beings. We can engage with the themes of the Exodus and be impressed by the drama without being distracted by any claims to historical reality.

Does this put the narratives of the Bible in the same class as the story of King Arthur and the knights of the Holy Grail? It doesn't, because these moral 'histories' became the religious basis of Western culture. Does reading the Bible as fiction then undermine the very foundations of Judeo-Christian civilization? It doesn't, because they have already had their impact. Does this approach threaten the faith of believers? Yes, but only the faith of those who are awaiting the fulfilment of those divine promises, especially that of eternal life. But I have no interest in demolishing the fundamentals of their faith. Reading it as a goldmine of literary and moral creativity and not as god-given truth enhances my own enjoyment of biblical literature and the edification I receive from its insights into human behaviour. Even fundamentalists should welcome the attempt to persuade the masses of the biblically ignorant to read it as a human text when they refuse to as a holy one, if only in the hope that the inspiration of its words will convince non-believers of its divine source.

*   *   *

The story of Israel's liberation by Moses is a tale of human redemption. Moses is God's midwife in forming a people who will bear his message. Only through serving him can humanity ever achieve fulfilment, peace and security. It is a quest for meaning in life. Ironically, while we are told that Moses spoke to God face to face, he pleads with him to reveal to him his glory, to which God replies that he can only show him his 'back'. If the attempt to understand the source and meaning of our being is not even given to the man closest to God, then it follows that the nature of the relationship to God is that of an eternal quest. God instructs Moses to tell the Israelites that 'I will be what I will be' is the name of the deity who has sent him to deliver them. If God is a dynamic and developing force, so are his human creatures. God's reaction to the cowardice and waywardness of Israel and the frustration of Moses indicates that God's future is intertwined with that of his chosen people. Having stepped out of human history after the great flood, he re-enters it by choosing Abraham and waits patiently until his descendants become a nation who cry out to him for salvation from the land of their captivity.

Because the character of the God of the West has been refined in the course of centuries, it came as a surprise to me in translating the Bible as literature to see how much he is like the Olympians in his human characteristics and emotions. Mount

Sinai is the Hebrew Olympus, where Moses ascends to receive the Tablets of the Law and to intercede on behalf of his erring people. It is abundantly apparent and, therefore, very surprising that our perception of God as being almighty has prevented us from realizing that God *cannot* act without the benefit of human agents. The people of Israel had been suffering long and hard before God listened to their pleas for help. If he did not respond sooner, it was because he had to wait for the man Moses to come on the scene. It is this interaction between the divine and the human, which can give us spiritual refreshment in an age when the relationship with God appears so one-sided and sterile. Then God becomes only the object of our prayers and praise but not a challenge to be engaged. The anthropomorphic faith of our ancestors provided the imagery for the cut and thrust of human engagement, which reveals the excitement in the encounters between god, Moses and the Israelites.

The story of Moses is a story but it is the most important ever told. It inspired the Judeans in Babylonian captivity to believe that, as their God had redeemed them from Egyptian bondage, he would redeem them again. This belief gave them the strength to maintain their identity as a people, and to return and rebuild Zion. It is significant that, without this faith in the power of divine redemption, Christianity would never have been born.

Index of subjects

Index of subjects

EXODUS

EXODUS

These are the names of the sons of Israel who entered
Egypt – every son with his family came with Jacob,
Reuben, Simeon, Levi and Judah,
Isaachar, Zebulun and Benjamin,
Dan, Napthtali, Gad and Asher.
All the lives that came out of Jacob's loins were seventy.
Joseph, **of course**, was already in Egypt.

Joseph died, all his brothers and all of that generation.
The people of Israel were fertile, increasing in numbers.
They became very powerful: the land was filled with them.

A new king reigned over Egypt,
Who had no regard for **what** Joseph did for Egypt.
He said to his counsellors:
"The people of Israel are becoming more numerous
And stronger than us. Let us be clever with them,
Lest they ever become more numerous.
If a war breaks out, they will join our foes to fight against us,
And leave the land **to unite with the invaders.**"

They set them under a levy of forced labour.
Taskmasters were placed over them
To break their backs with hard work.
They built store cities for Pharaoh – Pithom and Raamses.
But however hard they worked them,
The more they increased and populated a larger area.
The Egyptian horror at the sight of the Israelites grew.
So they increased their misery with hard labour,
Forcing them to make mortar and bricks and
To do all their labour on their farms,
Loading them with buckets of water to irrigate their fields –
Their purpose was to destroy them by oppression.

The king of Egypt instructed the Hebrew midwives,
Whose names were Shiphrah and Puah,
"When you deliver the child of a Hebrew woman,
And see that she is giving birth to a son – kill him;
But if it is a daughter – keep her alive."
The midwives, however, revered God.
They did not obey the command of the king of Egypt,
But allowed the boys to live.

The king of Egypt summoned the midwives,
"Why have you behaved so – to save the boys?"
The midwives replied to Pharaoh,
"The Hebrew women are not like the Egyptian women.
They are very active and deliver their sons
Before the midwives can reach their homes."
God rewarded the midwives.
The Israelites continued to increase in great numbers.
Because the midwives revered God,
He made their issue into great families.
Pharaoh then gave this order to all his people:
"Every Israelite son who is born – cast into the river,
But allow every daughter to live."

Because of this edict men and women did not lie together;
They feared having sons who would be killed.
In spite of this, a man of the family of Levi
Took to wife a woman who was also a Levite.
The name of the Levite was Amram
The name of the woman was Jochebed
She was the sister of Amram's father.[1]
The woman conceived and bore a son.
When she saw how beautiful he was
She hid him for three months.
When she could no longer keep his existence a secret,
She made for him a basket out of papyrus.

[1] This information is revealed in Exodus 6:20. See footnote on p. 17.

She strengthened it with mud and pitch.
In it, she placed the little boy in the bulrushes
On the river edge.
His sister waited at a distance
To see what would be his fate.

The Pharaoh's daughter was coming to bathe in the river.
Her ladies walked along the riverside **to find a good place.**
She, however, saw the basket in the bulrushes
And sent off one of her ladies to fetch it.
When she opened it, she saw the little boy –
He was crying. She had pity on him and reflected,
"He is one of the Hebrew children."
Seeing the Princess holding the child with such love,
His sister came near, bowed and asked Pharaoh's daughter,
"Would you like me to go and find for you a Hebrew nurse,
Who would breast-feed the child?"
Pharaoh's daughter agreed, "Go."
The girl went and fetched the child's mother.
Pharaoh's daughter instructed her,
"Take this young fellow and give suck to him for me.
I will pay your wages."
The woman took the child and nursed him.

When the child had grown, she brought him to
Pharaoh's daughter. He became a son to her.
She named him Moses because she said,
"I saved him out of the water."

Now, Moses knew that he was a Hebrew,
For the nature of his birth was not hidden from him.
In time, when Moses was an adult,
He went to visit his kinsmen and saw their oppression.
Once he saw an Egyptian beating a Hebrew kinsman.
He looked about **to see that there were no Egyptians.**
When he saw no one, he killed the Egyptian
And buried him in the sand.

The next day when he returned,
Instead of an Egyptian beating a Hebrew,
There were two Hebrews fighting each other.
He remonstrated with the bully,
"Why are you beating your brother?
Is it not sufficient to be beaten by the Egyptians?"
The man rebuffed him, "Who appointed you to be our
Leader and judge? Do you intend to kill me as
You killed the Egyptian?" Moses became anxious:
"The thing that I have done is known."

When word of these events came to Pharaoh,
He decided to have him killed.
He had indulged his daughter's love for Moses,
But now he had proved himself to be a Hebrew –
Not an Egyptian! Pharaoh's daughter warned Moses.
Moses fled from Pharaoh's presence
And lived in the land of Midian.
Once he was sitting down by a well.
The priest of Midian had seven daughters.
They would go there to draw water to fill
The troughs to water their father's flocks.
Shepherds always arrived and drove them away
Until they had watered their own herds.
But Moses stood up in their defence
And helped them; he watered their father's flocks.

When they returned to Reuel, their father, he asked,
"How did you do it so quickly today?" They replied,
"An Egyptian defended us against the shepherds.
Not only that, he drew all the water for us from the well,
And watered all the flocks." He criticised them,
"Why did you leave the man behind?
Bring him here and let him eat with us."
Moses was happy to live in the man's home.
In time, he gave his daughter Zipporah to Moses.

She bore him a son, whom she named Gershom,[1]
For he said, "I have been an alien in a foreign country."

After many years, the king of Egypt died. **The new king**
Did not know Moses, but oppressed the Hebrews even more.
The Israelites were moaning from their hard labour
They cried out and their cries reached God –
All because of their hard labour.
God recalled his covenant with Abraham, Isaac and Jacob.
God again took notice of the People of Israel
God decided to involve himself in their suffering.[2]
Now, Moses had not forgotten his kinsmen in Egypt.
He thought, "I have left the Pharaoh's court.
I was a prince and enjoyed everything:
The science of the wise priests and magicians;
The art of painters and sculptures;
The luscious fruits of Pharaoh's feasts;
The beauty of dancing women and music.
I gave this up because I suffered
The affliction of my brothers and sisters.
And now, what am I but a shepherd in Midian
When I should have been a shepherd to my kinsmen
To save them from slavery?
Where is the God of my ancestors of whom my mother spoke,
Who promised to bring them back to Canaan?
So did Moses wait for God to answer his question –
His prayer for the deliverance of his people.

"Here am I"

One day when Moses was shepherding the flock of
Jethro[3], his father-in-law, he led them beyond the wilds.
He approached the mountain of God – Horeb.

---

[1] Hebrew meaning: *stranger – there.*
[2] Literal translation of this line: God took knowledge of them.
[3] Previously called Reuel – a different account integrated into this narrative?

That is Sinai – where God would reveal his laws.
A Messenger of the L ORD appeared to him
In a flame of fire leaping out of the centre of the bush.
He saw the bush burning from within with fire,
But the bush was not burning down.

Moses said, "I will go closer to see this great sight,
To discover why the bush does not burn down."

When the L ORD saw that Moses had come to see it,
He[1] summoned him from the centre of the bush,
"Moses, Moses." He answered, "Here I am."
The L ORD said, "Do not come any closer,
Take the sandals from off your feet.
The place upon which you stand is holy ground.
I am the God of your father, the God of Abraham,
The God of Isaac and the God of Jacob.
[Moses turned away because he was afraid
To look at the face of God.]
"I have taken serious note of the oppression
Of my people who are in Egypt.
I have heard their outcries caused by their persecutors.
I have experienced their suffering.
Now I am coming down to save them
From the might of the Egyptians,
To bring them up from that land
To the good and spacious land –
A land flowing with milk and honey –
The place of the Canaanites, the Hittites, the Amorites,
The Perizzites, the Hivites and the Jebusites.
Now that the cries of the Israelites have touched me,
And I have seen how the Egyptians persecute them,
Now, go, for I am sending you to Pharaoh.
Take out from Egypt my people, the Israelites."
Moses replied to the supreme God,

[1] The Messenger of the L ORD becomes the L ORD himself.

8

"Who am I, to go to Pharaoh ·
To bring out the Israelites from Egypt?"
The LORD said, "**True**, but I will be with you.
This is the proof that I have sent you:
When you take out this people from Egypt,
You will serve the supreme God on this mountain."
– "See, when I come to the Israelites and tell them,
'The God of your ancestors sent me to you,'
They will question me, 'What is his name?'
What shall I tell them?"
– "EHYEH ASHER EHYEH, I will be what I will be.
This is what you will tell the Israelites,
'EHYEH has sent me to you'
This is what you will tell the Israelites,
'YHWH[1], the LORD the God of your ancestors,
The God of Abraham, the God of Isaac and
The God of Jacob sent me to you.'
This is my name for all eternity, and
This is how I am to be remembered
From generation to generation."

Go, assemble the elders of Israel and tell them,
'The LORD, the God of your ancestors appeared to me –
The God of Abraham, Isaac and Jacob saying,
"I have most certainly come down amongst you
To see what the Egyptians are doing to you.
I have decided that I will bring you up out of
The misery of Egypt to the land of the
Canaanites, the Hittites, the Amorites, the Perizzites,
The Hivites and the Jebusites to a land

[1] Hebrew has only consonants and the vowels were supplied by the intelligent reader. When, eventually, vowels were added in the form of dots and dashes, as God's personal name was ineffable, the four consonants were given the vowels of *Adonai*, a variant form of *Adon*, meaning master or lord to be read as such in the Hebrew, hence the translation of YHWH as the LORD. Some translators mistakenly connected the vowels of *Adonai* with YHWH and came up with Jehovah – the Hebrew "Y" being read in English as "J".

Flowing with milk and honey.'
They will listen to you – then you and the elders of Israel
Will go to the king of Egypt and say to him,
'The LORD, the God of the Hebrews has met with us.
Now, permit us to go for three days
Into the wilderness to offer sacrifices to the LORD our God.'
Now I know that the king of Egypt will not permit you
To go, and his refusal will be backed by great power.
So, I will send forth my power and
Strike Egypt with all my miracles which
I will perform in his country.
Then, after all this, he will send you off.
Not only this, I will make the Egyptians love
This people, so that they do not leave empty handed:
Every woman shall ask her neighbour,
And the woman in whose house she lives **as a servant**, for
Silver and gold jewellery and clothing. **They will agree.**
You shall put them on your sons and daughters;
So will you plunder the Egyptians."

– "But they will not believe me
Nor will they listen to me; they will deny it:
'The LORD has not appeared to you.'"
– "What is that in your hand?"
– "A staff."
– "Throw it on the ground."
[He threw it on the ground; it became a serpent
And Moses ran away from it.]
– "Put your hand out and grasp it by the tail."
[He put out his hand and took hold of it,
and it reverted to a staff in his hand.]
– "This is so that they believe that the LORD,
The God of their ancestors, the God of Abraham,
The God of Isaac and the God of Jacob has appeared to you.
Put now your hand on **the naked flesh of** your chest."
[He put his hand on his chest; when he removed it,

his hand was leprous – white as snow.]
"Put your hand on your chest again.
[He put his hand on his chest again;
When he removed it from his chest, it became normal.]
"So it will be, if they still do not believe you-
Unimpressed by the first proof,
They will believe because of the second proof.
And if they do not believe in either of the proofs,
And still refuse to listen to you,
You will take water out of the Nile and
Spill it on the dry ground. The water you have taken
From the Nile will turn to blood on dry land."
– "Please, my lord, I have never been a man of words,
Not before, nor even since you began to speak to your
     servant.
Because I am slow and hesitant in speaking."
– "Who gave man a mouth, makes one dumb, deaf, seeing,
     blind?
Is it not I, the LORD?
So go now, I will be with your mouth
I will teach you what to say!"
– "**I can no longer argue with you; I am not ready,**
But send whomever you decide to send."
The LORD was angry with Moses,
Because he was not confident of saving Israel.
He said to him, "What of Aaron your brother, the Levite?
I know that he speaks well; he is coming to meet you.
When he sees you, he will rejoice. You will speak to him.
You will put words into his mouth.
I will be with your mouth and with his mouth,
And will show you what you are to do.
He will speak for you to the people.
He will be your spokesman and you will be to him as God.
Take this rod in your hand, with which
You will perform all the proofs **of your mission.**"

Moses went back to his father-in-law, Jethro: "Please
Allow me to return to my kinsmen who are in Egypt
So that I will know whether they are still alive."
Jethro agreed to Moses's request, "Go in peace."
The LORD then said to Moses before he left Midian,
"You can now go and return to Egypt for the men
Who have sought your life have all died."
Moses took his sons[1] and had them ride on a donkey.
He set out for his return to Egypt
With the staff of God in his hand.

The LORD advised Moses, "When you return to Egypt
Make certain to perform all the magic I have shown you.
In spite of this display of magic, I will harden his heart;
He will not send the people away.
You will then tell Pharaoh, 'So says the LORD:
My son Israel is my **favourite and** first-born, and
I say unto you, send away my son to serve me.
Because you have refused to send him away,
I will kill your own first-born son.'"[2]

As he set off for Egypt, Moses lost faith in himself.
"How can I persuade Pharaoh to let Israel go
When Zipporah refuses to let Gershom be circumcised,
So that he enters into the covenant with God,
Which he made with Abraham?"
He pleaded with her, 'Now that we go to Egypt
To do the Lord's will – to deliver the
Israelites from their hard labour and oppression
Let me circumcise our son in the covenant of Abraham.'
– "I will not. I have agreed to go with you,
To take my son, to leave my father's house and my sisters
And go to a foreign land from which you fled,

[1] Strange as we are only told of the birth of one son – Gershom.
[2] God here informs Moses that he need not be discouraged at Pharaoh's constant refusal, in spite of all the plagues (to follow), to let the Israelites go. Only after the death of the Egyptians' first-born, will Pharaoh relent.

Where your kinsmen are slaves who rejected you.
Must I also shed the blood of my son?
I have done enough for your ancestral God.
I will not allow you to circumcise our son."
– "But if we do not, I cannot make Israel remember its
Covenant with God, if Gershom is not a Son of the Covenant!"
So Gershom was not circumcised.

The Lord was angry with Moses,
"I regret that I have chosen him to deliver Israel."
So the LORD struck him as he came to a lodging place.
He came near to killing him.
Moses fell into a deep sleep, as if to die.
Zipporah pleaded with him, "Please do not die.
I will circumcise your son, only live and be my husband."
So Zipporah took a flint, cut off the foreskin of her son.
She threw it by Moses's feet, so that he might live.
She said, "Now because of what I have done
To save your life, you are my bridegroom in blood."
So he, the LORD, allowed Moses to recover.
Then she thought, "The child is a bridegroom of blood
To the Lord because of his circumcision."[1]
From that time until now the circumcised child is
Known as the Bridegroom of the Covenant.

The LORD instructed Aaron, "Go towards the wilderness to meet
Your brother, Moses." He went and met him by the
Mountain of God, Horeb. He embraced and kissed him.
Moses explained to Aaron all that the LORD had said to him
When he sent him on his mission to Egypt;
Also the acts the LORD had instructed him to perform
To show that he had indeed sent him.
Moses and Aaron assembled the elders of the Israelites.

---

[1] My intervention was necessary to make sense of the story, to explain why
God, having sent Moses on a mission should suddenly decide to kill him.

Aaron told them all that the LORD had said to Moses.
He revealed all the proofs **that the Lord had shown him**
Before all the people. The people believed.
They heard that the LORD had taken note of the Israelites,
That he had seen their affliction.
They bowed and prostrated themselves in prayer.
After this, Moses and Aaron came to Pharaoh,
They said to him, "Thus says the LORD, the God of Israel:
'Send forth my people to observe a festival for me
In the wilderness.'" Pharaoh replied contemptuously,
"Who is the LORD that I should obey him,
To send off the Israelites!
I know not the LORD!
I will not send Israel forth."
– "The God of the Hebrews has appeared to us,
Please let us go on a journey of three days
In the wilderness to offer sacrifices to the LORD our God;
Otherwise he might strike us by plague or sword."
– "Moses and Aaron, why do you distract the people from
Their work? Get on with your own problems!
They are now more numerous than the Egyptian people;
You would have me allow them a respite from their work!"

That day Pharaoh instructed the people's taskmasters
And overseers, "No longer give the people straw
With which to make bricks. Let them go and
Gather the straw for themselves.
Furthermore, the same number of bricks they made before,
You must continue to demand of them.
You shall not accept any less, for they are shirkers.
That is why they have time to plead:
'Let us go and offer sacrifices to our God.'
Make the men work even harder.
Let them stick to their work, without time
To believe in false hopes **of redemption.**"
So the taskmasters and overseers instructed the people,

"This is Pharaoh's command, 'I will not give you straw.
You go, find straw wherever you can,
But no less will be demanded of you in
The number of bricks you must deliver."'

So the people scurried throughout all of Egypt
Gathering stubble for straw.
The taskmasters were insistent, "Meet your old quotas
Each and every day, as when you were given straw."
The Israelite overseers appointed by Pharaoh's taskmasters
Were beaten as they said,
"Why have you not met your quotas –
The bricks you should have made yesterday as well as today?"
The Israelite overseers cried out to Pharaoh,
"Why are you doing this to your servants?
Your servants receive no straw and
We are told, 'Make for us bricks.'
Then, we your servants are beaten,
But the blame belongs to your people."
– "Shirkers, you are shirkers,
Otherwise, you would not have the time to say,
'Allow us to go and offer sacrifices to the LORD.'
Now, get back to work.
You will receive no straw
But you will deliver your quota of bricks."
The Israelite overseers knew that they were making mischief,
When they said, "Do not reduce the daily quota of bricks."

They found Moses and Aaron waiting to meet them
As they were leaving Pharaoh's court. They said to them,
"Let the LORD look **at what** you **have done** and judge:
You have made Pharaoh and his ministers
Turn away from us as though we stank.
You have given them an excuse for killing us,
**For they say, 'If you had enough work to do,
You would not be talking of sacrificing to the Lord.'**"
Moses withdrew **on his own** to speak to the LORD,

"My lord, why have you been so wretched to this people?
Why have you sent me?
From the moment I went to Pharaoh
To speak in your name, he has treated the people even worse.
As for saving them, you have not saved your people."
– "Just wait and see what I will do to Pharaoh,
Because of my great power, he will send them away,
Because of my strength, he will expel them from his land."

"By my name YHWH I did not make myself known . . ."

God sought to reassure Moses. He said to him,
"I am Yahweh [The LORD]
I appeared to Abraham, Isaac and Jacob as El Shaddai
But my name, YHWH, I did not make known to them.[1]
All the same, I made my covenant with them
To give them the land of Canaan, the land where they lived.
Also, I heard the moaning and groaning of the Israelites
Whom the Egyptians are enslaving.
I then remembered my covenant **with the patriarchs.**
Therefore, reassure the Israelites,
'I am the LORD and I will release you from Egyptian bondage.
I will deliver you from your labours.
I will redeem you with an outstretched arm
And with great judgements **against the Egyptians.**

[1] This passage is as mysterious as it is significant. A name in biblical narrative reflects the qualities of one's nature or destiny. A change of personality is revealed by a change in name, e.g. Abram becomes Abraham and Jacob becomes Israel. What new characteristics is God revealing to Moses that he did not reveal to the patriarchs? Did Moses have a unique appreciation of the deity denied to his ancestors? If so, what was it? Or are we being told that the deity known as Yahweh was the same deity who was known as El Shaddai? The narrative in *Genesis* and *Exodus*, etc., fluctuates between referring to the deity as God; as the LORD [YHWH] and, often, the LORD God.

I will take you to be my people
And I will be your God.
You will then know that I am the LORD your God
Who released you from Egyptian bondage.
Not only this, but I will bring you to the land,
Which I raised my hand **in an oath** to give it
To Abraham, Isaac and Jacob,
To give it to you for **an eternal** inheritance." '

Moses spoke these words **of promise** to the Israelites,
But they did not listen to Moses –
So depressed were their spirits by their hard labour.
The LORD ordered Moses, "Go speak to Pharaoh, king of Egypt,
To make him send the Israelites out of his land."
– "But the Israelites are not listening to me,
Why should Pharaoh, as I cannot speak persuasively?"
The LORD, **however**, spoke both to Moses and Aaron, and
Commanded them what to say to the Israelites
And to Pharaoh, the king of Egypt to bring
The Israelites out of the land of Egypt.[1]

This is the same Aaron and Moses to whom the LORD said,
"Bring out the Israelites from the land of Egypt,
Troop by troop, **tribe by tribe and clan by clan.**
They shall leave Egypt like the Lord's army."
These are the very same who spoke to Pharaoh,
The king of Egypt, to bring out the Israelites
From Egypt – these are those very Moses and Aaron!

On that day when the LORD spoke to Moses in Egypt,
When he said to Moses, "I am the LORD,

---

[1] See Appendix 1 for 6:14–25 which now follows in the traditional text of the
genealogical table of the heads of the tribes of Reuben, Simeon and Levi,
Jacob's first three sons, and concludes with Aaron's family. 6:25 in the text
explains that this is the genealogy of the two heroes, Moses and Aaron. It
would appear that the purpose of the genealogical insert at this point is to
validate the historicity of these men as the descendants of Levi, the founders of
the priestly clan.

Speak to Pharaoh, king of Egypt
All that which I tell you." Moses protested,
"I cannot speak eloquently, why should Pharaoh listen to me?"
But the LORD said to Moses, "See,
I will make you as a god to Pharaoh,
And Aaron your brother will be your prophet.[1]
You will say all that I command you.
Through you, Aaron your brother will address Pharaoh,
So that he may send the Israelites out from his land."

"But I will harden the heart of Pharaoh
So that I have an excuse to increase
The proofs of my power and wonders in Egypt.
Still Pharaoh will not listen to you. Then
I will lay down my hand on Egypt; then will
I bring out my troops – my people, the Israelites
From Egypt with harsh judgements **against her.**
Then will Egypt know that I am the LORD
When I stretch out my hand against Egypt
To bring the Israelites out from her midst."
Moses and Aaron did just as the LORD had told them.
Moses was eighty years old, Aaron was eighty-three
When they spoke to Pharaoh.

The LORD instructed Moses and Aaron,
"When Pharaoh tells you, 'Show me a miracle of yours,'
You will instruct Aaron, 'Take your staff and throw it
Before Pharaoh' and it will turn into a serpent."
Moses and Aaron came to Pharaoh and did as
The LORD had said. Aaron threw his staff before Pharaoh
And before his ministers. It turned into a serpent.

---

[1] The Hebrew for prophet is Nah-vee, meaning speaker. The sense of its
meaning is God's spokesman or representative. The Hebrew prophets foretold
events on the basis of their knowledge of God's will and intentions. This
episode appears out of place here and may be an insert to give status to Aaron
as Moses's spokesman. Later in this narrative it is Aaron who is to turn the
staff into the serpent, and not Moses, as reported earlier (p. 10).

Exodus 7:11–21

Pharaoh then summoned his wise men and sorcerers.
The magicians of Egypt did likewise with their spells.
Every one of them threw down his staff.
They too became serpents but
Aaron's staff-**turned-serpent** swallowed up their staffs.
Pharaoh's heart however was stubborn.
He paid no heed to them as the LORD had foretold.

The LORD said to Moses, "Pharaoh is stubborn.
He refuses to send forth my people.
Go to Pharaoh in the morning,
As he comes out to view the Nile.
You will be standing by the river edge to meet him,
Take the staff, which turned into a serpent.
Say to him, 'The LORD, the God of the Hebrews
Has sent me to you, saying, "Send forth my people
To serve me in the wilderness."
As you have not yet agreed to this,
Thus says the LORD, 'By this you will know that I am the
  LORD.'
I, **Moses**, will strike the waters of the Nile
With the staff in my hand and they will turn into blood.
The fish in the river will die – the river will stink
And the Egyptians will not be able to drink from the Nile."

So it happened. Moses met Pharaoh by the Nile
And told him the words of the Lord, the God of Israel.
Then the LORD instructed Moses, "Tell Aaron, take your staff,
Stretch out your hand over the waters of Egypt –
Its rivers and canals, its ponds and pools of water
To turn them to blood. All of Egypt will be soaked in blood –
Covering all its vessels of wood and stone."'

Moses and Aaron did so, just as the LORD had ordered.
He raised his staff, struck the river waters before Pharaoh
And his ministers, and all the river waters were transformed
Into blood. The fish in the river died, the river reeked **with the**

Dead fish and the Egyptians could not drink from the rivers.
All of Egypt was saturated with blood.
To prove that Aaron was practising magic,
The Egyptian magicians did the same with their
Own spells **on water from the wells.**

So Pharaoh hardened his heart and did not listen to them
Just as the LORD had foretold.
Pharaoh turned away, returned to his palace
And did not give these events any further thought.
But all the Egyptians dug near the river for drinking water
Because they could not drink from the Nile.
Seven days passed from the time that the LORD struck the Nile,
And the blood became water again.

The LORD spoke to Moses, "Go unto Pharaoh, say to him,
'Thus commands the LORD, "Send forth my people,
So that they may worship me.
If you refuse to send them out
I will smite the land within your borders with frogs.
The Nile will swarm with frogs, which will leave it
To go into your palace, into your bedroom,
Into your very bed, into the homes of your Ministers
And of all your people, even into your ovens and vessels.
The frogs will ascend both against you and your people
And against all your Ministers."'
But Pharaoh took no notice of the Lord or of
The words of Moses and Aaron, his servants.

So the LORD told Moses, "Command Aaron, 'Stretch forth
The staff in your hand over the rivers of Egypt
Over their canals and pools of water.
Cause frogs to come up and cover Egypt.'"
Aaron did so and the frogs came up and
Covered the land of Egypt.
But the magicians did the same with their spells –
They too brought **a plague of** frogs over Egypt.

Exodus 8:4–14

Pharaoh was angry with his magicians,
"I do not need your magic to give me more frogs,
But to magic away the frogs brought by Moses and Aaron."
But they could not remove the frogs.

Pharaoh summoned Moses and Aaron, "Entreat the LORD,
That he take away the frogs from me and my people,
And I will send away your people,
To offer sacrifices to the LORD."
Moses replied to Pharaoh, "I will pay you this tribute:
Tell me the time when you wish your entreaty –
For the frogs to be cut off from you, your Ministers,
Your people and your homes – to be answered,
So that they remain only in the river."
He said, "Let it happen tomorrow."
Moses replied, "It will be as you say,
So you may know that none is like the LORD our God.
The frogs will leave you and your houses
And the houses of your Ministers and people.
They shall be found only in the river beds."

Moses and Aaron went out from Pharaoh's presence, and
Moses prayed to the LORD about the frogs
With which he had plagued Pharaoh.
The LORD did as Moses had entreated him.
The frogs in the houses, the courtyards and fields died.
They collected them into heaps and the land stank from them.
But when Pharaoh saw that there was relief **from the frogs**
He again became stubborn and did not listen to them,
Just as the LORD had foretold.
The LORD ordered Moses, "Tell Aaron, 'Stretch out your staff.
Strike the dust of the earth, so that fleas cover all Egypt.'"
They did this. Aaron stretched out the staff in his hand,
Struck the ground and the fleas infected man and beast,
As though every particle of dust became a flea
Throughout all the land of Egypt.
The magicians tried to do the same with their spells

21

To make fleas to swarm but they could not.
The fleas infected every man and beast.
Then did the magicians admit to Pharaoh,
"This is the finger of God, **send them away.**"
But Pharaoh's heart was stubborn.
He did not listen to them as the LORD had foretold.

The LORD instructed Moses, "Get up early in the morning
And stand in the way of Pharaoh as he goes to the river.
Say to him, 'Thus says the LORD: send forth my people
So that they may worship me, because if you do not
Send my people forth, I will send you and
Your Ministers and your people beetles[1]
Which will fill the houses of Egypt as well as
The ground from which they come.
But I will distinguish on that day between Goshen,
The land in which my people are settled, **and your land.**
They will suffer no beetles, so that you realise that
I, the LORD, am a power in your country.
My people will I save **from this plague** but not yours.
Tomorrow will this sign **of my power** happen."'

Moses did as the Lord said, but Pharaoh did not listen.
So the LORD did it. A great infestation of beetles
Struck Pharaoh's palace and the houses of his Ministers –
The whole of Egypt was consumed by hosts of beetles.
Pharaoh summoned Moses and Aaron. He said,
"Go make sacrifices to your God in this land."
But Moses refused, "It would not be proper to do so.
It would be offensive to the Egyptians for us
To sacrifice to the LORD our God animals
Which are sacred to Egyptians. If we offended the

---

[1] Hebrew is *ha-arob* from a root, meaning 'to mix'. Scholars differ on the nature of this plague. The medieval Jewish commentator, Rashi, explained it as a 'mixture of noxious animals.' I opted for beetles, which is the rendition of others. There may be some irony in the fact that the beetle or scarab was sacred and regarded as the emblem of the Sun-god.

Exodus 8:23–9:4

Egyptians by offering sacrifices before them –
Will they not stone us? Rather will we make a
Three-day journey into the wilderness.
There we will sacrifice to the LORD our God
As he will command us."

"Send forth my people so that they may worship me"

Pharaoh said, "I will send you forth.
Offer sacrifices to the LORD your God in the wilderness.
Be sure not to go too far away. Now plead on my behalf."
Moses replied, "See, I leave you now. I will entreat the LORD.
He will remove the beetles from Pharaoh, his Ministers
And his people tomorrow.
But let not Pharaoh be deceitful again,
By not sending forth the people to sacrifice to the LORD."
Moses left Pharaoh and entreated the LORD.
The LORD did as Moses had asked.
He removed the beetles from Pharaoh, his Ministers and
    people.
There did not remain even one of them.
Pharaoh, however, hardened his heart even this time.
He did not send the people away.

The LORD said to Moses, "Go to Pharaoh and tell him,
'Thus says the LORD, the God of the Hebrews.
Send forth my people so that they may worship me.
But if you refuse to send them forth
And persist in holding on to them,
The hand of the LORD will smite your livestock in the field,
The horses, donkeys, camels, herds and flocks,
With deadly pestilence.
But the LORD will distinguish between the livestock of Israel
And between the livestock of Egypt.
Not one will die from all that belongs to the Israelites.

The LORD has appointed a time for this –
Tomorrow will the LORD do this in the land."'

Moses went to Pharaoh but he did not listen to him.
The next day the LORD did this: Egyptian livestock died.
But of the Israelite livestock not one died.
Pharaoh sent messengers to see – of all
The Israelite livestock not one had died.
But Pharaoh's heart was hard and he did not let the people go.

The LORD then said to Moses and Aaron, "Fill your hands
   with soot
From the furnace and let Moses toss it to the heavens
In the presence of Pharaoh and it will become a dust storm
Over Egypt, causing an inflammation of boils on
Man and beast throughout the land of Egypt."
They took soot from the furnace and stood before Pharaoh.
Moses tossed the soot to the sky and it caused an
Inflammation of boils in man and beast.
The magicians were not able to stand up to Moses
Because of the boils which had afflicted
The magicians as well as all the Egyptians.
But the LORD strengthened the will of Pharaoh.
He did not listen to them as the LORD had foretold to Moses.[1]

The LORD said to Moses, "Get up early in the morning,
Stand before Pharaoh. Say to him, 'Thus says the LORD of
The Hebrews: Send forth my people to worship me!
Because this time I will send all my plagues against you,
Your Ministers and your people so that you will know –
There is none like me on all the earth.
By now I could have stretched forth my hand and smitten
You and your people with a pestilence that
Would have wiped you off the face of the earth.
But for this very reason I have allowed you to survive –

---

[1] The LORD wants the opportunity to display his full bag of tricks.

To show off my power so that the story of
My fame will spread throughout all the earth.'

"Since you make yourself into an obstacle against my people –
Not to send them forth, tomorrow at about this time
I will cause a severe hailstorm to fall,
The like of which has not been seen in Egypt
From the day it was established until now.
Now, therefore, hurry and fetch in your livestock
And whatever you have in your fields.
All man and beast found outside and not brought home,
The hail will pound down on them and they will die."
Pharaoh's Ministers who respected the Lord's word
Had their servants and livestock taken indoors.
Those that had no regard for the word of the Lord
Allowed their servants and livestock to remain outdoors.

The Lord ordered Moses. "Stretch out your hand towards the
    heavens
So that hail may overwhelm Egypt, man and beast –
On all vegetation throughout the land of Egypt."
Moses pointed his staff towards the heavens.
The Lord sent thunder and hail and lightning struck the
    earth.
So did the Lord cause hail to rain down upon Egypt.
So there was hail and fire caused by the lightning-
Hail of such severity that had not been in
The land of Egypt from the time it became a nation.
The hail struck the whole of Egypt – all that was outdoors
From man to beast and all vegetation. It broke every tree.
Only in the district of Goshen, the Israelite settlement,
Was there no hail.

Pharaoh sent to summon Moses and Aaron. He said to them,
"This time I have sinned. The Lord is righteous.
I and my people are the wicked ones. Entreat the Lord.
There has been enough of these divine blasts of hail.

I will send you away. You need stay no longer."
Moses said to him, "When I leave the city
And stretch out my hands to the LORD,
The thunder will cease, there will be no more hail
So that you may know that the earth belongs to the LORD.
Though I do this, I know that as for you and your Ministers
You still do not respect the LORD."

Now, the flax and barley, **Egypt's two mainstays,** were ruined,
For the barley was still in ear and the flax in bloom.
But the wheat and spelt were not ruined
Because they had not yet ripened.
Moses left Pharaoh and the city.
He stretched out the palms of his hands towards the LORD.
The thunder and hail ceased.
The rains stopped pouring over the land.
But when Pharaoh saw that the rains, the hailstorms
And thunder had stopped, he sinned again.
He hardened his heart – he and his Ministers.
He did not send out the Israelites
Just as the LORD had foretold to Moses.

The LORD instructed Moses, "Go to Pharaoh.
I have hardened his heart and the heart of his Ministers
So that I have reason to display my wonders amongst them.
Also, so that you can retell them to your child and grandchild:
How I performed against Egypt – the wonders I did there,
That you **and your descendants** should know that I am the
    LORD."
Moses and Aaron went to Pharaoh and said to him,
"This is what the LORD, the God of the Hebrews, says:
'Until when will you refuse to submit to me?
Send forth my people so that they may worship me.
Now, if you persist and do not send out my people,
Tomorrow will I set locusts within your borders.
They will cover the face of the land so as not to see it.
They shall consume the residue which has survived

The hailstorm. They shall consume every tree in the field.
Your houses and those of your Ministers and all the Egyptians
Will be filled with them, as neither your fathers nor
  grandfathers
Have ever seen, since the day that they were
Placed upon this earth until this very day."'

After saying this, he turned and left Pharaoh.
Pharaoh's Ministers said, "Until when will this man
Be a nuisance to us? Send off these men
To serve the LORD their God.
Are you not aware that until then Egypt is a lost cause?"
So Moses and Aaron were again summoned to Pharaoh.
He said to them, "Go, serve the LORD your God.
Tell me, who of you will be going?"
Moses replied, "With our young and old will we go,
With our sons and daughters, with our flocks and herds
We will go to observe the festival of the LORD."
He replied, "The LORD be with you **if you think** that
I will send you out with your little ones.
For I see evil intentions on your faces.
If I let you all go, you will never return.
Not so. Let only the menfolk go to worship the LORD,
For that is what **you say** you want."
But Moses and Aaron refused, "No, all of us will go
Or none of us. You must decide, Pharaoh."
They were expelled from the presence of Pharaoh.

The LORD instructed Moses, "Stretch out your hand against
  Egypt
To bring the locusts into the land of Egypt.
They will consume all the vegetation of the earth,
Everything which survived the hail storm.
Moses stretched out his staff over the land of Egypt.
The LORD hurled an east wind across the land
All that day and all that night.
When morning came the east wind brought in the locusts.

The locusts invaded all of Egypt.
They settled in all of the territories of Egypt.
The swarms were so dense –
Never had there been so many locusts as then,
Nor would there ever be again.

They covered every surface of the land –
Darkened by them **as if covered by a black carpet.**
They consumed every bit of vegetation,
All the fruit trees which had survived the hail.
Not a green thing, neither tree nor grass
Remained in the entire land of Egypt.
Pharaoh hastened to summon Moses and Aaron.
He said, "I have sinned against the LORD your God
And against you. Please, forgive my sin this one time;
Entreat the LORD your God that he remove this death from me."
Moses left Pharaoh and entreated the LORD.
The LORD altered the wind into a powerful west wind
Which lifted the locusts and cast them into the Red Sea.
Not one locust remained in the whole territory of Egypt.
But the LORD hardened Pharaoh's heart
And he did not allow the Israelites to go.

The LORD instructed Moses, "Raise your hand to the heavens
So that darkness may descend upon Egypt –
A darkness which can be felt."
Moses raised his hand to the heavens.
A fog descended and the darkness was thick
Throughout all of Egypt for three days.
They could not see one another
Nor move from where they were for three days.
But for all the Israelites – they had light in their homes.
Pharaoh summoned Moses, "Go, worship the LORD,
Only leave your flocks and herds behind.
Your little ones can also go with you."
Moses replied, "You must also allow us to take with us
Animals for sacrifices and burnt offerings

To prepare for the LORD our God.
Our cattle will also go with us – not a hoof shall remain!
For we must take them to worship the LORD our God.
We cannot know with what we must worship the LORD
Until we reach the place."[1]

The LORD hardened Pharaoh's heart.
He did not agree to send them off.
Pharaoh said to him, "Get out from my presence!
You lie to me. Once you leave, you will not return to Egypt.
Take heed for your safety.
You will not see my face anymore
Because on the day you see me again
You are dead."
Moses retorted, "You have spoken the truth
I will never again see your face."
[The LORD had told Moses, "One more plague will I bring upon
    Pharaoh
And on Egypt. After it, he will send you out from this **place.**
He will cast you out; he will drive you out of here.
Speak now to the people, instructing them, every man, to ask
Of his neighbour, and every woman of her neighbour,
Articles of silver and articles of gold."
The LORD made the Egyptians look favourably upon the people.
Also the man Moses was very great in the eyes of
Pharaoh's Ministers and in the eyes of the people.]

Moses said to Pharaoh, "Thus says the LORD:
'At the strike of midnight I will go out into Egypt
And every firstborn in the land of Egypt will die,
From the firstborn of Pharaoh who sits on the throne
To the firstborn of the maid servant who turns the mill,

---

[1] Why Moses, according to the narrative, is not prepared to admit that the
Israelites have no intention of returning to Egypt is strange. It does, however,
increase the dramatic interplay because Pharaoh is justified in his suspicions of
Moses's sincerity.

And the firstborn of all the cattle.
There shall be a great outcry throughout all Egypt
Such as has never been nor ever will be![1]
But a dog will be afraid to bark
Against the Israelites, either against a man or his beast.
So that you may know how God has distinguished between
The Egyptians and the Israelites.
All these, your Ministers, will come down to me
And bow themselves down before me, saying,
"Get out, you and all the people who follow you." '
After this, I will go."
He left Pharaoh fuming with anger.
The LORD told Moses, "Pharaoh will not listen to you,
So that my wonders can increase in the land of Egypt."
So did Moses and Aaron do all these wonders before Pharaoh:
   Turning the water to blood
   Frogs
   Fleas
   Beetles
   The wasting of the cattle
   Boils
   Hail
   Locusts
   Darkness
   Deaths of the first-born.
The LORD, **however**, hardened Pharaoh's heart
He did not send the Israelites out of his land
Until the deaths of all the first-born in Egypt.
The LORD said to Moses and Aaron, in the land of Egypt,
"This month shall be the first of all months for you –
The first month of the year for you **and all Israel.**

---

[1] This last plague is brutally indiscriminate, indicating the moral acceptance of collective punishment which takes a deadly toll among the innocent – the very thing that Abraham protested against when he tried to save Sodom and Gomorrah. The story of the Ten Plagues is meant to demonstrate God's power to save his chosen people, rather than the morality of his methods.

Exodus 12:3–11

Instruct the entire community of Israel:
On the tenth day of this month each man shall take
A lamb for his family – one lamb per household.
If a family is too small to consume the lamb,
Then he and his closest neighbour shall take a smaller one.
By the needs of each person you will decide, and
According to the number of participants, the size of the lamb.

The lamb[1] you choose should have no blemish –
A one-year old male either from your sheep or goats.
You will keep it until the fourteenth day of this month
When all the groups of the community of Israel
Will slaughter it at dusk.

You will take some of its blood and smear it on
The doorposts and on the beam of the doorway
Of the houses in which you eat the lamb.
They shall eat its meat, **that night** roasted by fire,
That night with unleavened bread and
Bitter herbs – they shall eat it.
Eat not any part which is raw
Or boiled with water – only entirely roasted by fire –
Its head with its legs and innards.
You shall not let any of it remain until morning.
Whatever remains you shall burn with fire before the morning.

This is how you shall eat it –
With your robes belted up, your sandals on your feet
And your staffs in your hands.
You shall eat quickly –
It is the Paschal offering[2] to the LORD.

---

[1] The Hebrew *seh*, translated as lamb was a generic term for young kids as well.
[2] The origin of the Paschal lamb is shrouded in mystery. Was it the primitive sacrifice of a lamb to celebrate the beginning of Spring? Whatever its origin, it became identified with Israel's first salvation from Egyptian bondage and God's redemption of the first-born of the Israelites. As a consequence of 'the last supper,' it became identified with Jesus as God's sacrifice of his own son to achieve the redemption not only of the Israelites but of all humanity.

I will go through the land of Egypt on that night
And strike every first-born in the land of Egypt –
From humankind to beasts.
Against all the gods of Egypt
Will I execute my judgements.
I am the LORD!
The blood **you smeared on the doorposts** will be your sign
On the houses in which you are dwelling.
I will see the blood and leap over **your houses.**
The plague will not destroy your **first-born**
When I strike out at the land of Egypt."[1]

Moses summoned the elders of Israel and instructed them
"**Go to the sheep folds** and draw out lambs for every family.
Slaughter the Paschal lamb; take bunches of hyssop
And dip them into the blood in the basin and
Brush them on the door-beam and the two doorposts.
None of you must leave his house before morning.
The LORD will cross through to strike Egypt.
When he sees the blood on the door beam and doorposts,
The LORD will leap over the doorway and not permit
The Destroyer[2] to enter your homes to plague you."
When Moses told the elders that God would deliver them,
The people bowed down and worshipped **the Lord.**
So the Israelites set off and did as the LORD had
Commanded Moses and Aaron, exactly as they were told.

At midnight, the LORD struck down all the first-born
In the land of Egypt – from the first-born of Pharaoh
Sitting on his throne to the first-born of the prisoners
Living in the dungeon and the first-born of every beast.

---

[1] Further instructions regarding the celebration of the Passover, *Exodus* 14:20; 24–27, are to be found in the *Laws of Moses*, page 1.
[2] Who is the Destroyer? The 'Angel of death' or a manifestation of the godhead?

Pharaoh got up that night,
He, all his Ministers and all Egypt.
There was a great cry in Egypt
Because there was no home without its dead.
He summoned Moses and Aaron during the night,
"Rise up, leave the midst of my people –
Both you, and all the Israelites –
Go, worship the LORD as you have spoken.
Take your flocks and your herds as you have demanded.
Be gone and ask **his** blessings upon me."

The Egyptians pressed the Israelites to go quickly
From the land because they said, "We will all die."
The Israelites took their dough before it had leavened,
The kneading bowls were already bound up
With their clothes on their backs.
The Israelites did as Moses had instructed them:
They asked the Egyptians for silver and gold items and clothes.
The LORD made the Egyptians look favourably upon them,
So they gave them whatever they asked.
So did they plunder the Egyptians.

The Israelites set off on their journey from Rameses
To Sukkoth – six hundred thousand men on foot
Besides the children **and women.**
A large mixed group **of slaves** went up with them,
Also flocks, herds – an enormous amount of cattle.
On their way, they baked unleavened cakes of the dough
They brought out of Egypt for it had no leavening.
Because when they were expelled from Egypt
They had no time to make preparations –
They prepared no food for themselves.[1]

---

[1] This appears to be a contradiction, as they had ten days warning to prepare
the Paschal lamb and also sufficient time to blackmail the Egyptians into
surrendering to them their silver and gold. Is this a later attempt to link the
ceremonial eating of *Matzah* to the Exodus from Egypt, when it was already
part of the natural spring harvest festival?

Now the time the Israelites lived in Egypt was
Four hundred and thirty years. At the end of the period,
On the exact day, all the LORD's armies left Egypt.
It was a night of vigilance for the LORD
In order to bring them out of the land of Egypt.
This is that very night of the LORD's **vigilance**
Which is to be vigilantly observed through all generations.[1]
On that very day the LORD brought out the Israelites
From the land of Egypt, army by army.[2]

Now, when Pharaoh expelled the Israelites
God did not lead them through Philistia – the shortest route –
For God thought, "The Israelites may have misgivings
About going to war and will return to Egypt."
God made the Israelites take a circuitous route,
Through the wilderness by the Red Sea.
All the same, the Israelites left Egypt armed with spears.
Moses took the bones of Joseph with him
Because he had caused the Israelites to take an oath,
"God will certainly remember you; **when he does**
And leads you out of Egypt, take these my bones with you."

They moved on from Sukkoth and encamped in Etham,
By the edge of the wilderness. The LORD went before them –
During the day in a pillar of cloud, and
During the night in a pillar of fire to give them light,
That they might travel by day and by night.
The pillar of cloud by day and
The pillar of fire by night
Never departed from before the people of Israel.

The LORD spoke to Moses, "Tell the Israelites to turn back

[1] *Exodus* 12:43–50 enumerates further laws for the observance of Passover. See *The Laws of Moses*, page 2.
[2] Chapter 13:1–16 repeats the laws of the Passover and declares that all first-born animals belong to God and all first-born Israelites must be redeemed from God, i.e. his priests, in recognition of their being spared when he struck down the first-born of Egypt. See *The Laws of Moses*, page 3.

And camp between Migdol and the sea, before Baal-zephon.
You shall encamp facing it by the sea. **When he hears of this,**
Pharaoh will say of the Israelites,
'They are lost in the land;
the wilderness has closed in on them.'
Then I will harden Pharaoh's heart – he will go after them.
And I will gain more fame because of Pharaoh
And **the downfall of his** armies.
The Egyptians will then know that I am the LORD."
The Israelites did this. The king of Egypt was told that the
Israelites had fled; the mind of Pharaoh and his Ministers
Changed regarding the Israelites. They asked themselves,
"What have we done in expelling Israel from serving us?"
He prepared his chariot and took all his people with him.
He assigned six hundred of the best chariots –
Indeed, all the chariots of Egypt
Each with its own captain **and crew.**
The LORD hardened the heart of Pharaoh, king of Egypt.
He pursued the Israelites for they had gone out triumphantly.
The Egyptians pursued them and overtook them –
Encamped by the sea beside Pi-hahiroth by Baal-zephon –
With all Pharaoh's cavalry and chariots,
All his charioteers and armies.

As Pharaoh approached, the Israelites looked up
And saw – the Egyptians were coming after them.
They were overcome with fear and the Israelites
Cried out to the LORD. They grumbled to Moses,
"Is it because there are not enough graves in Egypt
That you have taken us to the wilderness to die?
What is this that you have done to us to take us out of Egypt?
Is this not what we said to you when we were in Egypt,
'Leave us be, let us serve the Egyptians
For it is better for us to serve the Egyptians
Than that we should die in the wilderness!"'

"Why do you cry out to me?

Moses replied, "Do not be afraid, stand your ground
And behold the LORD's salvation that he will perform
For you today. While you see the Egyptians now
You will never ever see them again.
The LORD will fight for you. You need only keep your peace."
The LORD said to Moses, "Why do you cry out to me?
Just instruct the Israelites to journey on.
You – raise your staff and stretch out your hand
Over the sea to divide it. The Israelites will
Go through the sea on dry land.
As for me, I will harden the hearts of the Egyptians,
They will go after you and I will win fame
Through Pharaoh and all his army – his chariots and cavalry.
When I cause their destruction in the sea;
The Egyptians will know that I am the LORD
When I have won honour over Pharaoh – his chariots and
    cavalry.

Now, the Messenger of God who went before the Israelite camp
Turned and moved behind them.
The pillar of cloud before them moved to stand behind them.
It came between the Egyptian and Israelite camps.
The cloud was dark – yet it gave light
By night, but only to the Israelites.
The distance between the camps remained the same
Throughout the night. Then Moses stretched out his hand
Towards the sea. The LORD forced the sea back
By a fierce east wind throughout the night.
He made the sea into dry land – the waters divided.
The Israelites marched into the sea on dry ground.
The waters were for them **protecting** walls
On their right and left sides.

The Egyptians pursued and went after them –
Every one of Pharaoh's horses, his chariots and charioteers –

Into the sea. At the morning watch
The LORD gazed at the Egyptian camp
Through the pillars of fire and cloud and
Threw the Egyptian camp into confusion.
He removed their chariot wheels which made them immobile.
The Egyptians shouted, "Let us flee from the Israelites
For the LORD fights for them against the Egyptians."

The LORD instructed Moses, "Stretch your hand over the sea
That the waters may return to cover the Egyptians –
Their chariots and charioteers."
Moses stretched out his hand over the sea and
The waters returned to their original strength by morning.
The Egyptians **in their confusion** fled towards them.
So did the LORD overwhelm the Egyptians in the sea.
The waters returned and covered the chariots and
    charioteers,
Even the whole army of Pharaoh who followed them
Into the sea – not one of them remained **alive.**

But the Israelites went on dry land in the midst of the sea.
The waters became walls for them on their right and left.
So the LORD saved Israel from Egypt on that day.
The Israelites saw the dead Egyptians on the sea shore.
So did Israel see with what a mighty hand
The LORD acted against the Egyptians.
The people then feared the LORD.
They believed in the LORD
And in Moses, his servant.

Then did Moses and the Israelites sing this song to the LORD,
    "I will sing unto the LORD for his glorious triumph –
    Horse and rider he has cast into the sea.
    The LORD is the source of my strength and
    The reason for my song – he is my deliverer.
    This is my God and I will build him a sanctuary –
    My father's God. I will elevate him with praise.

"The LORD is a man of war, the LORD is his name.
Pharaoh's chariots and his army – he flung into the sea.
The best of his captains are sunk in the Red Sea.
The deeps cover them, they sank in the depths like stones.
Your right hand, O LORD, is armoured with power.
Your right hand shatters your enemies.
In the greatness of your majesty you overwhelm your
    opponents.

"When you express your wrath, it burns them into dust.
With the puff of your nostrils the waters mounted up,
The floods stood upright like walls,
The deeps became solid in the heart of the sea.

"The enemy boasted, 'I will pursue, overtake, divide the
    plunder.
My life will be fulfilled **by their destruction.**
I will draw my sword, my strength will wipe them out.'
But you blew your wind and the sea covered them,
They sank as lead in majestic torrents.

"Who is like you among the gods, O LORD,
Who is like you, glorious in divinity?
Awesome beyond praise, working wonders.
You stretched out your right hand –
The earth swallowed them.

"In your compassion, you led forth this people
Whom you redeemed. With your might you led them
To your divine dwelling place.[1]
The peoples have heard **of your wonders** – they shake.
Pain grips the citizens of Philistia.
The chiefs of Edom are astounded.
The warriors of Moab – they cannot stop trembling.
All the citizens of Canaan melt away **in fear.**
Terror and dread descend upon them

[1] This would appear to be Mount Sinai, which they had not yet reached.

Because of the strength of your arms,
They turn as silent as stone.

"Until your people, O LORD, go beyond their territories,
Until the people you have acquired pass them by.
You will bring them in and plant them
In the mountain of your inheritance,
The place you have made for their dwellings.
Also, the sanctuary, O LORD, which your hands have made.
The LORD will reign forever and ever."

When Pharaoh's horses, chariots and charioteers went into
The sea because the LORD turned the water against them,
The Israelites walked on dry ground on the floor of the sea.
So Miriam the prophetess, Aaron's sister, took a
Timbrel into her hand. All the women followed her
Dancing with timbrels and dances and Miriam chanted,
"Sing ye to the LORD for his glorious triumph,
The horse and his rider he has cast into the sea."[1]
Moses led Israel from the Red Sea into the wilderness of Shur.
They went for three days in the wilderness and found no
    water.
When they reached Marah, they could not drink its waters
Because they were bitter – hence its name: Marah.[2]
The people grumbled to Moses: "What shall we drink?"
He cried out to the LORD who showed him a tree.
He threw it into the waters and they became sweet.
There he **God**, made for them an established judgement.
And there he put them to the test. He told them,
"If you will fully obey the LORD, your God,
Behaving righteously in his sight,
Heeding his commandments and keeping all his laws,
All the plagues with which I afflicted Egypt

---

[1] Was Miriam then repeating the song led by Moses to involve the women in the celebration of Israel's triumph? Or is this an indication that it was she who led the singing?
[2] Meaning 'bitterness'.

Will not fall upon you for I the LORD am your healer.
Remember then: I will sweeten your waters
But only if you believe in me and walk in my ways."
They then came to Elim where there were twelve water springs
And ten palm trees. There they camped by the waters.

They made their way from Elim. The whole community of
Israel entered the wilderness of Sin, between Elim and Sinai
On the fifteenth day of the second month after leaving Egypt.
The entire community of Israel grumbled against
Moses and Aaron in the wilderness, "Would we had died
By the hand of God in Egypt
Where we sat by the fleshpots,
When we ate bread to the full,
But you have brought us out to this wilderness
To kill the entire community by starvation."

The LORD said to Moses, "See, I will make bread
To drop like rain from the heavens
For the people to collect day by day to prove
Whether they will walk according to my teaching or not,
In how they obey my instructions regarding the food.
For on the sixth day, **the day before the Sabbath,**
They shall prepare **for the next day** what they gathered –
Double of that which they collect every day."

Then Moses and Aaron remonstrated against the Israelites,
"You say that we brought you out of Egypt
From your fleshpots to starve in the wilderness.
In the evening you will learn that it is the LORD
Who has taken you out of the land of Egypt
And in the morning you will witness the LORD's glorious
  power
For he hears your grumblings against the LORD.
Who are we that you turn against us?
We are but servants of the Lord."
Moses continued, "**You will see** when the LORD gives you

Meat in the evening and bread in the morning to eat your fill.
Because the LORD has noted your grumblings against him.
I say again: Leave us be! Grumble to the LORD – not to us."

Moses ordered Aaron, "Instruct the whole community of Israel,
'Come close to the LORD for he has heard your mutterings.'"
When Aaron was speaking to all the Israelites,
They turned to look towards the wilderness and
The glorious power of the LORD appeared through a cloud.
The LORD spoke to Moses, "I have noted the mutterings of the
Israelites. Tell them that at dusk you will eat meat;
In the morning you will eat your fill of bread;
You will **finally** accept that I am the LORD your God!"

Evening approached, and stocks of quails flurried about,
They swarmed over the camp **and were easy prey.**
In the morning dew was lying all about the camp.
When the dew dried, look: on the floor of the wilderness
Were thin flakes as delicate as hoar frost on the ground.
When the Israelites saw it, one said to the other:
"*Mahn* – what is it?"[1]
Because they did not know what it was.
Hence it was called manna. Moses told them,
"It is the bread which the LORD has given you for food.
This is what the LORD has commanded, let every person
Gather according to his needs, an omer[2] per person,
According to the number of people living in your tent."
The Israelites obeyed; some gathered more and some less.
Miraculously, however much or little they gathered
When they took its measure by the omer **in their tents,**
He that had collected more had no more **than an omer**
And he that took less had no less **than an omer.**

---

[1] 'What' in Hebrew is *mah*. But the text has *mahn*, so the literal translation is:
it is man[nah]. As the next verse says that they did not know what it was,
how could they call it manna? The Authorised Version makes a question of it.
It is possible that *mahn* was the superlative of *mah* to express surprise.
[2] An omer is a measure of about two quarts.

In the end, each man gathered enough for his needs.

Moses ordered them, "Leave nothing for the next day,
Believe in the LORD that he will provide more manna."
In spite of this, they did not obey Moses.
Some held part in reserve until the next morning.
It bred worms and stank and Moses was angry with them.
So they gathered it every morning,
Each in accordance with his need.
When the sun rays were fierce, it melted.

On the sixth day, **according to the Lord's command,**
They gathered double the amount of bread,
Two omers for each one. The heads of the community came to
Moses **for an explanation of this instruction.** He said,
"This is what the LORD has commanded:
Tomorrow is to be a total rest – a Sabbath[1]
Dedicated to the LORD. Bake and boil it however you like.[2]
Keep **enough** leftovers for the next day,
When you are not permitted to cook." They did this,
As Moses had instructed. It did not stink
Nor did it become mouldy with worms.

Moses said, "Eat it today because today is a Sabbath
To the LORD; today you will not find manna in the field.
Six days you will gather it, but the seventh day is the
Sabbath – on it none shall be found." **Nonetheless,**
On the seventh day, some people went out to gather **the
  manna,**
But they found nothing. The LORD reprimanded Moses,
"How long will you refuse to keep my laws and teachings?"
And Moses thought, "It is not I who is breaking

---

[1] The three-letter consonantal root of the Sabbath is Sh-b-t, which means to rest.
[2] The manna, being a miraculous food, could be prepared in any way, and according to rabbinic tradition was to everyone's particular taste at the time of its being eaten.

The Law of the Lord," but he remained silent.
"See, the LORD has given you the Sabbath **to rest on it.**
Therefore, he gives you on the sixth day a double portion.
Let everyone stay at home; let no one leave his place
On the seventh day." So the people rested on the seventh day.[1]

The Israelites called its name manna.
It looked like coriander seed in its whiteness,
Its taste was like wafers soaked in honey.
Moses said, "This is what the LORD commands.
Let an omerful be kept for future generations to see
The bread with which I fed you in the wilderness,
When I delivered you out of the land of Egypt."
So Moses instructed Aaron, "Take a pot and put
An omerful of manna in it to place before the LORD,
To be kept **as proof** for future generations."
As the LORD instructed Moses, so did Aaron place it in
The Ark of the Testimony in the Tabernacle to be stored.
(The Israelites ate the manna until they came
Into the borders of the land of Canaan.
Now an omer is a tenth of an ephah.)

"What shall I do with this people?

The whole community of Israel travelled from
The wilderness of Sin by stages, as the LORD instructed **them.**
They **first** pitched their camps in Rephidim.
There was no water there for the people to drink.
For this reason the people quarrelled with Moses,
"Give us water so that we may drink."

---

[1] The command to observe the Sabbath is first mentioned here in connection
with the collection of the manna. It is the fourth of the Ten Commandments.
See p. 51. The version of the Ten Commandments found in *Exodus* bases the
Sabbath on God resting on the seventh day from the six days of creation, and
not to the Exodus from Egypt, which is the reason given in the Deuteronomic
version, see p. 131 and footnote.

Moses rebuffed them, "Why are you angry with me?"
Why are you putting the LORD to the test?"
But the people were thirsty for some water.
The people grumbled against Moses, they complained,
"Why have you brought us out of Egypt to kill us,
Our children and our cattle through thirst?"[1]

Moses cried out to the LORD, "What shall I do with this
    people?
In a little time, they will stone me!"
The LORD ordered Moses, "Go before the people and
Take with you some of the elders of Israel and
The staff with which you struck the water,
Take it in your hand and go.
See, I will stand before you on the rock in Horeb.
You will strike the rock and water will gush out –
So that the people may drink from it."
Moses did this in the sight of Israel's elders.
Moses struck the rock in the presence of the elders,
The waters gushed out and made a pool of water.
Moses said, "Speak to the people and tell them,
'The Lord has given you waters to drink, go drink
And stop grumbling against Moses, the servant of the Lord."'
He named the places Massah [test] and Meribah [strife]
Because of the strife of the Israelites **against Moses**
And because they tested the LORD, saying,
"Is the LORD among us or is he not?"

The Amalekites were mustering to attack Israel at Rephidim.
Moses told Joshua, "Choose men to fight the Amalekites.
Tomorrow I will stand on the hill top
With the staff of God clasped in my hand."
Joshua did as Moses had told him,

---

[1] This raises an interesting question. When the Israelites previously complained
that they would die of starvation, why could they not have eaten their cattle?
It is a mystery, or are these tales metaphors to reveal the LORD's wondrous
power contrasted to Israel's lack of faith in him?

To do battle against the Amalekites.
Moses, Aaron and Hur[1] climbed to the hilltop.
When Moses raised his hands, Israel prevailed, but
When he rested them, Amalek prevailed.
Moses became tired. They brought a rock, placed it
Under him and he sat on it; Aaron and Hur on either side of
  him
Held up his arms which remained firm
Until the setting of the sun.
Joshua defeated the Amalekites by their military might.

The LORD instructed Moses, "Write this down in a book
As a perpetual reminder. Fix it into Joshua's mind
For he will succeed you that I intend to wipe out any
Memory of Amalek from under the heavens.
Without cause they attacked an innocent people.
Amalek is the sign of all evil which will be destroyed,
Perhaps not in the time of Joshua or his children,
But in the day that I become King over all the earth.
On that day, Moses built an altar. He named it:
"The LORD is my banner," for he declared,
"There is an evil force against the LORD's kingdom.
The LORD will battle against Amalek for all generations."

Jethro, the priest of Midian and Moses's father-in-law, heard
Everything that the LORD had done for Moses and Israel
His people – how the LORD delivered Israel from Egypt.
Jethro, Moses's father-in-law, took Zipporah, Moses's wife,
After he sent her home and her two sons.
The name of one was Gershom [stranger there] as he had said,
"I have been a stranger in an alien country."
The name of the other was Eliezer [my God helps] for he said,
"The God of my father will be my help
And will save me from the might of Pharaoh."

---

[1] An unidentified character needed to prop up one of Moses's arms. According to rabbinic tradition, he is Miriam's son. He never gets a speaking part.

As Jethro, Moses's father-in-law, with his sons and his wife
Approached Moses where he was camping in the wilderness
By God's mountain, he sent word to Moses,
"I, your father-in-law Jethro, am come to you –
With your wife and her two sons with her."
When Moses heard this, he did not wait for them to come,
He rushed out to meet his father-in-law **and his family.**
Though he was the prince of Israel, he bowed down to him
And kissed him **and his wife and two sons who followed him.**[1]
They asked after each other's welfare and went into his tent.

Moses related to his father-in-law everything that the LORD
Did to Pharaoh and to Egypt for the sake of Israel –
All the problems they had faced on the way
And how the LORD had delivered them **from them all.**
Jethro rejoiced for all the good things the LORD did for
   Israel –
How he had saved them from the might of Egypt. He said,
"The LORD is the source of all blessings, he who saved
Your people from under the domination of Egypt.
Now I recognise that the LORD is greater than all the gods,
Because they behaved arrogantly against them [**the
Israelites], the Lord humbled them with his power.**
Jethro, Moses's father-in-law made a burnt offering
And sacrifices for God. Aaron and all the elders of Israel
Came and broke bread with Moses's father-in-law before God.

The next day, Moses sat to judge the people, who stood
Before Moses from morning until nightfall. When
Moses's father-in-law saw all he was doing for the people,
He said, "What is this that you are doing for the people?
Why do you **sit in judgement** all on your own and
Everybody stands before you from morning until nightfall?"

[1] The biblical text makes no reference to the reunion of Moses and his family.
This does not indicate the cold-heartedness of Moses; only that the narrator
has but one purpose in mind, which is to reveal the conversion of Jethro and
the good advice a foreign priest gives to Moses.

Moses replied to him, "Because they come to enquire of God,
To judge their disputes by the authority of the Lord.
When they are in dispute, they come to me and I judge
Between a man and his neighbours. I tell them
The statutes of God and his teachings."

Moses's father-in-law rejoined, "What you do is not good, for
You will exhaust yourself and the people with you
Who will become tired and impatient because of the waiting.
The task is too burdensome for you; you cannot do it alone.
Now, listen to me; I will advise you. God will be with you.
You must be God's deputy for the people to bring
Their **collective** causes to God. You shall give them warnings
Of the statutes and teachings and reveal to them how
They must behave and the obligations they must undertake.
Choose through inspiration competent men from among the
 people
Who fear the LORD – honest men who despise bribery.
You will set them over them to be judges over thousands,
Judges over hundreds, over fifties and over tens.[1]
Let them judge the people at all times; difficult disputes
They will bring to you. The smaller disputes they will judge
So it will be easier for you as they will share your burden.
When you do this, if God instructs you so to do,
You will endure; also all the people will go home happy."
Moses listened to what his father-in-law advised.
He did as he suggested; he chose competent men from all
The Israelites and appointed them as heads over the people –
Officials over thousands, hundreds, fifties and tens.
They judged the people all the time. The challenging cases
They brought to Moses; the easy ones they judged themselves.
Moses let his father-in-law go and he returned to his country.

To the very day, three months after the Israelites left Egypt,
They reached the wilderness of Sinai from Rephidim.

---

[1] 'Tens' means up to fifty, fifties up to a hundred, and so on .

When they arrived at the wilderness of Sinai, they camped
   there.
There Israel encamped at the foot of the mountain.
Moses went up to God**'s mountain** and the LORD called to
Him out of the mountain, "Say this to the house of Jacob,
Recount this to the children of Israel:
'You have seen what I did to the Egyptians,
How I carried you on eagles' wings to bring you to me.
Now, if you listen to me to keep my covenant,
You shall be for me more special than all the nations,
For the earth belongs to me **and it is I who decide.**
You shall be for me a kingdom of priests, a holy nation.'
This is what you will say to the children of Israel."

Moses proceeded to summon the elders of Israel and set
Before them all the words that the LORD told him to say.
The whole people answered him in unison:
"All that the LORD has commanded, we will do."
Moses took back to the LORD the words of the people.
The LORD told Moses, "I will come to you in a thick cloud,
So that the people can hear when I speak to you,
But without seeing me, lest they die,
So that they also believe in you forever."
Moses related the words of the LORD to the people.[1]

The LORD then instructed Moses, "Go to your people
And dedicate them today and tomorrow.
Let them wash their clothes and be ready for the third day.
On the third day the LORD will descend in the sight of
All the people on Mount Sinai; set limits for the people
Around **the mountain** with the warning: Beware of going on to
The mountain or of touching its edges, for
Anyone who touches the mountain will surely die.
No one shall touch the trespasser; he will be stoned

---

[1] The original text has Moses telling the words of the Israelites to the LORD,
which is not consistent with the preceding lines.

Or shot through. Be it beast or man, he shall not live.
But, when the ram's horn makes a long blast,
They shall come up the mountain". Moses descended from
The mountain to the people, and made them holy.
They washed their clothes. He ordered the people,
"Be ready for the third day. Do not approach a woman."
On the morning of the third day there was thunder and
    lightning
And thick cloud covering the mountain and
A very great blast of a horn.
All the people in the camp trembled.
Moses brought the people out of the camp to meet God.
They stood at the foothills of the mountain.
Mount Sinai was all covered with smoke
Because the LORD came down on it in flames of fire.
Its smoke rose up as the smoke of a furnace.
The whole mountain quaked exceedingly
When the sound of the horn became louder and louder,
Moses spoke and God answered him with a loud voice,
To be heard over the thunder and lightning flashes.
The LORD descended on to Mount Sinai
To the mountain's summit. The LORD summoned Moses
To the top of the mountain and Moses went up.

The LORD, **after giving him his instructions**, said to Moses,
"Go down and warn the people not to cross the limits
To look upon the LORD – lest many of them perish.
Also, the priests who **are allowed to** come near to the LORD
Must sanctify themselves lest the LORD lash out against them."
Moses said to the LORD, **"Is it necessary? You already said,**
The people cannot come up Mount Sinai. You charged us,
Set limits to the mount to sanctify it, **not to be trespassed."**
The LORD answered him, "Nevertheless, go down! Then
    ascend,
You with Aaron, but the priests and the people must not
Trespass the limits to go up to the LORD lest

He lash out against them." Moses descended to the people
And told them **of the dangers of going on the mount.**[1]
All the people, witnessing the thunder and lightning,
The sound of the trumpet and the smoking mountain –
The people, seeing this panicked and stood far off.
They pleaded with Moses, "You speak to us
And we will obey but let not God speak to us,
Lest we die!" Moses reassured the people, "Be not afraid,
Because God came to put you to the test,
So that the dread of him might be upon you –
To prevent you from sinning **against him**."
The people stood far away and Moses went near to
The deep darkness – where God was.

The Ten Commandments

God uttered all these words:
  1. I am the LORD your God who brought you out of Egypt –
     From the house of slaves.[2]
  2. You shall have no other gods but me.
     You shall not make yourself any sculpted image or
     Any physical representation of any body in the heavens
        above,
     On the earth beneath or in the waters under the earth.
     You shall neither bow down to them nor worship them.
     Because, I, the LORD your God, am a jealous God
     Who remembers the sins of the fathers
     Of them that hate me
     To the second, third and fourth generations,
     But who behaves kindly for a thousand generations
     To those who love me and keep my commandments.

---

[1] In the traditional text verses 20:15–18 follow the Ten Commandments, but it
reads more sensibly to have them prior to the great revelation of God's law.
[2] According to the Jewish tradition, this is the first commandment. Christians
view this as part of the introduction: The first commandment is not to have
other gods and the second is not to make idols.

3. Do not abuse the name of the LORD[1]
   For he will not exonerate those who use his name
   For perverse purposes, **but will punish him.**
4. Remember the Sabbath day to make it holy.[2]
   During six days you may work to do all your tasks
   But the seventh day is the Sabbath to the LORD your God –
   You shall not work, you, nor your son, nor your daughter,
   Nor your male or female servant, nor your cattle,
   Nor the stranger within your gated walls.
   Because in six days the LORD made the heavens, the earth,
   The sea and all that live in them, but
   He rested on the seventh day.
   Therefore, the LORD made the Sabbath into a blessing
   And declared it as holy.
5. Honour your father and mother
   So that you may long live on the land
   Which the LORD your God is granting you.
6. You shall not murder.
7. You shall not commit adultery.
8. You shall not steal.
9. You shall not bear false witness against your neighbour.
10. You shall not covet your neighbour's house,
    His wife, his male or female servant,
    His ox, his donkey nor for anything
    That belongs to your neighbour.

The LORD said to Moses, "This is what you should say to
The Israelites, 'You yourselves saw that I spoke to you

---

[1] The accepted translation is 'not to take the LORD's name in vain.' This would be trivial. It must be a more serious crime such as using the power of God's name [The LORD] and the respect it commands for evil purposes such as curses and false oaths. The modern equivalent is the use of religious belief to justify bigotry and ethnic wars.

[2] A special day dedicated to rest and the emulation of God. Sabbath means 'desist from labour'.

From heaven. Do not make with me gods of silver or gold.[1]
"See, I am sending a Messenger[2] to go before you
To guard you on the road and to bring you to the place
I have prepared for you. Pay attention to him and obey him.
Do not rebel against him, **for if you do** he cannot
Pardon your sins, for my name[3] is in him.
But if you will truly obey him, I will do all that I said.
I will be an enemy to your enemies and a foe to your foes.
For my Messenger, **invested with my power,** will go before you,
To bring you to the land of the Amorites, the Hittites,
The Perizzites, the Canaanites, the Hivites and Jebusites.
I will cut them down. **When you come there** you will not
Bow down to their gods nor serve them **for they cannot help.**
And do not behave as they do. You will raze them
To the ground and shatter their monuments.

"But you shall worship the LORD your God and
He will bless you with food and water
And keep away sickness from your thresholds.
None shall miscarry or be childless in your land.
I will grant your lives fullness of years.
I will send the dread of me before you and weaken
All the nations you come to; your enemies will show you
Their backs **as they flee from you**. I will send my forces
Before you to drive out the Hivites, the Canaanites and
Hittites. I will not drive them out in a year's time.

---

[1] Chapter 20:21–23:19 contain ritual, civil and humanitarian legislation which may be found in *The Laws of Moses*, page 5ff.
[2] This messenger never materialises. Herbert Brichto, *Towards a Grammar of Biblical Poetics, OUP 1992*, pp 109–111, makes a convincing case that the Messenger is Moses himself. The divine presence in him is attested to by the radiance of his face after coming down from Mount Sinai. The religious implications of this are enormous. As Moses has divinity in him, so do all the authentic prophets to a greater or lesser degree. The idea that man can become divine is therefore not unique to the New Testament.
[3] i.e. divinity

For the land would become desolate **without inhabitants**
And the wild beasts would increase against you.
Little by little will I expel them before you until
Your numbers increase. Then you shall possess their land.
I will make your borders reach from the Red Sea
To the Sea of the Philistines:
From the wilderness until the great River Euphrates.
I will give the inhabitants of the land into your hand.
You will drive them out when you invade their lands.
You will make no treaty with them nor with their gods.
They shall not inhabit your land for they might make
You sin against me; and, if you worship
Their gods, they will lure you into destruction."

Moses descended the mountain; he summoned the elders
And told them all the words of the Lord.
They asked him, "When will the Lord's Messenger come?"
Moses replied, "I do not know but he will, for all of
The Lord's words will be fulfilled. Only keep
His commandments so that you may possess
The land he has promised to give to your fathers."

The LORD said to Moses, "Ascend to the LORD, you and Aaron,
His sons, Nadab and Abihu, and seventy elders of Israel;
And worship from a distance. Only Moses shall come near to
The LORD. They shall not come near. The people shall not
Ascend with him. **So Moses ascended the mountain**
And the Lord told him his laws and statutes.
Moses came down and told the people the words of the LORD –
All his judgements. The people were united in affirmation:
"All that the LORD has commanded we will do."

Then Moses wrote down all of the LORD's words.
He rose early in the morning and built an altar below
The mountain with twelve pillars of stone –
The same number as the tribes of Israel.
He ordered the young men of Israel to sacrifice oxen as

Burnt and peace offerings to the LORD.
Moses gathered half of the blood into a basin;
The other half he sprinkled onto the altar.

He took the Scroll of the Covenant **in which he wrote**
The Lord's promises to fight Israel's enemies.
To give her the land of the Canaanites as an inheritance;
To bless Israel with abundant food and water;
To increase her numbers and protect her from pestilence.
In it were written the laws of the Lord for Israel to obey –
Neither to worship the gods of the land nor to make
Covenants with them but to destroy their altars.
He read it to the people. They declared:
"All the LORD has commanded we will observe and obey."
So Moses took the blood **in the basin** and sprinkled it on
The people[1], and said, "See the blood, **sign** of the
    covenant –
The LORD has made **between you and him**
Confirming all these matters: **that you will obey him**
And he will be your God as you will be his people.

God entertains the elders of Israel on Mount Sinai

Only then did Moses, Aaron, Nadab and Abihu and
Seventy elders of Israel go up and they saw the God of Israel.
Under his feet was what appeared as **a footstool of**
Bright sapphire but as transparently clear as the heavens.
He did not lay a hand on the nobility of Israel to harm them.
They looked upon God.[2]
They dined and drank **with him.**

---

[1] An extraordinary event which never became part of Jewish ritual in future generations as a sign of the covenant between God and Israel. Circumcision is the sign of the covenant which has carried on till present times.
[2] The visibility of God attested to by this passage is usually ignored or minimised to a visionary appearance.

**When they descended the mountain they told the
Israelites what they had seen and they were amazed.**

Then the LORD summoned Moses, "Come up to me on the
    mountain
And remain there **with me** and I will give you stone tablets –
The teachings and commandments which I have inscribed **on
    them,**
For you to teach them **to the Israelites."**
Moses got up with Joshua, his chief-of-staff.
He ascended onto the mount of God.
He said to the elders **who had accompanied them,**
"Stay down here until we return to you.
Aaron and Hur are with you. Let any litigant approach
    them."
Moses ascended the mountain which was covered by cloud.
The glory of the LORD rested on Mount Sinai.
The cloud covered it for six days,
On the seventh day, he summoned Moses from within the
    cloud.
The appearance of the glory of the LORD to the Israelites
Was like a consuming fire at the top of the mountain.
Moses entered the density of the cloud, and
Went on to the mountain top.
Moses was on the mountain for forty days and forty nights.[1]
When he had finished speaking to him on Mount Sinai,
The LORD gave the two tablets of testimony,[2]
Witness to the covenant between the Lord and Israel –
Tablets of stone inscribed with the finger of God.

---

[1] The Mosaic laws relating to the building of the sanctuary, the tabernacle, the
priestly cult, Ch. 25 to 31:17, are in *The Laws of Moses*, page 14ff.
[2] The two tablets are symbolic of the two witnesses required to confirm the
validity of a contract or treaty.

The Israelites break their covenant with the Lord

The people saw that Moses did not come down the mountain,
They assembled together as a group against Aaron,
"Come make us gods who will go before us
Because this Moses, the man who brought us out of Egypt,
We do not know what has happened to him."

– "He is on God's mountain receiving the laws of the Lord.
He will return. Do not break the Lord's covenant."
– "We will worship him too. Only make for us an image –
A representation of his power that we may honour him."
– "But the Lord said to you, 'Make no graven image.'"
– "We are frightened! Where is the Lord? Do as we say."
Aaron thought, "I will ask them for their golden rings
They will not wish to give them up to me."
Aaron instructed them, "Take off the golden earrings
Which are on the ears of your wives, sons and daughters
And bring them to me." All of them took off the
Golden rings in their ears and brought them to Aaron.
He took them, **melted down the gold.**
With a sculpting tool, he formed it into a golden bull.
When they saw it they shouted, "This is your God, O Israel,
Who brought you up out of the land of Egypt."[1]
Aaron, when he saw this, built an altar before it.
Aaron cried out, "Tomorrow will be a feast for the LORD."
**For he thought, "Let them think this is the Lord's image
Lest they forget that the Lord delivered them from Egypt."**

---

[1] Looking forward, in the first Book of Kings, 12:26–30, Jeroboam rebelled against Solomon's heir Rehoboam and became king over the ten tribes of Israel. To discourage the Israelites from going to Jerusalem, the capital of the kingdom of Judah, to offer sacrifices at the Temple, he makes two bulls of gold and sets them up at Beth-el and Dan, and he says to his subjects almost identical words: 'Behold your God O Israel who brought you out of the land of Egypt.' Is this a coincidence or is it a retrospective attack on Jeroboam, which suggests that a later prophet wrote this narrative long after Jeroboam's crime?

They got up early the next day and sacrificed
Burnt and peace offerings. The people sat down
To eat and to drink and then got up to dance.

The LORD exhorted Moses, "Go, go down, for your[1] people
Whom you brought up out of Egypt have behaved perversely.
They did not wait very long before turning away from
The path which I commanded them to take.
They have made for themselves a molten image,
Bowed down to it and sacrificed to it. They said,
'These are your gods who brought you up out of Egypt.'
I have considered this people. It is a stiff-necked people,
Now let me be and my anger will burn and consume them.
But I will make you into a great nation."

Moses implored the LORD his God, "Why are you
So intensely angry against your people
Whom you brought out of the land of Egypt
With great power and a mighty arm?
Why should the Egyptians say, **as they will**,
'He took them out to do them evil,
To kill them in the mountains and to wipe them off
The face of the earth?' Turn away from your fierce anger
And turn back from harming your people.

"Cast back your memory to Abraham, Isaac and Israel,
Your servants, to whom you swore by your own person,
Saying to them, I will increase your descendants
As the stars of heaven and all this land, of which
I have spoken, will I give to your offspring –
They will possess it forever." So the LORD turned back
From committing the evil which he said
He would do to his people.

---

[1] A very human touch: when Israel sins, she becomes Moses's people whom he,
and not the LORD, delivered out of Egyptian bondage; very much like a mother
saying to her husband, "Darling, your child is crying."

Having persuaded the Lord not to destroy his people,
Moses turned to descend the mountain with the two tablets of
The Testimony in his arms. [The tablets were engraved on
Both sides – on the one side and the other they were engraved.
The tablets were the work of God – the inscriptions were God's
Graven upon the tablets.] When Joshua[1] heard the noise of
The people shouting, he said to Moses, "These are
The sounds of war in the camp," but he replied,
"It is not a triumphant shout, nor the cry of defeat;
It is the sound of responses in song that I hear."

When he came closer to the camp, he saw the bull and
The dancing; Moses went into a wild rage.
He threw the tablets out of his arms
And broke them at the foot of the mountain.
He took the bull they had made and smelted it down with fire.
When it was dry, he pounded it into powder, mixed it in water
And made the Israelites drink it **as punishment.**

Moses questioned Aaron, "What did this people do to you
To make you allow them to sin so grievously?"
Aaron pleaded, "Do not be so furious with me, my lord.
You know this people – how intent they are to do evil.
They demanded of me, 'Make us gods who will go before us,
Because this Moses, the man who brought us up out of Egypt,
We know not what has happened to him; and
I said to them, 'Whoever has gold, let them pull it off them
And give it to me.' **I thought that they would not want to
Part with their gold but they did,** so I threw it into
The fire and out comes this bull.[2] I said to them,

---

[1] Was Joshua, according to the narrator, with Moses, or had he encamped on a
lower mountain slope for forty days to await his master? It is unclear.
[2] According to the earlier narrative, Aaron formed the image. Could Aaron get
away with such a lie; or has God made the bull appear miraculously to put the
people to the test? Had he not just commanded them not to worship any
images and had they not sworn to obey the commandments coming out of the
fire on Mount Sinai? They should have resisted the temptation as the image is
eventually imagined to be the 'real thing', for they had shouted, 'This is your
God, O Israel, who brought you up out of the land of Egypt.' See p. 56.

'Go to your tents, tomorrow will be a festival to the Lord.'
Because they still believed in the Lord
And I hoped that you would return before then."

"Whosoever is for the Lord . . ."

Moses forgave Aaron for he saw that the people
Were running riot and that Aaron could not stop them
From making themselves foolish in the eyes of their enemies.[1]
Moses stood up at the head of the camp and declared,
"Whosoever is for the LORD, let him come to me."
The men of the tribe of Levi assembled together before him.
He exhorted them, "Thus says the LORD, the God of Israel,
'Let every man put his sword on his thigh,
Let him go from door to door in the camp even
To kill his kinsman, neighbour or close one **who**
Broke the Lord's commandment to make a graven image."'
The Levites did as Moses had ordered them.
That day about three thousand men were killed

Moses said, "You have ordained yourselves to the
LORD on this day by being zealous for him:
A father against his son and his brother that he may today
Grant you blessings." The next day, Moses addressed the
     people,
"You have sinned grievously. Now I will go up to the LORD.
Perhaps I can appease the LORD regarding your sin."
So Moses returned to the LORD, **"How well I know that**
This people have sinned most grievously in making
For themselves golden gods. If you will draw a line
Under their sins, well and good. If you cannot,
Blot me out from the scroll you have written,
For I have given my life to this people.
If you destroy them, you destroy me."

---

[1] By a foolish betrayal which would lead to their destruction.

The LORD replied to Moses, "He who has sinned against me,
Will I blot out from my scroll, **not you nor anyone else.**
Go now, lead this people to the place of which I have spoken.
See, my Messenger will go before you. Nevertheless,
In the day of my visitation **which is to come**
When their sins become unpardonable,[1]
I will punish them for their sins."
So the LORD made a plague come down on those people
Who made the bull which Aaron had fashioned.
Then did the LORD instruct Moses, "Go up from this place,
You and the people whom you brought out of Egypt,[2]
To the land which I swore to give to Abraham, Isaac and
Jacob; I will give it to your descendants.
[I will send my Messenger before you. I will drive out
The Canaanites, the Amorites, the Hittites, the Perizzites,
The Hivites and the Jebusites] a land of milk and honey.
But I will not go up with you for you are an obstinate people,
Lest I lose my temper and wipe you out on the way."
When the people heard this bad news they went into
    mourning
And no one wore their fancy jewellery.
For the LORD had said to Moses, "Say to the Israelites –
You are an obstinate people. If I were to go up with you,
In a moment, **your behaviour could anger me and**
I would wipe you out. Now take off your fancy ware
And I will decide what to do with you!"
So, in repentance, the Israelites stripped themselves of
Their fancy ware from the time they were at Mount Horeb.

Moses used to take the Tent and pitch it outside the camp,
At some distance from the camp. He named it *Ohel Moed.*[3]

---

[1] When God ultimately destroys the kingdoms of Israel and Judah in the years
622 and 586 BCE respectively, he will take this sin into account.
[2] While previously God takes the credit for Israel's liberation, as their sinfulness
increases, he distances himself from Israel and turns her into Moses's
responsibility.
[3] Tent of meeting or testimony. It was the seat of judgement.

All who wished to approach the LORD with a petition
Would go to the *Ohel Moed* which was outside the camp.
When Moses went to the Tent, all the people rose up –
Each standing by his tent opening, looking at Moses
Until he reached the Tent. When he arrived there,
The pillar of cloud **descended and** stood at the Tent's door.
Then the people stood and bowed down – each by his tent
   door.
The LORD spoke to Moses face to face
As a man speaks to his friend. He would then
Return to the camp. His chief of staff – Joshua ben Nun,
A young man, did not leave the Tent.

Moses remonstrated with the LORD, "See, you say to me,
'Bring up this people' and you have not informed me
Who you will send with me – **the Messenger you promised.**
You also said, 'I know you intimately and you please me.'
Now, if I really please you, show me your purposes,
So that I may know and please you even more.
This nation is your people **and I am its guide.**"
He replied, "I myself will go with you and give you ease."
But he insisted, "If you do not go with me,
Do not take us up from this place. For how will it be known
That I have found favour with you – I and **also** your people?
Is it not the proof that you go with us – so that I and
Your people are distinguished from all the nations
Who are on the face of the earth?"

The LORD said to Moses,
"Because you have won favour with me,
And I know you 'by name',[1] I will also do what you ask."

---

[1] Previously I have translated this as 'I know you intimately'. I have kept the
literal translation here because I want to share the problem with the reader. Is
the impact of the phrase intended to be that God chooses to have personal
relationships with only a few choice individuals and treats the others as a
collective entity who benefit from the divine selection of their ancestors, i.e. the
Patriarchs? I am not sure, but this is my guess.

– "**Then**, please reveal to me your glory."
– "I will make all my goodness pass before you
And will reveal the essence [1] of the LORD before you:
I will be gracious to those to whom I wish to be gracious;
I will be merciful to those to whom I wish to be merciful.
You cannot see my face;[2] for a man shall not see me and live.
See that place by me – you will stand on the rock.
Now when my glory passes by you,
I will put you in the cleft of the rock;
I will protect you by covering you with my hand
You will see my back, but not my face."
The Lord did as he had said and
A cloud of radiant light passed before Moses.
When it became blinding, a cool shadow covered his face
The shadow disappeared and he saw a soft light
Which enveloped him as a mother holds a child.
His face was suffused with light.
A hand went over his face and he slept.

The LORD instructed Moses, "Hew out two tablets of stone
As the first and I will inscribe on the tablets that
Which was on the first ones which you shattered.
Let them be ready in the morning when you will ascend
Mount Sinai where you will stand by me on the
Top of the mountain. No one shall go up with you.
Equally – no one shall be on any part of the mountain
Nor shall their flocks and herds graze near the mountain."
So he hewed two tablets of stone like the first ones
And ascended Mount Sinai as the LORD had told him.
In his arms, he took the two tablets of stone.

---

[1] Literally: proclaim the name . . .
[2] Does this contradict the previous story of Moses seeing and eating with God in the company of the seventy elders of Israel? Or should we suppose that they only saw his feet on the pedestal? Traditional commentators believe that what was previously described was a vision. I think not. There the elders saw only a physical presence of God. Here God reveals to Moses his divine aura.

The LORD came down in a cloud and stood there with him.
He proclaimed the name [the essential nature] of the LORD.
The LORD passed by him as he called out:
"The LORD! the LORD! a God full of compassion and gracious,
Slow to anger, totally kind and loyal;
Showing mercy to the thousandth generation **because of**
The virtues of one's ancestors – patiently coping
With **human** iniquity, rebelliousness and error,
Remembering the sins of the ancestors upon their descendants,
When they too sin to the third and fourth generations."
On hearing these words, Moses quickly prostrated himself on
The ground and worshipped, "If I really have found
Favour in your eyes, O LORD, please let the LORD
Go with us. I know it is an obstinate people
But pardon our sins and errors and make us
Your special possession." He replied,
"See, I have made a covenant with you.
Before all your people, I will perform wonders
Which have never previously been created on earth,
Nor experienced by any nation. The whole people with you
Will witness the work of the LORD.
What I do with you will be awesome.[1]
Keep in mind what I command you this day.
I will chase out from before you the Amorites,
The Canaanites, the Hittites, the Perizzites,
The Hivites and the Jebusites. Beware of making treaties with
The inhabitants of the land to which you go,
Lest they be a snare among you. You shall
Grind down their altars, shatter their monuments and
Cut down the **wooden** images of **their goddess,** Ashera.
You will worship no other god except me because

---

[1] One is stimulated to ask: Have not the Israelites experienced enough miracles to make them believe? Can any more help when the others failed? My conclusion: the miracles are intended to prove the power of Israel's God to generations yet unborn, and their obligation to keep his commands.

The LORD – Jealousy is one of his attributes[1] – is a jealous God.
Other nations may worship more than one god but
My people has a covenant only with me and
I have made a special covenant only with Israel.

"If you make treaties with the land's inhabitants
You will go whoring after their gods **and**
Be unfaithful to the Lord, the God of your ancestors
And will sacrifice to their gods. One will invite you and
You will eat of their sacrifice. You will marry your
Sons to their daughters. When they go astray
After other gods, they will make your sons go
Astray after their gods **as well.**
Also, you shall not make for yourself any graven gods."[2]

The LORD said to Moses, "Inscribe these words, for on their
Foundation have I made a covenant with you and Israel."
He remained with the LORD for forty days and forty nights.
He neither ate nor drank. He inscribed upon the tablets
The conditions of the covenant – the Ten Commandments.
When Moses came down from Mount Sinai with the
Two tablets of the testimony **of the covenant** in his arms –
Moses was not aware that his face **still** shone as it did
When he, **the Lord**, was speaking to him.
When Aaron and the Israelites saw Moses – his face shone
And they were frightened of drawing near to him.

Moses summoned them. **Only** Aaron and the leaders of Israel
Came to him. Moses spoke to them **and they were not**
Injured by his divine aura. After this all the
Israelites drew near and he reported all the commandments of

---

[1] Literally 'Jealousy is his name'.
[2] Chapter 34:18–26 are a repetition of laws regarding the celebration of
Passover, the firstborns which belong to God, i.e. the priests, the Sabbath, other
festivals; also the law forbidding the boiling of a kid in its mother's milk – this
law which was a sensitive piece of legislation became the basis of Jewish
dietary laws which forbid eating meat and dairy products together. See the
Laws of Moses, page 30.

Which the LORD had spoken when he was with him on Mount
  Sinai.
When Moses finished speaking, he covered his face with a veil.
When Moses came before the LORD to speak with him,
He removed the veil until he came out **from the Tent.**
On his coming out, he would tell the Israelites what
He was commanded. The Israelites saw his face –
That his skin shone. Then Moses put on his veil again
Until he went in again to speak to him, **the Lord.**[1]

*   *   *

Then, **when the Tabernacle and all its furnishing had been
Completed,** the cloud covered the *Ohel Moed.*
The LORD's glorious majesty filled the tabernacle.
Even Moses was not able to go to the *Ohel Moed*
Because the cloud rested upon it and the
Glorious majesty of the LORD filled the tabernacle.
When the cloud ascended from the tabernacle
The Israelites carried on with their journey.
But if the cloud did not rise, they did not proceed
Until the day it rose, because the cloud of the LORD
Was on the tabernacle by day and by night.
A flame burnt within the cloud.
This was seen by all the Israelites
In the course of all their journeys.[2]

---

[1] Ch. 35 to 40:33 are for the larger part a repetition of instructions regarding
the construction of the Tabernacle and its furnishings, including the breastplate
worn by the High Priest. See *The Laws of Moses,* page 173.
[2] See Appendix 2, *Numbers,* 9:15–10:10 for an elaboration on how the
Israelites set out on their journeys.

NUMBERS

NUMBERS[1]

On the twentieth day of the second month of the second year
After the Exodus the cloud rose up from above the
Tabernacle of Testimony, and the Israelites set off on to
The next stage of their journeys out of the Sinai wilderness.
The cloud then stopped at the wilderness of Paran.
They proceeded on their journey according to
The LORD's direction revealed to them by Moses.
This was the nature of their procession:
1. Foremost was the flag of Judah with all its people
    Leading them was Nahshon ben Amminadab.
2. Leading all the Issacharites was Nethanel ben Zuar.
3. Leading all of the Zebulunites was Eliab ben Helon
    Then came the dismantled Tabernacle led by
    The sons of Gershon and the sons of Merari who carried it.
4. Then came the flag of Reuben's camp with all its forces.
    Leading them was Elizur ben Shedeur.
5. Leading all the Simeonites was Shelumiel ben Zurishaddai.
6. Leading all the Gadites was Eliasaph ben Deuel
    Then the Kohathites[2] marched carrying the regalia of the
    Sanctuary. Those who carried the Tabernacle would set it up
    Before their arrival **when they ended their march.**
7. Then followed the flag of the Ephraimites with its people.
    Leading them was Elishama ben Ammihud.
    Leading the tribe of Manasseh was Gamaliel ben Pedahzur.
8. Leading the Benjaminites was Abidan ben Gideoni.
9. The flag of the Danites was at the rearguard of the camp.

---

[1] See Appendix Two for the opening chapters 1–2:34 which record the first
census and how they encamped and broke camp for their journeys; 3:1–9:14
which describe priestly duties and the offerings of the tribes at the dedication of
the Tabernacle and various other rites are to be found in *The Laws of Moses*,
page 99ff. For 9:15–10:10, also see appendix 2. This text begins at 10:11.
[2] A clan of the Levites.

They marched led by Ahiezer ben Amishaddai.
10. Leading the Asherites behind them was Pagiel ben Ochran.
11. Leading the Naphtalites was Ahira ben Anan.
This was the order of the Israelites as they moved forward.

Moses said to Hobab[1] ben Reuel the Midianite,
Moses's father-in-law. "We are going to the place of which
The LORD has said, 'I am giving it to you.'
Come now with us and we will treat you well
Because the LORD has determined to be kind to Israel."
He replied, "I will not go, but I will return to my
Own country and birthplace." But he persisted,
"Do not forsake us. You know how we are camping in
The wilderness and you can be eyes for us,
To tell us what lies ahead of us and where we might rest.
And if you go with us, however generously the LORD
Behaves towards us, so shall we behave towards you."
– "But the Lord directs you. His cloud leads you."
– "No, it only tells us in what area to encamp
But not how we should proceed day by day."
And Hobab ben Reuel listened to Moses and stayed with him.

They made a three-day journey from the LORD's mountain;
The Ark of the LORD's Covenant preceded them for three days
To find a comfortable place for them to rest.
The LORD's cloud was above them every day as they broke
  camp.
When the Ark was carried forward, Moses would say,
  "Rise up O LORD
  Let your enemies be dispersed

[1] According to rabbinic tradition, Hobab is assumed to be another name for Jethro and Reuel would therefore be Jethro's father. In *Exodus*, see p. 6, Jethro's daughters refer to their father as Reuel, but this need not be considered as a contradiction as grandfather in the biblical narratives can be called father, perhaps like Papa. What is more troubling is that in *Exodus* we are told of the visit and departure of Jethro. Here Hobab suddenly reappears. As Moses had more than one wife, he could have had more than one father-in-law, and their names could have been confused in the handing down of traditional lore.

Let your enemies flee from you."
When it returned to its resting place, he said,
"Return O LORD to the ten thousands of
Thousands of Israelites **who welcome you.**"

The people were ceaselessly moaning,
Speaking maliciously in the LORD's hearing.
When the LORD heard this, his nostrils were aflame with fire.[1]
The flames of the LORD burnt them,
Consuming them throughout the camp.
The people wept before Moses.
Moses interceded before the LORD and the fires burnt out.
The name of the place was called Burning [Taberah]
Because the flames of the LORD were aflame there.

Once again, the riff-raff among them
Had a great lust **for meat. Influenced by them,**
The Israelites again began complaining and wailing,
"Who will give us meat to eat?
We remember the fish we ate in Egypt for nothing.
The cucumbers, the melons, the leeks, the onions
And the garlic; now our lives are dried up.
There is nothing for us here except this manna before us!"
To appreciate the extent of their ingratitude,
You should know that:
The manna was like coriander seed – It sparkled as bdellium.
(The people would go about and collect it,
They would grind it in mills or beat it in mortar.
They boiled it in pots and made it into cakes.
It tasted like cakes of wafers baked in honey.
After the dew fell on the camp during the night,
The manna fell over it.)

---

[1] This is the literal translation of the Hebrew text, which is usually translated, *his anger was kindled.* The image is similar to that of a dragon whose nostrils are flame throwers. In the present context, the literal translation seemed appropriate because of its anthropomorphic imagery.

"Did I conceive this people . . . ?"

Moses heard that the people were weeping – every family
And every man by the entrance of his tent.
The LORD was enraged nor was Moses pleased.
Before the Lord struck out in anger against the Israelites
Moses complained to the LORD, "Why have you treated
Your servant so badly. In what have I displeased you
That you have laid upon me the burden of this people?
Did I conceive this people, did I give birth to it –
That you should say, 'Carry them in your bosom –
As a nurse carries a suckling babe –
To the land which you promised to give to their ancestors.
Where am I to get the meat to give to all the people?
They cry to me, 'Give us meat to eat.'
I am not able to suffer this people on my own –
They are too difficult to endure.
If this is the way you intend to treat me –
If I please you – kill me straight away –
And let me not wallow in my misery!"
The LORD replied to Moses, "**I hear what you say,**
You alone should not bear the burden of this people.
Pick for me seventy men from the elders of Israel
Whom you know to be worthy elders and officers over them.
Assemble them at the Tent of Meeting.
Let them stand there by you.
I will descend to speak to you there.
I will take some of your **divine** spirit and place it on them.
They will share the burden of the people with you
So that you will not have to endure it alone."

As for the people, say to them, "**Prepare** for tomorrow,
Sanctify yourselves. You *will* eat meat because you have
Groaned in the hearing of the LORD, 'Who will feed us meat?
It was better for us in Egypt.' The LORD *will* give you meat,
And you *will* eat. Not on one day will you eat, or on two days

Or on five, or on ten or twenty but for a whole month,
Until it is coming out of your nostrils until it disgusts you –
Only because you despised the LORD who was with you
And you groaned before him, complaining,
'Why have we come out of Egypt?'"'

Moses interjected, "The people whom I lead number
Six hundred thousand men on foot, and you say,
'I will give them enough meat for a whole month.'
Shall whole flocks and herds be slaughtered for them?
Will that suffice? Or shall all the fish in the sea be caught
For them and will that even be enough for them!"
The LORD retorted to Moses,
"Has the LORD's hand lost its power?
Now you will see whether my promise will be fulfilled or not!"
Moses went out and told the people the words of the LORD.

He **also** assembled seventy men from the elders of Israel.
He stood them in a circle around the Tent.
The LORD descended in a cloud and spoke to him
And removed some of his spirit which was in Moses.
And granted it to the seventy elders.
When the spirit rested upon them, they prophesied;
But they did not continue to do so **after that day.**
When the elders dispersed, there were two men in the camp.
The name of one was Eldad, the other's name was Medad.
The spirit rested upon them; they were listed **among the elders**
But had not gone to the Tent **as had the others,**
Now, they were prophesying within the encampment.
Seeing them, a young man rushed with the news to Moses,
"Eldad and Medad are prophesying in the camp."[1]
Joshua bin Nun, Moses's minister since his youth, said,
"Moses, my lord, restrain them." Moses replied,

---

[1] The nature of their prophecy is a mystery: was it the moral utterances of an Isaiah, or was it the spiritual ecstasy which seizes King Saul when he is caught up with whirling dervishes? It would appear from Moses's response that they were revealing the knowledge and will of God.

"Are you jealous for my sake!
Would that all the LORD's people were prophets
And that the LORD would bestow his spirit on them all!"

Moses returned to the camp with the elders of Israel.
The LORD sent forth a wind carrying in quails from the sea.
The wind lessened and they fell **from exhaustion**
Flying around the camp a distance of a day's march
No higher than two yards from the ground.
Throughout that day and night and the next day
The people gathered the quails **into nets.**
He who caught the least caught a hundred bushels.
They spread them out in piles all about the camp.
The LORD was incensed with anger against the Israelites
For their greed and lack of faith in him as their provider.
So the LORD afflicted the people with a great plague
Even while the meat was between their teeth,
While it was still being chewed.
The name of that place was called Graves of Gluttony
[*Kibroth-hattaavah*] because there they buried
The people who lusted **after meat.** From *Kibroth-hataavah*
The people journeyed to Hazeroth where they stopped.

Moses was sad for Zipporah, his wife, was distraught,
She said to him, "When you took me to wife
You were not a man of God, but only a man.
I gave you two sons but they are nothing for you
And nor am I. You speak only to the Lord
And bear the burden of your people Israel.
I have no place in your life, neither I nor your sons."
From that day Moses did not know his wife.
Among the slaves that came out with the Israelites
Was a virgin, an Ethiopian beautiful to look at.
Her eyes sparkled and he loved her.

He sent a message to her father to say,
"Give me your daughter to be my wife."

She was brought to him and came into his tent.
And Moses was comforted for the loss of Zipporah.
Miriam and Aaron were murmuring against Moses
Because of the Ethiopian wife he had taken –
For she was an Ethiopian woman **black as night:**
"Why has he not taken to wife a daughter of Israel?
First he marries a Midianite woman and now this one!
How can he lead Israel when he rejects his own flesh,
And takes an Ethiopian woman to wife!
Now, what shall we do before the people rebel?
Think, has the LORD only spoken to Moses;
Has he not spoken also to us!" **Miriam said to Aaron,**
"Did he not also make you into a prophet
To do wonders in his name before the Egyptians!"

The LORD heard how they were colluding against him.
Now, the man Moses was very humble,
More so than any man on earth.
Suddenly, the LORD spoke to Moses, Aaron and Miriam,
"You three, go to the Tent of Meeting."
They went there and the LORD descended in a pillar of cloud.
He stood by the opening of the Tent and summoned
Aaron and Miriam. They both came out and he said,
"Hear my words: with any prophet of the LORD among you
I reveal myself to him in a vision.
In a dream I speak to him. Not so with my servant Moses.
In my entire household, he is the most trusted.
Mouth to mouth, I speak to him distinctly
Not in ambiguities. He gazes on the reflection of the LORD,
Why were you then not afraid to reproach my servant Moses?"
The LORD was incensed against them and he withdrew.
The cloud ascended from the Tent, and look –
Miriam became as leprous as snow.
When Aaron looked at Miriam – she was a leper.
Aaron pleaded with Moses, "Please, my lord,
Do not punish us for our sin;

We acknowledge our foolishness and our sinfulness.
Let her not be as though she were dead,
Who leaves his mother's womb as flesh half wasted."
Moses implored the LORD,
"Please, God, please heal her."
The LORD answered Moses, "Had her father spat in her face,
Would she not be humiliated?
Let her be locked away outside the camp seven days,
Then she may re-enter the camp again."
Miriam was put out of the camp for seven days,
She returned to the camp cured of leprosy.
The people stayed their journey until Miriam's re-entry.
After this the people departed from Hazeroth
And pitched their tents in the wilderness of Paran.

The LORD instructed Moses, "Send men to spy out the
Land of Canaan which I am giving to the descendants of Israel.
From each ancestral tribe send one man – a prince among
   them."
Moses sent them from the wilderness of Paran according to the
LORD's instruction – all were head-men of the Israelites:

These were their names tribe by tribe:

1. *Reuben*: Shammua ben Zaccur
2. *Simeon*: Shaphat ben Hori
3. *Judah*: Caleb ben Jephunneh
4. *Issachar*: Igal ben Joseph
5. *Ephraim*: Hosea bin Nun
6. *Benjamin*: Palti ben Raphu
7. *Zebulun*: Gaddiel ben Sodi
8. *Manasseh*: Gaddi ben Susi
9. *Dan*: Ammiel ben Gemalli
10. *Asher*: Sethur ben Michael
11. *Naphtali*: Nahbi ben Vophsi
12. *Gad*: Geuel ben Machi.

These are the names of the men whom Moses sent to spy out
The country. **No one was sent from the tribe of Levi.**[1]
(Now Moses called Hoshea bin Nun, Joshua.)

---

[1] The tribe of Moses and Aaron. They were to become the special caste of priests.

When Moses sent them to spy out the land of Canaan,
He instructed them, "Go up this way towards the south.
Go through the mountain passes; view the land –
What is it like, and as for the people who live there –
Are they strong or weak, few or many;
As for the land in which they live – is it good or bad?
And the towns in which they live – are they camps or fortified;
The country – is it rich or poor; has it forests or not?
Be courageous and bring specimens of its fruit."

The time was the season of the first ripe grapes.
They left to spy out the land from the
Wilderness of Zin to Rehob at the entrance of Hamath.
They went southward and reached Hebron.
The clans of Ahiman, Sheshai and Talmai,
The descendants of **the demigod** Anak,[1] lived there.
(Now, Hebron was **an ancient town** built seven years
Before **the great city of** Zoan in Egypt.)
They reached the valley of Eshkol and cut down
A branch with one cluster of grapes of such a size
It required two men to carry it on a staff.
They also brought branches of pomegranates and figs.
That place was named the valley of Eshkol because of
The cluster [eshkol] which the Israelites had cut down.
After forty days they returned from their spying expedition.

They came to Moses, Aaron and to the entire
Community of Israelites at Kadesh in the Paran wilderness,
To report to them and the community and show them the
Fruit of the land. This is what they said,
"We went into the land where you sent us.
Indeed it is a land which flows with milk and honey,
But the people who live there are powerful.

---

[1] Plural: 'Anakim' – The name given to the giants who were the issue of the mating of the sons-of-God with the daughter of Man. See *Genesis, The People's Bible.* pp. 11,12.

The towns are fortified and very large;
There we saw the descendants of Anak.
In the southern part of the land live the Amalekites,
The Hittites, Jebusites and Amorites live in the hill country.
The Canaanites live by the sea and along the Jordan."

The people began to moan: "We will never defeat them."
Caleb silenced the people before Moses. He shouted,
"Let us go up immediately to possess it –
We can certainly conquer it."
But the men who had gone up with him said,
"We are not able to attack the people.
They are mightier than us."
So they returned with a negative report concerning the land
They had spied out for the Israelites, "The land we have
Spied out is a place unable to sustain its inhabitants.
All the men we saw were of enormous stature.
We saw the giants, the descendants of Anak –
One of the *Nefilim*, **the children of the sons-of-God.**
Compared to them, we appeared to ourselves like grasshoppers
And so must we have appeared to them."

The whole community wailed and wept.
The people wept throughout the night.
The Israelites complained bitterly against Moses and Aaron,
"Better we had died in Egypt or even in the wilderness.
Why does the LORD bring us here to put us to the sword –
Our wives and our infants will be spoils **for the victors.**
Is it not better for us to return to Egypt?"
They said to each other, "Let us appoint a captain
Who will lead us back to Egypt."

Moses and Aaron fell on their faces before the Israelites.
Joshua bin Nun and Caleb ben Jephunneh who were of the
    spies
Ripped their clothes **as do those in mourning.**
They pleaded with all the Israelites, "The land we spied out

Is a very good land. If the LORD takes delight in us,
He will bring us to this land and give it to us.
It is a land which flows with milk and honey.
Just do not rebel against the LORD!
Do not be afraid of the natives of the land,
For they will be like bread for us **to chew up.**
All their defences will disappear for the LORD is with us –
Do not be in awe of them!"
But they urged each other to stone them
And the glory of the LORD appeared to
The Israelites at the Tent of Meeting.

The LORD said to Moses,
"Until when will this people despise me,
Until when will they not believe in me
Despite all the wonders I have done for them?
I will strike them down with a pestilence
And disown them; but I will make you
Into a great people – more numerous than they."

Moses replied to the LORD, "**This will not be wise.**
The Egyptians know that by your power
You have brought out this people from among them.
They will speak of it to those who live in this land.
They **too** know that you, O LORD, are among this people,
That you reveal yourself to their sight, O LORD.
As your cloud stands over them and that
You lead them by a pillar of cloud by day
And a pillar of cloud by night.
Now, if you kill this people as if it was one man,
The nations who have heard of your fame will say,
'Because he was unable to bring this people into the land
He promised them, he slaughtered them in the wilderness.'

"Now I beg of you, my LORD, reveal your even greater power,
Of which you yourself have spoken:
'The LORD is full of forbearance, exceedingly kind,

Forgiving iniquity and transgression.
However, he does not exonerate the guilty
But imposes **the consequences of** the sins of the fathers
On their descendants to the third and fourth generation.'
Please pardon the iniquity of this people
In accordance to your kindness which is so great,
Just as you have forgiven this people
From her time in Egypt until now."
The LORD said, "Because of your words, I have forgiven.
But, as I live and as the earth is filled with my glory:
All these people who have seen **the revelation of** my glory,
My signs, which I performed in Egypt and in the wilderness,
Yet tested me at least ten times by not obeying me –
They will never see the land I promised to the patriarchs,
Not one of them who despised me will see it!
But my servant, Caleb, because there was another spirit in
    him,
And he was fully behind me, I will take him to the land
Which he has entered and his descendants will inherit it.
Now, the Amalekites and Canaanites live in the valley –
Go back into the wilderness by way of the Red Sea."

"How long must I suffer this wicked people?"

[1]The LORD spoke to Moses and Aaron, "How long must I suffer
This wicked people who continually rail against me?
I have heard their moaning and groaning against me.
Tell them, 'By my life,' says the LORD, 'as you have said
In my hearing, just so will I deal with you.
You will turn into corpses in this wilderness –
All of you from the age of twenty upwards

---

[1] What follows appears repetitive, but it does expand on God's previous speech
to Moses and is addressed to Aaron as well as Moses to be reported back to the
sinning Israelites.

Who have moaned and groaned against me
You will most certainly not go into the land which
Through my power you were to possess to live in.
Only Caleb ben Jephunneh and Joshua bin Nun –
The two spies who believed in me – shall enter it.[1]
But your infants whom you said would be for spoil –
Them will I bring in and they will live in the land
You have rejected. But as for you –
You will turn into corpses in the wilderness.'

'Your children will wander in the wilderness forty years,
Suffering for your errors until your bodies
Die in the wilderness. For as many days
You took to spy out the land – forty days –
So for forty years, a year for each day,
Will you know what it is to be alienated from me.
I, the LORD, have spoken, so will I behave towards
This wicked community who joined together against me.
In this wilderness they will be eaten up. Here will they die!"'

The men whom Moses sent out to spy out the land
Who, on their return, made the Israelites conspire
Against him because of their pessimistic report –
These men died immediately by a plague from the LORD.
[But Joshua bin Nun and Caleb ben Jephunneh remained alive
Of all the men that went to spy out the land.]

Moses reported these words to all the Israelites
And they went into deep mourning. Early next morning
They ascended the high places, "Here we are,
We will go up to the place the LORD has promised
Because we have sinned." Moses was contemptuous,
"Why do you again transgress the word of the LORD –
You will not succeed in so doing. Do not go up because

[1] It would appear that God had already decided that Moses and Aaron would also die in the wilderness, though this deprivation is attributed to a later peccadillo on their part.

The LORD is not with you to prevent you from being beaten
By your enemies. The Amalekites and the Canaanites
Are there facing you; you will fall by the sword
Because you turned your backs on the LORD –
Therefore the LORD will not be with you."

Still they had the temerity to go up into the hill country.
But the Ark of the LORD's Covenant did not leave the camp.
The Amalekites came down as did the Canaanites
Who lived in those hills. They struck them down
And cut them back as far as Hormah.[1]

The Rebellion of Korah

Korah ben Izhar ben Kahath, the descendant of Levi,
Along with Dathan and Abiram the sons of Eliab and
On ben Peleth, the descendants of Reuben,[2] took men
Who with certain Israelites conspired against Moses –
Two hundred and fifty chieftains and well-known councillors.
They joined together against Moses and Aaron saying,
"You take too much upon yourselves as
The entire community – all of them are holy!
The LORD is with them. **Did you not tell us so!**
Why then do you exalt yourselves over the LORD's assembly?"[3]

[1] Those who read this as pure historical narrative would maintain that the Israelites did not have the strength to conquer Canaan for a long period of time, as their defeat proved, and thus remained as nomads in the wilderness. The biblical view is that their lack of faith in the Lord is what condemned them to remain nomads. The result is the same. Chapter 15 which follows describes aspects of the sacrificial rite and is to be found in *The Laws of Moses*, page 115ff.
[2] Reuben, being Jacob's [Israel's] first-born, his descendants would have an interest in achieving more authority as their hereditary right.
[3] Following the events of Miriam's and Aaron's attacks on Moses, this rebellion is even more fantastic when one considers that Moses's face was so radiant with the divine light that he had to keep it covered lest it blind the onlookers. On this basis and on other inconsistencies the ancient rabbinic sages maintained that there is no chronological order in the Torah. Indeed, the exuberance of the rebels appears unrealistic after the news that they are to die in the wilderness.

When Moses heard this he fell on his face. He said to Korah
And to his group, "In the morning the LORD will show
Who are his, who is holy. He will bring him close to him –
He whom he has chosen will he bring near to him.

"Do this – you, Korah, and all in his group – take censers.
Tomorrow put burning incense on them before the LORD.
The man whom the LORD does choose – he is holy.
You have taken too much upon yourselves – you sons of Levi!"
Moses continued speaking to Korah,
"Listen now, you descendants of Levi,
Does it seem but a small thing to you that the God of Israel
Has distinguished you from among the community of Israel.
To bring you near to himself to minister at the
Tabernacle of the LORD – to stand before the congregation
To minister to them. He brought you and all your
Kinsmen of the descendants of Levi near to him.
Now, do you also demand the priesthood?[1]
You and your entire group have joined against the LORD.
What has Aaron done that you conspire against him?
It is not his choice but the Lord who has selected him."

Moses summoned Dathan and Abiram, the sons of Eliab,
But they said, "We will not come up to you.
Is it a small matter that you brought us up from
A land flowing with milk and honey to kill us in
The wilderness[2] – does this entitle you to rule over us?
You have not brought us to a land flowing with milk and
  honey

---

[1] The priesthood belonged solely to Aaron and his descendants. So Moses is not
defending his own position but that of his brother. Later narratives indicate
that it was much later that the priesthood was restricted to the descendants of
Aaron. For a period it seemed to have been the prerogative of the first-born.
[2] This now is a head-on attack on Moses. Confronted by the hardships of the
wilderness, in retrospect oppression in Egypt appears idyllic. The Reubenites
decide to make their own altar on which to offer sacrifices. Korah, the
rebellious Levite, however, heeds Moses's instructions.

Nor given us the possession of fields and vineyards.
You may throw dust into the eyes of your followers.
We will not obey your summons. We will not come to you!"

Moses was very angry. He petitioned the LORD,
"Do not accept their offering. I have not taken a donkey from
   them,
Nor have I hurt any of them." Moses instructed Korah,
"You and your group will come before the LORD tomorrow.
You, all of them and Aaron as well.
Let everyone bring his censer filled with incense –
Let every man bring his censer before the LORD –
Each man with his censer – that is two hundred and fifty
Censers – you and Aaron, each with his censer."

The next day, each man brought his censer, lit it
And placed incense on it. They stood at the entrance of
The Tent of Meeting together with Moses and Aaron.
So Korah's group confronted them at the Tent of Meeting.
The LORD's glory appeared to the whole group.
The LORD spoke to Moses and Aaron,
"Distance yourself from this mob and
I will consume them in a moment."

They fell on their faces and said, "God, the God of
The spirits of all flesh, will you consume in anger
All of them for the sin of one man?"
The LORD answered Moses, "Say this to them,
'Distance yourself from the Tabernacle[1] built by
Korah, Dathan and Abiram.'" Moses went to Dathan and
   Abiram,
The elders of the Israelites following him.
He warned the men about them, "Leave the encampment of

[1] Had Dahan and Abiram built their own tabernacle to promote their right to
be priests because they were the descendants of Jacob's first-born, Reuben? This
would explain their refusal to accept Moses's summons to attend on him. They
rejected his priestly authority over them.

These wicked men! Do not touch anything of theirs
Lest you be engulfed together with their sins."
From every side they left the tabernacle of Korah,
Dathan and Abiram. Dathan and Amiram came out and stood by
The entrance of their tents, with their wives, sons and babes.
Moses said, "This is how you will know that
The LORD has sent me
To do all these things **to have authority over you.**
I have not done them voluntarily.
If these men die as do most men or if they share
The fate of all men, the LORD has not sent me.
But if the LORD makes something unique happen –
If the earth opens up its mouth and swallows them up
With everything that belongs to them and they descend to
Sheol alive, you will know that these men despised the LORD
By rejecting me and Aaron, my brother."

As soon as he finished saying this, the ground under them
Split open – the earth opened up her mouth and
Swallowed them and their households –
All the people who followed Korah and all their belongings.
They went down with all they had, alive to Sheol.
The earth covered them up and they disappeared from
Amidst the assembly. All the Israelites who were close by
Fled at their cry for they were afraid that the earth
Would swallow them up. Fire emitted from the LORD
And consumed the two hundred and fifty men
Who were offering up the incense.[1]

---

[1] Two stories of destruction seem to be intertwined: 1) the earthquake which
swallows up Dathan and Abiram and their cohorts; 2) The divine fire that
burns up Korah and his followers. Are they based on two separate attempts to
wrest the priesthood from the Aaronites, one by the firstborn represented by
Reuben and one by a different clan of Levites? This speculation is strengthened
by the fact that later in *Numbers* 26:11, the narrator tells us that the sons of
Korah were not killed. They may have been too young to be carrying censers;
they would, however, have been swallowed up by the earthquake. In any
event, God has rejected Moses's plea to spare the group and only to punish the
instigators.

The LORD instructed Moses, "Tell Eleazar ben Aaron the priest
To remove the censers from the embers of the flames,
And disperse the other embers. The censers are holy –
Even the censers of these who have sinned to the
Cost of their own lives. Let them be beaten into plates for a
Covering for the altar. As they have offered them to the LORD,
They are holy – they will be a symbol for the Israelites."
Eleazar the priest took the brass censers offered by the
Rebels who had been burnt up and had them beaten out
For an altar covering – a reminder to the Israelites that
No alien – that is someone who is not a descendent of Aaron –
Should offer up incense before the LORD so that they
Do not end up as Korah and his company –
Just as the LORD had ordained through Moses.

The following day, **once again,** all the Israelites complained
Against Moses and Aaron, "You have killed the LORD's
    people."[1]
When the community joined together against Moses and
    Aaron,
They looked at the Tent of Meeting and over it was a cloud
And the glory of God was seen.
Moses and Aaron approached the front of the Tent of Meeting.
The LORD commanded Moses, "Quickly, leave this congregation
And I will in the space of a moment consume them."
They **did not do so but** fell on their faces **in prayer.**
Moses ordered Aaron, "Take the censer and set it aflame
From the altar; place incense upon it and quickly go to
The congregation and do atonement for them.
The LORD's wrath is pouring over – the plague has
    commenced."

---

[1] In the light of the miracles just witnessed, the self-destructive nature of the
Israelites is hard to believe! Whatever their grievance, how can the narrator
have them attack Moses for killing the 'Lord's people', when it is the Lord who
is responsible. It would appear that these episodes and the one to follow are
designed to repeat *ad nauseam* the rights of the tribe of Levi, and especially the
family of Aaron over the Temple service.

Aaron did as Moses had bidden – he ran into the midst of
The community, but the plague had begun to strike the people.
He put on the incense and made atonement for the people.
He was standing between the dead and the living.
The plague ended. Those that died by plague were
Fourteen thousand and seven hundred excluding those
Who had died because of Korah. When Moses and Aaron
Returned to the Tent of Meeting the plague had ended.

The LORD instructed Moses, "Tell the Israelites each to take
Staves, one for each tribe; all the tribal chieftains –
Twelve staves. Write each chieftain's name on his staff.
You will write Aaron's name[1] on the staff of Levi,
For there is to be one staff for each tribal chieftain.
And you will plant them in the Tent of Meeting before the
Ark of the Testimony **in which are the**
Two Tablets of The Law –
Where I meet with you. The man whom I choose
His staff shall flower, so will I end the complaints of the
Israelites who are constantly murmuring against you."
Moses instructed the Israelites: all the chieftains
Gave him staves, one for each tribal chieftain –
Twelve staves and Aaron's staff was among them. Moses
Planted the staves before the LORD in the Tent of the
    Testimony.
Aaron's staff of the tribe of Levi blossomed.
Its sprouted buds turned into blossoms
Bearing ripe almonds. Moses took out all the staves
From before the LORD as the Israelites looked on.
Each chieftain fetched his staff. The LORD told Moses,
"Put back Aaron's staff before the **Ark of** Testimony
To be kept as a reminder of the seeds of rebellion,

---

[1] It is of interest that it is not Moses's name but Aaron's – a further indication
that this was intended to establish the authority of the descendants of Aaron as
Israel's priests.

To put an end to their complaints so that they do not die."
So Moses did just as the LORD had instructed him.

The dread of the Lord fell upon the Israelites.
They said to Moses, "We are all dead men.
We are utterly lost if everyone who comes near the Tabernacle,
Who seeks to approach God dies.
Will there ever be an end to our dying?"
Moses replied to them, "You will not die now,
But you will never see the Promised Land."[1]

The Israelites, the entire people, reached the wilderness of Zin
In the first month **of the fortieth year of their wanderings.**
The people encamped in Kadesh where Miriam died and was
   buried.
There was no water there for the people to drink.
They joined together to protest to Moses and Aaron.
The people quarrelled with Moses. "We would be better off if
We had died with our kinsmen by the hand of the LORD.
Why did you bring the LORD's people into this wilderness,
That we should die here, we and our cattle?
Why did you make us come out of Egypt
To bring us to this evil place – not a place for planting seed,
Or for figs or for vineyards or pomegranates?
There is not even any water to drink."
Moses and Aaron left the people to go to the entrance of the
Tent of Meeting; they prostrated themselves with their faces
To the ground and the glory of the LORD appeared to them.

Moses said to the Lord, "What am I to do with your people?
They say, 'Would that we had died as did our fathers.'
Then they condemn me for taking 'your' people from Egypt,
As if you had not sent me as your messenger to save them.

---

[1] Chapters 18 and 19 confirm the privileges of the tribe of Levi. To the
descendants of Aaron will go the rich benefits that come from representing God
on earth. These are to be found in the *Laws of Moses*, page 119ff.

This generation is no better than their fathers.
How can they go up to the land you have promised to
Give to Abraham, Isaac and Jacob?
They are not worthy of your graciousness.
Let them also die in the wilderness.
I am weary to death of their wickedness."

The Lord replied to Moses, "They will enter and conquer
The land I promised to their ancestors.
They are a stubborn people but they are mine.
I have chosen the children of Abraham, my friend,
To serve me so that I may watch over them,
So that they will walk in my ways
And be a blessing for all the nations of the earth."
Then the LORD instructed Moses, "Take your staff;
Order the people to assemble. You and Aaron, your brother,
Will speak to the rock before their very eyes.
You will make water come out of the rock and
You will give water to all the people and their cattle."
Moses was not pleased. He did not wish to perform miracles
For the people of Israel because of their rebelliousness.
But he obeyed the Lord. Moses took his staff from
Before the LORD as he had instructed him.

"Because you did not trust me . . ."

Moses summoned the people to come to the face of the rock.
He was very angry and did not want to give them water.
He shouted at them, "Listen, you rebels,
Shall we bring you water out of this stone?"
And, instead of speaking to the rock as the Lord had
Instructed him, he raised his hand and twice
Did he strike the rock and streams of water
Gushed out of the rock, so the people and their cattle drank.

The LORD said to Moses and Aaron,
"Because you did not trust me,

To sanctify me in the sight of the Israelites, **for you said,**
'Shall *we* **bring you water' when it is I who saves Israel –**
You will not bring this people into the land I am giving them."
These are known as the waters of Meribah[1] because
The Israelites quarrelled with the LORD.
Still his holy power was revealed because of them,[2]
As he created water from the rock
To satisfy the thirst of a whole people and its cattle.

The Lord comforted Moses, "You will not enter the land
But you will see it. You have been my Messenger
To bring my people to their land.
But you are tired and weary of bearing the burden
Of this people. It will be enough for you.
Another man will bring them across into their inheritance.
But your work is not yet done.
You will need to conquer the nations who will not
Permit my people Israel to enter the land I promised
To give to their ancestors, Abraham and Israel.

So Moses sent messengers from Kadesh to the king of Edom,
"So speaks your brother Israel, **for did not Esau [Edom]**
His brother come out of the same womb?
You have heard of all the sufferings that have befallen us,
How our ancestors went down into Egypt.
Where we lived many years.
The Egyptians treated us badly – our ancestors too.
We cried out to the LORD. He heard our voices.
He sent a Messenger[3] and he took us out of Egypt.
Now we are in Kadesh, the town closest to your border.

---

[1] Meaning *strife.*

[2] Literal translation: 'and he was sanctified in them.' I believe that my
translation makes sense of the narrator's intention.

[3] The messenger, *angelus* in Greek [thus angel in traditional translations], could
only have been Moses, as no other messenger is ever mentioned. This indicates
that God may send a man or woman to do his work, just as he may send a
representative or reflection of his divine being.

Please allow us to pass through your territory.
We will not go over your fields or vineyards.
We will not drink the waters of your wells.
We will march on the king's highway.
We will not turn aside to the right or to the left –
Until we leave your territory."

Edom sent back this reply, "You shall not cross my land,
Unless you want me to greet you with the sword of war."
The Israelites responded, "We will go on the highway.
If we drink your water, we and our cattle,
We will pay the proper price. Let us only, nothing more,
Pass through on our feet." But Edom said,
"You will not be allowed to pass through."
So the Edomites confronted them with a great army
And great weaponry. So did Edom refuse to
Grant Israel the right to pass through
Their territory. So Israel turned back from Edom.
They then set off from Kadesh and all the Israelites came to
Mount Hor, which was by the border of the land of Edom
Where the LORD informed Moses and Aaron:[1]
"Aaron shall be gathered to his people,
He will not enter the land I am giving to the Israelites
Because you rebelled against me at the waters of Meribah.
Take Aaron and Eleazar his son and bring them to Mount Hor.
Strip Aaron of his vestments and put them on Eleazar his son.
Aaron will be gathered to his people and die there."

Moses did as the LORD had commanded.
They went up to Mount Hor in the sight of all Israel.
Moses stripped Aaron of his vestments[2]

---

[1] From what follows, it would appear that God is only speaking to Moses. It has been suggested that later priestly scribes coupled Aaron's name to that of Moses in order to enhance the importance of the founder of the priestly hierarchy.

[2] The absence of human feeling suggests that the only purpose of this story is to validate the inheritance of the high priesthood through Aaron's line. We are not even told that he was buried.

And put them on his son Eleazar.
Aaron died there on the top of the mountain.
When Moses and Eleazar came down
The whole community knew that Aaron had died.
All of Israel mourned over him for thirty days.

The Canaanite king of Arad who reigned in the Negev
Learnt that Israel was coming by way of Atharim.
They attacked the Israelites **as had Amalek**
By ambushing them; they took some captives.
Israel vowed an oath to the LORD:
"If you deliver this people into our hand
We will utterly destroy all their towns
And give all the booty to the Lord's sanctuary."
The LORD heeded Israel's petition and
Delivered up the Canaanites to them.
They and their towns were utterly destroyed
So that place was named Hormah.[1]

They set out from Mount Hor by way of the Red Sea
To circle around Edomite territory.
But the people became impatient on the journey:
"Why had not the Lord enabled us to go through Edom,
Where there was plenty of food and water!"
So the people spoke against God and Moses,
"Why did you bring us up out of Egypt
To die in the wilderness because there is no bread or water –
We are fed up with this revolting bread."[2]
The LORD sent flying[3] serpents against the people.

---

[1] A place with its booty being under a ban, as was Jericho. This episode is
misplaced. It should have happened after they left Sinai, as the south of
Canaan – the Negev – would be on this route.

[2] They are referring to the manna from heaven – an ironic reflection on
human nature.

[3] The Hebrew is *seraph*, often translated as fiery, which is doubtful. On the basis
of an analogy with the *Seraphim* – winged celestial creatures – I have chosen
'flying' because they would not be creatures from which the Israelites could
flee.

They bit the people and many Israelites died.
The people came to Moses and said, "We have sinned in that
We spoke against the LORD and against you.
Pray to the LORD so that he rid us of these serpents."
Moses interceded for the people.
The LORD instructed Moses, "Make a *Seraph* figure
And mount it on a standard.
Anyone bitten who looks at it will live."
Moses made a copper *Seraph* and set it on a standard.
So it was, if a serpent bit a person and
He looked at the copper serpent, he lived.

The Israelites journeyed and camped at Oboth.
From Oboth they encamped at Iye-abarim,
In the wilderness before Moab where the sun rises.
From there they camped at the wadi of Zered
From there they encamped beyond the Arnon,
In the wilderness on the border of the Amorites;
For Arnon is the border of Moab between her and the
    Amorites.
Therefore the 'Book of Wars'[1] speaks of:
Waheb in Suphah, and the wadis of Arnon
Whose tributaries stretched to the settlement of Ar,
Hugging the territory of Moab.

From there to Beer, the well where the LORD said to
    Moses,
"Assemble the people that I may give them water."
Then Israel sang this song,
    "Spring up, O well; be a chorus
    To the sound of the waters gushing forth
    The well that the chieftains dug
    Which the notables of the people laid open

---

[1] Another authoritative book, which has been lost. It would appear that the
only guarantee of ancient works being preserved was their inclusion in the
Canon. How wonderful it would be were these to be found in some buried
urns!

With their maces and staffs –
A gift from the wilderness"[1]

From Beer they journeyed to Nahaliel, to Bamoth,
Then to the valley that is in the territory of Moab,
To the peak of Pisgah,[2]
Overlooking the wasteland.
Israel sent messengers to Sihon, king of the Amorites,
"Let me pass through your land
We will not stray into your fields or vineyards
We will not drink the waters of your wells.
We will follow the king's highway
Until we have crossed your territory."
But Sihon did not allow Israel to do so.
He mustered all his forces and
Marched against Israel in the wilderness.
He reached Jahaz where he attacked the Israelites.

And Israel felled him with its swords
And took possession of his land
From Arnon to Jabbok up to the boundaries of the Ammonites.
For the borders of the Ammonites were impenetrable.
Israel captured all their towns.
Israel lived in the Amorite towns,
In Heshbon and all its villages.
Heshbon was the city of Sihon, king of the Amorites
Who had warred against the former king of Moab,
Who had wrested from him all his land
As far as the Arnon, wherefore the bards would sing,
  "Come to Heshbon.
  Let the city of Sihon be built and fortified.
  For a fire has gone out of Heshbon –

[1] The involvement of the people in the digging of the well would indicate that it was more than God's command which brought forth the water. God told them where to look, but humans had to do the work.
[2] The mountain range called the mountain of Arabim [*Deuteronomy* 32:49] of which Mount Nebo, the place of Moses's death, was the highest point.

A flame from the city of Sihon.
It has consumed Ar of Moab,
The lords of the heights of Arnon.

Woe to you, O Moab
You are finished, O inhabitants of Chemosh,
His sons have become fugitives.
His daughters are taken captive
By an Amorite king, Sihon.

But we have brought them down[1]
Heshbon along with Dibon
We have laid waste Nophah
Which reaches as far as Medeba."

So Israel settled in the land of the Amorites.
Moses sent to spy out Jazer, **after which**
They captured their villages and
Dispossessed the Amorites who lived in them.

They turned to proceed along the road to Bashan.
Og, king of Bashan, marched to attack them –
He and all his forces to do battle at Edrei.
The LORD said to Moses, "Do not fear him!
As I have delivered him and his people and his land
Into your hand; you will do to him as you did to
Sihon, the king of the Amorites, who reigned in Heshbon."
They struck him down – his sons and all his people,
Not one of his men remained alive.
So did they conquer his land.
The Israelites moved on and camped in the steppes of Moab
Across the Jordan from Jericho.

Balak ben Zippor saw all that the Israelites
Had done to the Amorites. Moab was terrified of them
Because there were so many of them.

---

[1] The defeat of the Amorites is all the more impressive because of their earlier conquest of Moab.

Moab was in dread of the Israelites.
The leaders of Moab consulted with the leaders of Midian,
"Now this horde shall lick clean all that is about us
As the ox licks clean the grass of the field."
Balak ben Zippor was king of Moab at that time.
He sent messengers to Balaam ben Beor in Pethor
Which is by the River [Euphrates], the home of his kinsmen,
To fetch him, "See, a people have come out of Egypt.
It casts its shadow over the entire countryside.
It is now settled **threateningly** close to me.
Please come now, curse this people for me
Because he is stronger than me.
Then, I might succeed to strike him down –
To expel them from our territory for I know:
He whom you bless is blessed
And he whom you curse is cursed."

The elders of Moab and the elders of Midian,
Experts in divination, set out and came to Balaam
And gave him Balak's message.
He replied to them, "Stay here tonight.
I shall respond to you as the LORD instructs me."
So the officials of Moab stayed with Balaam.
God came to Balaam and said,
"Who are these men with you?"
Balaam replied to God, "Balak ben Zippor, king of Moab
Sent them to me **with these words:**
'See, the people who have come out of Egypt
Have cast its shadow on the whole earth.
Come now, curse them for me. Then I might succeed
In fighting them and driving them out.'"
God said to Balaam, "Do not go with them,
Do not curse the people for they are blessed."

Balaam got up in the morning and spoke to Balak's officials:
"Return to your land for the LORD will not let me go with
   you."

The officials of Moab got up, returned to Balak and said,
"Balaam refused to come with us."
Balak sent more officials of even greater standing.
They came to Balaam, "Thus says Balak ben Zippor,
'Let nothing prevent you from coming to me, for
I will load you with honours and do whatever you ask of me.
Please come and curse this people for me.'"
Balaam answered the ministers of Balak,
"Were Balak to give me his house full of silver and gold,
I could not transgress the command of the LORD my God,
Whether it be in an insignificant or major matter.
So now, please stay here tonight and I will learn
If the LORD has anything more to say to me."

God came to Balaam that night and said to him,
"You really want to go for you could have sent them away.
So, if the men have come for you, go with them
But you will only act according to my instructions."
**God was not pleased with Balaam because he wanted
The riches that Balak ben Zippor would give him.**[1]
Balaam got up in the morning and saddled his donkey
And went with the officials of Moab.

Now God was burning with anger because he went.
So a Messenger of the LORD stood in his path to oppose him.
He was now riding on his ass with two servants beside him.
The ass saw the Messenger of the LORD standing in his way,
With his sword drawn in his hand.
The ass turned from the path into the fields.
Balaam whacked the ass to direct her back to the path.
Then the Messenger of the LORD stood in an alley-way
Between the vineyards with fences on both sides. Seeing the

---

[1] My intervention is to reconcile the textual contradiction for God will soon
place obstacles in Balaam's path. It is possible that two stories are interwoven
here. Another interpretation is that what follows is a dream in which Balaam
finally receives God's permission to go to Balak.

Messenger of the LORD, the ass lurched to the wall,
Pressing Balaam's foot against the wall. He whacked her again.

The Messenger of the LORD went ahead and stood in a
Narrow place where there was no way to swerve right or left.
The ass saw the Messenger of the LORD.
She lay down with Balaam's feet crushed under her belly.[1]
Balaam burnt with anger and he whacked the ass with his
     staff.
The LORD opened the mouth of the ass who said to Balaam,
· "What have I done to you that you should hit me three
     times?"
– "You have made a fool of me.
If I had a sword in my hand,
I would have killed you by now."
– "Am I not your ass on whom you have been riding
All along until this very day?
Had I ever done such things to you?"
– "No, **that is true**."

Then the LORD opened Balaam's eyes and he saw
The Messenger of the LORD standing in the way
With his sword drawn in his hand.
He bowed and fell with his nose to the ground.
The Messenger of the LORD said to him,
"Why have you hit your ass these three times?
See, I have come to oppose you
For the path you are taking is abhorrent to me.
The ass saw me and turned from me three times.
Had she not turned away from me,
You are the one I would have killed –
I would have allowed her to live."
– "I have sinned because I did not know you stood in the way.
If it displeases you I will return home."

---

[1] Literally: She lay down under Balaam. This does not convey Balaam's
discomfort.

– "Go with the men, but only the words I say to you –
Those will you utter."
So Balaam went with the officials of Balak.[1]

Balak heard that Balaam had arrived **in Moab.**
He went out to greet him at Ir-moab
By the Arnon, which is at the furthest border.
Balak challenged Balaam, "Did I not urgently summon you!
Why did you not come to me **immediately**?
Am I not able to load honours **and riches** on you?"
– "Look, I have come to you
But be warned, I can say nothing, but
The words which God puts into my mouth
Only those may I speak."

Balaam went with Balak and they came to Kiriath-huzoth.
Balak sacrificed sheep and oxen
And sent for Balaam and officials who were with him
To eat of the sacrifices he offered.
In the morning, Balak took Balaam up to Bamoth-baal.[2]
From there he could see some of the Israelites.
Balaam said to Balak, "Build me seven altars.
Prepare for me seven bulls and seven rams."
Balak did as Balaam had instructed.
Balak and Balaam offered a bull and a ram on each altar.
Balaam instructed Balak, "Stand by the burnt offering.
I will go now. Perhaps the LORD will manifest himself to me.
Whatever he reveals to me, I will tell you."
He went off to a secluded high place.

God made himself known to Balaam. He said to him,
"I have erected seven altars. On each of them
I have offered up a bull and a ram."

---

[1] Where was the company of Moabites during Balaam's tribulations? Could this be the dream/nightmare, which gives him permission to go, or is it just a matter of literary licence?
[2] Literally: the high places of Baal – the local male deity.

And the LORD put words into the mouth of Balaam,
"Return to Balak and this is what you will say."
He returned to him; he was standing by his burnt offering,
He and all the officials of Moab.

Balaam's Oracles

He began his oracle:
    "From Aram has Balak led me here –
    Moab's king **brought me** from eastern hills,
    'Come, curse Jacob for me
    Come and damn Israel.'
    But how can I curse whom God has not cursed
    And how can I damn whom God has not damned!

    "From the mountain tops I see him
    From the peaks I look on them.
    It is a people who dwell alone.
    Among the nations, they are discounted.
    Who can count the dust[1] of Jacob
    And number the descendants of Israel?
    Let me die, **like them,** die the death of the upright
    May my destiny be as theirs."

Balak cried to Balaam, "What are you doing to me?
I brought you here to curse my enemies
But instead you have given them a great blessing."
– "I understand what you say
But if the LORD puts words into my mouth
Must I not be sure to express them?"
– "Please, go with me to another place
Which may be more favourable
A change in place may bring a change in fortune.
From there you will see them,

---

[1] God promises Abraham that his descendants will be as numerous as the dust of the earth . . . *Genesis* 13:16.

But only a small number of them – not all of them
And curse them for me from there."

He took him to a lookout point at the peak of Pisgah.
Again he built seven altars
And offered a bull and ram on each of them.
Balaam said to Balak, "Stand this way by your burnt offering,
While I wait for the LORD over there."
The LORD met Balaam and put words into his mouth.
He said, "Return to Balak and tell him this."
He came to him who was still standing by his offering.
His officials were with him. Balak asked him,
"What did the LORD say?"

Balaam uttered his oracle:
  "Stand up, Balak, and listen.
  Hear me, you son of Zippor.
  God is not a man to act with deceit,
  Nor a mortal to change his mind.
  Will he make a commitment and not do it?
  Will he make a promise and not fulfil it?
  My command was to bless,
  He has blessed and I cannot reverse it.

  "He has not seen any faults in Jacob[1] –
  Nothing deserving misfortune in Israel.
  The LORD his God is with him,
  Acclaimed among them as king.
  God had brought him out of Egypt
  With the thrusting power of wild oxen.

  "Jacob is in no need of wizardry
  Nor are there divinations in Israel.
  The time is coming and it will be said of Jacob and Israel
  How wonderfully God has acted **for them**.

---

[1] A great exaggeration if one considers that God wanted to destroy all the Israelites. But is this the new generation?

The people are rearing up like a lioness;
Like a lion, he arouses himself
He will not lie down before eating the prey
And drinking the blood of the slain."

And Balak said to Balaam, "**In that case,**
Do not curse them but **at least** do not bless them."
– "Did I not tell you that I must do whatever the LORD says?"
– "Come then, I will take you to another place
Perhaps God will approve you cursing them for me there."
Balak brought Balaam to the summit of Peor
Which overlooks the wastelands. Balaam instructed Balak,
"Build here another seven altars.
Prepare another seven bulls and rams."
Balak did so and offered a bull and ram on every altar.

As Balaam realised that the LORD wished to bless Israel,
He no longer went as before in search of omens.
He turned his face towards the wilderness **for inspiration.**
When he looked up, he saw Israel camped in tribal formation.
The divine spirit came on him and he prophesied,
  "The word[1] of Balaam ben Beor
  The word of a man whose eyes have been unveiled
  The word of he who has heard the words of God
  Who had visions of Shaddai[2]
  Who fell down **in awe**
  Whose eyes were unveiled.

  "How impressive are your tents, O Jacob
  Your encampments, O Israel!
  Like palm groves spreading far and wide,
  Like gardens by the river banks,

[1] The Hebrew *n'oom* is always used by the Hebrew prophets before God's name to express their conviction that they are declaring the *word of the Lord.* Though Balaam is inspired, the narrator, most likely a prophet himself, does not allow him to claim such authority.
[2] Another name for God. Meaning unknown, traditionally translated as almighty.

Like aloes planted by the LORD,
Like statuesque cedars beside the waters,
Their branches drip with moisture,
Their roots are well watered.

"His king shall rise higher than Agag.[1]
His kingdom will be exalted.
God brought him out of Egypt
With the thrusting power of wild oxen.
They shall consume hostile nations.
They shall shatter their bones
After breaking their arrows.

"He crouched down, he lay down as a lion.
And like a lion, who will dare to rouse him?
Blessed are those who bless you
Cursed are those who curse you!"

Balak was consumed with anger against Balaam.
He clapped his hands together and cried out to Balaam,
"I summoned you to curse my enemies
But instead you have now blessed them three times.
Therefore, flee home **for your life!**
I thought to load you with honours and riches,
But the LORD has denied you any benefits."

Balaam retorted: "Did I not tell your messengers,
'If Balak were to give me a house filled with silver and gold
I could not transgress the word of the LORD
To do good or evil according to my own will.
What the LORD speaks – that is what I will say.
Now, I return to my people.
But come, let me advise you as to what this people
Will do to your people in days to come.'"

---

[1] Agag, king of the Amalekites, was slain by Samuel. Was Agag a generic name for Amalekite monarchs like Pharaoh or Caesar? Or is it an indication of the time of the composition?

So he began his oracle,
"The word of Balaam son of Beor
The word of the man with unveiled eyes
The word of he who listens to the words of God,
Who has knowledge of the Most High
Who had visions of Shaddai
Who fell down **in awe**
Whose eyes were unveiled!

"What I see for him is yet to be.
I behold him but not soon.
A star emerges out of Jacob
A king's sceptre shall rise out of Israel
And smash the heads of Moab
And break down the sons of Seth.
Edom will be occupied.
Seir will be possessed by its enemies
While Israel is victorious[1]
From Jacob will come a victor
And destroy the survivors of Ar."

He looked at **the land of** Amalek and uttered this oracle:
"Amalek was first among the nations
But his fate is utter destruction."

He looked at **the land of** the Kenites and uttered this oracle:
"Your habitations are well-fortified.
Your nest is set in the cliffs.
Yet Kain's fate is to be burnt
When Assur takes you captive."
He then uttered this oracle:
"Who shall live unless God desires it?
Ships come from the coast of Kittim.

[1] The allusions seem to be to David's monarchy, during which time Moab and Edom were badly defeated and made servile states. The comparison of Israel to a lion supports this supposition as the lion was the emblem of Judah, David's ancestor, and Jacob on his deathbed refers to Judah as a lion.

> They shall oppress Assur and Eber
> But they too will end in utter destruction."[1]

Then Balaam set out on his return journey home and
Balak also went on his way.
The Israelites settled down in Shittim and
Degraded themselves by having intercourse with Moabite
    women
For they invited them to the sacrifices of their gods.
The Israelites ate and worshipped their gods.
When Israel submitted to the rites of Baal – **the god** of Peor,
The LORD went into a fiery rage against Israel.
The LORD instructed Moses, "Take out all the ringleaders
And impale them before the LORD in the face of the sun,
So that the LORD's burning anger may turn away from Israel."
Moses ordered the judges of Israel**'s tribes,**
"Kill every one of your men who have attached themselves to
Baal of Peor." **While they were in counsel,**
An Israelite came and brought over to his friends
A Midianite woman – **this he did** in the sight of Moses
And in view of the assembly of the Israelites
While they were weeping at the entrance of the
Tent of Meeting **over the tragedy that had befallen them.**

When Phinehas ben Eleazar ben Aaron the priest saw this,
He stood up from the assembly and grabbed a spear.
He went after the Israelite into the tent and
Transfixed the two of them through the belly
Pinning them together as they had intercourse.
So the plague that had struck Israel ceased.
Twenty-four thousand died from the plague.

The LORD spoke unto Moses, "Phinehas ben Eleazar ben Aaron

---

[1] The reference to nations is obscure. Kittim is identified with Greece. Could this
be referring to Alexander the Great? Is this prophecy or an indication of the
time of authorship? The theme seems to be that nations will destroy nations
and all is by the will of God.

The priest has abated my rage against the Israelites.
Because of his zealous passion among them on my behalf,
I did not consume the Israelites in my own jealousy.
Therefore, declare this: I am giving him my covenant of peace.[1]
He and his descendants will enjoy the priestly covenant
Forever because he was zealous for his God
And by his action achieved atonement for the Israelites.
The name of the slain Israelite with the Midianite woman was
Zimri, son of Salu, a chieftain of a leading Simeonite family.
The slain Midianite woman was Cozbi the daughter of Zur –
He was the chief of a clan, an ancestral house in Midian.
The LORD instructed Moses, "Harass the Midianites
And strike them down for they have harassed you
By their guile in the Peor affair when Cozbi, their sister,
The daughter of a chieftain of Midian, was killed
At the time of the plague because of Peor.
For it was their intention to turn me away from you
By seducing you into the worship of Baal
So that I would forsake you
And deliver you into their hands.[2]

After the plague, the LORD spoke to Moses
And Eleazar ben Aaron the priest,
"Take a census of all the Israelites
From twenty years and upwards, by their ancestral houses –
All able fighters in Israel." Moses and Eleazar the priest
Spoke to them in the steppes of Moab by the Jordan at Jericho,
"From the age of twenty years up take a census,"

---

[1] God again confirms that he has made a contract with Aaron's descendants
that they are to be his high priests, i.e. the government of Israel. It is often not
appreciated that, in a theocratic state, ultimate power must rest with the
priests. This is one more opportunity for justifying the hereditary right of the
Aaronites to rule over Israel, by being God's intermediaries.
[2] The instruction to attack the Midianites seems to be out of place here,
otherwise, why does God need to remind Moses of the background as it had
just happened! My addition to the text is based on the Midianites being accused
of guile in turning the Israelites to the worship of Baal.

As the LORD had instructed Moses and the Israelites
Who had come forth out of the land of Egypt.[1]

The LORD said to Moses, "Ascend the mountain of Abarim,
And look upon the land I am giving to the Israelites.
When you have seen it, you too will be gathered to your
  people,
As was Aaron your brother;
Because you rebelled against me in the wilderness of Zin,
In not making known my sanctity before them,
When the people were contentious
At the waters, which **sprang forth at my command.**"
[These are the waters of Meribah at Kadesh
In the wilderness of Zin.]

Moses responded to the LORD, "Let the LORD, the God of spirits
Who gives life to all creatures, appoint a man over
The community who will lead them in all matters,
Who shall lead them out and bring them in
So that the LORD's people be not like sheep without a
  shepherd."
The LORD said to Moses, "Appoint Joshua bin Nun –
One who is inspired and lay your hand upon him.
Place him before Eleazar the priest and the community.
Commission him before them.
You shall give him some of your authority
So that the entire community of Israel will obey him.
He will stand before Eleazar the priest
Who shall ask **at his request the judgement** of the LORD
Through the Urim.[2]

[1] See appendix 3 for 26:5–65 which follows in the traditional text recording
details of the second census and the policy of the division of the Promised
Land. For 27:1–11 which prescribes the rights of inheritance of daughters, see
The Laws of Moses, page 124.
[2] Either a pouch worn over the head priest's chest which held two lots which
indicated 'yes' or 'no' or according to rabbinic tradition, they were twelve
precious or semi-precious stones on the priest's breastplate which would sparkle
to give more complicated answers according to a code.

At his command they shall go out.
At his command they shall come in – he, the Israelites
With him, even the entire community."
Moses did as the LORD instructed him.
He took Joshua and placed him before Eleazar the priest.
He laid his hands on him and gave him his commission
As the LORD had commanded through Moses.[1]

The LORD ordered Moses, "Exact full vengeance for Israel
On the Midianites **for leading them into sin.**
Afterwards you will be gathered to your people."
Moses commanded the people, "Arm yourselves for war
To go and attack Midian to exact the LORD's vengeance on it.
Send to war a thousand from every tribe."
So there were conscripted out of the thousands of Israelites,
One thousand from each tribe – twelve thousand men
Armed for war. Moses dispatched them to war –
A thousand from each tribe. With them went Phinehas ben
    Eleazar,
The priest, equipped with the holy vessels – **the Ark –**
And the trumpets for sounding the battle cry.

They fought against Midian as the LORD had ordered Moses.
They killed every male. Along with the slain soldiers,
They killed the kings of Midian – Evi, Rekem, Zur,
Hur and Reba, the five kings of Midian.
They also put Balaam ben Beor to the sword.[2]
The Israelites took the women and children of Midian captive.
All their cattle, flocks and goods were taken as booty.
They burnt down all their towns, settlements and
    encampments.

---

[1] Chapters 28–30 of *Numbers* with laws regarding sacrificial offerings, the festivals, the High Holydays and making vows are to be found in *The Laws of Moses*, page 125ff.
[2] This contradicts the previous information that Balaam returned home to Mesopotamia. Later, Moses holds Balaam responsible for the seduction of the Israelites to the worship of Baal at Peor.

They gathered together all the spoil and booty – man and
  beast.
They brought them to Moses and Eleazar the priest and to
The community of Israelites – the captives, the spoil and
  booty –
To their camp in the steppes of Moab by the Jordan at Jericho.

Moses and Eleazar the priest and all the chieftains of the
Community went out to greet them outside the camp.
But Moses was furious with the commanders of the army –
The officers of thousands and hundreds who had returned from
The campaign, "Have you allowed all the women to live?
Were they not the ones, who, at the counsel of Balaam,
Led the Israelites to rebel against the LORD at Peor
Which in turn caused the plague in the LORD's people?
Now, therefore, kill every male child.
Also, kill every woman who has slept with a man, but
Keep alive for yourselves every virgin.
The Israelites did as Moses had commanded them.[1]

"Will your brothers go to war while you remain here?"

The Reubenites and the Gadites owned very many cattle.
When they saw the lands of Jazer and Gilead,
They reckoned it as an ideal place for cattle-raising.
The Gadites and the Reubenites approached Moses and

[1] The ruthlessness of Moses in this episode is chilling and cannot be justified.
Vengeance against the women who turned the Israelites away from God is at
least subject to rationalisation but not that of innocent male children. This
story is a product of an age, which viewed other peoples as not entitled to the
same justice and compassion as they would afford to members of their own
community. Sadly, in many respects, contemporary ethnic wars reveal the
same moral backwardness. *Numbers* 31:19–24 which follows in the traditional
text can be found in *The Laws of Moses*, page 130 as they deal with purification
rites for men returning from battle. See appendix 4 for 31:25–54, which
records the sharing of the booty after the Midianite war.

Eleazar the priest and the chieftains of the community,
"The land which the LORD conquered for the Israelites –
Ataroth, Dibon, Jazer, Nimrah, Heshbon,
Elealeh, Sebam, Nebo and Beon –
Is an ideal place for cattle raising and
Your servants have **an exceeding amount of** cattle.
If you would act kindly to us, grant this land to your servants
To be their portion. Do not make us cross the Jordan."
Moses replied to the Gadites and Reubenites,
"Will your brothers go to war while you remain here!
Why would you discourage the Israelites from crossing
Into the land which the LORD has granted them?
This is just what your fathers did when I sent them from
Kadesh-barnea to spy out the land.
They went up to the wadi of Eshcol and explored the land.
They discouraged the Israelites from going into the land
Which the LORD had granted to them."
The LORD burnt with anger and he swore this oath:
'No men from the age of twenty who came out of Egypt
Will ever see the land which I promised to Abraham, Isaac and
    Jacob
Because they had no confidence in me.'
Only Caleb ben Jephunneh, the Kenizzite, and Joshua bin Nun,
Because they had full confidence in the LORD.

"The LORD burnt with anger against Israel.
He made them wander for forty years in the wilderness,
Until all that generation which sinned against the LORD died.
Now, you rise up in the place of your fathers –
A brood of sinners – to fuel further the burning anger of the
LORD against Israel, for if you resist following him,
He will let them stay even longer in the wilderness,
And you will cause the destruction of the whole people."

They came privately to him and explained,
"We will build folds for our cattle
And villages for our little ones,

But we will go with all our weapons before the Israelites
Until we have brought them to their places.
Only our youngsters will live in fortified towns
Because of the hostile inhabitants of the country.
We will not return to our homes until every man of Israel
Has received his inheritance. But we will not take possession
With them on the other side of the Jordan and outwards
Because our inheritance has fallen to us eastward of Jordan."
Moses replied, "If you do as you say,
If you go out before the LORD armed for war and
Every armed man will cross the Jordan before the LORD
Until he has disinherited his enemies before him –
And the land being conquered before the LORD and if
Afterwards you return, you will be exonerated before the LORD
And before Israel – this land will be yours before the LORD.
But if you do not do so, know that you have sinned
Against the LORD and know that your sin will find you out.
Build cities for your little ones and sheepfolds for the sheep.
As you have spoken, proceed to do."

The Gadites and the Reubenites assured Moses,
"Your servants will do as our lord has commanded.
Our youngsters, our wives, our flocks and all our cattle
Will remain in the land of Gilead.
But your servants will go over fully armed for war
Before the LORD to do battle as my lord has spoken."

So Moses gave this instruction to Eleazar the priest
And to Joshua bin Nun and to the heads of the
Ancestral houses of the tribes of Israel,
"If the Gadites and the Reubenites
Cross the Jordan with you –
Armed for battle before the LORD and the land is conquered
Before you – then you shall grant them the land of Gilead
To be their possession; but if they do not cross over with you
Armed for battle, their possession will be with you in Canaan
For the Lord will not allow them to possess Gilead."

The Gadites and the Reubenites responded,
"As the LORD has spoken to your servants, so we will do!
We will prepare to cross over armed before the LORD into the
Land of Canaan, but our possession will be in Trans-Jordan."
So Moses allocated to them – the Gadites, the Reubenites and
Part of the tribe of Manasseh, the son of Joseph[1] –
The land of Sihon, the Kingdom of the Amorites,
And the land of Og, the Kingdom of Bashan;
All the countryside – the towns with their borders
And all the towns in the area.[2]

The LORD said to Moses in the plains of Moab,
"Speak to the Israelites and tell them this,
'You are now crossing the Jordan to the land of Canaan.
You shall dispossess all the inhabitants in your way.
You shall destroy all figures carved in stone and
All their molten images you shall also destroy.
You shall demolish all their high places **of worship.**
You shall possess the land and live in it,
Because to you I have given the land
For an inheritance. You shall divide the land
Among all the clans by lot.
You will allocate more land to the larger clans
And less land to the smaller clans.
However the lot falls, that shall be his.
You will divide the land by tribal allotments.
If you do not drive out all the inhabitants of the land
From before you, **but let them live in your midst,**
Those that remain will be like splinters in your eyes
And thorns in your side.

[1] As members of the tribe of Manasseh did not enter into the negotiations with
Moses, this allocation probably takes into account the fact that they were
ultimately to conquer parts of Gilead and live there.
[2] See appendix 5 for 32:33–42, which describes the towns built by the two
tribes and the territory conquered by Manasseh. See appendix 6 for 33:1–49,
which summarises the stages of the journey of the Israelites from Egypt to the
Promised Land.

They will be irritants for you
By seducing you in the worship of their gods so that
The evil I intended to do to them, I will do to you.' "[1]

---

[1] See appendix 7 for ch. 34 which follows in the traditional text, which records instructions to Moses regarding the boundaries of the land to be possessed by the Israelites and the tribal representatives in charge of allocating the land by lots; ch. 35 with instructions regarding towns designated for the Levites and towns of sanctuary for manslaughterers, in fear of revenge and ch. 36 with the laws permitting daughters to inherit are *The Laws of Moses*, page 131ff.

DEUTERONOMY

DEUTERONOMY

The Farewell Speeches of Moses

These are the words which Moses spoke to all of Israel
Across the Jordan – in the wilderness – the Arabah near Suph
Between Paran and Tophel, Laban, Hazeroth and Di-zahab –
A journey of eleven days from Horeb to Kadesh-barnea
Using the route of Mount Seir.

On the first day of the eleventh month of the fortieth year
Since the Israelites first left Egypt,
Moses told the Israelites all that the LORD had
Instructed him to say to them.
This was after he had struck down Sihon, king of the Amorites,
Whose capital was Heshbon, and Og, king of Bashan,
Whose capital was Ashtaroth at Edrei.
Moses began to utter these teachings in the
Land of Moab across the Jordan river:

[1]The LORD our God said to us in Horeb,
'You have remained at this mountain long enough.
Make your journey until you reach the hill-country of
The deep valley running north and south of the Dead Sea.[2]
The Amorites and all the nearby places
In the Arabah, in the hill-country, in the low-lands
In the Negev [the South] and by the sea shore –
The land of Canaan and Lebanon as far as the great river –
The Euphrates. I have prepared this land for you.
Come and possess the land which the LORD

---

[1] Moses addresses the children of those who died in the wilderness as though
he were speaking to their dead ancestors. This is a literary device for greater
oratorical effect. As the narrative of *Deuteronomy* consists almost entirely of the
speeches of Moses, I will omit quotation marks.
[2] 'The deep valley, etc. is what is described as 'the Arabah' in the first verse of
Deuteronomy.

Swore an oath to grant to your patriarchs, to
Abraham, Isaac and Jacob and to their descendants.'

I told you then, I cannot cope with you on my own –
The LORD your God has increased you,
So that today you are as numerous as the stars in the sky.
May the LORD the God of your ancestors increase you a
Thousandfold and bless you as he promised you –
But how was I alone to carry the responsibility for you,
The burden **of providing for you** and your disputes?
Nominate men of wisdom and insight whom you respect,
Tribe by tribe, and I will appoint them as your headmen.
You replied, 'What you have proposed to do is good.'
So I appointed the heads of your tribes
Who were wise and enjoyed your respect
And made them your chieftains, officers of thousands,
Officers of hundreds, officers of fifties and tens.
All the officers according to their tribes.

At that time, I charged your appointed judges,
'Heed carefully the disputes between your kinsmen,
Give honest judgement between a person and his kinsman
Or between a person and a resident alien who lives with him.
You shall not show favour towards the influential –
You shall be equal in your judgements
Towards the rich and poor.
You shall not be frightened by the face of any man,
For you are enforcing God's judgement.
If you find the case too difficult for you
Bring it before me and I will hear it.'
At that time, I gave you detailed instructions on what to do.

We journeyed from Horeb and travelled through that
Large and awful wilderness which you experienced –
The route being the hill-country of the Amorites,
As the LORD our God told us until we reached Kadesh-
    barnea.

Then I said to you, 'You have reached the hill-country of
The Amorites which the LORD our God has given to us.
See, the LORD your God has prepared this land for you.
Rise up and inherit it as the LORD the God of your ancestors
Promised you, do not be frightened or discouraged **at the task.**'
Nevertheless, you all approached me and said,
'Let us send scouts ahead of us to reconnoitre the land for us,
To advise us on the route to take and the cities on the way.'

Your proposal pleased me and I appointed from you
Twelve men, one man for each tribe.
They ascended the hill-country and reached the wadi Eshkol,
And reconnoitred there. They collected the land's produce
And brought it down to us along with their report,
'The land which the LORD our God has given us is good,'
But you did not want to go up **and possess it**
Because you were frightened and did not trust the Lord.
You rebelled against the command of the LORD your God.
You sat moaning in your tents, 'The LORD must hate us
To bring us out from Egypt to hand us over to the Amorites to
Slaughter us. Why should we go up **to fight!**
Our kinsmen made our hearts melt on their report:
The men are of greater stature than we.
The cities are great with their fortifications reaching heaven.
We also saw the giants – the descendants of the *Anakim*.'
I said to you: 'Do not be terrified nor frightened of them.
The LORD your God is he who goes before you.
He will fight for you just as he did for you in Egypt
Before your very eyes – and in the wilderness
You saw how the LORD lifted you up as a father does a son,
Everywhere you went until you came to this place.'
Yet, in spite of this, you did not trust the LORD your God,
Who always went out before you on the journey
To find places for you to pitch your tents;
At night, by a ball of fire he pointed out the way,
By day through a **moving** cloud.

The LORD heard what you said and he was furious.
He swore then, 'Not one of these men of this wicked generation
Will see the good land I promised to give their forefathers –
Only Caleb ben Jephunneh[1] will see it.
I will give him and his sons the ground on which he trod
Because he was fully prepared to follow the LORD.'
The LORD was also angry with me because of you,
'You too will not go over there.
Joshua bin Nun who stands by you, he will go there.
Give him of your strength for he will lead Israel to their
Inheritance; and the infants who you said would be booty
And your babes who do not know good or evil –
They will go there. To them will I give it.
They will possess it. As for you – turn back.
Go back into the wilderness by the route of the Red Sea.'
Then you confessed to me, 'We have sinned against the LORD,
We will go up and fight just as the LORD our God
Has charged us; every man girded himself with his weapons,
And brazenly went up into the hill-country.'
The LORD said to me, 'Tell them, do not go up or fight
For I am not with you and you will be routed by your
    enemies.'
So I told you but you would not listen.
You rebelled against the LORD's command.
Arrogantly you descended into the hill-country.
The Amorite inhabitants of the hill-country came out and
Attacked you and pursued you as bees do.
They kept beating you in Seir as far as Hormah.
You returned and cried before the LORD
But the LORD would not listen to you or take any heed of you.

So you remained in Kadesh the many years you lived there.
We turned around and travelled through the wilderness
By the Red Sea route as the LORD told me to do.

[1] Caleb and Joshua were the scouts who were not discouraged by the strength
of the Amorites.

We lived in the hill-country of Seir for many years.
The LORD then instructed me, 'You have wandered long
      enough
Around these hills. Turn towards the north.
Tell the people, "You are about to pass through the territory of
Your kinsmen, the descendants of Esau who live in Seir.
They are anxious about your coming; take care of yourselves.
Do not fight with them. I am not giving you their land,
Not even so much as a foot of land on which you could step,
Because I have given the hill-country of Seir to Esau
As their inheritance.[1]
You will buy food from them with money
To eat and you will buy their water with money to drink." '

The LORD your God has blessed you in all you have
      undertaken.
He has cared for you during your travels in this great
Wilderness. The LORD your God has been with you for forty
      years.
You have lacked nothing. We moved beyond our kinsmen,
The descendants of Esau who dwell in Seir by
The route of the Arabah from Elath and Ezion-geber.
We then turned and went through the wilderness of Moab.
The LORD told me, 'Do not harass Moab or do battle with
      them
Because I have given Ar as the inheritance for Lot's children.[2]
So, decamp and cross the Wadi Zered which we did.
From the time we left Kadesh-barnea until we reached Zered
      was
Thirty-eight years – by which time a whole generation of
Warriors had died inside the camp as the LORD had sworn.

---

[1] The reader should remember that Esau was Jacob's elder brother who was entitled to the birthright and superiority over his brother. See *Genesis, The People's Bible*, p. 61.
[2] See appendix 8 for 2:10–12, which follows in the traditional text and describes the previous inhabitants of Ar.

They did not die at a ripe old age for the LORD struck them –
To root them out in the camp until they all perished.

When all the former warriors had met their deaths
Among the people, the LORD declared to me,
'Today you will pass by Ar, on the boundaries of Moab.
When you reach the Ammonites, do not harass them
For I am not granting you their land as an inheritance,
Because I have given it to the descendants of Lot
To be their inheritance.[1] So set out **instead**
Through the wadi Arnon which I hand over to you –
The land of Sihon the Amorite, king of Heshbon.
Prepare to conquer it; gird yourselves for battle with him.
This very moment, I will begin to instil trembling
And fear of you in the peoples under the heavens, who
When they hear of your coming, shall tremble and
Panic because of you.'
But I sent messengers from the wilderness of Kedemoth to
Sihon king of Heshbon carrying words of peace,
'Let me pass through your land on the highways.
I will not turn to the right or to the left,
You will sell me food for silver so that I may eat
And water for silver you will give me so that I may drink.
Only let us go through **your territory**
As we did with the Edomites who live in Seir,
And as we did with the Moabites who dwell in Ar
Until I cross over the Jordan into the land which
The LORD our God is giving us.'

But Sihon king of Heshbon would not let us pass by him
For the LORD had stiffened his spirit and puffed him up

---

[1] As has been mentioned before, while Moab and Ammon did not behave
towards Israel in a fraternal fashion and were calumniated as descendants of
an incestuous relationship, they were still the sons of Lot, who was the nephew
and ward of Abraham and, therefore, enjoyed favour from the God of Israel.
See appendix 9 for 2:20–23, which follows in the traditional text – a
description of the previous inhabitants of the territory of Ammon.

In order to deliver him into our hands, as he did.
So the LORD said to me, 'See, I have begun to deliver up
Sihon and his land to you so that you may possess it.'
So, when Sihon came out to attack us, he and his army
At Jahaz, the LORD surrendered him to us.
We struck down not only him, but his children and his people.
We captured all his towns at that time,
We proscribed every inhabited town together with
Women and children. We left no one alive.[1]

Of living creatures, it was only the cattle we took as spoil,
Along with the plunder we had taken from other towns.
From Aroer which is by the Wadi Arnon,
And the city in the valley itself up to Gilead,
There was not a town too powerful for us.
The LORD delivered them all into our hands.
Only into the land of the Ammonites, you did not trespass,
Nor the towns of the hill-country and whatever places
The LORD our God forbade us **to conquer.**

We then proceeded on the road to Bashan, and
Og, king of Bashan came out to attack us –
He and all his army to give us battle at Edrei.
The LORD reassured me, **for Og was Rephah – a giant,**
Descendant of the sons of God who lay with mortal women,
'Do not fear him for I will deliver him into your hand
And all his forces as well as his country.
I shall do to him what I did to Sihon, the Amorite king
Who reigned in Heshbon.' The LORD gave into our hand
Og, king of Bashan and all his armies.
We struck them down until they had no survivors.

---

[1] Another staggering brutality as the price for refusing an offer of peace. Ironically, the narrator credits God for making Sihon obstinate to give the Israelites the excuse for wiping her out. The 'justification' is that the Amorites like Sodom and Gomorrah were so sinful as to deserve utter destruction, but what of Abraham's plea for the innocent who lived in the twin cities of sin! [*Genesis, The People's Bible* pp 37–8]

We conquered all his cities at that time
There was not a city which we did not capture from them –
Sixty towns, the whole region of Argob –
The kingdom of Og in Bashan.
All these cities were fortified with towering walls,
With gates and barriers as well as many open towns.
We wiped them out as we had done to Sihon,
The king of Heshbon – destroying every town's inhabitants –
The women and infants as well.

All the cattle and goods of the cities we took as spoil.
At that time we captured the lands from the two Amorite kings
Across the Jordan, from the Wadi Arnon up to Mount Hermon.
(The Sidonians called Hermon, Sirion; and the Amorites, Seir.[1])
All the cities of the tableland (the Plateau of Moab).
All of Gilead, all Bashan as far as Salecah and Edrie,

Towns of the kingdom of Og in Bashan.
You should know that Og king of Bashan was the
Only remaining descendant of the Rephaim –
His bed was made of iron **to carry his weight.**
[Is it not still to be seen in Rabbah,
The capital of the Ammonites!]
It was over thirteen feet long and six feet wide.
We took this country into our control,
From Aroer by the Wadi Arnon.[2]
I charged Joshua at that time, 'You have seen all that
The LORD your God has done to these two kings,
So will the LORD do to all the kingdoms to which
You are crossing over **the Jordan to possess.**
You shall not fear them, for the LORD your God –
It is he who fights for you.'

---

[1] All three names suggest a majestic mountain, the equivalent of a 'Mont Blanc'.
[2] See appendix 10 for 3:12–20, which follows in the traditional text, describing the land allocated to the tribes of Reuben, Gad and Manasseh and the stipulation that they would have to join the other tribes in their conquest of Canaan.

"Please allow me to cross over."

And at that time I pleaded for the Lord's compassion,
'O Lord, my lord, you have begun to reveal to your servant
The power of your great deliverance.
What God is there in heaven or earth who equals your works
And mighty deeds. **Now that I have seen it all,**
Please allow me to cross over. Let me see the good land
Across the Jordan – the majestic hills and the Lebanon.'
But the Lord was cross with me on your account.
He would not listen to me.

The Lord said to me, 'Enough!
Do not continue to speak any longer on this matter!
Go up to the top of Pisgah and let your eyes wander
To the west, to the north, to the south and to the east.
See it with your eyes for you will not cross this Jordan.
Charge Joshua. Encourage him and give him strength
For he will cross over before this people;
He will conquer for them the land which you will see.'
So we remained in the valley by Beth-peor.

Now, Israel, be mindful of the laws and judgements
Which I am teaching you so that you might live
And reach the land of your inheritance
Which the Lord the God of your fathers gives to you.
Your eyes saw what the Lord did at Baal-peor,
For every man who worshipped Baal at Peor
The Lord your God wiped out from among you.
But you who clung to the Lord your God –
All of you are alive today.

See, I have taught you laws and judgements
As the Lord my God commanded me – to do so
In the midst of the land to which you go to possess.
Observe and practice them –
For this will be your wisdom and understanding.

In the view of the peoples who, when they hear these laws,
Will remark, "This great people is very wise and perceptive."
For what great nation is there to whom God is so close
As the LORD our God whenever we call upon him!
Is there anywhere such a great nation
Which possesses such righteous laws and judgements –
As this teaching – all of which I put before you today?

Only take care; keep watch over how you conduct your life
So that you never forget what you yourself have seen and
Let it never be forgotten all the days of your life.
Rather, tell **what you have seen to** your children and
Grandchildren – the day you stood before the LORD your God at
Horeb, when the LORD said to me,
"Assemble all the people and I will make them hear my
    words –
To learn to revere me all their years on earth;
And that they may teach their children."

So you approached and stood at the foot of the mountain.
The mountain was burning with its flames reaching heaven,
Amid darkness, cloud and a deep mist.
The LORD spoke to you from the heart of the fire.
You heard the sound of words but saw no image –
Only a voice. He told you of his covenant **with you,**
Which he instructed you to observe – the Ten Commandments
Which he inscribed on the two tablets of stone.
It was me whom the LORD commanded at that time
To teach you to observe the laws and judgements
In the land to which you are crossing over to possess.

Keep a close guard over the conduct of your lives –
You did not see any image when the LORD
Spoke to you at Horeb from the midst of the fire.
Therefore it is not images that you should obey.

Do not act self-destructively[1] by making sculpted images of
Any creatures – in male or female form,
Whether it be of beasts that straddle the earth
Or winged creatures that fly through the sky;
Or creatures that crawl on the ground
Or swimming things in the water below the earth.

Nor should you, when you look up to the skies and see
The sun, moon and stars – the whole array of the heavens;
Nor be seduced by them to bow down and worship them.
The LORD your God has allocated them to be worshipped
By all the other peoples who live under the heavens.[2]
But you are different. The LORD took you out of an
Iron furnace – from Egypt to be his very own people,
As is the situation to this very day.

As for me, the LORD was angry with me due to your actions.
He swore not to permit me to cross this Jordan –
Not to reach the good earth which the LORD your God
Is giving to you as your **eternal** inheritance.
I must die in this land.
I will not cross this Jordan.
But you are crossing it and you will possess this good earth.
In my absence, take care of yourselves.
Do not forget the covenant the LORD your God made with
    you –
Do not **forfeit it** by making sculpted images in
The form of anything which the LORD your God has forbidden.
For the LORD your God is a devouring flame – a jealous God.

---

[1] The Hebrew verb is *Shahat* meaning: destroy. Translations have been 'mar'
(Tyndale); deprave yourself (Moffatt); 'corrupt' (the New Jerusalem Bible); act
wickedly (Jewish Publication Society). In the sense that the worshipping of
other gods would break Israel's covenant with God – to do so would be an act
of self-destruction – hence my translation.
[2] An ironical twist: God appreciates that their majesty will inspire the worship
of the nations in whom he has not taken such an interest – an indication of a
tolerance for the worship of the celestial bodies.

Now, when you sire children and they sire children
And you are very secure in the land **and forget the Lord**
Who made a covenant with you to give you this land
And you act self-destructively and make sculpted images
And do that which is wicked in the sight of the LORD your
   God
To incense his fury, I call as witnesses against you today –
The heavens and the earth – you will quickly perish
In the land you are crossing the Jordan to possess.
You shall not live in it for long, but will perish utterly.

The LORD will scatter you among foreign peoples.
You will be left as a minority among the nations,
To whose places the LORD will lead you **into exile**.
There you will be serving gods – the work of human hands –
Made of wood and stone, who neither see nor hear
Nor eat nor drink. From there you will seek
The LORD your God; and you will find him
If you look for him with all your heart and soul.[1]
When you are in straitened circumstances –
When all these catastrophes befall you-
Then will you return to the LORD your God and listen to him.
For the LORD your God is a compassionate God.
He will not abandon you or destroy you;
He will not forget the covenant with your patriarchs –
The agreement, which he promised them by an oath.

Now, look into the past, that which came before you –
From the very day that man created Adam on the earth
Between the two ends of heaven:
Has there ever been such a great happening as this –
Has anything of such magnitude ever been heard!
Had a people ever heard the voice of God
Speaking from the midst of the fire as you heard

[1] The heart is the seat of intelligence; the soul is the 'life force'. God will be found if he is sought with the utter dedication of mind and body.

And lived?[1] Or, has God ever before attempted
To pluck out one people from the domain of another people
By tribulations, by extraordinary events and miracles
And by war with a mighty hand, an outstretched arm –
With unbelievable terrors – indeed, all that the
LORD your God did for you in Egypt before your very eyes?

This was revealed to you to prove to you that the LORD –
He is God! There is no one else except him alone.
Out of the heavens he made you hear his voice to teach you,
And on earth, he made you see his great fire,
Why? Because he loved your patriarchs, he
Chose their descendants after them to bring you out of
Egypt through his presence and with enormous power –
To disinherit nations, larger and more powerful than you,
To bring you there to give you their land to be
Your possession, as is the case this very day.

So, on this day you should especially realise this and
Take it to heart that the LORD – he is the God in the
Heavens above and on the earth beneath – no one else!
Give heed to his laws and commandments which
I am confirming now, so that you will prosper,
And your descendants after you – so that you may
Long live in the land which the LORD your God
Has granted you for evermore.[2]

The Second Discourse

Moses summoned all of Israel and addressed them,
Hear, O Israel, the laws and judgements which
I now speak into your ears. Learn to keep and observe them.

---

[1] Moses is addressing those who were under the age of military service. All those over eighteen to twenty years would have died because of their lack of faith in God to disinherit the natives of Canaan.
[2] See appendix 11 for 4:41–49 which follows in the traditional text on the appointment of the three cities of sanctuary for the manslaughterer.

The LORD our God made a covenant with us in Horeb –
That he would deliver us from his enemies – in turn
We, as his people, were to serve him as our God.
He made the heavens and the earth his witnesses
To the Covenant between him and us.
Not only with our fathers did the LORD our God
Make this covenant but with us, even us –
All of us who are here today.

Face to face the LORD spoke to you on the mountain from
Amidst the fire. [I stood then between the LORD and you
To tell you the words of the LORD because you were
Frightened of the fire and did not ascend the mountain][1]:
1. I am the LORD your God who brought you out of Egypt
    From a house of slaves.
2. You shall have no other gods but me.
    You shall not make yourself any sculpted image or
    Any physical representation of any body in the heavens
        above,
    On the earth beneath or in the waters under the earth.
    You shall not bow down to them or worship them
    Because I, the LORD your God, am a jealous God
    Who remembers the sins of the fathers.
    Of them that hate me
    To the second, third and fourth generations.
    But who behaves kindly for a thousand generations
    To those who love me and keep my commandments.
3. Do not abuse the name of the LORD
    For he will not exonerate those who use his name
    For pernicious purposes, **but will punish them.**
4. *Observe* the Sabbath day to make it holy
    As the LORD your God has commanded you.

[1] In the description of the pronouncement of the Ten Commandments in *Exodus*, God does *not allow* the Israelites to touch the mountain. For comparative purposes of the two versions see p. 50. Italicised words indicate differences with the *Exodus* version.

During six days you may do all your tasks
But the seventh day is a Sabbath to the LORD your God.
You shall not work, you, nor your son nor your daughter
Nor your male or female servant, *nor your ox,*
Nor your donkey nor any of your cattle
Nor the stranger within your gated walls
So that your male and female servants may rest as you do.
You should remember that you were a slave in Egypt
And that the Lord your God brought you out from there
With a mighty hand and an outstretched arm.
Therefore does the Lord your God command you
To observe the Sabbath day.[1]

5. Honour your father and mother
   As the Lord your God commanded you
   So that you may live long *and prosper*
   In the land which the LORD gives to you.

6. You shall not murder.

7. You shall not commit adultery.

8. You shall not steal.

9. You shall not bear false witness against your neighbour.

10. You shall not covet your neighbour's wife
    Nor desire your neighbour's house, his field,
    His male or female servant, his ox, his donkey
    Or anything that belongs to your neighbour.

The LORD uttered these words to your whole assembly
At the mountain from amid the fire, the cloud and deep mist
In a thundering voice – **not only this** – he did more.
He inscribed them on two tablets of stone and gave them to me.
When you heard the voice coming out of the darkness

---

[1] The reason given for the observance of the Sabbath is significantly different from the previous version. In *Exodus*, humanity is to rest because God, in whose image man was created, rested: *imitatio dei*. In *Deuteronomy*, it is the equality of all creatures in God's sight and therefore their equal rights to freedom and leisure. The two concepts from both versions express the basic foundations of a moral society.

And the mountain was burning in flames
You came close to me – all the heads of your tribes
And elders. You exclaimed, "Yes, the LORD our God
Has revealed to us his glory and his majesty.
We heard his voice out of the fire. Today we saw that
God does speak to Man and he remains alive!
But now, why should this great fire consume us?
For if we continue to listen to the voice of
The LORD our God we shall die.
Who is there of any mortals who has heard the voice of the
Living God speaking out of the fire as we have and lived?
You go closer and hear what the LORD our God is saying –
Then you tell us what the LORD our God tells you –
We will listen and obey."

The LORD heard what you said to me and he said to me,
"I have listened to the words of this people –
What they said to you. All they said is well said.
Oh, if only they always were of the same mind to revere me,
To observe all my commandments and enjoy prosperity
Together with their descendants forever. Go tell them,
Return to your tents. But you, stand here by my side.
I will tell you all the commandments, laws and judgements
For you to teach them to obey in the land I am giving them
For an inheritance."

Therefore, you shall carefully observe what the LORD your God
Commanded you, without turning to the right or left.
You shall walk religiously in the way that the LORD your God
Has instructed you that you may live and prosper
And prolong your years in the land you are inheriting.
Now this is the instruction – the laws and judgements
Which the LORD your God has instructed **me** to teach you
To practise them in the land which you are to possess,
So that you revere the LORD your God by keeping
All his laws and commandments which I tell you,
Your children and grandchildren all the years of your

Life so that you may increase your years.
Listen, O Israel, and take care in doing them,
So that you may prosper and increase immeasurably
As the LORD the God of your fathers has promised you –
In a land overflowing with milk and honey.

"The LORD is our God the LORD alone"

[1] Hear, O Israel: The LORD is our God, the LORD alone!
You shall love the LORD with your entire heart, life and might.
These words which I command you now shall be on your
    mind.
You shall rehearse them to your children
And talk them through when you are at home;
When you are walking down the path,
When you go to bed and when you get up.
They shall be as signs bound to your hand.
They shall be like amulets between your eyes.[2]

You shall write them on the doorposts[3] of your homes and
    gates.
Now, when the LORD your God brings you into the land
He promised to your patriarchs, Abraham, Isaac and Jacob
To give you – with grand and prosperous towns which
You did not build and houses filled with luxuries that
You did not furnish and hewn-out cisterns which
You did not hew out and vineyards and olive trees which

---

[1] The *Shema Yisroel* has become the rallying cry of Jews since time immemorial.
[2] Traditional male Jews base on this text the wearing of phylacteries –
leather-bound boxes containing this paragraph and several other biblical texts
hand-written on parchment – on their forehead and left arm during morning
prayers, except on the Sabbath. The boxes are tied to them by thin leather
straps.
[3] In Hebrew *Mezuzah* (singular). On this basis, this paragraph and other
scriptural verses are hand-written on a parchment scroll and inserted in a
rectangular case affixed to the right door-post of a Jewish home or room.
Jewish women often wear a silver *Mezuzah* – the name given to the case – as
an ornament around their neck, very much as Christians would wear a cross.

You did not plant – you will eat and be satisfied.
Then, amid all this plenty, which I have given you,
Take care not to forget the LORD who brought you
Out of the land of Egypt, out of the house of slavery.

You will **continue to** revere the LORD your God.
You will serve him and by his name you will take oaths.
You will not go after other gods –
The gods of your neighbouring peoples.
Because a jealous god is the LORD your God who is
Always in your midst – lest the anger of the LORD your God
Be inflamed against you and demolish you from off
The face of the earth. Do not test the LORD your God
As you tested him at Massah.[1]

You will carefully observe the LORD's commandments –
His testaments and laws which he has commanded you.
You will do what is right and proper in the sight of the LORD,
That you may prosper when you enter and possess
The good land which the LORD promised to your patriarchs –
To expel all your enemies before him as the LORD spoke.

When your son in the future asks you,
"What is the reason for these testaments, laws and judgements
Which the LORD our God has commanded you?"
You will then answer your son,
"We were slaves to Pharaoh in Egypt.
And the LORD brought us out of Egypt with a mighty hand.
The LORD performed great and terrifying signs and wonders
On Egypt, on Pharaoh and his court before our eyes.
He brought us out from there to the land which
He had sworn to our patriarchs **to give us.**"
The LORD **then** commanded us to obey all these laws,
To revere the LORD our God for our lasting benefit,
To sustain our lives as **he has done** at this time.

---

[1] *Exodus* 17:7 – see p. 44.

We will be credited as righteous[1]
by the Lord our God
Because we took care to observe this whole instruction
As he has commanded us.

When the LORD your God passes on to you the land you enter
To possess – and he casts out many nations before you:
The Hittites, the Girgashites, the Amorites, the Canaanites,
The Perizzites, the Hivites and the Jebusites –
Seven nations more numerous and mightier than you-
The LORD your God will deliver them up before you-
You shall strike them down into utter destruction.[2]
You shall make no treaties with them nor show them any
    mercy.
You shall not make marriages with them –
Do not give your daughters to their sons
Nor take their daughters to your sons
Because they will turn your sons from following me –
To serve other gods, which will make the LORD burn with
    anger
Against you, leading to your quick destruction.

But this is what you must do to them:
Overthrow their altars, shatter their pillars,
Cut down their Asherim – **the trees dedicated to Astarte-**
And melt down with fire their graven images
Because you are a people consecrated to the LORD your God.
It is you that the LORD your God has chosen to be his
Singular people from among all the peoples dwelling on earth.
It is not because you were more numerous than other peoples

---

[1] How different from Paul's interpretation of the Torah as a barrier to grace
and salvation! Obedience is the basis of righteousness, entitling a person to the
divine reward of peace and security.
[2] The Hebrew phrase has the force of a ban. It is by divine decree that the
Israelites show no quarter to the native inhabitants. God is punishing them for
their idolatry and proving his supremacy by disinheriting them to make room
for a people who will worship him and keep his laws.

That the LORD bonded in love with you
And chose to be his – no, you were the smallest of
    peoples!
But out of the LORD's love for you and in keeping the oath
Which he swore to your patriarchs – **that is why**
The LORD took you from Egypt with a mighty hand
And redeemed you from a colony of slaves
From Pharaoh, king of Egypt.
So know that the LORD your God – he is God,
The loyal God who keeps his covenant,
Who is gracious to those who love him and who keep
His commandments for a thousand generations; but
He confronts his enemies – punishing them with
    destruction.
He does not delay in dealing with his enemies –
He will pay them back immediately.
So keep the command and the laws and the judgements
Which I am instructing you today to do.

When you obey these judgements and observe them
    fully,
The LORD your God will fulfil for you the faithful
    covenant
He made on oath with your patriarchs.
He will love you; he will bless you; he will increase you.
He will bless the fruit of your womb;
The fruit of your land, your grain, your wine and oil,
The calves of your herds and the lambs of your flocks
In the land which he swore to give to your patriarchs.

You will be blessed more than all the peoples.
No male shall be sterile or female barren among you
Or among your herds of cattle.
The LORD will remove from you all sickness
He will not afflict you with the terrifying diseases of Egypt
Which you witnessed – these he will impose upon your
    enemies.

You will consume all the peoples the LORD your God
Is handing over to you; do not pity them.[1]
Do not serve their gods for they will be a trap for you.

But if you think to yourselves, "These nations are greater
Than we; how shall we dispossess them?"
Do not fear them; just recall what the LORD your God
Did to Pharaoh and to the whole of Egypt –
The great trials and tribulations which you witnessed –
The miraculous signs, the wonders, the mighty hand,
The outstretched arm with which the LORD your God
Delivered you – just so will the LORD your God
Do to all the peoples of whom you are afraid.

Not only this, but the LORD will send a plague against them
Until even those who remain and hide from you perish.
Do not be frightened of them because the LORD your God
Is among you – a great and awesome God.
The LORD your God will cast out these nations bit by bit.
You will not be able to finish them off quickly;
Else, wild beasts would roam in the wastelands to your cost.
The LORD your God will deliver them up before you.
They will be in a great panic until they are destroyed.

He will deliver their kings into your hands.
You will cause their very names to be forgotten under the
    heavens.
No man shall be able to stand up to you
Until you have utterly destroyed them.
You shall melt down in fire the images of their gods.
You shall not lust after the silver and gold on them
To keep for yourselves lest you be seduced by them,
Because they are an abomination to the LORD your God.
You should not bring abominations into your homes,

[1] The narrator or prophet seems to believe that tolerance of the indigenous
people would lead or, if this was written after the event, did lead to idolatry
and moral wickedness.

Or you will be placed under the same doom.
You shall utterly despise and abhor them for they are
    doomed.

All the commandments, which I command you today –
You should strictly observe so that you may live and increase
When you come to possess the land
Which the LORD swore to give your patriarchs.
You shall remember the entire journey,
Led by the LORD your God,
These forty years in the wilderness to prove you by trials,
To learn what was in your minds.
Would you keep his commandments or not?
So he tested you through pangs of hunger,
Then fed you with manna – the like of which neither
You nor your ancestors had ever experienced
To teach you that man lives not on bread alone;
But humankind is sustained by everything
Which comes out of the mouth of the LORD.[1]
Because the Lord your God watched over you
Your clothes never wore out nor did your feet swell
During all your journeys these forty years.
Think of it in this way: just as a man rebukes his son,
The LORD your God chastens you, so that you obey
The instructions of the LORD your God,
To follow in his footpaths and to revere him.
Because it is the LORD your God who brings you to
A good land with flowing streams, fountains and deep wells,
Both in the plains and in the hills,
A land growing with wheat and barley, vines and figs and
Pomegranates, a land full of juicy olives and honey;
A land where you suffer no scarcity of food.
The land will meet all your needs –
A country whose rocks contain iron, whose hills yield brass.

---

[1] The image is of God feeding nestling chicks as a mother bird does. Humanity
is totally dependent on God for survival.

You will eat, be satisfied and bless the LORD your God
In the land of prosperity which he has given you.

Beware, lest you forget the LORD your God by not obeying his
Rules and judgements; lest when you eat and are satiated
And dwell in the secure homes you have built,
And when your herds and flocks increase and you have
Quantities of silver and gold – you become big-headed and
Forget the LORD your God who brought you out of Egypt –
A slave camp; who led you through a vast and
Frightening wilderness – of flying serpents and scorpions,
A parched earth with no water – but who made
Water flow for you out of flint boulders;
Who fed you manna in the wilderness – experiences that
Your ancestors had not known – to prove and test you
For your own future good.

Do not even think, "It was my own strength and skill
That has achieved this wealth."
Just remember that it was the LORD your God
Who gave you the ability to achieve riches
In order to fulfil his covenant on this day,
Which he swore to your patriarchs **to give you this land.**
But if you totally forget the LORD your God and
Stray after other gods to worship and bow down to them,
I am witness today that you will certainly perish,
No less than the nations which the LORD destroys before you,
So will you be destroyed because you did not obey
The voice of the LORD your God.

Hear, O Israel, you are now crossing the Jordan to begin
To disinherit nations greater and mightier than you,
Whose cities are majestic and fortified to the skies –
Stout and gigantic men, descendants of the Anakim of
Whom you know and have heard speak:
"Who is able to stand up to the descendants of Anak?"
Know that it is the LORD who precedes you –

He is a consuming flame; he will wipe them out.
He will make them cower before you – you will soon
Dispossess and cause them to perish as
The LORD has told you. Therefore, do not even think,
After the LORD your God has expelled them before you,
"Because of my righteousness, the LORD brought me
To inherit this land!" No! Because of the wickedness of
These nations, the LORD dispossessed them for you.
Not because of your righteousness or your integrity
Do you succeed in possessing their land,
But because of the wickedness of these nations,
The LORD your God dispossessed them before you.
Also to fulfil what the LORD promised your patriarchs,
Abraham, Isaac and Jacob."[1]

Know then that it is not due to your righteousness that
The LORD gives you this prosperous country to inherit –
Because you are a stiff-necked people.
Remember, do not forget how you provoked the LORD your
    God
In the wilderness from the very day you left Egypt
To the time you came to this place.
You were always rebelling against the LORD.
In Horeb, you especially provoked the LORD
And made the LORD angry enough to wipe you out.
This was when I ascended the mountain to receive
The two stone tablets of the covenant which
The LORD had made with you.

I stayed in the mountain forty days and forty nights.
Bread I did not eat nor did I drink water
The LORD gave me the two tablets of stone
Written by the finger of God.

[1] The appreciation of this theme is essential for an understanding of God's relationship to the Israelites: It is only on the basis of the wickedness of the inhabitants of the land and God's promise to Abraham that they became entitled to the land. They must now earn the right to live there.

On them were all the words, which the LORD said to you
On the mountain from amid the fire in the day,
When you had assembled **to hear the words of the covenant.**
It was at the end of the forty days and nights,
When the LORD had given me the two stone tablets –
The tablets of the covenant – that the LORD said to me,
"Quickly get down from here because your people
Whom you[1] took out of Egypt have destroyed themselves.
They have quickly strayed from the way I instructed them –
They have made a sculpted image." The LORD continued,
"I see this people – it is a very stiff-necked people!
Leave me alone for a moment and I will destroy them.
I will cause their names to be forgotten under the heavens.
You will I make into a greater and more powerful people!"

I turned to descend from the mountain.
The mountain was burning in flames.
The two tablets of the covenant were in my hands.
I saw that you had sinned against the LORD your God.
You had made for yourselves a sculpted bull.
Quickly had you strayed from the way
Which the LORD your God had set out for you.
Had you not just heard his command from the fiery mount
Not to make any sculpted image of any creature
Of the earth beneath or in the heavens?
I tightened my grip on the two tablets
And threw them from my arms and
Broke them before your very eyes.

I threw myself down before the LORD as before –
Eating no food nor drinking any water
For forty days and forty nights because of your sins:
How you did wrong in the eyes of the LORD

---

[1] The reader should appreciate the ironic humour attributed to the Lord. He
will take all the praise for delivering the Israelites and dispossessing their
enemies in the Promised Land, but, when they sin, they become Moses's
people, whom he and *not* the Lord saved from Egyptian slavery.

To make him so angry; I was terrified in the presence of
His anger and burning rage which the LORD felt towards you,
Enough to destroy you totally.
But the LORD once again listened to my plea **on your behalf.**
The LORD was especially angry with Aaron,
Enough to kill him.
I also prayed for Aaron at that time.
And as for the source of your sinfulness –
The bull, which you made – I melted it down in fire.
I broke it into bits so small until they were like dust.
I scattered it into the brook descending the mountain.
Also at Taberah[1] and at Massah[2] and at Kibroth-hattaavah,[3]
You provoked the LORD's anger.

"So I threw myself down before the LORD . . . *"*

Also, when the LORD charged you at Kadesh-barnea,
"Go up and conquer the land which I give to you,"
You rebelled against obeying the LORD your God.
You did not believe in him, **his power**
To go before you and destroy your enemies.
You were rebels against the LORD from the first day I knew
  you.
So I threw myself down before the LORD for
Forty days and forty nights because the LORD was
Intending to wipe you out, but I prayed to the LORD,

"LORD God, do not destroy your people – your portion,
Whom you redeemed by your greatness,

[1] Where the Lord set part of the Israelite camp into flames to punish them for
their murmuring against him [*Numbers* 11:1–3].
[2] Where the Israelites attacked Moses for not providing them with water and
bringing them out of Egypt [*Exodus* 17:1–7].
[3] Where many Israelites died of plague from the quails God sent to meet their
demands for meat [*Numbers* 11:4–35].

Whom you brought out of Egypt with a mighty hand.
Remember your servants, Abraham, Isaac and Jacob.
Ignore the stubbornness of this people and her wrong-doings
Lest the people of the land from which you took them say:
'Because the LORD could not bring them to the land
He promised them; it was only because he hated them,
Did he bring them out – only to kill them in the wilderness.'
They are still your people and portion whom you delivered
With your enormous power and outstretched arm."
The Lord listened to my prayer. He did not destroy you
But decreed that the generation of fighting men
Would die in the wilderness and that the
Lord your God would conquer this land for you.

Then the LORD instructed me, "Carve out two tablets of stone
Like the first and come up to me in the mountain
And make a wooden ark **in which to keep them.**
I will inscribe on the tablets the same words
Which were on the first, which you shattered.
Then you will put them into the ark."
I made the ark from acacia wood and I carved out
Two tablets of stone like the first and went up
The mountain with the two tablets in my hands.

He inscribed the tablets as he had done at first –
The Ten Commandments that he addressed to you in
The mountain from amid the fire in the day of assembly.
The LORD then gave them to me. I went down the mountain
And placed the tablets in the ark I had made.
There they remain as the LORD had commanded.[1]
I had stayed on the mountain as at the first time –
Forty days and forty nights when the LORD also
Listened to me and agreed not to destroy you.
After this the LORD said to me, "Get up, and take

[1] See Appendix 12 for 10:6–9, an insert that follows to confirm the authority
of the Aaronite priesthood.

The journey at the head of the people to reach and
Possess the land, which I swore to their patriarchs
To give to them."[1]

And now, Israel, what does the LORD your God ask of you?
Only to revere the LORD your God and to follow in his paths –
To love him, to serve the LORD your God with all
Your heart and soul – keeping the commandments of the
    LORD-
Laws which I order you to keep today for your own benefit.

Consider that the LORD your God owns the heavens,
The heaven of heavens, the earth and all it contains.
Yet the LORD only clung to his love for your patriarchs,
And to choose their descendants after them from
All the nations as is proved today.
Circumcise the foreskin of your heart[2]
And give up your stubbornness for good
Because the LORD your God is the God of gods,
The LORD of lords, the great, mighty and awesome God
Who shows no favouritism to important people and is
Never to be bribed **by costly animal sacrifices to him.**
But he is just to the orphan and widow.
He loves the stranger and gives him food and clothing.

You should love the stranger because
You were strangers in Egypt.

---

[1] Note the belief that when God behaves favourably to his human creatures, he is doing this for their ancestors. This is a reinforcement of the concept that parents live on and achieve eternity through the survival and success of their genealogical line; also the Jewish concept of children benefitting from the 'merit of the patriarchs'.

[2] Jeremiah also calls on a person to be circumcised spiritually as well as physically. [*Jeremiah* 14:4] There is a Jeremaic resonance to this speech of Moses, which has led some scholars to attribute parts of *Deuteronomy* to his pen. The first mention of the discovery of *sefer Hatorah*, the books of the Torah, which must have been part of *Deuteronomy* is recorded in *II Kings* 22:8, in 622 BCE, the year when Jeremiah had begun to prophesy.

Revere the LORD your God. Serve him and clasp him to
   yourself
And swear by his name. He is your glory and he is your God
Who did for you these great and wonderful things
Which your eyes have seen – with seventy souls
Your ancestors went down to Egypt, but now the LORD your
   God
Has made you as numerous as the stars of the heavens.

Love the LORD your God, accept his charge, his laws,
His judgements and commandments forever.
Know then that now I am not speaking to your children
Who did not experience and did not see the instruction
That came from the LORD your God – his power,
His mighty hand and his outstretched arm – all the signs
And works he performed in Egypt to Pharaoh and his land.
Also what he did to the Egyptian army, horses and chariots –
How he made the waters of the Red Sea overwhelm them
When they pursued you and how he destroyed them –
And dead they are until this very day;
Also what he did for you in the wilderness
Until you arrived to this place.
And what he did to Dathan and Abiram,

The sons of Eliab ben Reuben –
When the ground opened up its mouth
And swallowed them up
Together with their households and tents and every creature
Who took their part among the Israelites,
Because they questioned my and Aaron's authority.
Your eyes have seen all the great deeds the LORD has done.
Therefore, obey his command, which I now give you
So that you may be strengthened when you approach
The land which you are soon to cross to possess,
So that you may lengthen your years on the land which
The LORD swore to your patriarchs to give to them
And their descendants – a land flowing with milk and honey.

For the land you are approaching to conquer is not like the
Land of Egypt from where you have come,
Where you used to plant your seed and water it
On foot **with your own labour** as one does a herb garden.
No, the land you are crossing over there to possess –
It is a land of hills and plains which drinks its water
From the rains of the heavens – a land looked after by
The LORD your God – his eyes are always on it from
The beginning until the end of the year.

If you carefully obey my commandments which I now give you
To love the LORD your God and to serve him
With all your heart and soul, I will give your land rain
In its proper season – the early and late rains –
So that you may harvest your new grain,
Your wine and your oil. I will provide grass in the fields
For your cattle so that you may eat and be satisfied.

Beware lest your heart be seduced and you stray
To serve other gods by bowing down to them.
The LORD will be incensed against you.
He will shut up the heavens and there will be no rain,
And the ground will not yield its produce.
You will soon disappear from off the good earth
Which the LORD has given you.

Place these words on your hearts and souls,
Bind them as a sign upon your hand
And let them be as symbols on your forehead between your
  eyes
So that you may know them well enough
To rehearse them to your children,
To talk them through when you are at home,
When you are walking down the path
When you go to bed and when you get up.
You shall write them upon the doorposts of your homes and
  your gates

So that your days and those of your descendants
Are as eternal in the land which the LORD swore to
The patriarchs as are the heavens above the earth.

If you carefully keep all this commandment
Which I give you this day to observe it –
To love the LORD your God, to follow in all his paths,
To cling to him – then will the LORD disinherit
All the nations before you and you will inherit
Nations greater and mightier than yourselves.
Every place upon which the sole of your foot treads
Will be yours – your own territory will extend from the
Wilderness to the Lebanon,
From the river Euphrates to the Western Sea.
No man shall stand up to you.
The LORD your God will place the fear and dread of you
On the face of the entire land on which you set foot –
Just as he has promised you.

See now, I have put before you today a blessing and a curse.
The blessing – if you obey the commandments of the LORD
Your God which I have now given you.
The curse – if you do not obey the commandments of
The LORD your God and stray from the path on
Which I have commanded you to walk, to go after
Other gods whom you have not known.
When the LORD your God brings you to the land
Which you have come to possess, you will pronounce
The blessing upon Mount Gerizim and
The curse on Mount Ebal[1] – they are across the Jordan
Beyond the Western Road in the land of the Canaanites
Who live in the Arabah near Gilgal
By the terebinths of Moreb. You are to cross the Jordan
To enter and to possess the land which the LORD your God
Gives to you – you will possess it and live in it!

---

[1] How this was done is described in *The Laws of Moses: Deuteronomy* 27

You will keep and observe all the laws and
Judgements, which I am laying before you now.[1]

Today, the LORD your God commands you to observe
All these laws and judgements.
Perform them diligently with all your heart and soul.
Today, you have affirmed that the LORD is your God,
By which you undertake to walk in his ways, to obey him,
By keeping his laws, commandments and judgements.
And today, the LORD, as he promised you, has affirmed that
You are his own treasured people, **chosen** to keep his laws,
So that you may be exalted in renown and glory
Over all the nations he has made; you shall be,
As he promised, a holy people to the LORD your God.

If you strictly obey the voice of the LORD your God to keep
And to do all his commandments which I now command you,
The LORD your God will lift you above all the nations on earth.
You will receive all these blessings; they will run after you
Because you have obeyed the voice of the LORD your God:
Blessed will you be in the town.
Blessed will you be in the countryside.
Blessed will be the fruit of your womb.
Blessed will be the fruit of the ground,
The fruit of your cattle, the yield of your calves
And the lambing of your flocks.
Blessings shall be in your basket and kneading bowl.
Blessed will you be in your coming home.
Blessed will you be in your going out.

The LORD will smite down the enemies who rise up against
   you.
They shall advance against you from one direction
But they will flee from you by seven.

---

[1] Excluding the paragraph 26:16–19, which follows, chapters 12–27
containing laws relating to ritual and civil laws are included in *The Laws of
Moses*, page 134ff.

The LORD shall order that your barns be blessed
And whatever you stretch out your hand to achieve.
He will bless you in the land the LORD your God is giving you.
The LORD will establish you as his holy people
As he has sworn to you but only if you observe
The commandments of the LORD your God to walk in his ways.

All the peoples of the earth will see that the LORD
Claims you as his own people and will be in awe of you.
The LORD will pile up favours on you –
The fruit of your womb, the yield of your cattle,
The fruit of your soil in the land the LORD
Swore to your patriarchs to give to you.
The LORD will open up his great treasures in the heavens,
To give rain in its season, to bless the works of your hand.
You shall be a lender to many nations but a borrower from
    none.
The LORD will make you the head and not the tail.
You will only be on top – never at the bottom;
If you will obey the commandments of the LORD your God
Which I now order you to keep and to do.
Do not deviate in any of these matters I now command you
Right or left, to follow other gods to serve them.

But, if you will not obey the voice of the LORD your God
To keep and to do all his commandments and the laws
I now command you, all these curses will descend,
Will come upon you and overwhelm you.
Cursed will you be in the town.
Cursed will you be in the countryside.
Curses will be in your basket and kneading bowl.
Cursed will be the fruit of your womb,
The fruit of the ground, the yield of your calves
And the lambing of your flocks.
Cursed will you be in your coming home.
Cursed will you be in your going out.
The LORD will lash out against you: disasters, anxiety and

Frustration in all that you stretch out your hand to achieve,
Until you are destroyed and quickly perish
Because of your evil deeds in that you have forsaken me.

The LORD will not stop plaguing you until he has put
An end to you on the land, which you enter to possess.
The LORD will strike you down with consumption,
Fever, inflammation, scorching heat, war, drought, blight,
Windblast and mildew – they will hound you to perdition.
The skies overhead shall be like copper **giving no rain.**
The soil under you will be like iron, **hard and infertile.**
The LORD will make the rain of your land into dust.
Sand will drop from the heavens until you are destroyed.

The LORD will strike you down before your enemies.
You will advance against them from one direction
But flee from them in seven.
You will be a terrifying example for all the earth's kingdoms.
Your corpses will be food for every bird in the sky.
And every beast in the field – no one will chase them away.
The LORD will strike you down with the boils[1] of Egypt –
With haemorrhoids, scurvy and the itch – there will be no
    cure.
The LORD will strike you with madness, blindness, distraction.
You will grope about at noonday as the blind do in darkness.
You will not find the right way.
You will be constantly downtrodden and robbed without relief.

You will pay for a bride and another man will lie with her.
You will build a house but not live in it.
You will plant a vineyard but not harvest its fruits.

Your ox will be slaughtered before your very eyes
But you will not eat any of it.
Your donkey will be taken from you and not returned.
Your enemies will confiscate your flocks.

---

[1] The sixth plague inflicted upon the Egyptians.

No one will come to save you.
Your sons and your daughters will be sold to other peoples.
Your eyes will watch and long for them the whole day long.
But your hand will be powerless **to bring them back.**
The produce of your soil and all your labours on it –
A people whom you never knew will consume it.
You will be downtrodden and crushed all the time.
You will be driven mad by the sights you will see.

The LORD will strike you with foul boils on knees and legs.
You will not be cured from the sole of your foot
To the top of your head. The LORD will lead you **into exile** –
You and the king you appointed over you[1] to a nation
Which neither you nor your ancestors ever knew.
There you will serve other gods made of wood and stone.
You will become a horror – a source for proverbs and jokes
Among all the peoples to which the LORD will lead you.

You will sprinkle much seed in your fields but your
Harvest will be small because the locusts will eat it.
You will plant and fill your vineyards but
You will not have wine to drink or store because
The worms will eat them; you will have olive trees
Throughout your land but you will have no oil for ointment
Because the olives will drop off **before they are ripe.**
You will sire sons and daughters but they will not be yours –
They will be taken captive. The crickets will inherit
All your orchards and the produce of your soil.

The aliens among you will rise higher and higher.
But you will sink lower and lower.
He will lend to you but you will not lend to him.
He will be the head and you will be the tail.
All these curses will come upon you –
They will chase you and overtake you until you are destroyed

[1] The fact that the king is spoken of as one appointed by the people and not by God reveals the prophetic disapproval of the monarchy.

Because you did not listen to the voice of the LORD your God
To keep the commandments and laws he gave you.

They will be a sign and proof for you and your descendants
Forever; because you did not serve the LORD your God
With joy and gladness for the abundance of everything.
You will serve your enemies whom the LORD will send to you –
In hunger, thirst, nakedness and deprived of everything.
He will set an iron yoke on your neck
Until he has destroyed you. The LORD will bring on you
A far-off nation – from the end of the earth – who will
Swoop down like an eagle – a nation whose language
You will not understand – a ruthless nation
Who will show no regard for the old or mercy for the
   young.

He will eat the offspring of your cattle and the produce of
Your soil until he destroys you – without any remaining
Grain, wine or oil, no increase in calves or lambs,
Until he completely devastates you.
He will lay siege against you within all your gates
Until your tall and fortified walls come down –
In which you have such confidence throughout your land
Which the LORD your God gave to you.
You shall eat the fruit of your own body[1] –

The flesh of your sons and daughters which the LORD your
   God
Gave you, because of the desperate straits
To which your enemy has reduced you.
The tenderest man among you – the gentlest – will look
   askance
At his brother, at the wife who lies in his bosom,
At the children who are left because he refuses to share with
Any of them the flesh of the children that he eats because

[1] This is reported in the dirge of '*Lamentations*', included in *The People's Bible*
under the title, '*Song of Songs*'. The mere reading of it sets one's hair on end.

He has nothing else because of the desperate straits
To which you will be reduced by your enemy in all your gates.

The most tender and refined woman among you, so delicate
And sensitive that
She would not venture to put a foot on the ground,
She will look askance at the husband she embraces,
Her son and her daughter; she will secretly eat them for
Lack of anything else – the after-birth and the babies
That come out between her legs because of the siege and the
Desperate straits imposed on you by the enemy in your gates.

This will be your future, if you do not keep and do all
The words of this teaching written in this scroll to revere
This glorious and awesome name – the Lord your God
The Lord will inflict terrible plagues on you and your children:
Severe and lasting plagues, malignant and chronic diseases.
He will bring on you all the plagues of Egypt which frightened
   you;
They will grip you. Even diseases and plagues not mentioned in
The scroll of this teaching will the Lord bring on you
Until your destruction. You will be left few in numbers,
Who before were as numerous as the stars of the heavens.
Why?
Because you did not listen to the voice of the Lord your God.

Then, just as the Lord delighted in being good to you
And in increasing your numbers, so will he delight
In causing your perdition and destruction.
You will be plucked from off the ground you came to possess.
He will scatter you among all the peoples
From one end of the earth to the other end.
There will you serve other gods unknown to you and
Your ancestors made of wood and stone.

You will not find peace among these nations.
There will be no rest for the sole of your foot.
The Lord will give you there an anxious heart,

Downcast eyes and a pining away of the soul.
Your lives will always appear vulnerable to you.
You will fear the night and the day.
You will have no confidence in your life expectancy.

In the morning you will exclaim, "If only it were night!"
At night you will exclaim, "If only it were morning!"
All because of your fearful heart and what your eyes will see –
With galleys will the LORD bring you back to Egypt
By a road of which I said to you, "You will not see it again."
There you would sell yourselves to your enemies
As male and female slaves – but none will buy you.[1]
[These were the words of **warning of the consequences of
Observing or breaking** the Covenant which the LORD
  instructed
Moses to make with the Israelites in the land of Moab beside
The Covenant he agreed with them at Horeb.

Moses summoned all the Israelites and said to them:
You have seen all that the LORD did before your eyes in Egypt
To Pharaoh, to all his ministers and to his entire land –
The great tribulations, the signs and great wonders.
But the LORD did not then give you the heart to fathom,
The eyes to perceive and the ears to understand until now –
**The purpose of your liberation from Egypt
Was to become the people of the Lord,
To serve him and to follow his paths,
To live in the land he promised to give the patriarchs.**

I have led you for forty years in the wilderness,
The clothes on you never got old and worn
The shoes on your feet did not become old and weather-beaten

---

[1] After the destruction of the first Temple many Jews fled to Egypt. Because of
their poverty they were prepared to sell themselves into slavery. Is this a
prophecy or written after the event? The certainty attributed to Moses that they
would be disloyal to God and his commandments suggests the latter. 28:69
which follows is in *The Laws of Moses*, page 174.

You had no bread to eat – **but manna.**
Neither did you have wine or liquor to drink.
This was for you to know that I[1] am the LORD your God
Who sustained you and kept you alive.
When you came to this place, Sihon, king of Heshbon and
Og king of Bashan attacked us and we defeated them.
We took their land and gave it as the inheritance
To Reuben, to Gad and to the half-tribe of Manasseh.
So, observe the words of this covenant and do them
In order that you may succeed in all you undertake.

You are all now standing before the LORD your God.
Your chieftains, your tribes, your elders, your administrators,
Every Israelite, your infants, your wives, the strangers in
The camp from the woodchopper to the water-carrier,
To confirm the covenant of the LORD your God and his oath
Which the LORD is confirming with you on this day;
In order to establish you today as his people and that
He will be to you a God as he told you and as
He swore to your patriarchs, Abraham, Isaac and Jacob.

Not only with you do I confirm this covenant and sanctions –
With those who are not now standing here with us as well
As with those who do not stand today before the LORD our
    God.
[For you know how we lived in the land of Egypt,
How we passed through the nations **on the way here.**
You have seen their abominable things, their idols –
Wood and stone, silver and gold – which they possessed].

I tell you this, in case there is among you man or woman,
Family or tribe whose heart turns away from the LORD our God
To serve the gods of those nations; in case there is among
You a root sprouting poison weed and wormwood,

---

[1] The switch to God as the speaker is surprising. Does the narrator want to
suggest that, in fulfilling the divine mission, Moses becomes almost akin to
God?

Who, when he hears the sanctions **for his disobedience,**
Thinks to himself, I will be safe though I do what I please –
To the final destruction of innocent and wicked[1] alike –
The LORD will never forgive him.
The wrath and zeal of the LORD will rise up like smoke
Against him and the curses written in this scroll will lurch
Upon him; the LORD will erase him from under the heavens.
If a tribe breaks the covenant – the LORD will single it out
For misfortune from among the tribes of Israel with all the
Sanctions for breaking the covenant written in this
Scroll of teachings. The generation to come, your descendants
Who will follow you, as well as the foreigner from far off
Will exclaim, when they see the plagues and diseases that
The LORD has inflicted upon her:

"Brimstone and salt!
The whole land is burnt out.
Nothing can be sown, nothing can grow.
No vegetation will ever sprout up.
It is like the overthrow of Sodom and Gomorrah!
Like Admah and Zeboiim
Which the LORD overthrew in his burning anger."
All the nations will say,

"For what reason has the LORD done so to this land?
What provoked the heat of this fierce anger?"
The answer:

Because they broke the covenant of the LORD
The God of their patriarchs, which he made with them.
When he took them out of the land of Egypt
They went and served other gods, bowing down to them –
Gods whom they did not know –
Whom he did not assign to them **as their gods.**[2]

---

[1] Literally: 'the moist together with the dry.'
[2] Earlier (p. 127) Moses explains that the Lord has assigned the worship of celestial bodies to other peoples. Implicit here is the acceptance that other nations are not sinning in worshipping other gods- only Israel when she does so. This goes against the view of Hebrew intolerance of other gods.

Therefore was the LORD incensed against that land
To bring upon her the curses written in this scroll.
The LORD uprooted them from their land
In anger, with a burning wrath and fierce indignation,
And exiled them to another land – their present situation.

Yet, we do not understand the ferocity of the Lord's anger.
These hidden things the LORD keeps close to himself.
What is revealed to us and our descendants forever
Is that we must observe the words of this Teaching.
When all this happens to you – the blessing and the curse
Which I have foretold to you – you will take it to heart
Among the nations to which the LORD has driven you.
You will return to the LORD your God and obey his voice
In all that I have instructed you today –
You and your descendants with all your heart and soul.

The LORD will then reverse your captivity and pity you.
He will return and gather you up from among the people
Where the LORD your God has scattered you.
Even if your outcasts are over the furthest horizon – from
There the LORD your God will gather you and bring you back.
The LORD your God will restore you to the land
Your ancestors possessed – **again** you will possess it –
You will prosper and increase even more than your ancestors.

The LORD your God will circumcise your heart and
The hearts of your descendants to love the LORD your God
With all your heart and soul for the sake of your lives.
The LORD your God will then place all these curses
On your enemies – those who hated and persecuted you.
You will return and obey the LORD's voice.
You will observe all his commandments which I now tell you.
The LORD will give success to all your undertakings –
The fruit of your womb, the yield of your cattle,
The produce of your soil – it will be good –
For the LORD will again delight in your well-being

As he delighted in that of your patriarchs.
Because you will listen to the voice of the LORD
To keep his commandments and laws written in this
Scroll of Instruction when you return to
The LORD your God with all your heart and soul.

The Commandment is not in heaven

For this commandment which I give you on this day
Is not beyond your **understanding** nor far away.
It is not in the heaven to make you exclaim,
'Who will ascend the heavens to take hold of it for us
To bring it to our attention so that we may practise it.'
Nor is it across the sea to make you exclaim,
'Who will cross the sea to take hold of it for us
To bring it to our attention so that we may practise it.'
No, the word is very close to you
Indeed, it is in your very mouth and heart for you to do it!

See, I am now offering you life and prosperity
Death and catastrophe – when I command you today:
To love the LORD your God, to follow his paths,
To observe his commandments, laws and judgements –
So that you may live and increase and so that
The LORD your God will bless you on the land
Which you enter to possess; but if you turn away your heart,
Cease to obey and are seduced in the worship and service of
Other gods – I tell you now you will be ruined.
You will not extend your years on the land to which
You are crossing the Jordan to reach and possess.
I now call heaven and earth as witnesses against you:
I am offering you life and death, the blessing and the curse,
Therefore choose life so that you and your progeny may live!
Only by loving the LORD your God, by obeying him,
By clinging to him because he is the source of your life and
Length of years, to inhabit the land which the LORD your God

Swore to give to your patriarchs, Abraham, Isaac and Jacob.

Moses proceeded to speak these words to all Israel:
I am now one hundred and twenty years old
I am no longer able to go in and out **before you as leader.**
Also, the LORD has said to me, 'You will not cross the Jordan.'
So it is the LORD your God who will cross before you.[1]
He will destroy these nations before you for you to disinherit.
Joshua will lead you as the LORD has spoken.
The LORD shall do to them as he did to Sihon and Og.
The kings of the Amorites and their lands which he destroyed,
The LORD will hand them over to you and you will act
Towards them as I have commanded you to do.

Be strong and courageous. Fear not!
Let them not frighten you because it is the LORD your God
Who goes before you. He will not fail or forsake you.
Moses called Joshua and said to him in the sight of all Israel,
Be strong and courageous for you will lead the people
To the land which the LORD swore to our patriarchs
To give them – but you will enable them to inherit it.
It is the LORD who goes out before you **in battle.**
He will be with you. He will not fail or forsake you.
Do not be afraid or anxious.[2]

The LORD said to Moses, "The day of your death approaches,
Summon Joshua and stand before me in the Tent of Meeting
So that I may give him a charge."
Moses and Joshua went and stood in the Tent of Meeting.
The LORD revealed himself in the Tent in a pillar of clouds –
The pillar of clouds stood by the entrance of the Tent.[3]
He charged Joshua bin Nun, "Be strong and courageous,

[1] The theme that it is God who is responsible for Israel's success is reinforced again and again. Moses and Joshua are only his agents.
[2] 31:9–13: instructions regarding the reading of the Torah on Tabernacles in the Sabbatical year are in *The Laws of Moses*, page 170.
[3] I now follow with v. 23 which, though it appears in the text six verses on, obviously belongs here.

You will bring the Israelites into the land I promised them
And I will be with you."

The LORD said to Moses, "You will sleep with your ancestors.
This people will proceed to play the whore with
The gods of the foreigners of the land in whose midst
They are going – they will forsake me and break my Covenant
Which I made with them.
For that my anger will consume them.
I will forsake them. I will hide my face from them.
They will be food **for vultures.** Much evil and trouble
Will happen to them, which will lead them to say
On that day, 'It is because our God is not with us
That these evils have come upon us.'
I will certainly hide my face at that time
Because of their wickedness in turning to other gods.

"Now, write for them this poem and teach it to the Israelites,
Make them memorise it so that this song will be
A testimony for me against the Israelites.
For **I know that** when I bring them into the land
I swore to their patriarchs – flowing with milk and honey –
They will eat, be satisfied and grow fat and turn to
Other gods and serve them.
They will despise me and break my covenant.
When great evils and trouble befall them, this song
Will act as a testimony against them for the
Mouths of their descendants will not forget it.
I know their inclination even on the day
Before I bring them to the land which I have promised."
Moses then wrote this poem and taught it to the Israelites.

When Moses had finished writing the words of this instruction
On a scroll, he ordered the Levites who were the bearers of
The Ark of the Covenant of the LORD:
"Take this Scroll of Instruction and put it on the side of
The Ark of the Covenant of the LORD your God

To be a testimony against you, for I know your rebelliousness
And your stubbornness – even while I am still alive
You have been rebels against God –
How much more after my death!

"Gather together all the elders of your tribes and officials.
I will speak these words into their ears and
Summon heaven and earth to witness against them,
Because I know that after my death they will self-destruct –
They will stray from the path which I have commanded them.
Evil will befall them in the future for they will act sinfully
In the sight of the LORD to provoke his anger through
What your hands get up to."
So did Moses speak into the ears of the congregation of
Israel the words of this poem until its conclusion:

Give ear, O heavens. Let me speak.
Let the earth hear the words of my mouth.
Let my discourse descend like rain.
Let my speech distil as the dew –
Like light showers on grass,
Like light rain on the green,
For it is the name of the LORD I proclaim:
Oh proclaim the greatness of our God!

The Rock – his works are perfect
All his ways are just –
A loyal God without **fault**.
He is righteous and straight.
Is their destruction his fault?
No, his sons were corrupt!
A crooked and perverse generation.

Do you blame the LORD for this?
O foolish and naïve people,
Is he not your father who has acquired you?
He is your maker and sustainer.

Remember ancient days,
Seek to understand the meaning of past generations.
Inquire of your father and let him tell you –
Your elders and see what they say to you:
When the Highest One gave allotments to the nations,
When he divided **the earth** among the descendants of Adam
He assigned borders for the peoples,
In keeping with the needs of Israel's numbers.
Because the LORD's portion is his people.
Jacob is the chain of his inheritance.
He came upon him in a desert land,
In an empty wasteland where the wild beasts howl.
He flew around him and watched over him.
He protected him as the apple of his eye.

As an eagle stirs up his nest,
As he flutters over his brood,
Spreading out his wings, he takes him,
Lifting him up, carrying him on his pinions.
So it was the LORD alone who led him –
There was no foreign god by his side!

He made him drive over the high places of the earth.
He foraged among the choicest of the fields.
He gave him to suck honey out of rocks
And oil out of flint stones;
Curd of cattle and milk of flocks
With the fat of lambs,
Rams of Bashan and goats,
The rich taste of wheat kernels.
From the blood of grape you drank wine.
But Jeshurun[1] became fat and kicked **his master.**

You have grown fat and thick and bloated.
And he forsook the God who made him.

---

[1] Jeshurun, meaning 'straight and honest', is another name for Israel. It is a
literary irony to use this name in the present context of sinfulness.

He despised the Rock of his salvation.
They made him jealous with foreign **gods.**
They provoked his anger with their abominations.
They made sacrifices to demons who were not divine –
To gods whom they never experienced,
To new gods who came up of late.
Their patriarchs had no regard for them.

You neglect the Rock who fathered you.
You forgot the God who bore you in labour.
The LORD saw this and spurned **them**
Provoked to anger by his sons and daughters.
He said, 'I will hide my face from them.
I will consider their future
For they are a treacherous generation –
Children with no loyalty in them.

"They have moved me to jealousy with no-gods.
They have provoked me with their vain things.[1]
As for me, I will make them jealous of a no-people.
I will provoke them with a stupid nation.
For flames are burning in my nostrils,[2]
Whose fires reach the depths of Sheol.
It will consume the earth and its bounty.
It will set alight the foundation of mountains.

"I will pile up evils upon them.
I will use up my arrows on them.
Wasted by hunger, eaten away by plague and bitter
    pestilence,
I will send against them the fangs of wild beasts
And the poison of snakes that slither in the dust.
The sword shall cause bereavement outside

---

[1] Meaning 'idols of no worth'.
[2] The word for anger in Hebrew is literally 'nostril', originating from the image of the nose being the source of anger, as one breathes in and out of it when angry. Fire coming out of the dragon's nostrils is the popular image.

While inside terror will reign.
No one will be spared – neither lads nor virgins,
Suckling babes and men with hoary heads.

"I thought to reduce them to nothing,
Make their memory to disappear from humanity,
Except I feared the taunts of the enemy,
That their opponents would misjudge the situation:
Lest they say, 'Our power is exalted –
The LORD has not done all this.'
For they are bereft of comprehension.
They have no understanding at all.
If they were wise enough they would consider this,
They would comprehend their final fate.
How is one able to pursue a thousand
And to put ten thousand to flight?
If their rock had not sold them **up for slaughter**
If the LORD had not delivered them up!
[For their rock is not like our Rock
Even our enemies accept this judgement[1]]

"Their [**the enemies of Israel's**] vine is of the stock of
    Sodom,
And from the fields of Gomorrah:
Their grapes are poisonous grapes.
Their clusters are a bitter growth.
Their wine is the poison of asps,
The cruel venom of vipers.
Is not their fate laid up in store by me,
Sealed off in my storehouses?
Vengeance and retribution are mine.
As soon as their foot falters
For the time of their ruin is approaching.
Their fate is catching them up.

---

[1] In this sentence and perhaps several of the previous lines, Moses and not God
is the speaker.

"The LORD will vindicate his people,
And repent of what he did to his servants,
When he sees that they are powerless:
Nothing – no slave or free man – remains.
He will ask, 'Where are their gods,
The rock in whom they sought refuge,
Who ate of the fat of their sacrifices
And drank of the wine of their libations?'
Let them get up and help you
Let them be a shield for you.

"See, now, that I, I am he,
And there is no god with me!
I kill and give life.
When I wound, it is I who heals.
No one rescues anyone out of my hand.
I lift up my hand to heaven,
And I say, 'As I live forever!'
When I whet my glittering sword
And my hand lays hold on **the staff of** judgement,
I will wreak vengeance on my foes
And retribution on those who hate me.
My arrows will be drunk with blood.
My sword will devour flesh
With the blood of the slain and captive,
From the wild-haired enemy chieftains.
Nations – rejoice with his people
Because he will take vengeance for the blood of his servants.
Wreak vengeance on his foes
And purify the land of his people."

Moses recited the words of this poem to the people –
He and Joshua bin Nun. Moses concluded his words to all
 Israel.
He said to them, "Pay closer attention to the words which
I gave you as testimony today.
You will command your children to practise all

The things of this Instruction. It is not without meaning
For you – it is your very life. Through it you will lengthen
Your years on the land to which you are crossing
The Jordan to reach and possess."

The LORD spoke to Moses on that very day saying,
"Go up into this mountain of Arabim – to Mount Nebo in the
Land of Moab facing Jericho, and see the land of Canaan,
Which I am giving to the Israelites as their possession.
Die on the mount which you are ascending,
And be gathered to your people as Aaron your brother
Died on Mount Hor and was gathered to his people;
Because you broke faith with me in the midst of the Israelites
At the waters of Meribah of Kadesh, in the wilderness of Zin;
Because you did not sanctify me among the Israelites.[1]
You will see the land before you but you will not go there –
To the land, which I am giving to the Israelites."

Moses blesses the Israelites

This is the blessing with which Moses,
The man of the supreme God,
Blessed the Israelites before his death. He said,
"The LORD came from Sinai, he dawned for them at Seir.
He shone upon them at Mount Paran and appeared out of
Tens of thousands of divine creatures.
In his right hand he had a fiery law to give them.[2]

[1] A rather petty reason for not allowing Moses to enter the promised land. Fed up with the moaning Israelites, he does not feel they deserve to be the beneficiaries of the water God has promised to come out of the rock. Considering that God wanted to wipe out the Israelites, Moses should have been forgiven. The fact is that, according to tradition, it was Joshua and not Moses who conquered Canaan and therefore a divine reason must be given for this. It was probably better for Moses to have died with the promise in his heart than to have to confront the harsh reality of its fulfilment.
[2] This translation is based on the traditional Hebrew reading. An alternative translation is: Streaming along at his right hand (Revised English Bible)

He loves the nations. He keeps his holy ones in his hand.
They sat down at your feet – they received your words."[1]

(An instruction Moses commanded us –
As an inheritance for the community of Jacob)

"So was he, **the Lord**, King of Jeshurun, **at Sinai**
When the chieftains of the people assembled
Together with all the tribesmen of Israel.
Let **the tribe of** Reuben live **and prosper** and not die.
Let not his men be few in number **but strong!**
This is Judah's blessing. He said,
"Be attentive, O LORD, to the plea of Judah.
Bring his warriors safely back to the people.
With his might, he fought for them all.
You will be his help against his foes."

Regarding Levi, he said **to the Lord**,
"Your Thummim and Urim are with your pious one,
Whom you tested at Massah, with whom you did
Contend at the waters of Meribah,
Who said of his father and of his mother,
I do not know them.[2]
He did not take regard of his brothers
He ignored his own children –
Because they observed your commandment
And kept **their part of** your Covenant.

"They, **the Levites**, shall teach Jacob your judgements
And your Instruction to Israel.
They will put the incense before you **to enjoy its smell**,[3]
The whole-burnt-offering on your altar.

---

[1] Is this a reference to the Elders going up to Mount Sinai and eating and drinking with the Lord? See p. 54.
[2] As priests and judges they had to be scrupulously fair and objective. Their loyalty to the Lord superseded love of parents, etc.
[3] I add this because literally the Hebrew says 'to put the incense in your nose'. The Lord is portrayed in very anthropomorphic terms.

Bless, O LORD, his substance and favour his undertakings,
Smite the loins of his foes;
Let those who hate him rise up no more."

Regarding Benjamin, he said,
"**Benjamin,** the beloved of the LORD – he rests securely by Him.
He protects him for all time.
He is nestled between his shoulders."[1]

Regarding Joseph, he said,
"His land will be blessed by the LORD
With the best things from the heavens above
And of the deep which couches below;
The best **harvests** mustered by the sun,
The best harvests influenced by the moon,[2]
The choice fruit growing on the ancient mountains,
The treasures of the eternal hills.
The treasures of the earth and its fullness –
The favour of he who dwells in a bush.[3]
May these **blessings** rest on Joseph's head,
And on the crown of him who was elected over his brothers.
Like the first-born bull in all his majesty,
With horns like the horns of a wild ox **ready for battle.**
With them he gores the peoples –
All together to the ends of the earth –
These are the myriads of Ephraim
These are the thousands of Manasseh."

Regarding Zebulun **and Issachar**, he said,
"Rejoice, O Zebulun, in your **maritime** expeditions.
And Issachar in **the peace of** your tents.

---

[1] This may be a reference to the fact that God's house – the Temple – was within the territory of Benjamin. For the sake of clarity, I have in this instance capitalised pronouns referring to God.

[2] The moon was perceived as the source of the change of months and seasons.

[3] The reference is to the burning bush [Exodus 3:1 ff]. This suggests that there was a tradition that the God of the Israelites revealed himself from a humble bush on more than one occasion.

They will summon the people to the mountain **for worship.**
There they will offer the appropriate sacrifices
In thanksgiving, for they will draw out the sea's bounty
And the hidden treasures – **the glass** – of the sand."

Regarding Gad, he said,
"Praise be he who expands **the territory of** Gad.
He is poised **to jump** like a lioness
To savage the body and head of his enemies.
He saw the first portion **of the spoils**
Due to him as the respected chieftain.
He arrived as head of the people's chieftains.
He executed the justice of the LORD **on the nations**
And the judgements on Israel."

Regarding Dan, he said, "Dan is a lion's whelp
That leaps out of Bashan."
Regarding Naphtali, he said,
"O Naphtali, you overflow with **divine** favours.
Full of the LORD's blessings
Your domain is in the west and south."

Regarding Asher, he said,
"Asher is more blessed than all the sons.
Let him be his brothers' favourite.
And let him bathe his feet in oil.
May your **protecting** bars be iron and brass
And your security as long as your years."

Moses then said: There is none like the God of Jeshurun
Who rides the heavens to your rescue –
Through the skies in all his majesty.
The God of antiquity is your refuge.
Below **on earth** is his everlasting arm **of might**
Which drives away the enemy from before you.
It is he who commands, "Destroy the enemy."
Thus Israel dwells in security,
Undisturbed is Jacob's **living** fountain

In a land of grain and wine,
With his heavens dropping with dew.
O fortunate Israel, who is like you –
A people saved by the LORD,
A shield who protects you,
A sword who makes you triumphant?
Your enemies shall come crying before you,
And you will trample on their backs."

"No prophet has ever arisen in Israel like Moses"

Moses went up from the plains of Moab to Mount Nebo,
The top of Pisgah opposite Jericho.
The LORD showed him the entire country –
Gilead as far as Dan, all Naphtali;
The lands of Ephraim and Manasseh;
All the land of Judah as far as the Western Sea,
The Negeb, the Plain – the valley of Jericho,
The city of palm trees – as far as Zoar.

The LORD said to him, "This is the land I swore to
Abraham, Isaac and Jacob with these words,
'To your descendants will I give it.'
I have allowed you to see it with your eyes
But you shall not cross over there."
Moses, the servant of the LORD, died there.
He buried him in the valley in the land of Moab,
Near Beth-peor. No one knows of his burial place even now.
Moses was one hundred and twenty years old when he died.
His eyes were undimmed, his strength undiminished.

The Israelites wept for Moses on
The Plains of Moab for Thirty days.
The time of weeping and mourning for Moses ended.
Now, Joshua bin Nun was filled with the spirit of wisdom

Because Moses had laid his hands upon him.
The Israelites heeded him, doing as the LORD told Moses.

No prophet has ever arisen in Israel like Moses
Whom the LORD knew face to face,
In all the signs and wonders which the LORD sent him to do
In the land of Egypt to Pharaoh, to all his ministers
And to all his country; for all the power of his hand
And the great dread that Moses wielded
In the sight of all of Israel.

APPENDIX

Appendix

APPENDIX ONE
EXODUS 6:14–25
Genealogy of Reuben, Simeon and Levi[1]

These are the heads of their respective clans: the sons of Reuben, the firstborn of Israel, Hanoch and Pallu, Hezron and Carmi – the families of Reuben. The sons of Simeon: Jemuel and Jamin and Ohad, Jachin, Zohar and Shaul – the son of a Canaanite woman. These are the families of Simeon. These are the names of the sons of Levi according to their lineage: Gershon, Kohath and Merari. The span of Levi's life was a hundred and thirty-seven years. The sons of Gershon: Libni and Shimei according to their genealogies. The sons of Kohath: Amram and Izhar, Hebron and Uzziel. The span of Kohath's life was a hundred and thirty three years. The sons of Merari: Mahli and Mushi. These are the families of the Levites according to their genealogies

Amram took to wife Jochebed – his father's sister.[2] She bore him Aaron and Moses. The span of Amram's life was a hundred and thirty-seven years. The sons of Izhar: Korah, Nepheg and Zichri. The sons of Uzziel: Mishael, Elzaphan and Sithri. Aaron took to wife Elisheba bath Amminadab, the sister of Nahshon. She bore him Nadab, Abihu, Eleazar and Ithamar. The sons of Korah: Assir, Elkanah and Abiasaph – these are the families of the Korahites. Eleazar, Aaron's son, took to wife a daughter of Putiel. She bore him Phinehas. These are the heads of their fathers' houses, of the Levites, by their genealogies.

---

[1] The fact that this genealogy starts with Jacob's first-born, proceeds to his second and third sons and stops with the descendants of Aaron, a Levite, seems to indicate that this was a priestly insertion. It is given an air of authenticity by the genealogy of the previous two sons. The genealogy of the other sons of Jacob is not of interest to the priests of the day who are seeking to justify their own claim to the priesthood.

[2] The marriage to an aunt is prohibited in *Leviticus* 18:12. One could argue in defence of Amram that the Torah – the law – had not yet been given. It is fascinating and of political significance that there is no record here of the great lawgiver's progeny.

APPENDIX TWO
NUMBERS 1:1–46
The First Census

On the first day of the second month in the second year following
their departure from the land of Egypt, the LORD instructed Moses
in the Sinai wilderness in the Tent of Meeting: "Take a census
of all the Israelites by tribes and clans recording the name of
every male individually. You and Aaron shall register all the
Israelites by their groupings from the age of twenty upwards
– all fit to bear arms: one man from each tribe – the head of
his clan will assist you. These are the names of the men who
will assist you; from Reuben – Elizur ben Shedeur; from Simeon
– Shelumiel ben Zurishaddai; from Judah – Nahshon ben
Amminadab; from Issachar – Nethanel ben Zuar; from Zebulun
– Eliab ben Helon; from the sons of Joseph: Ephraim – Elishama
ben Ammihud; Manasseh – Gamaliel ben Pedahzur; from Benjamin – Abidan ben Gideoni; from Dan – Ahiezer ben Ammishaddai; from Asher – Pagiel ben Ochran; Gad – Eliasaph ben Deuel;
from Naphtali – Ahirah ben Enan. These were the community's
elected, the chieftains of their ancestral tribes – they are the heads
of the myriads of Israel. So Moses and Aaron took those men
who had been named, and on the first day of the second
month they mustered the entire community: every male aged
twenty had their names registered according to their ancestral
clans. As the LORD had instructed Moses, so did he record
them in the wilderness of Sinai. They totalled as follows: the
descendants of Reuben, Israel's first-born, the registration of the
clans of their ancestral house individually listed – all males aged
twenty years and over bearing arms. Those enrolled from the
tribe of Reuben were 46,500; the descendants of Simeon, the
registration of the clans etc. Those enrolled from the tribe of
Simeon: 59,300; the descendants of Gad, the registration of the
clans etc. Those enrolled from the tribe of Gad: 45,650; the
descendants of Judah, the registration of the clans etc. Those
enrolled from the tribe of Judah: 74,600; the descendants of

Issachar, the registration of the clans, etc. Those enrolled from the tribe of Issachar: 54,400;

The descendants of Zebulun, the registration of the clans, etc. Those enrolled from the tribe of Zebulun: 57,400; the descendants of Joseph: the descendants of Ephraim, the registration of the clans, etc. Those enrolled from the tribe of Ephraim: 40,500; the descendants of Manasseh, the registration of the clans, etc. Those enrolled from the tribe of Manasseh: 32,200; the descendants of Benjamin, the registration of the clans, etc. Those enrolled from the tribe of Benjamin: 35,400;

The descendants of Dan, the registration of the clans, etc. Those enrolled from the tribe of Dan: 62,700; the descendants of Asher, the registration of the clans, etc. Those enrolled from the tribe of Asher: 41,500; the descendants of Naphtali, the registration of the clans, etc. Those enrolled from the tribe of Naphtali: 53,400. These are those who were enrolled by Moses and Aaron and by the chieftains of Israel – twelve in number, one man from each ancestral tribe. All the Israelites aged twenty years and over able to bear arms – all who were enrolled came to 603,550.

NUMBERS 1:47 – 2:34
The Encampment of the Israelites

The Levites, however, were not recorded by their ancestral tribe, for the LORD had instructed Moses: "On no account enrol the tribe of Levi or take their census with the Israelites. Put the Levites in charge of the Tabernacle of the Testimony, they shall tend all its furnishings; they shall encamp around the Tabernacle. When the Tabernacle is to set out, the Levites will take it down; when the Tabernacle is to be pitched, the Levites will erect it. Any layman who comes near it is to be put to death. The Israelites shall encamp by companies each man with his division and each under his standard. The Levites will encamp around the Tabernacle of the Testimony; otherwise **God's** wrath may strike the Israelite community." The Israelites acted so just as the LORD had instructed Moses.

The LORD spoke to Moses and Aaron: "The Israelites will encamp each with his standard under his ancestral house banners. They will camp around the Tent of Meeting at a distance: encamped in the front on the east side – the division of Judah company by company. Judah's chieftain: Nahshon ben Amminadab, his company's enrolment: 74,600; camping next to it – the tribe of Issachar – its chieftain: Nathanel ben Zuar, his company's enrolment: 54,500; **on its other side,** Zebulun, its chieftain: Eliab ben Helon, his company's enrolment: 57,400. The total enrolment in Judah's division: 186,400 by companies. They shall break camp first. On the south side: the standard of the division of Reuben, company by company. Reuben's chieftain: Elizur ben Shedeur, his company's enrolment 46,500; camping next to it – the tribe of Simeon – its chieftain: Shelumiel ben Zurishaddai; his company's enrolment: 59,300; On **its other side,** Gad.

Gad's chieftain: Eliasaph ben Reuel, his company's enrolment: 45,650. The total enrolled in the division of Reuben: 151,450 in their companies. They shall break camp second. Next, the Tent of Meeting will move with the Levites.

As they camp, so will they march in order – each man in position by his standard. On the west: the standard of the division of Ephraim, company by company. Ephraim's chieftain: Elishama ben Ammihud; his company's enrolment: 40,500; next to it – the tribe of Manasseh – its chieftain Gamaliel ben Pedahzur; his company's enrolment: 32,200; **on its other side** – Benjamin, his chieftain: Abidan ben Gideoni; his company's enrolment: 35,400. The total enrolled in the division of Ephraim: 108,100 in their companies. They shall be the third to break camp. On the north: the standard of the division of Dan, company by company; Dan's chieftain: Ahiezer ben Ammishaddai; his company's enrolment: 62,7000. Camping next to it – the tribe of Asher – its chieftain: Pagiel ben Ochran; his company's enrolment: 41,500; **on its other side** – Naphtali – its chieftain: Ahira ben Anan; his company's enrolment: 53,400. The total enrolled in the division of Dan:

157,600 in their companies. They shall be the last to break camp by their standards. This is the tally of Israelites by their ancestral houses: the total enrolled in the divisions, for all companies: 603,550. The Levites, however, were not included in the census among the Israelites as the LORD had instructed Moses. The Israelites did just as the LORD had instructed Moses. So they pitched camp by their standards, and broke camp each man with his clan according to his ancestral house.

NUMBERS 9:15–9:23
A cloud guides the Israelites

On the day the Tabernacle was Tabernacle was raised, the cloud covered the Tent of Testimony. During the evening, it remained over the Tabernacle but appeared as a burning flame until morning. It was a regular occurrence: covered by the cloud, which appeared as a fiery flame by night. When the cloud lifted itself from above the Tent, only then did the Israelites set out on their journey. Where the cloud rested, there did the Israelites encamp. So it was at the LORD's command that the Israelites set out and at the LORD's command they pitched camp. As long as the cloud remained above the Tabernacle, they remained in their camps. When the cloud rested over the Tabernacle for an extended period, the Israelites still heeded the LORD's instruction and did not move on. Sometimes the cloud would be over the Tabernacle for only a few days; whatever the case, they acted as the LORD commanded, **as indicated by the cloud,** whether to remain in camp or to set out on their journey. Sometimes, the cloud only rested from evening to morning. When the cloud rose up in the morning, they set out on their journey; **even** if the cloud kept moving throughout the day and the night – so long as the cloud remained on the move – they continued their journey. **Equally,** whether it was for as little as two days, or a month or even a year, so long as the cloud hovered over the Tabernacle, the Israelites remained rooted to their camps and did not set out. But when it rose –

they set out.[1] By the LORD's command, they pitched their tents and by his command they decamped. They heeded the LORD's charge conveyed to them by Moses on the LORD's instruction.

NUMBERS 10:1–10

The silver trumpets to give the clarion call

The LORD instructed Moses: make two trumpets of silver; hammer each of them out **from silver.** They are to be used the community to set out in divisions. When they are both blown the whole community to set out in their divisions. When they are both blown, the whole community shall join you at the gateway to the Tent of Meeting. If only one is blown, the chieftains, the heads of Israel's contingent.[2] shall assemble before you. When you blow the call, the divisions stationed on the east side **of the Tabernacle** shall set out. When you blow the call a second time, the divisions on the south side shall set out. Short blasts shall be blown for setting them out on their journeys. But, to assemble the community **for any other reason,** you shall blow long clarion calls, not staccato ones. The descendants of Aaron, the priests, shall blow the trumpets. This is to be a perpetual commandment throughout the generations. Also, when you go forth in your land to engage in war against your enemies who seek to oppress you, you will sound the clarion call with short blasts, so that the LORD your God will be reminded of you and will save you from your enemies. Also, at the time of your rejoicings – the appointed festivals and at the celebration of the New Months – you shall sound the trumpets during your whole offerings and your peace offerings. They shall be a reminder of you before your God: I am the LORD your God.

---

[1] The tiresome repetition of this theme begs for an explanation. It is as though a teacher was drilling home a lesson. The attempt is to persuade the Israelites that God is their constant and unfailing guide whose guidance, however demanding must be accepted.

[2] Literally: thousands.

APPENDIX THREE
NUMBERS 26:5–65
The second census

Reuben is Israel's first-born. The descendants of Reuben: of Hanoch; the clan of Hanoch; of Pallu, the Palluite clan; of Hezron, the Hezronite clan; of Carmi, the Carmites clan –these are the clans of the Reubenites – numbering 43,730. Of the son of Pallu – Eliab; of the sons of Eliab – Nemuel, Dathan and Abiram – the same Dathan and Abiram, highly regarded in the community, who conspired against Moses and Aaron, as part of Korah's band, who rebelled against the LORD. The earth opened her mouth and swallowed them with Korah, when that company died, when the fire consumed the two hundred and fifty men as a warning. Yet, the descendants of Korah[1] did not die. The descendants of Simeon, according to their clans: of Nemuel, the Nemuelite clan; of Jamin the Jaminite clan; of Jachin, the Jachinite clan; of Zerah, the Zerahite clan; of Shaul, the Shaulite clan. These are the clans of the Simeonites, numbering 22,200. The descendants of Gad, according to their clans: of Zephon, the Zephonite clan; of Haggi, the Haggite clan; of Shuni, the Shunite clan; of Ozni, the Oznite clan; of Eri, the Erite clan; of Arod, the Arodite clan; of Areli, the Arelite clan. These are the clans of Gad numbering 40,500.

The descendants of Judah: Er and Onan who died in Canaan. The descendants of Judah according to their clans were: of Shelah, the Shelanite clan; of Perez, the Perezite clan; of Zerah, the Zerahite clan; the descendants of Perez were: of Hezron, the Hezronite clan; of Hamul, the Hamulite clan. These are the clans of Judah numbering 76,500. The descendants of Issachar according to their clans; of Tolah, the Tolaite clan; of Puvah, the Punite clan; of Jashub, the Jashubite clan; of Shimron, the Shimronite clan. These are the clans of Issachar numbering 64,300. The descendants of Zebulun according to their clans; of Sered, the Seredite clan; of Elon, the Elonite clan; of Jahleel, the Jahleelite clan. These

---

[1] A number of Psalms bear their name.

are the clans of the Zebulunites numbering 60,500. The descendants of Joseph according to their clans: Manasseh and Ephraim. The descendants of Manasseh: of Machir, the Machirite clan; Machir sired Gilead: of Gilead, the Gileadite clan; the descendants of Gilead. of Iezer, the Iezerite clan; of Helek, the Helekite clan; of Asriel, the Asrielite clan; of Shechem, the Shehemite clan; of Shemidah, the Shemidaite clan; of Hepher, the Hepherite clan; Zelophehad ben Hepher had no sons – only daughters: the names of Zelophehad's daughters were Mahlah and Noah, Hoglah, Milcah and Tirzah. These are the clans of Manasseh numbering 52,700. These are the descendants of Ephraim according to their clans: of Shuthelah, the Shuthelahite clan; of Becher the Becherite clan; of Tahan, the Tahanite clan. These are the descendants of Shuthelah: Eran, the Eranite clan. These are the clans of the Ephraimites numbering 32,500 – these are the descendants of Joseph according to their clans.

The descendants of Benjamin according to their clans: of Bela, the Belaite clan; of Ashbel, the Ashbelite clan; of Ahiram, the Ahiramite clan; of Shephupham, the Shephuphamite clan; of Hupham, the Huphamite clan. The descendants of Bela were Ard and Naaman: of Ard, the Ardite clan; of Naaman, the Naamite clan. These are the descendants of Benjamin according to their clans numbering 45,600. These are the descendants of Dan according to their clans: of Shuham, the Shuhamite clans numbered 64,400.[1]

The descendants of Asher according to their clans: of Imnah, the Imnite clan; of Ishvi, the Ishvite clan; of Beriaah, the Beriite clan; of Beriah's descendants; of Heber, the Heberite clan; of Malchiel, the Malchielites; the name of Asher's daughter was Serah.[2]

---

[1] For some reason we are not given any details as to the names of Shuham's descendants. It would appear that in the tribe of Dan there was only one super-clan. One is left to wonder why they were not just known as the Danites or the Shuhamites.

[2] The inclusion of Asher's daughter is puzzling, as no other daughters of the sons of Jacob are mentioned. She is also one of the two women mentioned among the seventy who went down to Egypt. See *Genesis, The People's Bible* p. 144–5 and my footnote.

These are the clans of the Asherites numbering 53,400. The descendants of Naphtali according to their clans: of Jazheel, the Jazheelite clan; of Guni, the Gunite clan; of Jezer, the Jezerite clan; of Shillem, the Shillemite clan; These are the clans of Naphtali numbering 45,400. These were they that were counted of the Israelites: 601,730.

The LORD instructed Moses: the land will be shared out among these as a heritage proportionate to the number of names. To the more numerous you will increase the share; to the smaller you will reduce the share; to each a share in proportion to its size in the census. The sharing out of the land is to be implemented by lot. **This will determine the site.** The size of their portion will be in proportion to the census of their ancestral tribes. Portions will be assigned by lot regardless of their numbers.

This is the census of the Levites by clans: of Gershon, the Gershonite clan; of Kohath, the Kohathite clan; of Merari, the Merarite clan; out of these clans of Levi: the clans of the Libinites, the Hebronites, the Mahlites, the Mushites and the Korahites. Kohath sired Amram.

Amram's wife was Jochebed, the daughter of Levi, born to Levi in Egypt. She bore for Amram Aaron and Moses and Miriam, their sister. To Aaron was born Nadab and Abihu, Eleazar and Ithamar. Nadab and Abihu died when they offered alien fire to the LORD. Their census was 123,000 including every male over a month old.[1] They, **the Levites,** were not part of the Israelite census since no portion was given to them with the Israelites. This is the census taken by Moses and Eleazar the priest who registered the Israelites in the plains of Moab by the Jordan near Jericho. Among them was no man whom Moses and Aaron the priest had registered when they took the census of the Israelites in the wilderness of Sinai because the LORD said of them: they

---

[1] The census of the other tribes was from the age of twenty, because the size of the allotments depended on the numbers of adults. As the Levites were given towns and villages amongst all the tribes, regardless of their numbers, details regarding age had no significance.

will die in the wilderness. Not one survived of them, excepting Caleb ben Jephunneh and Joshua bin Nun.

APPENDIX FOUR
NUMBERS 31:25–54
Distribution of booty following the war with the Midianites

The LORD instructed Moses: You, Eleazar the priest, and the heads of the ancestral clans of the community are to take an inventory of the booty captured, both human and animal. Divide it between the warriors and the rest of the community. You shall levy a tribute for the LORD: from the warriors one out of every 500 persons, oxen, donkeys and sheep shall be taken from their half share for Eleazar the priest as a contribution to the LORD. From the half share of the other Israelites, **the non-combatants,** you shall withhold one in 50 persons as well as cattle, donkeys and sheep, and all other animals to give to the Levites who attend to the duties of the LORD's Tabernacle. Moses and Eleazar the priest did as the LORD instructed Moses. The booty remaining from the spoil that the warriors had taken came to 675,000 sheep, 72,000 heads of cattle, 61,000 donkeys, and a total of 32,000 persons, namely virgin women. So, the half-share of the warriors: 337,000 sheep – of which the LORD's tribute was 675; the cattle came to 36,000 – of which the LORD's tribute was 72; 30,500 donkeys, the LORD's tribute: 61; the number of persons was 16,000, the LORD's tribute 32. Moses gave the tributes levied for the LORD to Eleazar the priest as the LORD had instructed Moses. As for the half-share of the other Israelites which Moses had withheld from the warriors – the half-share was 337,500 sheep, 36,000 head of cattle, 30,500 donkeys and 16,000 persons. From this half-share of the Israelites, Moses withheld one in every 50 persons and animals. He gave them to the Levites who attended to the duties of the Tabernacle as the LORD had instructed Moses. The commanders of the troop divisions, officers of thousands and officers of hundreds came to Moses and said to him: "Your servants have counted the warriors under our charge – and not one is missing. Therefore we have brought an offering **of thanksgiving** to the LORD, whatever a man may have: gold ornaments, armlets, bracelets, rings, earrings and necklaces to make expiation for ourselves before the LORD.'' Moses and Eleazar took the gold from them – all kinds of crafted articles. All the gold offered by the officers of thousands and the officers of hundreds to the LORD were the weight of 16,750 shekels. [The troops had all taken plunder for themselves.] So, Moses and Eleazar the priest accepted the gold from the officers of thousands and hundreds and brought it to The Tent of Meeting for the LORD to remember Israel.

APPENDIX FIVE
NUMBERS 32:33–42
Moses's allocation to the Gadites, Reubenites and the half tribe of Manasseh

Moses assigned to them – to the Gadites, the Reubenites and the half tribe of Manasseh ben Joseph – the kingdom of Sihon, king of the Amorites and the kingdom of Og, king of Bashan, the land with its **major** towns and all their surrounding towns within the borders of their land.

The Gadites built Dibon, Ataroth and Aroer, Atroph-shophan, Jazer, Jogbehah, Beth-nimrah and Beth-haran as fortified towns and as enclosures for their flocks. The Reubenites built Heshbon, Elealeh, Kiriathaim, Nebo, Baal-meon – some names being changed – and Sibmah. They gave **their own** names to the towns they rebuilt. The descendants of Machir ben Manasseh captured Gilead. They dispossessed the Amorites who lived there. Moses then allocated Gilead to Machir ben Manasseh. He settled there. Jair, a Manassehite, went and captured the villages in Transjordan and named them Havroth-jair. Nobah went and captured Kenath and its villages. He called it Nobah, naming it after himself.

APPENDIX SIX
NUMBERS 33:1–49
The itinerary of the Israelites

This is how the Israelites journeyed from place to place when they departed from the land of Egypt with all their forces under the supervision of Moses and Aaron. Moses recorded the starting points of their journeys that were according to the LORD's instruction. They set out from Rameses on the fifteenth day of the first month. The day after the Passover offering, the Israelites departed defiantly in the view of all the Egyptians. The Egyptians were burying those who the LORD had struck down – every first-born, whereby the LORD executed his judgement against their gods. When the Israelites had set out from Rameses, they encamped in Sukkoth. From Sukkoth they moved on to Etham which is on the edge of the wilderness. They moved from Ethan, turning back to Pene-hahiroth which is before Baal-zephon where they encamped before Migdol. They set out from Pene-hahiroth and passed through the river into the wilderness; they made a three-day journey in the wilds of Ethan and encamped at Marah. They set out from Marah and arrived at Elim. At Elim were twelve springs of water and seventy palm trees; so they encamped there. They set out from Elim and encamped by the Red Sea. They set out from the Red Sea and encamped in the wildernesss of Sin. They set out from Sin and encamped at Dophkah. They set out from Dophkah and encamped at Alush. They set out from Alush and encamped at Rephidim, where there was no water for the people to drink. They set out from Rephidim and encamped in the wildernesss of Sinai. They set out from the wilderness of Sinai and encamped at Kibroth-hattaavah. They set out from Kibroth-hattaavah and encamped at Hazeroth. They set out from Hazeroth and encamped at Rithmah. They set out from Rithmah and encamped at Rimmon-perez. They set out from Rimmon-perez and encamped at Libnah. They set out from Libnah and pitched at Rissah. They set out from Rissah and encamped at Kehelathah. They set out from Kehelathah and encamped at Mount Shepher.

They set out from Mount Shepher and encamped at Haradah. They set out from Haradah and encamped at Makheloth. They set out from Makheloth and encamped at Tahath. They set out from Tahath and encamped at Terah. They set out from Terah and encamped at Mithkah. They set out from Mithkah and encamped at Hashmonah. They set out from Hashmonah and encamped at Moseroth. They set out from Moseroth and encamped at Bene-jaakan. They set out from Bene-jaakan and encamped at Hor-haggidgad. They set out from Hor-haggidgad and encamped at Jotbathah. They set out from Jotbathah and encamped at Abronah. They set out from Abronah and encamped at Ezion-geber. They set out from Ezion-geber and encamped in the wilds of Zin, that is Kadesh. They set out from Kadesh and encamped at Mount Hor, on the edge of the land of Edom.

Aaron the priest ascended Mount Hor at the command of the LORD and died there in the fortieth year after the Israelites went out of the land of Egypt, on the first day of the fifth month. Aaron was one hundred and twenty-three years old when he died on Mount Hor. The Canaanite king of Arad who lived in the Negeb, in the land of Canaan, heard of the coming of the Israelites.

They set out from Mount Hor and encamped at Zalmonah. They set out from Zalmonah and encamped at Punon. They set out from Punon and encamped at Oboth. They set out from Oboth and encamped at Iye-abarim in the territory of Moab. They set out from Iyim and encamped at Dibon-gad. They set out from Dibon-gad and encamped in Almon-diblathaim. They set out from Almon-diblathaim and encamped in the hills of Abarim, before Nebo. They set out from the hills of Abarim and encamped in the plains of Moab at the Jordan near Jericho. They encamped by the Jordan from Beth-jeshimoth as far as Abel-shittim in the plains of Moab.

APPENDIX SEVEN
NUMBERS 34
The division of the land

The LORD said to Moses, "Instruct the Israelites in this manner: when you enter the land of Canaan, which comes to you as your portion – Canaan, stretching to all its borders. Your southern sector will be the wilderness of Zin near Edom,your southern border will be from the Dead Sea's eastern tip. Your border shall turn south towards the ascent of Akrabbim, and pass by Zin and extend in the south to Kadesh-barnea. It will go to Hazar-addar and pass through Azmon; from Azmon the border shall turn to the Wadi of Egypt and end at the Sea. The great Sea will be your western border. This will be your northern border: from the Great Sea you will mark your line to Mount Hor; from there you will mark it out to Lebo-hamath up to Zedad. From there it will run to Ziphron ending at Hazar-enan – this will be your northern border. You will mark out your eastern border from Hazar-enan to Shepham – from there to Riblah, the east side of Ain, running down to the eastern ridge of the sea of Kinnereth. The border shall run down to the Jordan ending at the Dead Sea. This will be your land with its surrounding borders."

Moses instructed the Israelites, "This is the land; your portion will be determined by lot, as the LORD has ordered to be granted to the nine and a half tribes, as the Reubenites, Gadites and the half-tribe of Manasseh have taken possession of their portion, family by family. These two and a half tribes have received their portion in Trans-jordan, east of Jericho toward the sunrise." The LORD said to Moses, "These are the names of the men who will apportion the land for you: Eleazar the priest and Joshua bin Nun; also appoint one chieftain from every tribe through whom the land will be apportioned. These are the names of the men from each tribe: Judah – Caleb ben Jephunneh; Simeon – Shemuel ben Ammihud; Benjamin – Elidad ben Chislon; Dan – the chieftain Bukki ben Jogli; Joseph's tribes: Manasseh – the chieftain Hannaniel ben Ephod; Ephraim – the chieftain Elizaphan ben

Parnach; Issachar – the chieftain Paltiel ben Azzan; Asher – the chieftain Ahihud ben Shelomi; Naphtali – the chieftain Pedahel ben Ammihud." These are they whom the LORD instructed to allocate portions to the Israelites in the land of Canaan.

APPENDIX EIGHT
DEUTERONOMY 2:10–12
The Emim people

In ancient times the Emim lived there – a people – powerful and numerous and of enormous height as the Anakim. Like the Anakim they are reckoned as Rephaim but the Moabites called them Emim. The Horites also lived in Seir in antiquity but the descendants of Esau dispossessed them, wiping them out, and settled in their land as Israel did in the land they were to possess which the LORD gave to them.

APPENDIX NINE
DEUTERONOMY 2:20–23
The Rephaim

That is reckoned to be in the land of the Rephaim. The Rephaim lived there in antiquity. The Ammonites called them Zamzummim – a great people – powerful and numerous, as tall as the Anakim; but the LORD destroyed them before them. They supplanted them and lived in their place. So did he do for the descendants of Esau who lived in Seir, when he destroyed the Horites from before them. They supplanted them and live in their place even now. Also, the Avvim, who lived in villages up to Gaza – the Caphtorim, who came from Caphtor, destroyed them **and now live in their place.**

APPENDIX TEN
DEUTERONOMY 3:12–20
Allocation of land to Reuben, Gad and Manasseh

This is the land we allotted at that time from Aroer, by the Wadi Arnon, part of the hill-country of Gilead and its surrounding towns, I gave to the Reubenites and to the Gadites. The rest of Gilead and all Bashan, the kingdom of Og, I gave to the half-tribe of Manasseh – the whole district of Argob – all that part of Bashan called Raphaim country. Jair the Manassehite received the entire district of Argob (Bashan) – as far as the borders of the Geshurites and the Maacthites and named it after himself – Havvoth-jair, its name to this very day. I assigned Gilead to Machir. To the Reubenites and the Gadites, I assigned part of Gilead down to the Wadi Arnon, the middle of the wadi, being its border up to the Wadi Jabbok, the border of the Ammonites. **We also captured** the Arabah from the foot of the slopes of Pisgah on the east to the edge of the Jordan and from Chinneretz down to the Sea of Arabah – the Salt Sea.

APPENDIX ELEVEN
DEUTERONOMY 4:41–49
The cities of refuge for the manslaughterer

Moses set aside three towns on the east side of the Jordan to which the manslaughterer might flee – he who kills his neighbour without intent – who was not a former enemy, so that by escaping to one of these towns – he could live-: Bezer in the wilds of the Tableland, belonging to the Reubenites; Ramoth in Gilead for the Gadites; and Golan in Manasseh for the Manassites.

This is the instruction of Moses which Moses set before the Israelites. These are the testimonies, the laws and judgements which Moses declared to the Israelites when they left Egypt, beyond the Jordan, in the Valley of Beth-peor in the land of Sihon, the Amorite king who reigned in Heshbon, who Moses and the Israelites struck down when they left Egypt. They took possession of his land and the land of Og, the king of Bashan – the two Amorite kings, who ruled on the east side of the Jordan from Aroer on the edge of the wadi Arnon up to Mount Sirion, that is Hermon, and all the Arabah, east of the Jordan as far as the sea of Arabah, at the foot of the slopes of Pisgah.

APPENDIX TWELVE
DEUTERONOMY 10:6–9
The itinerary of the Israelites, the death of Aaron and the selection of the Levites

The Israelites set out from Beeroth-bene-jaakan[1] to Moserah. Aaron died and was buried there Eleazar, his son became the priest in his place. From there they set out towards Gudgodah –from Gudgodah to Jotbathah – a region of running brooks. At that time the LORD designated the tribe of Levi to carry the Ark of the Covenant of the Lord; to stand before the LORD and to minister to him and to ask blessings in his name which they do to this very day. Therefore, the Levites have no **hereditary** portion with their kinsmen. The LORD is their portion[2] just as the LORD your God spoke to him.

---

[1] Literally, 'wells of the Jaakanates.'
[2] The taxes paid to the Lord through offerings and tithes etc which went to the Levites.

2 *The Laws of Moses*

Introduction

Readers who are expecting in this introduction a scholarly review of the origins of the various codes of law will be disappointed. Our interest is not in giving credit or attributing blame for the plethora of laws and rites which follow. Their inclusion in a Torah as a reflection of God's eternal will is what concerns us, not how they came into existence. Three statements from the Mosaic narrative set their moral benchmarks for me at the time in my life when I believed that the Laws of Moses came directly from God.

You shall be holy for I the LORD your God am holy

See, I am now offering you life and death . . . choose life and live

You shall be to me a kingdom of priests – a holy nation.

These are bedded in Moses's exhortation to Pharaoh in the name of God: "Let my people go so that they may serve me."

The plethora of laws which are irrelevant to modern life should not distract the reader from their over-riding purpose: The Israelites should use their newly won freedom from slavery to serve a god who desires them to live in internal harmony while he in turn protects them from all external natural and human dangers. The LORD, who created Man in his own image, expects his human children to be like him, stewards of the earth, enfranchised to rule the earth but with respect for their fellow creatures. They are to be special – holy, for he is holy. They were to be "a kingdom of priests, a holy nation". Obedience to his guidelines – the Torah – is the way to peace and prosperity. The alternative is self-destruction.

There is one disturbing factor to the LORD's benevolence – it is limited to his chosen people, Israel. Why? The children of Adam and Eve had corrupted their ways on the face of the earth. The punishment was the flood. Noah and his family alone were saved. God vowed never again to intervene on such a destructive scale.

The rainbow is the sign of his agreement to allow humanity, for better or for worse, to go its own way. After permitting Noah's progeny to eat animal flesh (without drinking its blood which is the life-giving force,) and forbidding the murder of human beings, he absents himself from human life. However, after ten generations of brooding over his failure to set humanity on the right path, the LORD decided on another course of action. He chose one man, Abraham, to be his messenger on earth. From his grandson Jacob, the nation of Israel was born. The people of Israel was nurtured in the slave camps of Egypt, liberated at the Red Sea and brought into an eternal contract with the LORD at Sinai. On the positive side any resident alien could become part of the people by joining the covenant through the worship of Yahweh and circumcision.

Other nations, submerged in the worship of earth, daemons and capricious gods, were outside the portholes of grace and were not subject to punishments or rewards. Seen in this light, the nations of the world are suffering no deprivation other than being independent of a caring and demanding father, king and master. And, for all we know, they too may have felt chosen by their own gods, from whose grace the Israelites had been excluded. The survival of Israel alone and the testimony of Jews, Christians and Muslims, her spiritual descendants, means that we only hear her side of the story. There can be little doubt, however, that the great empires of Egypt and Assyria and the Persians believed, and perhaps more realistically, that it was their nations and not Israel, who were chosen. But they are no longer here to tell their tale.

While the equality ordained for all the Israelites was a wonderful concept, it was beset by pragmatic problems of divine and human governance. Some group had to be in charge of the ritual through which an individual and a people communicate with their god – to offer him the required observance and to receive his directives. The election of a priestly class did not rest easily with the prophets, some of whom were themselves priests, who were the authors of Jewish theology immediately before, during and after the Babylonian exile. Their belief was that God, like all monarchs, required some tribute. In his case, it was the first fruits of all human produce, including that of their male children. The first-born would serve as his ministers. In an obscure narrative in the text, the Israelites fear that, because of their sinfulness, those who enter Yahweh's sanctuary will suffer death. The solution is that the family of Aaron will assume, in the place of Israel's first-born, the awesome responsibility of looking after God's sacrificial rites – for one slip in the observance of the ordained order could lead to instant death. Henceforth the first-born male Israelites would be redeemed from entering the Temple service by a ransom of five shekels.

Before anyone dismisses the rigmarole of the sacrificial rites as senseless, let them consider, for example, the great detail and panoply of a Christian cathedral service or the intricacies involved in a Jain wedding. Ceremonial increases in impressiveness in ratio to the number of ministrants and the tasks they perform. The power of a ritual lies in the minutiae of observance which leaves the ignorant seeking to comprehend the layers of mystery unfolding before him.

In the Israelite community, sacrifice was the means of coming close to God. A king is never approached without a present to express gratitude for favours received or being sought. As the king of the Israelites, the LORD would expect no less, and from his erring subjects he would expect offerings of penance. The variations of these sacrifices and the methods of presentation can try our patience, but it should be seen in the perspective of our elaborate preparations in all matters of ceremonial attached to state and church. We must also appreciate that the sacrificial and ritual codes were written down as a guide for priests and not intended for laymen. Ordinary people would have acted on instructions on all ritual matters from the cradle to the grave as they do to this very day. They still rely on priests and officials to tell them what to do in any crisis. The fact that there is in the entire Mosaic code only one reference to the appointment of a king, and no instructions as to his privileges, limitations and responsibilities to his subjects, is evidence that this code was not put into it final form until some time after the return from exile when the monarchy had ceased to exist. By that time the prophetic view that God alone was king had become part of the Jewish ethos.

The Laws of Moses can *not* be treated as have been other volumes in this series of translations. It is not intended to be read as one does histories, fiction, plays or poetry. It is a reference book to give the curious reader the opportunity to consider those laws, which through Christianity became one of the foundation stones of Western civilisation. By use of the indexed Table of the Laws, the reader is able to pick and choose and so find the gems of Hebrew law which have redeemed the rest from obscurity. Laws declaring the Jubilee and the liberation of slaves, the exhortation not to return run-away slaves, as well as a most sensible set of civil laws indicate why the Mosaic law has been applauded for its contribution to Western legal codes.

Lex talionis – "The law of an eye for an eye and a tooth for a tooth, and a life for a life" – has been used to malign Old Testament law as one of vengeance, when the very opposite is the case. The reader will see from instances when this principle is applied that it was not meant to be taken in the literal sense, but in terms of monetary value, for it is apparent that while one person would survive the loss of an eye, another could die from the wound through loss of blood, etc. What benefit would there be to the victim if his attacker was blinded? Furthermore, an 'eye for an eye', even in the literal context, is not vengeance but justice, for it is indisputable that individuals will feel justified in killing an attacker if they thought he was posing a threat to their family and property even when his ultimate objectives are not clear. *Lex talionis* is the law of retribution and as such is the basis of all Western criminal and civil law.

The concept of justice underpinning *Lex talionis* is put into its proper perspective when considered in the light of those extreme legal measures which are meant to deter anyone from disturbing the foundation stones of biblical society. Adultery and incest are capital offences because the threat to the marital contract is an attack on community values, as is the worship of strange gods. If the trust between a man and his wife or between a people and its god disappears, the consequence is seen to be moral chaos. This was the basis for stigmatising the offspring of such forbidden intercourse as *mamzerim*, those unable to marry within the normal community. This deterrent originated during a period when the individual was subsumed in the collective and is in flagrant contradiction to the enlightened law, also found among the Laws, that a child should not be punished for the sins of his parents.

Once the individual took on an identity independent of the family and the community, these harsh reprisals for anti-social crimes became inoperative. The Oral Torah, codified in the Talmud, make the implementation of the death penalty extraordinarily difficult as it required two witnesses to warn the potential criminal of the punishment he would suffer before he commits the act. When a person rebels against God, death is the penalty, but there is no post-biblical record of this ever happening. In this sense the laws often served as metaphors to illustrate the scale of moral priorities.

The laws of Moses, interspersed as they are within the narratives of *Exodus*, *Leviticus*, *Numbers* and *Deuteronomy*, are inaccessible. I appreciate that their consolidation into one volume, while making the narratives – *Moses, Man of God*– more readable, may not excite the ordinary reader of prose literature, but it is now there for students and the curious to consider with ease. The Table of Laws will help them find those statutes which are still far more advanced than those practised in large sections of the world. The demand that on the Sabbath there should be utter equality, that on that day the poor do not serve their rich masters (for time belongs to God and as he rested on the seventh day, so must all his creatures emulate him); the proclamation of freedom in the jubilee year for all slaves to go free and for all property to return to their original owners (for property belongs to God and humans are only leaseholders); the resting of the land on the Sabbatical year, when all produce belongs to everyone – reinforcement of the principle that we all are equal before God and that all that derives from him must be shared; the laws to provide for the poor; guidelines for respect for the disadvantaged: the aged, the deaf and the blind, and the runaway slave – all these are now at the reader's fingertips. They may not read *The Laws of Moses* from cover to cover – but they would be dismissing one of the foundations of Western civilisation if they chose to ignore them altogether. If this volume has saved them in some part from this ignorance, it will have served its purpose.

Table of the Laws

Table of the Laws

Table of the Laws

EXODUS

1. The Passover

This day shall be for you a **day of** remembrance. Celebrate it as the LORD's festival in all your generations. You shall observe it as a festival, instituted forever. For seven days you will eat matsot [unleavened bread]. From the very first day you will clear out all leaven from your houses. Whoever eats leavened bread from the first to the seventh day, that person shall be cut off from Israel. The first day will be a sacred occasion; similarly the seventh day will be a sacred occasion for you. No work shall be done on them, except that which a person must do to prepare food to eat. You will observe the Festival of Matsot, for on this very day I brought your rank and file out of the land of Egypt. Therefore, you shall observe this day in all your generations as a perpetual law. On all evenings from the fourteenth day to the twenty-first day of the first month you shall eat matsot. For these seven days, leavened bread must not be found in your homes, for whoever eats anything leavened, that person shall be cut off from the community of Israel, be he a resident alien or a native of the land. You shall eat nothing leavened; you shall only eat matsot in all your dwellings. [12:14–20]

You shall observe this rite as a perpetual law for you and your descendants. So, when you arrive at the land the LORD will give you as he has promised, you must observe this rite. And when your children will say to you, "What does this rite mean to you?" You shall say, "It is the Passover sacrifice to the LORD who passed over the houses of the Israelites in Egypt when he struck down the Egyptians but spared our homes **from the plague.**" The people, **on hearing this,** bowed and worshipped. [12:24–27]

2. The Passover offering

The LORD said to Moses and Aaron: "This is the ritual law of the Passover offering – no resident alien shall eat of it. However, any slave purchased for money – once you had him circumcised – he will be able to eat of it.[1] A foreigner and a hired hand must not eat of it. It shall be eaten **by every household** in one **and the same** house. None of its meat shall be carried outside the house, nor may you break any of its bones. The entire community of Israel shall observe it. If an alien who is living with you wishes to observe the LORD's Passover, let **him and** all the males of his household be circumcised, and then let him come and observe it. He will then be just as the native born. But, **remember,** no uncircumcised may eat of it. One law shall be for the native and the resident alien **[who has been circumcised]** who lives with you."[2] So all the Israelites did as the LORD instructed Moses and Aaron; they did so. [12:43–50]

3. The first-born and matsot

The LORD spoke to Moses: "Dedicate to[3] me all the first-born, both of humankind and beasts. The first issue of the womb of the Israelites belongs to me." Moses said to the people: "Remember this day when you came out of Egypt – that place of slavery – how with a mighty hand the LORD brought you out of it. For this reason no leavened bread shall be eaten. You go out on this day during the month of Abib. When the LORD brings you into the land of the Canaanites, the Hittites, the Amorites, the Hivites and the Jebusites which he swore to your Patriarchs to give to you – a land flowing with milk and honey – you shall celebrate this rite in this month. For seven days you shall eat matsot. The seventh day will be a festival for the LORD. Matsot will be eaten for seven days; no leavened bread shall be found with you, nor

---

[1] There is no reason to assume that this was a forced conversion, as it would have been of no benefit to the owners. More significantly it does show that no distinction was made between a born Israelite and an alien convert.

[2] An indication that a converted alien could celebrate the Passover even though his ancestors were not redeemed from Egypt. Judaism, even when a purely national religion, was not racist but welcomed all to worship its God and to become part of its people.

[3] Literally: *sanctify* or *make holy*. The meaning is to dedicate something to God. The sparing of the Israelite first-born during Passover is the justification for this edict. Thus, they become ministers in God's Sanctuary or monetary compensation for them was to be given to the priests. Possibly before the Levites became the priestly class, the first-born fulfilled this function.

Exodus

shall any leaven be found within all your borders. You shall tell your son **about the matsot on** that day and say, 'This is because of what the LORD did for me when I came out of Egypt.' It shall be as a sign for you on your hand and as a remembrance between your eyes[1] so that the LORD's instruction may be in your mouth, for it was with a mighty hand that the LORD brought you out of Egypt. Therefore, you shall observe the ritual laws of this institution at this season every year." [13:1–10]

4. The first-born and firstlings
When the LORD brings you into the land of the Canaanites as he swore to you and your Patriarchs – and he gives it to you, you shall dedicate to the LORD all that first opens the womb: every firstling that issues from the beasts you own – only the males shall belong to the LORD. You will redeem the firstling of a donkey with a lamb.[2] If you will not redeem it, you will have to break its neck **because you are to have no benefit from it.** You will also redeem all the **male** first-borns among your children. And when, in the future, your son should ask you, "What is this **that you are doing?**" you will say to him, 'With a mighty hand, the LORD brought us out of Egypt, that place of slavery. **You see,** when Pharaoh hardened himself, not to let us go, so that the LORD killed all the first-born in the land of Egypt, both the first-born of humankind and beasts – for this reason I sacrifice to the LORD all that opens the womb when they are males, but the first-born of my children, I redeem with money. It shall be as a sign on your hand and as a symbol between your eyes, that with a mighty hand the LORD brought us out of Egypt." [13:11–16]

[1] For traditional Jews this is the basis for the rabbinic ordinance to wear phylacteries – leather boxes, containing spiritual passages, affixed to the forehead and left arm by leather straps – by males over the age of thirteen at daily morning prayers, excepting the Sabbath and festivals. In my view, the intention of the text is symbolic. In this passage, it is the eating of the matsot as the reminder of God's salvation. Further down, it is the payment to redeem the first-born which is the reminder of divine intervention.
[2] Redemption is the monetary value or a substitute tax. As the priests could not eat donkeys, a lamb was required..

5. The Ten Commandments

God uttered all these words:

1. I am the LORD your God who brought you out of Egypt –
   From the house of slaves.[1]

2. You shall have no other gods but me.
   You shall not make yourself any sculpted image or
   Any physical representation of any body in the heavens above,
   On the earth beneath or in the waters under the earth.
   You shall neither bow down to them nor worship them.
   Because, I, the LORD your God, am a jealous God
   Who remembers the sins of the fathers.
   Of them that hate me
   To the second, third and fourth generations
   But who behaves kindly for a thousand generations
   To those who love me and keep my commandments.

3. Do not abuse the name of the LORD.[2]
   For he will not exonerate those who use his name
   For pernicious purposes, **but will punish him**.

4. Remember the Sabbath day to make it holy[3]
   During six days you may work to do all your tasks
   But the seventh day is the Sabbath to the LORD your God –
   You shall not work, you, nor your son, nor your daughter,
   Nor your male or female servant, nor your cattle,
   Nor the stranger within your gated walls.
   Because in six days the LORD made the heavens, the earth,
   The sea and all that live in them, but

---

[1] According to the Jewish tradition, this is the first commandment. Christians view this as part of the introduction: The first commandment is not to have other gods and the second is not to make idols.

[2] The accepted translation is 'not to take the LORD's name in vain'. This would be trivial. It must be a more serious crime such as using the power of God's name [Yahweh, translated as the LORD] and the respect it commands for evil purposes such as curses and false oaths. The modern equivalent is the use of religious belief to justify bigotry and ethnic wars.

[3] A special day dedicated to rest and the emulation of God. Sabbath means 'desist from labour'.

He rested on the seventh day.
Therefore, the LORD made the Sabbath into a blessing
And declared it as holy.
5. Honour your father and mother
So that you may long live on the land
Which the LORD your God is granting you.
6. You shall not murder.[1]
7. You shall not commit adultery.
8. You shall not steal.
9. You shall not bear false witness against your neighbour.
10. You shall not covet your neighbour's house,
His wife, his male or female servant,
His ox, his donkey nor for anything
That belongs to your neighbour. [20: 1–14]

6. Idolatry and the Lord's altar

In worshipping me, you shall not make gods of silver, nor should you make for yourselves gods of gold. Make for me an altar out of earth to sacrifice on it your burnt and peace offerings – your sheep and oxen. In all places where I cause my name to be invoked, I will come to you to bless you. But, if you want to make me a stone altar, do not build it out of hewn stones for if you put a tool to it, you have polluted it. Nor shall you climb stairs to reach my altar, so that your nakedness is not exposed on them.[2] [20:20–23]

7. Slavery of Hebrews

Now these are the judgements which you will set before them. If you buy a Hebrew slave, he will **only** serve you for six years. In the seventh year he goes free and without payment **for his freedom.** If

---

[1] The basis for forbidding murder is *Genesis 9:6:* 'Whoever sheds the blood of man, for that man his blood shall be shed, for in the image of God did he make man.'

[2] The LORD does not want ostentatious worship. When these laws were given, worship was not centralised, though there were places such as Shiloh where the Ark of the Covenant rested that had an aura of holiness.

he came **to you** single, he leaves single. If he was married, his wife shall leave with him. If his master gave him a wife and she bore sons or daughters for him, the wife and her children shall be her master's and he leaves single. But, if the slave says with conviction, "I love my master, my wife and my children. I do not want to go free," his master shall bring him before the judges **to affirm that it is his desire to remain a slave.** He will also bring him to a door or doorpost where he will pierce his ear with an awl and he will be his slave forever.[1] [21:1–6]

8. Slavery of females

A daughter sold into slavery will not go free as do male slaves. If he intended her for himself and is not happy with her, she must be bought back **by her family.** He cannot sell her to a foreigner because this would be to break faith with her. If she was intended for his son, she shall be treated just as other women **who are free.** If the man takes another wife, her food, clothing and sexual rights shall not be reduced.[2] If he does not fulfil these three obligations to her, she goes free without the need to be bought out of slavery. [21:7–11]

9. Murder

A man who strikes a man and kills him is to be executed. But if the man did not lie in wait **in order to murder him,** but his death was caused by an act of God,[3] I will designate to you a place to which he may escape. However, when a man treacherously kills his neighbour, you must even tear him away from my altar to execute him. [21:12–15]

---

[1] The rabbinic sages explain the custom: He is pierced in the ear because he did not listen when the LORD told the Israelites at Sinai that they should serve only him.

[2] This indicates that the woman was purchased to be a concubine. This law is extraordinary, first because it gives a slave-girl equal rights to a wife, and, secondly, it posits the rights of women to the fulfilment of their sexual needs, a relatively modern concept, at least in Christian society.

[3] From this, it would appear that accidental death was perceived as ordained by divine providence.

10. Kidnapping
A man who kidnaps a person, whether he has sold him into slavery, or if he is found still in his possession, shall most certainly be executed. [21:16]

11. Cursing parents
The one who curses his father or mother shall most certainly be executed.[1] [21:17]

12. Punishment for violent behaviour
1. If, while fighting, one strikes another with a stone while fighting together, or with a fist and the person is not killed but confined to bed but later can get up and walk about, even on a stick, the assailant will be acquitted of any crime; but must compensate him for his loss of time and the cost of treatment he requires until he is restored to health. [21:18–19]
2. If an owner strikes his male or female slave with his rod and he dies immediately, he shall certainly be avenged. But, if he survives a day or two, he is not to be avenged, since he is his property.[2] [21:20–21]
3. When men are fighting and a pregnant woman is hurt so that she miscarries but with no other injury, the one responsible shall certainly be penalised in accordance with her husband's claim against him as adjudicated by the judges. But, if she suffers any permanent hurt, then you must award **her according to the principle** 'life for life,[3] eye for eye, tooth for tooth, hand for

---

[1] A curse was more significant then than now. It meant invoking God's name to kill a person when the curser was not in a the position to do so. The use of magic to bring death upon an individual may have been considered as murder.
[2] The supposition here is that it was not intentional as he would not have wanted to 'destroy' his property. In the case of immediate death, the likelihood is that in his anger he did want to kill him.
[3] That this was never intended to be taken literally but meant as a monetary compensation is proved by the fact that the present case is referring to an injury to the woman, and not to her death. Even were she killed, it would have been a case of manslaughter. A life for a life, eye for eye, etc. is a general ethical principle, which is the highest principle of justice as one considers one's own person as of far greater value than that of another. Further proof is in

hand, burn for burn, wound for wound, blow for blow'. [21:22-5]

13. Cruelty to slaves
If a person strikes the eye of his male or female slave so that it no longer functions, he must let him/her go free because of the loss of the eye. Likewise, if he causes his male or female slave to lose a tooth by striking them, he shall let him/her go free because of the loss of the tooth. [21:26-27]

14. Injury caused by a beast
When an ox gores a man or a woman, so that they die, the ox must be stoned. Its flesh shall not be eaten but the owner will be acquitted **of any liability.** However, if the ox was a persistent gorer, and the owner had been advised of this but did not restrain him, so that he killed a man or woman, not only shall the ox be stoned, but his owner shall also be executed. **Should the next of kin** demand monetary compensation from him, as ransom for his life, he shall give whatever sum is demanded from him. The same judgement shall apply to the owner if it has gored a male or female child. If the ox gores **to death** a male or female slave, the owner shall give the master thirty silver shekels and the ox must be stoned. [21:28-32]

15. Injury caused to beasts by an uncovered pit or a goring ox
When a man opens a pit or digs a new one without covering it and an ox or donkey falls into it, he shall make good by giving monetary compensation to its owner. The dead beast, however, becomes his. When a person's ox gores another's so that it dies, they shall sell the live ox; divide the money of the sale and also the value of the dead ox. But if it was known that the ox was a persistent gorer and the owner did not restrain

---

Leviticus 24:18 (see **169**, p. 90); where in the case of the killing of an animal, life for life can only mean compensation.

him, he shall pay ox for ox but the dead ox will belong to him. [21:33–36]

16. Theft

When a person steals an ox, or a sheep, and kills it or sells it, he shall restore five oxen for an ox and four sheep for a sheep. If a thief is caught breaking in **at night** and dies as the consequence of being beaten, no blood shall be shed on his account, but if it happens during the day, his blood may be avenged.[1] A thief must make full restitution for **what he has stolen.** If he has nothing, then he must be sold into slavery to pay for what he has stolen. If the stolen article is found alive with him, whether an ox or a donkey or a sheep, he shall pay back double its value.[2] [21:37–22:3]

17. Beasts grazing in another person's field

If a person allows his animals to graze in a field or vineyard which is not his own, he must make restitution for **the loss of value to** that field or vineyard from the best of his own. When a fire is started and spreads to thorns so that stacks of grain or standing grain or grain which is still growing is consumed, the one that started the fire must pay restitution. [22:4–5]

18. Laws regarding guardianship and the expropriation of property

When a person entrusts money or goods to another to look after, if they are stolen out of the person's house, and the thief is found, he must pay back double. If the thief is not apprehended, the

---

[1] At night he may be excused for manslaughter, because in his fright, he struck out, but during the day he could see that it was only a thief and could call for help. Also, the thief, being recognised, could be apprehended even if he got away with his theft.

[2] In verse 21:37 we are told that he is to pay four or five fold, not just double. The Talmud rules that the larger penalty was in the case of a thief slipping in and stealing when he was not seen. The smaller penalty was for the thief who broke in. The logic is that a greater deterrent was required to discourage the surreptitious thief than the blatant robber.

house owner shall come before the judges[1] to determine if he has stolen his neighbour's goods. **If he is found innocent, he is not liable for making restitution.** In every case of misappropriation involving either an ox or donkey or sheep or any livestock or clothing or any other loss where the ownership is disputed, both parties will come before the judges. He whom the judges declare guilty will pay double to his neighbour. [22:6–8]

When a person entrusts to his neighbour a donkey, an ox, a sheep to look after and it dies or is injured or is carried off and there were no witnesses to these events, the custodian shall swear by the LORD that he has not laid his hands on his neighbour's goods. The owner must accept **the validity of the oath** without restitution being made. But, if it was stolen from him, the custodian will pay the owner its value. However, if the animal was torn to pieces, he must bring it as evidence **before the judges;** he is not required to make restitution for its value **because he could not be expected to risk his life to defend it from a wild beast.** When a man borrows **an animal** from his neighbour, if it is injured or dies in the absence of its owner, the borrower must make restitution. However, if the owner was present, he need not pay for it. But, if it was hired, the hiring fee is still due **to the owner.** [22:9–14]

19. The seduction of a virgin

When a man seduces a virgin who is not engaged to be married[2] and lies with her, he will pay the bride-price and marry her. If her father absolutely refuses to give her to him, he must pay him the bride-price for a virgin. [22:15–16]

---

[1] This contradicts the passage above, unless one presumes, as do the ancient rabbinic sages, that in this case we are talking of someone who was paid to guard the property. If marauders carried off the animal, he could not have been expected to prevent the crime, but in the case of theft, he was being paid to be more diligent.

[2] An engaged woman was as if married. Her seduction would be an act of adultery and both parties liable to execution.

20. Capital crimes: sorcery, bestiality, sacrifice to other gods
You shall not allow a sorceress to live. Whoever lies with a beast must most certainly be put to death. Whoever sacrifices to any god except the LORD shall be doomed to destruction.[1] [22:17–19]

21. Humanitarian exhortations
You shall not wrong a resident alien or oppress him for you were aliens in the land of Egypt.

You shall not wrong a widow or a fatherless child. If you wrong them in any way, I will respond to their outcry when they cry out to me. My anger will be kindled; I will have you put to the sword so that *your* wives will become widows and your children fatherless. [22:20–23]

22. Lending to the poor
When you lend money to any of my people,[2] to anyone who is poor among you, you shall not act towards them as a creditor. Do not charge them interest. If you go so far as to take your neighbour's cloak as security, you must return it to him before the setting of the sun, for it is his only covering which he has to cover his skin. How can he sleep **without a covering! If you oppress him,** and if he calls out to me, I will respond to his outcry for I am compassionate. [22:24–26]

23. Obligations to the Lord
You shall not revile God nor place a curse upon a chieftain of your people. Do not delay in making offerings from the fullness of your harvest of grain and wine. You shall give me your first-born of your sons, likewise with your cattle and flocks. Seven days will they, **the male first-born,** remain with their mothers. On the eighth day you will give them to me. Men of holiness you will be to me – you shall not eat the flesh of

[1] In **251, 252,** p. 138–9 they are stoned or put to the sword.
[2] The Hebrew of this command is unclear.

animals torn to pieces in the field; you shall feed it to the dogs.[1]
[22:27–30]

24. Exhortations to justice in human relationships

You shall not spread false rumours. Do not join the wicked to
become a witness to cause violence.[2] Do not follow the mob to
do evil. In a dispute, do not side with the powerful to prevent
justice; but, neither show partiality to a poor man in a dispute
when he is in the wrong. [23:1–3]

25. Helping your enemy

Should you come across your enemy's ox or donkey which has
gone astray, you must certainly bring it back to him. Should you
see the donkey of a man who has expressed his hatred for you
unable to rise because of its burden and are inclined to resist
helping him – all the same, you must help him **raise** the
donkey. [23:4–5]

26. Perversion of justice

Do not deprive your poor of justice in his disputes. Distance yourself from participating in false charges. Do not through the perversion of justice bring death upon the innocent and the righteous,
for I will not exonerate the wicked. Do not accept presents, for
bribes blind even the most clear-sighted and shatter the case of
righteous men. [23:6–8]

27. Oppression of resident aliens

Also, do not oppress a resident alien, for you know the heart of
the alien for you yourselves were once aliens in the land of Egypt.
[23:9]

[1] Israelites following the example of the LORD must not act like beasts, eating
like savages.
[2] i.e. a false witness which leads to the unjust execution of the innocent.

28. The Sabbath for the land and for Israel

For six years you shall sow your land and gather in its yield, but in the seventh you shall let it rest and lie fallow. Let the poor among you eat from it; and what they leave, let the wild beasts eat. This applies also to your vineyards and olive groves. For six days you may go about your business but on the seventh day you must rest, so that your ox and donkey may rest and so that your home-born slaves and resident aliens may have breathing space.[1] [23:10–12]

29. No mention of foreign gods

Be attentive to everything I have told you. Especially, make no mention of the names of other gods; their names are not even to cross your lips. [23:13]

30. The three pilgrim festivals

Three times in the year you will hold a festival for me.

1. You shall observe the Festival of Matsot[2] – eating matsot for seven days as I instructed you at the designated time of the month Abib,[3] for during it you came out of Egypt. None shall appear before me **at my Sanctuary** empty-handed.
2. The Festival of the harvest of the first fruits of your labour of what you sow in the field (Pentecost).
3. The Festival of Ingathering at the end of the year, when you gather in the produce from your fields (Tabernacles).[4] Three times during the year all males must appear before the supreme sovereign – the LORD. [23:14–17]

---

[1] The reason given here for the Sabbath suggests that the main purpose was to allow the labourers – animal and human – to have a day off. The others were not really 'working' even during the six days. For this reason I have translated *ma-ah-seh-chah*, literally 'the things you do', as business.

[2] Unleavened bread.

[3] The month is also called Nissan. Abib is now the modern Hebrew word for Spring.

[4] These three festivals, Passover, Pentecost, Tabernacles, are treated more fully in other sections of the *Laws of Moses*. Here, the agricultural aspects are emphasised.

31. No leaven with sacrifices

You shall not offer the blood of my sacrifices with anything leavened, nor shall the fat of my festal offering be left lying until the morning. The choicest of your first fruits of the ground shall be brought into the house of the LORD your God. [23:18–19]

32. Sympathetic compassion for animals

You shall not boil a kid in its mother's milk.[1] [23:19]

33. Gifts for the Sanctuary

The LORD spoke to Moses, "Tell the Israelites to bring me gifts. You shall accept gifts for me from every person whose heart so prompts him. These are the gifts you should accept from them: gold, silver and copper; blue, purple and scarlet yarns; fine linen, goats' hair, rams' skins dyed red, fine leather and acacia wood; oil for the lamp, spices for the anointing oil and for the fragrant incense; onyx and other gems to be set in the Ephod[2] and Breastpiece. So let them make me a Sanctuary that I may dwell among them. Just as I show you – the design of the Tabernacle and all its furnishings – so shall you make it." [25:1–9]

34. The Ark

They shall make the Ark of acacia wood, two and a half cubits long, a cubit[3] and a half wide and a cubit and a half high. Overlay it with pure gold – inside and out – and make a gold moulding all around it. Cast four rings of gold for it and fix them to its four feet, two rings on each side. Make staves of acacia wood and overlay them with gold and put them into the rings on the sides of the Ark, by which to carry it. The staves shall remain in the rings of the Ark, never to be removed. You shall put into the Ark the **Tablets of the** Testimony which I will give you. [25:10–16]

---

[1] This command is repeated in 34:26 and *Deuteronomy 14:21*.
[2] Priestly garment without sleeves, consisting of two parts for the front and back which were clasped together on the shoulder with a gem-studded buckle and a fine twined girdle at the waist.
[3] Measurement based on the length of an arm, roughly eighteen inches.

35. The 'Mercy-seat'[1] on the Ark

Make a cover plate of pure gold, two and a half cubits long and a cubit and a half wide.[2] Make two cherubim out of beaten gold to place on the two ends of the cover plate. Make one cherub at one end and one cherub at the other end; make the cherubim out of the cover plate on its two ends. The cherubim will have their wings spread out above, overshadowing the cover plate with their wings. They will face each other but their faces will incline downwards toward the cover plate. Put the cover plate on top of the Ark and put the **Tablets of the** Testimony which I will give you into the Ark. There will I meet you. I will give you, from above the plate between the two cherubim which are on the Ark of Testimony, all my instructions concerning the Israelites. [25:17–22]

36. The table, its vessels and the showbread

Make a table of acacia wood, two cubits long, a cubit wide and a cubit and a half high. Overlay it with pure gold and make a golden moulding to go around it. Surround it with a frame, a hand's breadth high with a gold moulding around the frame. Make four gold rings for it and fasten them on the four corners at its four legs. The rings shall be on the frame for the staves to carry the table. Make the staves of acacia wood and overlay them with gold that the table may be carried with them. Its bowls, ladles, jars and jugs with which to pour **out libations** must be made out of pure gold. The showbread[3] shall always be set on the table before me. [25:23–30]

---

[1] William Tyndale, the first English translator of the Bible, coined this expression for the solid gold cover which was to go over the Ark. This was an ingenious translation as the Hebrew for cover is also for forgiveness in the sense of God covering up human sins in order to show mercy. It thus has come to mean 'atonement'. It was identified with the seat of divine judgement.
[2] We are not given any indication of its thickness, but it would have been of sufficient substance to bear the weight of the golden cherubim, who most likely were winged beasts with human faces.
[3] The showbread was for a permanent display to symbolise that the LORD was the source of all foods.

37. The Menorah[1]

Make a Menorah of pure beaten gold, its base and central stem with its cups and calyxes and petals as of one piece of work. Six branches shall come out of its side, three branches from one side of the Menorah and three branches out of the other side. On one branch there shall be three cups shaped like almond blossoms, with inner and outer petals; and on the next branch there shall be three cups shaped like almond blossoms with inner and outer petals; so for all six branches coming out of the Menorah. On **the central stem of** the Menorah, there shall be four cups shaped like almond blossoms with inner and outer petals. There shall be outer petals, of one piece with it, under the six branches which come out of the Menorah, a single set of outer petals under each pair of branches. The outer petals and the branches are to be of one piece with it – all a single piece of pure beaten gold. Make its seven lamps and mount them so that they light up their front side. Its tongs and trays shall also be of pure gold. You will use a talent[2] of pure gold for the Menorah and its accessories. Make certain that you employ the designs that were shown to you on the mountain. [25:31–40]

38. The Tabernacle

Make the Tabernacle itself of ten hangings of finely twisted linen of blue, purple and scarlet yarns with the design of cherubim skilfully worked into them. The length of one hanging is to be twenty-eight cubits and the breadth of one hanging is to be four cubits. All are to be of the same measurement. Five of the hangings shall be joined to one another and the other five hangings are to be joined to one another. Make blue loops of yarn on the edge of the last hanging in each set and similarly on the edge of the last hanging of the other set. Make fifty loops on the one hanging and fifty loops on the edge of the last hanging of the other set. They must be opposite to each other; and make fifty

[1] The lampstand for the Tabernacle and later in the Temple.
[2] Josephus gives the weight as one hundred pounds.

golden clasps and join the hangings one to another with them, so that the Tabernacle becomes one. [26:1–6]

Make sheets of goats' hair, eleven in number, to form a tent over the Tabernacle. Each sheet shall be thirty cubits long and four cubits wide – the eleven sheets must be of the same size. Join five of the sheets together and similarly the other six; and fold the sixth sheet over the front of the tent. Make fifty loops on the edge of the last sheet in the first set and make fifty loops on the joining edge of the second set. Make fifty copper clasps and insert them into the loops and join up the tent so that it becomes one. There will be an extra half sheet of tent covering which should hang over the rear of the Tabernacle. The extra cubit on the length of the tent's sheets should hang over the bottom of the two sides of the Tabernacle to cover it. Make for the tent a covering of rams' skins dyed red and a covering of fine leather over that. [26:7–14]

Make upright frames of acacia wood for the Tabernacle. Each frame shall be ten cubits long and one and a half cubits wide. Each frame shall have two pegs to fit the frames together. You shall make these for all the frames of the Tabernacle. Make the frames for the Tabernacle: twenty frames for the south side with forty sockets of silver under the twenty frames, two sockets under each frame for its two pegs. On the second side of the Tabernacle on the north side shall also be twenty frames with their forty sockets of silver – two sockets under each of the frames. On the rear of the Tabernacle westward – make six frames. Make two frames for the corners of the Tabernacle at the rear. These shall be coupled together at the bottom and also at the top to the level of the first ring. Do the same for both of them to form the two corners. So there shall be eight frames with their silver sockets – sixteen sockets – two sockets under each frame. [26:15–25]

Make bars of acacia wood, five for the frames of one side wall of the Tabernacle and five for the frames of the other side wall of the Tabernacle and five for the frames of the wall of the Tabernacle at the rear towards the west. The centre bar halfway up the frames shall run from end to end. Overlay the frames with gold and make their rings of gold to hold the bars. Also, overlay the bars with rings of gold. You must erect the Tabernacle according to the design you were shown on the mountain. [26:26–30]

Make a curtain of fine twisted linen of blue, purple and scarlet yarn with cherubim skilfully worked into it. Hang it on four posts of acacia wood overlaid with gold – its hooks of gold set in four sockets of silver. Hang the curtain under the clasps and place the Ark of the Testimony there behind the curtain of so that the curtain shall be a divider for you between the Holy and the Holy of Holies. Place the table outside the curtain and the Menorah on the south side of the Tabernacle opposite the table which is to be placed by the north wall. Make a screen for the entrance of the Tent of fine twisted linen of blue, purple and scarlet yarn done in embroidery. Make for the screen five posts of acacia wood; overlay them with gold, with their hooks also of gold; cast for them five sockets of copper. [26:31–37]

39. The Altar
Make an altar of acacia wood, five cubits long, five cubits wide – the altar is to be square-shaped – and three cubits high. Make horns for its four corners and the horns shall be of one piece with it and overlaid with copper. Make the pans for removing its ashes, its shovels, basins, flesh hooks and fire pans – make all its utensils out of copper. Make for it a grating, a network of copper, and fit four copper rings, one on each corner. Set it below under the ledge of the altar so that it comes up to the middle of the altar. Make poles of acacia wood for the altar. Overlay them with copper. They are to be put through the rings on both sides of the altar, for carrying it. Make it hollow, of boards. You will make it as you were shown on the mountain. [27:1–8]

40. The Court of the Tabernacle
This is how you are to make the Court of the Tabernacle. On the south side, the court shall have curtaining of finely twisted linen one hundred cubits long with twenty posts and twenty copper

sockets. The hooks and bands of the posts are to be made of silver. The north side is also to have curtaining a hundred cubits long with its twenty posts and twenty copper sockets with silver hooks and bands for the posts. Across the breadth of the court on the west side, the curtaining is to be fifty cubits long with ten posts and ten sockets. The breadth of the court at its front – the east side – will be fifty cubits, fifteen cubits of curtaining on one side of the entrance with three posts and their three sockets and fifteen cubits of curtaining on the other side of the entrance with their three poles and sockets. The court gateway will be a twenty-cubit screen of linen embroidered with finely twisted blue, purple and scarlet linen with four posts and four sockets. All the posts around the court are to be banded with silver, with silver hooks; their sockets will be of copper. The length of the court will be one hundred cubits, the width fifty and the height five cubits, with curtains of fine twisted linen and sockets of copper. All the utensils of the Tabernacle's court for every use, as well as all the Tabernacle's pegs and those of the court, will be of copper. [27:9–19]

41. Oil for the lamps
Instruct the Israelites to bring you pure olive oil for the light to keep the flame of the lamp burning perpetually. Aaron and his sons are to keep it burning before the LORD from evening to morning in the Tent of Meeting outside the curtain, which is in front of the **Ark of Testimony**. This is a perpetual rite to be kept by the Israelites. [27:20–21]

42. The vestments of the priesthood
Appoint Aaron your brother together with his sons from among the Israelites to serve me in the office of High Priest, **not only** Aaron, **but also** Nadab and Abihu, Eleazar and Ithamar, Aaron's sons. You will make for Aaron your brother sacral vestments, which will be glorious in their splendour. You shall instruct all who are skilful, whom I have graced with artistic insights, to make a costume for Aaron, **to make him special** when he is

consecrated to serve me as my priest. These are the vestments they will make: a Breastpiece, an Ephod,[1] a robe, a fringed tunic, a head-dress and a sash. They will make these sacral vestments for Aaron your brother and his sons to act as my priests. They will use gold, blue, purple and scarlet yarns – and fine linen. [28:1–6]

43. The Ephod

The Ephod is to be made of gold, blue, purple and scarlet yarn and fine twisted linen worked into creative designs. **The front and back pieces** will be joined together by a pair of shoulder straps. Its band which joins them together **at the waist** will be of a creative design of similar work of fine gold, blue, purple and scarlet yarn. On two onyx stones, you will have engraved the names of the **twelve** sons of Israel: six names on each stone in order of their birth.[2] The quality should be like those achieved by a gem cutter, as in the engravings on a signet, with the names of the sons of Israel. Aaron will bear their names on his shoulder as a reminder before the LORD **of his covenant with them.** Make rosettes of gold filigree and two chains of pure gold twisted like cords to be fixed on to the rosettes. [28:6–14]

44. Breastpiece for the revelation of God's will.[3]

Order the making of a Breastpiece of Decision at the hands of an artisan and let it be made as was the – of gold, blue, purple and scarlet finely woven linen; its size will be a span [of a hand[4]] squared and doubled over **to form a pouch.** Set into it four rows of stones. The first row: ruby, chrysolite and emerald; the second row: turquoise, sapphire and diamond; the third row: jacinth, agate and crystal; the fourth row: beryl, onyx and jasper. They

---

[1] To be described in the following instruction.

[2] Distinction was not to be based on whether their mothers were Jacob's wives or concubines, i.e. each of the tribes was equal.

[3] In Hebrew it is the 'breastpiece of judgement', but it was used to learn God's will on all matters. In the body of the text I will refer to it as the 'Breastpiece of Decision', as does the Jewish Publication Society translation.

[4] Nine inches is the estimated modern size.

will be framed in gold mountings. The stones represent in number the names of the sons of Israel, one stone for each name. They are to be engraved like seals, each with its name, for each of the twelve tribes. On the breastpiece make braided chains of pure gold; make also two golden rings which are to be fastened to the two upper corners of the breastpiece to which the two braided golden chains are to be attached. Then fasten the two ends of the chains to the two settings which you will attach to the shoulder straps of the Ephod at the front. Make two rings of gold, attach them to the two ends of the breastpiece on the inside edge next to the Ephod . And make two other gold rings and attach them onto the two shoulder straps of the Ephod low down on its front along its seam just above its waistband. The breastpiece shall be bound by its rings to the rings of the Ephod with a violet braid so that the breastpiece rests on the embroidered waistband, so that it does not come loose from the Ephod. [28:15–28]

45. The Urim and Thummim
Aaron shall thus bear the names of the children of Israel in the Breastpiece of Decision over his heart, when he enters the Sanctuary as a continual reminder of them to the LORD. In the Breastpiece of Decision, you are to place the Urim and Thummim.[1] They shall be above Aaron's heart when he comes before the LORD. Thus Aaron will always carry the divine decisions in regard to the Israelites over his heart before the LORD. [28:29–30]

46. The robe of the Ephod
Make the robe of the Ephod all blue. In its centre will be the opening for the head. The border of the opening shall be woven to be as hard-wearing as that of the neck of a coat of mail so that it never gets torn. On its hem, design pomegranates in blue, purple and crimson yarns. In this way you are to make the

[1] These probably were lots saying 'yes' and 'no' which the High Priest would remove from the pouch in answer to questions put to God.

whole circumference of the hem with golden bells between all
the pomegranates – all around the hem. Aaron must wear it
while he officiates, so that its sound is heard when he enters
and leaves the Sanctuary before the LORD, so that he may not
die.[1] [28:31–35]

47. The medallion of gold
Make a medallion of pure gold and engrave on it as you would
do with a seal: 'Consecrated to the LORD.' Suspend it on a blue
cord to go on the head-dress on its front. This is to go on Aaron's
forehead so that he may bear whatever guilt the Israelites may
incur while consecrating the donations they have dedicated. That
is why he is to wear it at all times to win favour for these donations
before the LORD. [28:36–38]

48. The tunic and head-dress
The tunic will be woven from fine linen as will be the head-dress.
And the waistband will be embroidered. Also for Aaron's sons,
you will have made tunics and waistbands. You will also have
made for them head-dresses for their honour and adornment.
You will dress your brother Aaron and his sons in these; you will
anoint them, invest them into office and consecrate them that
they may serve me as priests. Make for them also linen under-
garments to hide their nakedness, reaching from their waists to
their thighs. Aaron and his sons must wear these when they
enter the Tent of Meeting and when they approach the altar to
serve in the Sanctuary, so that they do not incur guilt and die.
This is a law for all time for Aaron and his descendants after
him. [28:39–43]

49. Consecration of Priests
This is what you are to do to consecrate them as my priests: Take
a young bull from among the herd and two unblemished rams;

---

[1] Why should the tinkling prevent his death? Is it to give God warning of his
approach, so that he does not barge into the divine presence!

unleavened bread, unleavened cakes mixed with oil, unleavened wafers covered with oil made with choice wheat flour. Put them into a basket and bring it with the young bull and the two rams. Then lead Aaron and his sons to the entrance of the Tent of Meeting and bathe them. You will then dress Aaron in the tunic, the robe of the Ephod, the Ephod itself and the Breastpiece and you will tie the waistband of the Ephod around his waist. You will put the head-dress on his head, and on the head-dress fix the sacred diadem.[1] Then take the anointing oil, pour it on his head to anoint him. Then you are to take his sons, clothe them in tunics and wind turbans around their heads. Fasten the waistbands around their waists. The priesthood is their right for all time. [29:1–9]

50. The investiture into office

So in this way you will invest Aaron and his sons into office. You will bring the young bull before the Tent of Meeting. Aaron and his sons will lay their hands on its head. You will then slaughter it before the LORD at the entrance of the Tent of Meeting.[2] You will put some of the blood of the young bull and with your finger smear it on the horns of the altar; the rest of its blood you shall pour out at the base of the altar. Take all the fat covering the entrails, the long lobe of its liver, its two kidneys together with the covering fat, and turn them into smoke on the altar. But the flesh, the hide and dung of the young bull you will burn outside the camp – it is a sin offering.[3] [29:9 – 14]

51. The ram of investiture: the elevation offering

Then take one ram; Aaron and his sons will lay their hands on its head. Slaughter the ram, take its blood and sprinkle it on all sides of the altar. Cut it into parts, wash its entrails and its legs

---

[1] This must be the medallion with the engraved words: 'Consecrated to the LORD', referred to earlier.

[2] It is apparent that the priest did not actually do the slaughtering.

[3] The sin offering was totally burnt: it was an atonement, a repayment to God for their sins.

and place them with its other parts and its head. Then turn all of it into smoke on the altar. It is a burnt offering to the LORD,[1] of pleasing fragrance, an offering made by fire to the LORD. Take the other ram; Aaron and his sons will lay their hands on its head. Slaughter the ram, take some of its blood and place it on the tip of Aaron's right ear and on the tip of the right ears of his sons, likewise on the thumbs of their right hands and on the large toes of their right feet; sprinkle the rest of the blood on all sides of the altar. Then take from the blood on the altar and the anointing oil and sprinkle it on Aaron and on his vestments; also on his sons and his sons' vestments. So will he be consecrated together with his vestments as will be his sons and their vestments. Take from this ram its fat, the fat part of the tail, the fat that covers the entrails, the long lobe of the liver and the two kidneys with their covering fat and its right thigh – this is a ram of investiture **of the priests**. Also take out of the basket of unleavened bread set before the LORD one of the loaves of bread, one of the cakes made with oil and one wafer. Put all these into the hands of Aaron and his sons and offer them as an elevation offering before the LORD. Then take them from their hands and turn them into smoke on the altar on top of the burnt offering to give a pleasing fragrance before the LORD – it is a fire-offering to the LORD. Then take the breast of the ram of Aaron's investiture and offer it as an elevation offering before the LORD. This will be your portion **for food.** You will consecrate the breast that has been offered as an elevation offering and the thigh that has been set aside as a gift offering, whether this be from the ram of investiture or any other offerings belonging to Aaron and his sons. This shall be for Aaron and his descendants as a statute for all time. They are a gift – a gift from the Israelites, for it is a contribution set aside for the LORD from their peace offerings[2] - **those**

---

[1] *Leviticus* chapters 1 and 8 provide further details and explanations of the fire offering.

[2] These were the communal sacrifices in which individuals gave thanks to God, and from which the priests were given their share as deputies of the LORD.

which they eat rather than those they offer up entirely to the
LORD. [29:15–28]

52. The sacred vestments
Aaron's sacred vestments shall pass on to his sons after him
to be worn at their anointing investiture. Whoever of his
sons becomes a priest in his place, who enters the Tent of Meeting to officiate in the Sanctuary, will wear them for seven
days. [29:29–30]

53. Eating the ram of investiture
Take the ram of investiture and boil its meat in a holy place.
Aaron and his sons will eat the ram's meat, the bread that is in
the basket at the entrance to the Tent of Meeting. They alone are
to eat of these things by which atonement was made for them at
their investiture and consecration. No laymen must eat of them
for they have been consecrated. If any of the meat from the
investiture sacrifice or the bread is left over until the morning,
you are to burn the left-overs with fire. It is not to be eaten
because it has been consecrated. This is what you will do for
Aaron and his sons, as I have commanded you for seven days of
investiture. Each day you will offer up a young bull as a sin
offering to achieve atonement. You will purge the altar by performing purification rites on it, by anointing and consecrating it
by the sprinkling of the sacrificial blood on it. For seven days you
shall perform the purification of the altar to consecrate it so that
the altar will be most holy – whatever touches the altar shall
become consecrated. [29:31–37]

54. The daily sacrifices[1]
This is what you are to offer on the altar: two lamb yearlings
every day; one lamb in the morning and one lamb at twilight;
with one lamb a tenth of an ephah[2] of choice flour mixed with

[1] *Numbers 28:3–8*, gives the laws of the daily sacrifices in greater detail.
[2] About 6.5 pints.

a quarter of a hin[1] of beaten oil, and one fourth of a hin of wine for drink offerings. With the lamb that you offer at twilight you are to act likewise with the meal offering and the drink offering as in the morning – to give off a pleasing fragrance through the fire-offering to the LORD. It will be a regular burnt offering throughout the generations by the entrance of the Tent of Meeting before the LORD – there will I meet you; there will I speak to you[2] and there will I encounter the Israelites, and the Tent will be sanctified in my presence. I will sanctify the Tent of Meeting and the altar; also I will sanctify Aaron and his sons to officiate before me in the priestly office. I will dwell among the Israelites and be their God. They will know that I am the LORD their God, who brought them out of the land of Egypt so that I might dwell among them. I am the LORD their God. [29:38–46]

55. The incense altar

Make an altar for burning incense out of acacia wood – a cubit long and a cubit wide – it shall be square-shaped – and two cubits high; its horns are to be made of the same wood. Overlay it with pure gold – its top, all its sides and its horns – and with a gold moulding all around it. Make two gold rings for it under its moulding on the two side walls, opposite each other. They will be used to hold the poles with which to carry it. The poles are also to be made of acacia wood and to be overlaid with gold. Put it in front of the curtain that is before the Ark of Testimony, in front of the cover plate that is over the **Ark of** Testimony – where I will meet with you. On it, Aaron will burn sweet-smelling incense every morning when he prepares the lamps and at every twilight when he lights the lamps – a regular incense offering before the LORD throughout your generations. You shall not offer non-prescribed incense on it, nor whole-offering nor meal offering; nor shall you pour libations on it. Once a year, shall Aaron shall perform **the rite of** expiation on its horns. Once a year throughout

[1] About 2.6 pints.
[2] This referred only to Moses.

your generations he shall perform **the rite of** expiation for it with the blood of the sin offering. It is most holy to the LORD. [30:1–10]

56. Census by ransom

[The LORD told Moses] When you take a census of the Israelites who are to be registered **for battle**, let every man give a ransom for his life, on being registered, to the LORD, so that there be no plague among them when you count them.[1] Everyone who is registered should pay half a shekel[2] as a contribution to the LORD, according to the standards set by the weight of the Sanctuary shekel. (The shekel is the weight of twenty gerahs.) Everyone who passes before the census taken from the age of twenty and upwards shall give the LORD's offering. The rich shall not pay more nor the poor less, than the half-shekel when they make their gift to the LORD to make expiation for their lives. You are to take the expiation money from the Israelites to be used for the ministry at the Tent of Meeting. It will be as a reminder to the LORD of the Israelites for the expiation of your lives. [30:11–16]

57. The laver

[The LORD told Moses] Make a copper laver with a copper stand for washing. Place it between the Tent of Meeting and the altar. Fill it with water so that Aaron and his sons may wash their hands and feet from its water. When they enter the Tent of Meeting let them wash with water so that they do not die. When they approach the altar to minister, to light the fire-offering to the LORD, let them wash their hands and feet so that they do not die. This is for them an eternal law, for them and their descendants throughout their generations. [30:17–21]

---

[1] This seems to resonate with David's order that all the men of his kingdom be counted in order to see how large an army he could muster. This led to a great plague. See *Samuel, The People's Bible*, p. 156 ff for my translation and note of explanation. It would appear that the ransom served a two-fold purpose: the coins and not the individual would be counted, and God is being paid to spare the recruit from harm. It is also a gain for the priesthood who collect the money.

[2] Quarter of an ounce. A gold shekel would be similar to the British sovereign.

58. The anointing oil

[The LORD told Moses] Take to yourself the choicest spices: five hundred weights of flowing myrrh, half as much – two hundred and fifty weights – of sweet cinnamon, and two hundred and fifty weights of fragrant cane, five hundred weights – the Sanctuary standard – of cassia and a *hin* of olive oil. Of this you are to make anointing oil for sacramental use, a blend such as a perfumer would make – it shall be the anointing oil for sacramental use. With it, you are to anoint the Tent of Meeting, the Ark of the Testimonial, the table and all its vessels, the Menorah and all its accessories and the altar of incense and the altar for burnt offerings with all its implements and the laver and its stand. You shall sanctify them that they become most holy. Whoever touches them will be sanctified. You will anoint Aaron and his sons and sanctify them that they may serve me in the priestly office. So will you say to the Israelites: This will be the anointing oil for sacramental uses for me throughout your generations. It is not to be poured on the bodies of people, nor shall you make anything like it according to its blend. It is holy and it shall be treated as sacred by you. Whoever makes a blend like it or whoever uses it on a layman will be cut off from his people. [30:22–34]

59. The holy incense

[The LORD told Moses] Take to yourself sweet spices: stacte, onycha and galbanum – sweet spices and pure frankincense, each in like measure; make of it incense, such a blend as a perfumer would make, salted, pure and holy. Beat some of it into powder and put it before the **Ark of the** Testimonial in the Tent of Meeting where I shall meet with you. It will be most holy to you. Do not make any incense of a similar mixture for your personal use. It shall be regarded by you as sacred to the LORD. Whoever makes anything like it, to use as perfume, will be cut off from his people. [30:35–38]

60. Bezalel and Oholiab – the divine artisans

[The LORD told Moses] I have specifically appointed Bezalel ben Uri ben Hur of the tribe of Judah. I have filled him with the divine spirit – skill, ingenuity and expertise in every craft – to create artistic designs in gold, silver and copper; also in the cutting of stones for setting and in the carving of woods – every type of craftsmanship. I have appointed Oholiab ben Ahisamach of the tribe of Dan **to be his assistant.** I have given the required skills to all the craftsmen to implement all that I have commanded you **to make:** The Tent of Meeting, The Ark of Testimony, the plate over it and all of the Tent's furnishings, namely its table and vessels, the pure Menorah and all its utensils, the altar for incense, the altar of burnt offerings and all its utensils, the laver and its stand, the elaborately designed vestments for the sacral service of Aaron the priest, and the priestly vestments of his sons; the anointing oil and the sweet smelling **spices for** incense for the Sanctuary. They will execute what I have ordered you to make. [31:1–11]

60. The Sabbath

[The LORD told Moses] Speak also to the Israelites: You must above all keep my Sabbaths, for this is the sign **of the bond** between me and them for all your generations to come as proof that I am the LORD who sanctifies you.[1] Keep the Sabbath for it is sacred to you. Those who profane it will most certainly die, for anyone who works during it – that life will be cut off from his people.[2] On six days work may be done, but the seventh day will be one of total rest – holy unto the LORD. Everyone who works on the Sabbath day will most certainly be put to death. The Israelites will keep the Sabbath, to observe the Sabbath for all generations as an eternal covenant. It is a sign **of the bond**

[1] The Israelites, by resting on the Sabbath as God did after the creation, share in his divinity.
[2] If this means excommunication, which can lead to death, it would suggest that it was not an offence deserving of capital punishment, though Moses does have a person collecting wood on the Sabbath stoned. See

between me and the Israelites forever because in six days the LORD made the heavens and the earth and on the seventh day he rested and drew breath. [31:12–17]

61. The Sabbath, Festivals of Unleavened Bread and the First-born, and the Festival of Weeks (Pentecost)

You may work for six days, but on the seventh day you must rest regardless of whether it is the time for ploughing or harvesting.[1] [34:21]

Keep the Festival of Unleavened Bread; for seven days eat only unleavened bread as I commanded you on the designated time in the month of Abib,[2] for in that month you came out of Egypt. The first issue of the womb, of all cattle, of the firstlings of ox and sheep, belongs to me, but only if they are males. You will redeem the firstling of a donkey with a lamb. If you will not redeem it you will have to break its neck. Also you will redeem all the first-borns who are sons. None of you is to appear before me **in my Sanctuary** without any gifts. Observe the Festival of Weeks[3] which occurs at the first harvest of wheat, and also the Festival of Ingathering[4] at the turn of the year. Three times in the year, on **Passover, Pentecost and Tabernacles,** all males must appear before the LORD God, the God of Israel. Because I will dispossess the nations from before you and extend your frontiers, **do not be afraid to leave your homes,** for there will be no **danger of** people longing after **and stealing** your property when you go up to appear before the LORD your God three times annually. Do not offer the blood of my sacrifices with anything leavened, nor allow the remains of the paschal sacrifice to remain **overnight** until morning. The choicest of the first-fruits of the ground shall be brought into the house of the LORD your God. [34:18–20; 22–26]

[1] The pressure of necessity, i.e. to sow seed or to get the harvest in on time, is to be no excuse for the infringement of the Sabbath.
[2] Abib is the modern Hebrew word for Spring. Interestingly, the Hebrew month during which the Israelites left is 'Nissan'.
[3] Pentecost, which occurs seven weeks after Passover.
[4] Tabernacles, which occurs four days after the Day of Atonement.

62. Sympathetic compassion for animals
You shall not boil a kid in its mother's milk. [34–26]

63. Fires not to be ignited on the Sabbath[1]
Moses assembled the whole community of Israel and said to them: "These are the things which the LORD has commanded that you do. On six days you will do all your work, but the seventh day will be a holy one for you – a day of total rest **dedicated** to the LORD. Everyone who works on the Sabbath will be put to death. You will not make fire in any of your dwellings on the Sabbath day." [Exodus 35:1–3]

[1] See appendix for Chapter 35:3 to the conclusion of the Book of *Exodus*.

LEVITICUS

64. The animals which may be sacrificed
The LORD summoned Moses and spoke to him from the Tent of Meeting: Instruct the Israelites and say to them: When any one of you brings an offering[1] to the LORD, such an offering must be from your herd or flock.[2] [1:1–2]

65. The whole-offering of a bull
If his offering is to be a whole-offering,[3] it is to be a perfect male. He shall offer it at the entrance of the Tent of Meeting to find favour with the LORD. He will lay his hand on the head of the whole-offering so that it may be accepted as expiation for him, and then slaughter the bull before the LORD. Aaron's descendants, the priests, shall offer up the blood by splashing it round about the altar which is by the entrance to the Tent of Meeting. They will then skin the whole-offering and cut it into parts. The descendants of Aaron the priest will make a fire on the altar with burning embers and wood; they will then lay its parts – its head and fatty bits – on the wood on the burning embers on the altar; but its entrails and legs they will wash with water. The priest will then burn it all into smoke on the altar – a whole-offering, a fire-offering of pleasing fragrance to the LORD [1:3–9].

[1] The Hebrew word means 'to bring near or close'. The Hebrew for offering is *Korban*, that which is brought near to God. The power of the phrase, lost in translation, is the attempt to come closer to God by giving him a present, very much in a way that presents are an attempt to show or buy affection from those we love. This sacrifice was totally consumed by fire. Translations vary: 'burnt offering', 'holocaust', and whole-offering.
[2] The animals cannot be wild or stolen. They must present as a sacrifice a belonging of personal value.
[3] One which is totally burnt of which the donor does not eat any part in a communal meal. The Hebrew *olah*, here translated as 'whole', LORD can either mean that which ascends, i.e. it all goes up in smoke, or 'wrongdoing' [avel] in which case it would be, like guilt or sin offerings, a voluntary sacrifice in which the donor seeks expiation for something on his conscience. This can only be achieved when the sacrifice is total.

66. The whole-offering of smaller animals
If his offering is from his flocks – a sheep or goat for a whole-offering – he shall offer a perfect male. He will slaughter it on the northern side of the altar before the LORD. Aaron's descendants, the priests, will splash the blood round about the altar; he will cut it into parts; its head and fatty bits the priest will lay on the wood on the burning embers on the altar; but the entrails and the legs he will wash with water. The priest will then offer it all up until it turns into smoke on the altar: a whole-offering of pleasing fragrance to the LORD. [1:10–13]

67. The whole-offering of fowl
If his offering to the LORD is a whole-offering of birds, his offering must be either a turtledove or a pigeon. The priest shall take it to the altar, remove its head and turn it into smoke on the altar; its blood shall be drained out on the side of the altar. He shall remove its crop with its feathers and fling them to where the ashes are on the east side of the altar; the priest shall tear it by its wings without severing it **into two pieces** and burn it on the altar on the wood which is on the fire. It is a whole-offering, a fire-offering of pleasing fragrance to the LORD. [1:14–17]

68. A meal offering
When a person presents a meal offering, it shall be of the finest flour; he shall put oil and frankincense on it and bring it to Aaron's sons, the priests; the priest shall take a handful of fine flour covered in oil and frankincense, and turn it into smoke on the altar as an offering by fire, giving a pleasing fragrance to the LORD – as a reminder **to him of the donor's observance.** The remainder of the meal offering shall belong to Aaron and his sons – a most sacred part of the fire-offerings to the LORD. [2:1–3]

69. A prepared meal offering
When your offering is of a meal already oven-baked, it shall be of the finest flour: unleavened cakes mixed with oil or unleavened wafers with oil spread overthem. If your offering is of meal made

on a griddle, it shall be of fine unleavened flour mixed in oil. Divide it into pieces and spread oil over it – it is a meal offering. Equally, if the meal offering is made in a frying pan, it shall be made of finest flour with oil. You will present any of the meal offerings made this way to the LORD; it shall be brought to the priest who will take it to the altar. The priest shall remove from the meal offering the 'reminder-part'[1] and turn it into smoke on the altar – an offering of fire of pleasing fragrance to the LORD. The remainder of the meal offering shall belong to Aaron and his sons – a most sacred part of the fire-offerings to the LORD. No meal offerings which you present to the LORD shall be made with leaven, for no leaven nor honey may be turned into smoke as a fire offering to the LORD. You may present them to the LORD as an offering of first fruits but they shall not be offered up to give a pleasing fragrance. You must also season all meal offerings with salt; you shall not miss out from any of your meal offerings the salt of your covenant[2] with God; all your offerings must be salted. [2:4–13]

70. Meal offering of first-fruits

If you present a meal offering of first-fruits **of the harvest** to the LORD you shall bring roasted ears of wheat, the mushed meal from the fresh grain – as your meal offering of first-fruits. Sprinkle it with oil and place frankincense on it: it is a meal offering. The priest will let the 'reminder-part' of it go up in smoke: some of the grits and oil and frankincense, as a fire offering to the LORD. [2:14–16]

[1] See *68* p. 33 for explanation.
[2] An everlasting Covenant of Salt is also mentioned in *Numbers* 18:19. I would assume that, as salt is a preservative, it is the symbol of the enduring quality of God's Covenant with Israel. Her loyalty to the eternity of the Covenant is revealed by the use of salt on all offerings.

71. The peace[1] sacrifice:

If his offering is a peace sacrifice –

1. If his offering is of the herd, what he offers to the LORD, whether male or female, must be unblemished. He shall lay his hand on the head of his offering and slaughter it by the entrance to the Tent of Meeting: Aaron's sons, the priests, shall splash the blood against all sides of the altars. Of the offering of the peace sacrifice, **a part** shall be an offering through fire to the LORD: the fat that covers and is all about the entrails, the two kidneys and their fatty covering, that is by the loins. The lobe on the liver; he will remove this with the kidneys. Aaron's sons shall turn these into smoke on the altar with the burnt offering which is on the wood on the fire, as an offering through fire of pleasing fragrance to the LORD.

2. If his offering of a peace sacrifice to the LORD is from the flock, whether male or female, it must be unblemished. If he presents a sheep for his offering, he shall offer it before the LORD. [Repetition of previous commandment, except for the addition of the sheep's broad tail to be cut off close to its backbone – translator's note] The priest shall turn these into smoke on the altar as food, an offering through fire to the LORD.

3. If his oblation be a goat, then he shall offer it before the LORD. [Repetition of previous commandment with the exception of the broad tail] The priest shall turn these into smoke on the altar: it is the food of the offering made through fire for a pleasing fragrance. All fat belongs to the LORD. It is an everlasting law throughout your generations and in all your settlements. You must not eat any fat or any blood. [3:1–17]

[1] Other translations are 'wellbeing' or 'thanksgiving'. With the exception of the parts of the beast mentioned, the animal was eaten by the priests or by the donor, his family and guests. It linked the eating of a grand meal with an acknowledgement to God for his blessings.

72. The sin offering[1] for the High Priest

The LORD instructed Moses: speak to the Israelites thus: if a person commits a sin by breaking any of the LORD's commandments about what is not to be done – if the anointed priest[2] has sinned and brought blame on to the people; for the sin he has committed, he shall offer to the LORD an unblemished bull as a sacrifice to purge **him of** the sin. He shall bring the bull to the entrance of the Tent of Meeting before the LORD, place his hand upon the bull's head and slaughter the bull before the LORD. The anointed priest shall take some of the bull's blood into the Tent of Meeting; he shall dip his finger in the blood – seven times shall he sprinkle the blood before the LORD by the curtain of the inner Sanctuary. The priest shall put its blood upon the horns of the altar of sweet incense before the LORD which is in the Tent of Meeting; he will pour out the remaining blood of the bull at the base of the altar for burnt offerings, which is by the entrance of the Tent of Meeting. He shall remove all the fat of the bull of the sin offering – the fat that covers and is all about the entrails, the two kidneys and the fat on them, that is at the loins and the lobe on the liver. He shall take them as they are taken from an ox for a peace sacrifice; the priest shall turn them into smoke upon the altar of burnt offerings. But the bull's hide and all its flesh including its head, legs, its entrails and dung – all the rest of the bull – he shall have carried to a 'clean'[3] place outside the camp, to the ash heap to be burnt up in a wood fire; it shall be burned on the ash heap.[4] [4:1–12]

[1] Literally, an offering to purge away sins, i.e. a purgation offering.
[2] The fact that the priest is described as the anointed – *mashiah* – suggests that he was the High Priest.
[3] Probably a euphemism for an unclean place – the rubbish heap.
[4] It must be significant that the whole animal is not burnt as an offering to God. It suggests that the sacrifice was a symbol of the desire for atonement, the purgation of guilt. Thus, it required token parts to go up in smoke – in fact that which would burn most easily. Were the whole animal burnt, the donor might believe that he had obtained forgiveness from God by bribing him with the gift of an animal.

73. The offering of purgation for the community of Israel

If the entire community of Israel should unintentionally err and it escaped the attention of their assembly,[1] that they had incurred guilt by doing something that the LORD had forbidden and are guilty – when their sin is discovered, then the assembly shall present a bull for the sin offering before the Tent of Meeting. The elders of the community shall place their hands upon the bull's head before the LORD – it shall be slaughtered before the LORD. The anointed priest shall take some of the bull's blood into the Tent of Meeting; he will dip his finger in the blood and sprinkle it seven times before the LORD before the curtain **of the inner Sanctuary**; he shall put some of its blood on the horns of the altar **of incense** which is before the LORD, that is in the Tent of Meeting; he will pour out the remaining blood at the base of the altar of burnt offering, which is by the entrance of the Tent of Meeting. He shall remove all its fat and turn it to smoke on the altar. He shall do precisely to this bull as he did with the bull for the sin offering **for his own guilt.** The priest will make expiation for them and they will be forgiven. He shall then have the bull carried outside the camp and burn it in accordance with the instructions of the first-**mentioned** bull. This is the sin offering for the assembly **of tribal chieftains**. [4:13–21]

74. The sin offering for a chieftain

When it is a chieftain who sins unintentionally and had incurred guilt by doing something which the LORD had forbidden and is guilty, and he is made aware of the sin he has committed, he shall bring an offering of an unblemished male goat. He shall place his hand upon the goat's head and slaughter it in the place where they slaughter the burnt offering before the LORD: it is a sin offering. The priest will take with his finger some of the blood of the sin offering to put on the horns of the altar of burnt offerings and he shall pour out the remainder of the blood at its base. He shall turn all the fat into smoke upon the altar, as in the case of

[1] This must refer to the council of tribal chieftains.

the fat of the sacrifice of peace offerings. The priest will make expiation for him because of his sin and he shall be forgiven. [4:22–26]

75. The sin offering for a man of the people
And if anyone of the populace ... [repetition of previous conditions and instructions except that the offerings required are either a female goat or a lamb: translator's note]. The priest shall make expiation for him because of the sin he has committed and he shall be forgiven. [4:27–35]

76. Other sin offerings
If a person sins:
- A person hearing a public imprecation **against someone who is withholding evidence** and, although able to testify because he has either seen or knows of the matter, he does not give evidence, he incurs guilt.
- A person touching an unclean thing, whether the carcass of an unclean beast, cattle, or creeping thing – the fact that he was unaware of it, and then, being unclean, he realises his guilt **because in his state of uncleanness he entered the Sanctuary and participated in sacrificial rites;** or when he touches human uncleanness – any of which renders one unclean – and, though he was aware of it, he forgot about it **and had gone into the Sanctuary**, and only afterwards realised his guilt;
- Or when a person makes a rash oath whether to do evil or good – making any sort of oath as people will do, and though he would acknowledge it, but forgot about it, then he incurs guilt **for not fulfilling his forgotten vow.** In any of these matters, when a person realises his guilt, he shall confess what he has sinned and bring as amends to the LORD for the sin which he has committed: a female from the flock, sheep or goat for a sin offering; and the priest shall make expiation for him because of his sin. But if he cannot afford a lamb, he shall bring as amends for his sin two turtledoves or two pigeons to the LORD: one for a sin offering and one for a whole-offering; he shall

bring them to the priest who shall first offer the sin offering; he will wring its head close to the neck but without removing it. He shall splash some of the blood of the sin offering on the side of the altar; the remaining blood shall be drained out at the base of the altar – it is a sin offering. He shall prepare the second as a whole-offering according to the instructions.[1] So will the priest make expiation for him for the sin he has committed and he shall be forgiven. But, if he cannot afford two turtledoves or two pigeons, he shall offer for what he has sinned a tenth of an *ephah* of fine flour for a sin offering; he shall put no oil or frankincense on it because it is a sin offering.[2] He shall bring it to the priest who will take a handful of it as a reminder **of the sinner's penitence** and turn it into smoke on the altar, with the LORD's fire offering; it is a sin offering The priest will make expiation for him for whichever sin he committed and he shall be forgiven. What remains shall be the priest's as with the meal offerings.[3] [5:11–13]

77. Penalty for inadvertent fraud against God

The LORD instructed Moses: When a person without intent expropriates something which belongs to the LORD, i.e **by withholding tithes, etc.,** he shall bring, as his penalty to the LORD, an unblemished ram from his flock or its worth in silver according to the Sanctuary scales – this is the guilt offering. As to restitution for what he expropriated, he shall add a fifth to its value and give it to the priest, who shall make expiation for him with the ram of guilt offering,[4] and he shall be forgiven.

---

[1] See section on 'whole-offering of fowl', **67** p. 33.

[2] Not a whole-offering which would require oil and frankincense to make a pleasing fragrance for the LORD.

[3] It would appear that the priest only benefits from the sin offering of the poorest, as in the case of the other sacrifices: what is not burnt on the altar is disposed of on the ash heap on the rubbish dump. Would this have been an incentive for the priests not to dismiss the meagre offering of the poor but to value their penance even more?

[4] The guilt offering is slightly different from the sin offering in that its major intention is atonement as a supplement to monetary restitution.

- When a person without intent commits any sin by breaking any of the LORD's commandments about what is not to be done; and then realises his guilt – he is **nonetheless** subject to punishment. He shall bring to the priest an unblemished ram or its **monetary** equivalent as a guilt offering. The priest shall make expiation for him for the error that he unintentionally committed, and he shall be forgiven. It is a guilt offering because, **not withstanding his unawareness,** he has incurred guilt before the LORD. [5:14–19]

78. Penalties for fraud against one's fellow man

The LORD instructed Moses: When a person sins in trespassing against the LORD[1] by defrauding his neighbour in a matter of a deposit or security for a loan or through robbery or by exploiting his fellow; or by finding something lost and lying about it; if he swears falsely about any of those matters that one may do and so sin thereby – when one has sinned thus and has acknowledged his guilt and would restore what he gained through robbery and fraud, or the deposit that was entrusted to him or the lost item that was found, or on any matter of property on which he swore falsely, he shall pay the principal amount and add **as penalty** a fifth of its value. He shall pay it to the owner when he acknowledges his guilt. Then shall he bring to the priest as his penalty to the LORD an unblemished ram from his flock or its monetary equivalent as a guilt offering. The priest shall make expiation for him before the LORD, and he shall be forgiven for whatever he did to incur guilt. [5:20–26]

79. Fire for the daily whole-offering[2]

The LORD instructed Moses: Command Aaron and his sons thus: This is the ritual of the whole-offering: it shall remain on its firewood on the altar all night until the morning while the fire

[1] A trespass against one's fellow human is a trespass against God. He must pay a penalty to both.
[2] The first five chapters dealt with various sacrifices affecting the entire people. The next two chapters deal with the daily sacrificial rites of the Sanctuary.

on the altar is kept burning on it. The priest shall dress in a linen
garment with linen breeches next to his body; he shall lift up the
ashes to which the fire has reduced the burnt offering on the
altar and put them beside the altar. He shall take off his clothing
and put on other clothing and carry the ashes out of the camp
to a 'clean' place. The fire on the altar shall be kept burning and
not be allowed to go out. Every morning the priest will fuel it
with wood, lay out the burnt offering on it and turn into smoke
the fat of the peace sacrifice. A perpetual fire shall be kept burning
on the altar, never to go out. [6:1–7]

80. Further instructions regarding the meal offering
This is the law of the meal offering. Aaron's sons shall offer it before
the Lord before the altar. He shall take from it a handful of fine
flour, the oil and frankincense, which is on the meal offering and
turn it into smoke giving a pleasing fragrance as a reminder to the
Lord **of the donor's obeisance.** The remaining meal is for Aaron
and his sons. It shall be eaten without leaven in a sanctified place:
they shall eat it in the enclosure of the Tent of Meeting. It shall not
be baked with leaven. I have granted this as their portion of the fire
offerings sacrificed to me. Their portion is most holy, as **holy as** the
sin and guilt offerings.[1] Every male Aaronite may eat of it, as a right
– because it is an eternal statute, throughout the generations – to
partake of the fire offerings of the Lord. Whatever touches them
shall become ritually holy.[2] [6:7–11]

81. The daily meal offering required of the descendants of Aaron
The Lord instructed Moses: This is the offering of the descendants
of Aaron which they shall present to the Lord from the day of their

[1] This is to give status of holiness to that which the priests are eating, i.e. what
the priests get for their own consumption is as ritually important as what goes
up on the altar – an obvious attempt to minimise the resentment of the laity
for the priests receiving the lion's share of their donations.
[2] Subject to all the regulations pertaining to holy objects – those dedicated to
the Lord, the Sanctuary and the Priesthood.

anointment: a tenth of an *ephah* of fine flour for their regular meal offering – half in the morning and half in the evening. It shall be made soaked with oil on the baking pan; the meal offering shall be in cut up pieces, it shall be offered to give a pleasing fragrance to the LORD. So shall the priest anointed from among the descendants of Aaron to succeed him prepare it; it is an eternal statute to the LORD – to be turned entirely into smoke. Every priestly meal offering is to be wholly burnt – it is not to be eaten. [6:12–16]

82. The priestly sin offering

The LORD instructed Moses: Tell Aaron and his sons: This is the law in regard to the sin offering. In the same place where the whole-offering is slaughtered, that is where the sin offering is to be slaughtered before the LORD – it is most holy. The priest who offers it as a sin offering shall eat of it; he shall eat it in a holy place – in the enclosure of the Tent of Meeting. Anything which touches its flesh becomes holy. If its blood is sprinkled on any piece of clothing, it must be washed off in the place where it became stained – in a holy place. If it was boiled in an earthen vessel, that vessel shall be broken;[1] if it was boiled in a copper vessel, it shall be scoured and rinsed with water. Every male among the priests may eat of it – it is most holy. But no sin offering may be eaten, from which any of its blood is brought into the Tent of Meeting for expiation into the Sanctuary. Such sin offerings must be consumed by fire. [6:17–23]

83. Further instructions regarding the guilt offering[2]

This is the law in regard to the guilt offering – it is most holy. In the same place where they slaughter the burnt offering the guilt

---

[1] Even were it washed thoroughly, earthenware might absorb some of its contents.

[2] The guilt offering for civil trespass could not be expected on its own, like the sin offering to achieve the expiation of sin, as it required further restitution, monetary or otherwise. It would appear that it differs from the whole-offering, as it was compulsory for a known offence. While the offender could not eat of it, the priests could.

offering shall be slaughtered. Its blood shall be sprinkled on all sides of the altar. He shall offer up all its fat: the fat tail, the fat that covers up the entrails, the two kidneys with its covering fat which is near the loins; the lobe of the liver – **all this** with the kidneys shall be taken from it. The priest shall turn them into smoke on the altar as an offering by fire to the LORD – it is a guilt offering. Any male of the priests may eat of it. It shall be eaten in a sacred area – it is most holy. As with the sin offering, so with the guilt offering – one rule applies: the priest who makes expiation shall have it. The priest who offers up a man's whole-offering shall have the hide of the offering he has sacrificed. Also, any meal offering baked in an oven or prepared in a pan or griddle shall belong to the priest who offers it. All other meal offerings, whether mixed with oil or dry, shall belong equally to all descendants of Aaron. [7:1–10]

84. The peace offering for thanksgiving[1]

This is the law of the sacrifice of peace that one may offer to the LORD: If he offer it for thanksgiving, he shall offer together with the thanksgiving sacrifice unleavened cakes mixed in with oil, unleavened wafers spread over with oil and cakes of fine flour mixed in oil and well soaked. Also, with cakes of leavened bread, he shall offer his sacrifice of peace for thanksgiving. Out of this, he shall offer one of each kind as a gift to the LORD. This shall go to the **officiating** priest who sprinkles the blood of the peace offering. The flesh of the sacrifice of his peace offerings for thanksgiving shall be eaten on the day he made the offering. He shall not let any part of it remain by the next morning.

85. Peace offering for fulfilment of vow[2]
or out of spontaneous thanksgiving

If a vow or a voluntary donation is the basis for his offering, it shall be eaten on the very day he offers his sacrifice; he can eat the

---

[1] Perhaps for recovery from illness, etc.
[2] A vow made in time of emergency.

rest on the next day, but whatever flesh of the sacrifice remains to the third day shall be consumed by fire. But if any of the meat of the sacrifice of his peace offerings is eaten on the third day, it is not acceptable; it is an offensive thing and the person who eats it shall bear his guilt.[1] [7:15–18]

86. Ritually unclean meat

The meat that touches anything ritually unclean shall not be eaten; it shall be consumed by fire. But for other meat, anyone who is ritually clean may eat of it. The person that is ritually unclean who eats the meat of the sacrifice of peace offerings to the LORD will be cut off from his kin. Whatever person touches a ritually unclean thing, whether it be a man or beast or reptile, and then eats of the meat of the sacrifice of peace offerings – that person shall be cut off from his kin. [7:19–21]

87. Fat[2] is forbidden and so is blood

The LORD instructed Moses: Tell the Israelites: You shall eat no fat of ox or sheep or goat. Fat from animals that died or were torn by beasts can be used for other purposes but not to be eaten. Whoever eats of the fat of animals from which offerings of fire are made to the LORD will be cut off from his kin. You shall not consume any blood, either of bird or beast, in any of your dwellings. Whoever consumes any blood[3] shall be cut off from his people. [7:22–27]

88. More instructions regarding peace offerings

The LORD instructed Moses: Tell the Israelites: The offering to the LORD from the peace sacrifice shall be presented by him who

[1] Did the lawgiver realise that unpreserved meat could be dangerous by the third day? Unlikely, but possible.
[2] The fat intended is that referred to in **71** p. 35, i.e. the coarse fat, but not the ordinary fatty tissue which accompanies meat.
[3] Blood was perceived as the life force of an animal and therefore should not be eaten. For this reason, Orthodox Jews to this very day salt meat to extract the blood before cooking it.

offers his peace offering to the Lord.[1] His own hands shall present the fire offerings to the Lord. He shall present the fat with the breast so that the breast may be elevated as an offering of elevation before the Lord. The priest shall turn the fat into smoke on the altar; but the breast shall belong to descendants of Aaron. The right thigh, which is the best portion, you shall give to the priest as a gift from the sacrifices of your peace offerings. He, among descendants of Aaron, who offers up the blood and fat of the peace offerings shall have the right thigh for his portion. For the breast for the elevation offering and the thigh of the gift offering I have expropriated from the peace offerings of the Israelites to grant to Aaron and his descendants as their due from the Israelites for all time. [7:29–34]

*   *   *

These shall be the benefits accruing to the descendants of Aaron from the fire offerings to the Lord from the time he ordained them to be priests to the Lord – that which the Lord commanded be given to them from the day he anointed them as their due from the Israelites throughout the generations. These are the laws for the whole-offering, the meal offering, the sin offering and the guilt offering and the offerings of **the priests'** ordination and of the sacrifice of peace offerings – that which the Lord had instructed Moses on Mount Sinai at the time he instructed the Israelites to bring near their offerings to the Lord in the Sinai wilderness. [7:35–38]

*   *   *

89. The consecration of priests [8:1–36]
This describes the implementation with minor variants of the instructions regarding the ordination and consecration of priests in *Exodus*, chapters 29 and 30.

---

[1] This refers to the bits that are burnt on the altar to create a pleasing fragrance to the Lord.

90. The offerings after ordination of priests

On the eighth day,[1] Moses summoned Aaron and his sons and the elders of the Israelites. He instructed Aaron: Take a young bull for a sin offering and an unblemished ram for a whole-offering and offer them to the LORD. And instruct the Israelites: Take a he-goat for a sin offering and a calf and lamb who are unblemished yearlings for a whole-offering; an ox and a ram for peace offerings to sacrifice to the LORD; a meal offering mixed with oil because on this day the LORD will appear to you. They brought that which Moses had commanded to the front of the Tent of Meeting. The whole congregation drew near to stand before the LORD. [9:1–5]

91. The sin offering of Aaron

Moses said: this is what the LORD has ordered you to do, so that the Presence of the LORD may appear to you. Moses instructed Aaron: Come to the altar and offer your sin offering and your whole-offering and make expiation for yourself and for the people and execute the offering of the people and make expiation for them as the LORD has commanded. Aaron then approached the altar and slaughtered his calf of sin offering. The sons of Aaron brought the blood to him; he dipped his finger into the blood and put it on the horns of the altar and poured out the rest of the blood at the base of the altar; he turned the fat, the kidneys and the liver lobe of the sin offering into smoke on the altar, as the LORD had instructed Moses; he burnt the meat and the hide outside the camp. [9:6–11]

92. The whole-offering

Then he slaughtered the whole-offering. The sons of Aaron handed over to him the blood and he splashed it round about the altar. They then handed him the offering piece by piece and the head and he burnt it into smoke on the altar. He washed the

[1] The consecration of the priests with the accompanying sacrificial offerings lasted throughout the week.

entrails and the legs and turned them also into smoke with the rest of the whole-offering. [9:12–14]

93. The people's offering

He then brought the people's offering; he took the goat of the people's sin offering and slaughtered it and offered it up as a sin offering as with the first sacrifice. He then brought forward the whole-offering and sacrificed it according to the regulations; he brought forward the meal offering, took a handful and turned it into smoke on the altar – in addition to the **daily** morning whole-offering. He also slaughtered the ox and the ram for the sacrifice of the people's peace offerings. Once again, Aaron's sons handed the blood to him and he splashed it all around the altar. They placed the fatty parts of the ox and the ram, the broad tail, the fatty covering, the kidneys, and the lobes of the liver over the breasts, and he turned them into smoke on the altar. Aaron lifted up the breasts and the right thigh as an offering of elevation before the LORD, as Moses had instructed. [9:15–21]

94. The blessings of Aaron and Moses and the revelation of the Lord's presence

Aaron lifted up his hands toward the people and blessed them. He stepped down after sacrificing the sin offering, the whole-offering and the peace offering. Moses and Aaron then went into the Tent of Meeting, came out and blessed the people. The presence of the LORD was revealed to the whole people – for fire came forth from before the LORD and consumed the whole-offering and the fatty parts on the altar. When the people saw this, they raised their voices in praise and fell on their faces. [9:22–24]

*   *   *

Interlude: The deaths of Nadab and Abihu

95. Nadab and Abihu, Aaron's sons, each took his fire pan, put fire in it, and laid incense on it. They thus brought before the LORD alien fire, which he had not commanded them to do. Fire came forth from the LORD and consumed them; so did they die before the LORD. Moses said to Aaron **when they learnt of this misfortune**, this is what the LORD meant when he said, "Through those who are close to me will I be declared as holy and be honoured in the presence of the entire people." And Aaron was silent.[1] [10:1–3]

Moses summoned Mishael and Elzaphan, the sons of Uzziel, Aaron's uncle, and said to them, "Approach and carry your kinsmen from the front of the Sanctuary to a place outside the camp."[2] They approached and carried them out in their tunics as Moses had instructed. Moses then instructed Aaron and Eleazar and Itamar, his sons, "Do not dishevel your hair nor tear your clothes **in grief**, lest you die and so that he will not be angry with the community,[3] but let your kinsmen and all the Israelites weep over the conflagration that the LORD has sent. You must not even leave the Tent of Meeting lest you die for you shall have the LORD's anointing oil on you." They did as Moses said. [10:4–7]

*　　　　*　　　　*

[1] The sin of Aaron's two eldest sons was simply the abuse of their authority. They acted unilaterally and without authority on the basis that, as priests, they could do as they pleased. Whatever the historical basis for this tale, the moral is clear. While their priesthood was inherited and was not subject to democratic rule, their power was limited to the duties as prescribed by the Laws of Moses. They were enactors of the laws and not the legislators. Even if their motive was to give obeisance to God, they had no authority to design their own rituals. While the laity could not remove them from office, God would. Moses's statement affirms the fact that it is God who ultimately decides by whom his presence is sanctified. Aaron's silence is noted because, while as a parent he would question whether the punishment fitted the crime, he was persuaded by Moses that his sons had, through their insolence, forfeited their rights to the priestly office. As there were no laws of impeachment, this could only happen by the forfeit of their lives.

[2] The remaining sons who were priests could not touch their brothers' corpses as this would make them ritually unclean and unable to perform the Sanctuary's rituals.

[3] While it would be natural for them to grieve, their mourning could be interpreted as a protest against the LORD's action against Nadab and Abihu.

96. Priests forbidden to drink spirits in the Sanctuary

The LORD instructed Aaron: Drink no wine or liquor, neither you nor your sons with you, when you enter the Tent of Meeting so that you do not die. It is an eternal law throughout your generations, so that you learn to distinguish between what is sacred and what is ordinary and between what is defiled and what is ritually clean, so that you are in a position to teach the Israelites all the laws that the LORD has given them through Moses.[1] [10:9–11]

97. Perquisites enjoyed by the priests

Moses said to Aaron and his remaining sons, Eleazar and Ithamar: Take what remains of the meal offering of the fire offerings to the LORD and eat it without leavening by the altar because it is most holy; so eat it in a holy place because it is your due and your sons' due from the offerings of fire to the LORD, for so have I been commanded. The breast of the elevation offering and the thigh of the gift offering – you and your sons and daughters may eat in any ritually clean place, for they have been apportioned as due to you and your descendants from the peace offerings of the Israelites; together with the fat of the fire offering, they must present the thigh of the gift offering and the breast of the elevation offering which are to be raised up as an elevation offering before the LORD, but which are to be your due and that of your descendants as well as yours for ever – as the LORD has commanded. [10:10–15]

98. The conclusion of the story of Nadab and Abihu's deaths

Moses made enquiries regarding the goat of the sin offering, and he learnt that it was totally burnt **when part of it should have been eaten by the priests**; so he addressed his anger at Eleazar and Ithamar, the remaining sons of Aaron, "Why did you not

---

[1] The proximity of the directive against priests officiating under the influence of alcohol and the deaths of Nadab and Abihu might suggest that their sin was the consequence of being intoxicated.

eat the sin offering in the holiness of the Sanctuary, for it is most holy and was given to you to remove the guilt of the community and to make expiation for them before the LORD. Since its blood was not brought inside the Sanctuary **as should be done**, you should at least have eaten it in the Sanctuary, as I instructed you." Aaron replied to Moses, "Consider, today they offered their sin offering and whole-offering before the LORD, but when such things have befallen me, would it have pleased the LORD if I had participated in eating the sin offering **as my due**?" On hearing this, Moses approved. [10:16–20]

The Dietary Laws[1]

99. Permitted and forbidden quadrupeds
The LORD spoke to Moses and Aaron: Inform the Israelites: Of all animals living on land these are the creatures you may eat: Any animal that has proper hoofs with clefts through the hoofs and chews[2] the cud – of such you may eat. These, however, who either chew the cud or have cloven hoofs you may not eat: the camel – because while it chews the cud it is not cleft-hoofed – is unclean for you. The rock badger, while it chews the cud but does not have cloven hoofs, is unclean for you. The hare, while it chews the cud but does not have cloven hoofs, is unclean for you. The pig, while he has cloven hoofs, does not chew the cud and is unclean for you. You shall not eat their meat nor touch their dead bodies. They are unclean for you. [11:1–8]

100. Permitted and forbidden fish
Of all that lives in the waters, these you may eat: Anything in the waters, the seas or the streams that has fins or scales – you may eat them. But anything in the seas or streams without fins and scales among all that swim in shoals in the waters and the

[1] The permission to eat animal flesh was given to Noah, see *Genesis 9:1–4*. It has to be drained of its blood.
[2] Literally: 'brings up'.

larger living creatures[1] in the waters shall be repulsive to you and nothing but repulsive. You shall not eat their meat and you shall detest their carcasses. Everything in the waters that has no fins or scales shall be repulsive to you![2] [11:9–12]

101. Forbidden birds
These are the birds that you will consider repulsive. They shall not be eaten because they are repulsive: the eagle, the vulture, the osprey, the kite and every kind of falcon, every kind of crow, the ostrich, the nighthawk, the seagull and every kind of hawk, the little owl, the cormorant and the great owl, the horned owl, the pelican, the buzzard, the stork, all kinds of herons, the hoopoe and the bat. [11:13–19]

102. Forbidden and permitted insects
All winged insects that move upon all fours will be repulsive to you except those with the sort of legs above their feet which allow them to leap over the ground. Of them, you may eat all kinds of locusts, every kind of bald locust, all kinds of crickets and grasshoppers. But all other winged insects on four feet you shall detest **as food.** [11:20–23]

103. Forbidden animals which cause ritual defilement
These shall make you unclean; whoever touches their carcasses shall be unclean until evening. Whoever carries any of their carcasses shall wash his clothes and be unclean until evening: every animal that has proper hoofs but without clefts through the hoofs,[3] that does not chew the cud is unclean for you. Anyone who touches them becomes unclean. Those four-footed animals that walk on their paws are unclean for you. Whoever touches their carcass shall be unclean until evening. He that carries any

---

[1] Sea animals such as whales.
[2] This of course includes all the varieties of shell fish.
[3] That is: the hoofs have a division in them which does not go straight through the hoofs.

of their carcasses shall wash his clothes and be unclean until evening – they are indeed unclean for you. [11:24–28]

104. Forbidden creeping things

These are unclean for you among the creeping things that swarm upon the earth: the mole, the mouse and every kind of great lizard; the gecko, the land crocodile, the lizard, the sand lizard and the chameleon. These are unclean for you among all that creep. Whoever touches them when they are dead shall be unclean until evening. On whatever thing they fall when they are dead shall become unclean, whether it be a wooden vessel or clothes or a skin or a sack – whatever article which can be put to use must be put into water and it shall be unclean until evening. Then shall it be clean. If they fall into an earthen vessel, whatever is in it becomes unclean and you must break it **because as it absorbs the uncleanness, it cannot be washed away**. Edible food will become unclean only if water moistens it **because it spreads the uncleanness**; all drinkable liquid shall become unclean, if it was in a vessel **which has been contaminated by such contact**. Anything upon which such a carcass falls shall be unclean, whether an oven or stove – it shall be broken to pieces. They are unclean and shall be unclean for you. But a spring or cistern in which water is collected shall be clean[1] but he who touches the carcass inside it becomes unclean. If such a carcass falls upon seed grain about to be sown, it remains clean, but if it is moisturised with water when the carcass falls upon it, it becomes unclean for you. [11:29–38]

105. Creatures that defile and are repulsive

If an animal that you may eat dies, whoever touches the carcass shall be unclean until evening. The one who eats from the carcass

---

[1] Either because of the impracticality of making it unusable or because flowing waters were seen to be a source of purification.

shall wash his clothes and be unclean until evening.[1] Also, the one that carries the carcass shall wash his clothes and be unclean until evening.

Every creeping thing that swarms upon the earth is repulsive. It shall not be eaten. Whatever crawls on its belly or moves on all fours or has many feet – all the creeping things that swarm upon the earth – you shall not eat for they are repulsive. You shall not make yourselves repulsive by **eating** any creeping thing which crawls upon the earth. You shall not be defiled by them and so become unclean [11:39–43].

106. The imitation of God
Because I am the LORD your God: sanctify yourselves; be holy because I am holy. Therefore do not defile yourselves by any creeping thing which crawls upon the earth; for I am the LORD who brought you up from the land of Egypt to be your God so that you may be holy as I am holy.[2] [11:44–45]

Conclusion
This is the law pertaining to the **eating of** land animals, birds and every living creature that moves in the waters and swarms upon the earth – to make a distinction between the profane and the pure and between the creatures which may be eaten and those which may not be eaten. [11:46–47]

[1] This is strange as it is forbidden to eat an animal which has died [Deut. 14:21]. Is it assumed here that the eater was not aware that the meat came from an animal who had died?
[2] The juxtaposition of the demand that the Israelites be as holy as God to the prohibition of eating 'creepy crawlies' is interesting. It suggests that, by making Israel his people, he has bestowed upon them a dignity which the eating of reptiles, snakes and insects would diminish.

Laws of Purification

107. Defilement through conception and birth[1]

The LORD told Moses: Instruct the Israelites: When a woman conceives and bears a male child, she shall be unclean; similar as to the time of her menstruation, she shall be unclean for seven days. On the eighth day, the flesh of his foreskin shall be circumcised.[2] Her period of purification because of the blood **that issued from her** shall be thirty-three days. She shall not touch any consecrated thing nor enter the Sanctuary until her purification is completed. When she bears a female child, she shall be unclean two weeks as in menstruation for fourteen days.[3] Her period of purification because of her blood shall be sixty-six days.[4] When the days of her purification are completed, for a son or a daughter, she shall bring to the priest at the entrance to the Tent of Meeting a yearling lamb for a whole-offering and a pigeon or a turtledove for a sin offering.[5] He shall offer it to the LORD and make expiation for her and she shall be purified from her issue of blood. This is the law for her who bears a child, whether a male or female. If she cannot afford a lamb, let her bring two turtledoves or pigeons – one for a burnt offering and the other

---

[1] The reasons for these laws must be buried in the recesses of the ancient human mind. The attitudes towards birth are very complex, as indicated in the story of the Garden of Eden. The mystery of the association there of knowledge, sex, birth and death and their relationship to God's scheme of things is matter for an essay and not a footnote.

[2] The law of circumcision is given to Abraham as the sign of the Covenant between God and Abraham's descendants, see *Genesis 17:9–14*. For the observance of the rite on the eighth day, see *Genesis 21:4*.

[3] Seven days during the menstrual period and for another seven days. To this very day Orthodox Jewish men and women do not have sex during these fourteen days.

[4] The doubling of the time required for purification of a female birth suggests a male sexist attitude.

[5] Why was a sin offering required? Was it due to the belief that Eve was responsible both for human mortality and immortality through child-birth by persuading Adam to eat of the fruit of the Tree of Knowledge? I have heard one explanation; the labour pains are so great that a woman suffering them swears never to give birth again – and for this false oath a sin offering is required.

for a sin offering. The priest will make expiation for her and she shall be clean. [12:1–8]

The Law of Virulent Skin Diseases[1]

108. Diagnoses of the skin disease

If a person has on the skin of his body a swelling, a scab or a spot and it could develop into a virulent skin disease, that person shall be brought to Aaron the priest or one of his sons, the priests. The priest shall examine the sore on the skin of his body. If the hair on the affected part has turned white and the sore appears to be more than skin deep, it is a virulent skin disease; when the priest sees it, he shall declare him ritually unclean; but if the spot is white in the skin of his body and does not appear more than skin deep and the hair in it has not turned white, the priest shall quarantine the affected person for seven days. On the seventh day the priest shall examine him and if the sore has remained as it was and has not spread on the skin, the priest will extend the quarantine for a further seven days. On the seventh day the priest will again examine him and if the sore has faded and has not spread on the skin, the priest shall declare him as clean. If it is only a scab, he shall wash his clothes and be clean. But if the scab spreads over the skin after he has been examined by the priest and declared clean, he shall present himself again to the priest; if he sees that the scab has spread on the skin, the priest shall declare him unclean. It is a virulent skin disease. [13:1–8]

109. A dormant skin disease

Someone who has a virulent skin disease shall be brought to the priest who will examine him. If there is a white swelling in the skin and the hair **near it** has turned white and the flesh is ulcerated, it

[1] Traditional translations describe this as leprosy but, as scholars now agree that the Hebrew term can refer to several skin diseases, I am happier using 'virulent skin diseases' [*Revised English Bible*]. My preference is simply due to the fact that individuals suffering from leprosy have sufficient agony and should be spared reading of their ban from the community.

is a dormant skin disease. The priest shall declare him as unclean. He need not put him in quarantine for he is known to be unclean.[1] If the skin disease spreads over his skin from head to foot, wherever the priest can see – if the priest sees that the disease has covered all his body – he shall declare him as clean; he is clean for he has turned all white.[2] However, whenever it becomes ulcerated, he shall be unclean. When the priest sees the ulcerations, he shall declare him as unclean. The ulcerated flesh is unclean. It is a virulent skin disease. But if the ulcer becomes white again, he shall present himself to the priest who shall examine him: if the disease has turned white, he will declare the diseased person clean. He is ritually clean. [13:9–17]

110. Symptoms of virulent skin disease
When an ulcer appears on someone's skin and heals but is followed in its place by a white swelling or a reddish-white spot, he shall present himself to the priest; if the priest finds that it is deeper than the skin and that its hair has turned white, he shall declare him as unclean; it is a virulent skin affliction breaking out into ulcers. But, if the priest finds that there is no white hair on it and it is not deeper than the skin and it is faded, the priest shall quarantine him for seven days. If it should spread over the skin, the priest shall declare him unclean. It is diseased. But, if the spot has stayed where it was and has not spread, it is merely the scar of the ulcer and the priest will declare the person as clean. If someone had a burn on the skin, and the raw spot left by the burn becomes reddish-white or white, the priest shall examine it. If the hair has turned white on the spot and it goes deeper than the skin, a skin disease has broken out in the burn. The priest will declare him unclean because it is a skin disease.

[1] The quarantine is therefore not to prevent the sufferer from infecting others, but only so that he, through touch, etc., does not make others ritually unclean. Knowing that he is unclean, he will know what to avoid.
[2] This is obviously a less virulent form of skin disease leading to discoloration which disappears in time, though it may reappear and may also break out from time to time which would make him ritually unclean.

But, if the priest finds that there is no white hair on it or that it is no more than skin-deep and that it is fading, the priest shall quarantine him for seven days. He will examine the person on the seventh day and, if it has spread over the skin, the priest will declare him unclean; it is a skin disease. But, if the spot has remained where it was, has not spread over the skin and has faded, it is only a swelling from the burn. The priest will declare the person clean, because it is the scar of the burn. [13:18–28]

111. Skin diseases of head and beard

When a man or woman has a sore on the head or in the beard, the priest will examine the sore. If it is more than skin-deep and the hair in it is yellow and sparse, he will declare the person unclean; it is a scall,[1] a scaly disease of the head or beard. But if the priest finds that the scall is not more than skin-deep, even if the hair in it is not black, the priest shall quarantine the person with scall sores for seven days. On the seventh day the priest will examine the sore again. If the scall has not spread, has no yellow hair in it and is not more than skin-deep, the person shall shave himself but not where the scall is; the priest will put him into quarantine for a further seven days. On the seventh day, the priest shall examine the scall. If the scall has not spread over the skin and is not more than skin deep, the priest shall declare him clean; he shall wash his clothes and he shall be clean. If, however, the scall should spread over the skin once he has been declared clean, the priest shall again examine him. If the scall has spread on the skin, the priest has no need to look for yellow hair. He is unclean. But, if the scall has not changed colour and black hair has grown in it, the scall is healed; he is clean and the priest shall declare him as clean. [13:28–37]

---

[1] The Hebrew word suggests: that which inclines one to scratch or tear away, which is why the *New Revised Standard Version* translates it as an 'itch'.

112. A skin rash and baldness

When a man or woman has spots on their skin of a whitish colour, the priest shall make an examination. If the spots are white and are fading, it is a rash that has broken out on the skin. The person is clean. If a man loses the hair of the crown of his head and becomes bald, he is clean. If he loses his hair off the front of his head and is bald at the forehead, he is clean. If, however, there is a reddish-white sore on his bald crown or bald forehead, it is a disease that is breaking out of those parts. The priest shall examine him and if the sore of the bald spot is reddish-white, similar in appearance to the skin disease on the body, the person is also diseased. He is unclean. The priest shall declare him unclean because of the affliction on his head. [13:38–44]

113. Treatment of those suffering from virulent skin diseases

Anyone with a virulent skin disease, his clothes shall be rent and his hair dishevelled; he shall cover up his upper lip and he shall call out 'unclean, unclean'.[1] So long as the disease persists, such a person will be unclean and, being unclean, he shall live alone, outside the camp. [13:45]

114. Clothing affected by leprosy[2]

If marks of mould are on a cloth of wool or linen fabric, whether in the warp or woof of the linen or the wool, or in leather or

---

[1] This was to warn people against touching him. It is difficult to know whether this treatment was due to fear of physical contagion or ritual uncleanness. As it is the biblical view that 'leprosy' was a punishment from God, there would be no reason for an innocent person to catch the disease. The fact that only unblemished animals could be sacrificed and that priests with physical blemishes could not perform the sacred rites indicates a belief that illness was a judgement from God. As death from internal diseases could not be diagnosed and the death which could result even in early age could not be distinguished from natural dying of old age, it was primarily skin diseases which were seen to make one's disfavour with God manifest. Even today, one hears people say of skin spots, etc., 'The evil is coming out.' Skin ailments are also the most common of psychosomatic illnesses.

[2] The original Hebrew text suggests that the clothing can suffer from the same skin disease as humans. Modern translations such as the *Jerusalem Bible* and

anything made of leather; if the spot on the cloth or the leather, in the warp or the woof of the fabric or in any leather article, is greenish or reddish in colour, it is a contamination and it is to be shown to the priest. The priest after examining it shall put the article in quarantine for seven days. He shall examine the outbreak on the seventh day. If the outbreak has spread over the cloth, in the warp or woof, or in the leather – for whatever function the leather is used – it is malignant and is unclean. The cloth, whether warp or woof in wool or linen, or any leather article – in which the outbreak is found – shall be burnt, for it is mouldy; it shall be consumed in fire. But, if the priest sees that the outbreak has not spread in the cloth, whether in its warp or woof, or in any leather article, the priest shall order them to wash the article in which the outbreak appears and put it under quarantine for a further seven days. And if, after the article has been washed, the priest sees that the outbreak has not changed colour and that it has not spread, it is still unclean. It shall be consumed in fire, whether the diseased spot is on the inside or the outside. But if the priest sees that the outbreak, after it has been washed, has faded, he shall tear it out of the cloth, in warp or woof, or the leather; if it should re-occur in the cloth – whether in warp or woof – or in any leather article, it is breaking out again; the affected article shall be burnt in fire. If, however, the outbreak disappears from the cloth – warp or woof – or from the leather article that has been washed, it shall be washed again and shall be clean. Such is the law for contaminations of cloth, woollen or linen, either in warp or woof, or of leather articles for declaring them clean or unclean. [13:47–59]

115. The purification of the sufferer
The LORD instructed Moses: This is the law for the sufferer from a skin disease on the day of his purification. He shall be brought to the priest who will meet him outside the camp. The priest shall

---

The Revised English Bible prefer to consider the infections as mould, caused by a fungus.

examine him and if he has recovered from the skin disease, the priest shall order, for the man who is to be purified, two clean birds who are alive and cedar wood and scarlet wool and hyssop. The priest will instruct that one of the birds be killed over an earthen vessel containing water fresh from a spring, **so that its blood flows into it.** He shall then take the living bird, the cedar wood, the scarlet wool and the hyssop and dip them and the living bird in the blood of the bird slaughtered over the spring water. He shall then sprinkle the one who is to be purified from his skin disease seven times and declare him clean. He shall then let the living bird go free into the open field.[1] He that is to be purified shall wash his clothes and shave off all his hair and bathe himself and he shall be clean. Then he shall come into the camp but not go into his tent for seven days.[2] On the seventh day he shall shave all his hair off his head, his beard and eyebrows – even all his hair; he shall wash his clothes, he shall bathe his body in water and he shall be clean. [14:1–9]

116. The sacrifices of the one who is purified

On the eighth day, he shall take two unblemished he-lambs and one unblemished yearling ewe-lamb and three tenths of an *ephah* (bushel) of fine flour for a meal offering mixed in oil and one *log* (pint) of oil. The priest that purified him shall place the man who is to be purified and those things before the LORD at the entrance to the Tent of Meeting. The priest shall take one of the he-lambs and offer it up for a guilt offering with the *log* of oil and elevate them for an offering of elevation before the LORD. He shall slaugh-

---

[1] The symbolic meaning for the items is unclear, except for the two birds. The dead one represents his diseased person which has died and the living bird, which is allowed to fly free, the sufferer who has been reborn a free man, able to rejoin the community. The scarlet wool could represent the expiation of his sins which brought on the disease, cf. *Isaiah* 1:18: "Though your skins be as scarlet, they shall be white as snow, though they be red like crimson, they shall be as wool.' Hyssop leaves were used in purification rites. Cedar is a most durable wood and could suggest the ability to withstand the corruption of the disease.

[2] Why this interim period was necessary is not explained.

ter the he-lamb in the place where they slaughter the sin offering and the whole-offering in the designated place of the Sanctuary; as the sin offering belongs to the priest, so does the guilt offering. It is most holy.[1] The priest shall take some of the blood of the guilt offering and put it on the lobe of the right ear of him that is to be purified and also upon the thumb of his right hand and upon the big toe of his right foot.[2] The priest shall then take some of the *log* of oil and pour it into the palm of his own left hand; he shall dip his right finger in the oil and shall sprinkle the oil seven times before the LORD. Some of the oil left in his hand, he shall put upon the lobe of his right ear of him that is to be purified and on the thumb of his right hand and on the big toe of his right foot on **the place that he put** the blood of the guilt offering. The rest of the oil that is in the priest's palm, he shall put upon the head of him that is to be purified. Thus shall the priest make expiation for him before the LORD. The priest shall then offer the sin offering – the yearling ewe-lamb – and make expiation for the one being purified of his uncleanness; afterwards he shall slaughter the whole-offering; the priest shall offer the whole-offering – the second he-lamb – and the meal offering upon the altar: so shall the priest make expiation for him and he shall be clean. [14:1–20]

117. If the one who is to be purified is poor

If he be poor and cannot afford so much, then he shall bring one he-lamb for a guilt offering to be elevated in expiation for him, one tenth of an *ephah* of fine flour mixed with oil for a meal offering and a *log* of oil; also two turtledoves or two pigeons, such as he can afford. One shall be a sin offering and the other a whole-offering. On the eighth day, he shall bring them for his purification to the

---

[1] The repeated declaration that it 'is most holy' is an affirmation that the priest's right to a benefit from the sacrifices is as much part of the ordained holy rite, as when the entire sacrifice goes up in smoke before God.
[2] The ceremony is identical to that of the consecration of the priests [8:23]. The symbolism has been interpreted to mean that a person should hear what the LORD says, do what he says and walk in his ways.

priest, to the entrance of the Tent of Meeting before the LORD. The priest shall take the lamb for the guilt offering, and the *log* of oil, and the priest shall elevate them as an offering of elevation before the LORD. He shall then slaughter the lamb for the guilt offering; the priest shall take some of the blood from the guilt offering and put it on the lobe of the right ear of him that is to be purified . . . to make expiation for him before the LORD.[1] He shall then offer one of the turtledoves or pigeons, whatever one he could afford, the one for a sin offering and the other for a whole-offering, together with the meal offering; the priest shall make expiation for him who is to be purified before the LORD. This is the ritual for him who has been afflicted by a virulent skin disease and cannot afford what is required for his purification. [14:21–32]

118. Laws regarding a 'leprous' house[2]

The LORD instructed Moses and Aaron: when you come into the Land of Canaan which I give you for a possession, and I inflict a 'leprous' infection on a house in the land you possess, he who owns the house shall come and tell the priest, "It appears that my house is infected." The priest shall command that the house be emptied before the priest goes to examine it, so that all its contents need not become unclean. After this the priest shall go in the house to examine it. If, when he examines the outbreak, it is in the walls of the house and consists of yellowish or reddish streaks that appear to have penetrated the walls, he shall leave the house through its entrance and order the house closed for seven days. On the seventh day the priest shall return for a further examination. If the outbreak is spreading throughout the walls of the house, the priest shall order that they remove the infected stones and throw them away in a dump outside the town. He shall order that the house be scraped inside all around and they shall

---

[1] Verses 25–29 repeats the procedure of the anointment of the parts of the body with blood and oil, for which reason I have omitted them, except for the opening and closing words.

[2] Is this due to dry rot or other forms of fungi or chemical incrustations on the walls?

throw away the plaster which has been scraped off into a dump outside the town. They shall replace these stones with others and replaster the house.[1] But, if there is a further outbreak after the infected stones have been removed and the house has been scraped and replastered, the priest shall come in to examine it and if the outbreak has again occurred, its corrosive growth is in the house – it is unclean. He shall order that the house be demolished – its stones and timber and all its plaster and all of it shall be hauled to the dump outside the town.[2] Whoever enters the house while it is closed up shall be unclean until evening. Whoever sleeps in the house must wash his clothes; likewise whoever eats in the house. If, however, the priest comes and on re-examination sees that the outbreak has not spread after the house was plastered, the priest shall declare it clean because the infection has cleared. [14:33–49]

119. The purification of the house

He shall take two birds, cedar wood, scarlet wool and hyssop to purify the house. He shall kill one of the birds over an earthen vessel over spring water; he shall take the cedar wood, the hyssop, the scarlet wool and the living bird and dip them into the blood of the slaughtered bird diluted by the spring water and shall sprinkle the house seven times; he shall purify the house with the blood of the bird diluted by the spring water, and with the living bird, cedar wood, hyssop and the scarlet wool. But he shall let the living bird free outside the town into the open fields. So shall he make expiation for the house, and it shall be clean.[3] [14:50–53]

[1] All the plaster was removed because the fungus could be lying dormant throughout the house.
[2] This may have been a more practical measure than it appears. Were it an attached hut, the rot could spread to other houses in the row. Were it detached, it still may have been a waste to replace the house piecemeal without any guarantee that the source had been eliminated.
[3] The ritual for the purification of the house is identical to that of an afflicted individual. Why does a house require expiation? The fact that the altar also has to be expiated [*Exodus* 29:36] suggests that the intent is only ritual purification.

Conclusion

Such are the laws for every type of virulent skin disease and scall, for mould in clothes and fungus in houses, for a swelling or a scab or spot – to decide whether they are to be declared unclean or clean. This is the law in regard to diseases of the skin **and other surfaces.** [14:54–57]

120. Impurity caused by secretions

The LORD instructed Moses and Aaron: Tell the Israelites: Whenever a man has a discharge from his member,[1] he becomes unclean. The uncleanness from his discharge has this consequence whether the discharge is voluntary or **his member** is stopped up so he cannot have a discharge – his uncleanness means: any bedding on which the one suffering the discharge lies shall be unclean; anything on which he sits shall be unclean. Whoever touches his bedding shall wash his clothes and bathe and be unclean until evening. He who sits on anything on which a person with a discharge has sat shall wash his clothes, bathe in water and be unclean until evening. If one with a discharge spits on one who is clean, the latter shall wash his clothes, bathe in water and be unclean until evening. He who touches the body of him who is suffering from the discharge shall wash his clothes and bathe himself and be unclean until evening. Anything used as a saddle by the sufferer from the discharge shall be unclean. Whoever touches anything which was under him shall be unclean until the evening, whoever carries such things shall wash his clothes and bathe himself and be unclean until evening. Whomsoever the sufferer from the discharge touches, without having first rinsed his hands in water, he shall wash his clothes and bathe himself and be unclean until evening. Earthen vessels which he who suffers from the discharge touches shall be broken –wooden vessels shall be rinsed in water. [15:1–12]

[1] Hebrew says, 'his flesh', a euphemism for penis.

121. The ritual for purification

When he who suffered discharge becomes clean of his discharge, he shall himself count seven days from his cleansing, wash his clothes, shall bathe himself in spring water and become clean. On the eighth day he shall take for himself two turtledoves or two pigeons and come before the LORD into the entrance of the Tent of Meeting and give them to the priest; the priest shall offer them, one for a sin offering and the other for a whole-offering and the priest shall make expiation for him before the LORD for his discharge.[1] [15:13–15]

122. Uncleanness from sexual activity

When a man has an ejaculation, he shall bathe his entire body in water and be unclean until evening. Every piece of clothing and leather on which there is semen shall be washed with water and be unclean until evening. The same applies to the woman with whom the man has lain and has had an ejaculation – both of them shall bathe and be unclean until evening.[2] [15:16–18]

123. Uncleanness from menstruation

When a woman has a discharge and the discharge is blood, she shall remain in her impurity for seven days. Whoever touches her shall be unclean until evening. Everything that she lies on during her period of impurity and everything she sits on shall be unclean. Whoever touches her bedding shall wash his clothes and bathe himself and be unclean until evening. Whoever touches anything that she sits on shall wash his clothes and bathe himself and be unclean until evening. Whether it is the bedding or anything on which she has sat, on touching it, he shall be unclean until evening. If a man lies with her, her period of impurity

---

[1] Any known physical ailment is seen as punishment from the LORD, requiring a sin offering.
[2] The practical consequences of these ritual laws of cleanliness was that the Israelites and their descendants would be constantly washing and bathing themselves. This may well have been the reason they did not suffer the ravages of the black plague to the same extent as did their non-Jewish neighbours.

extends to him – he shall be unclean for seven days, and every bed on which he lies down shall be unclean. [15:19–24]

124. Uncleanness from irregular or lengthy menstruation
When a woman has a discharge of blood for many days not at the normal time of her impurity, or if she has discharges beyond the time of her impurity, she shall be unclean, as she was at the time of her impurity, as long as her discharge lasts. She is unclean. Every bed on which she lies during the days of her discharge shall be like the bed during her regular period of impurity, and likewise, with every object on which she sits. Whoever touches these things shall be unclean. He shall wash his clothes, bathe and be unclean until evening. But once she is cleansed of her discharge, she shall count for herself seven days and after that she shall be clean. On the eighth day she shall take for herself two turtledoves or two pigeons and bring them to the priest to the entrance of the Tent of Meeting. The priest shall offer one for a sin offering and the other for a whole-offering and the priest shall make expiation for her before the LORD for the discharge of her uncleanness. [15:19–30]

Concluding admonition
So shall you put the Israelites on guard against their uncleanness, so that they die not[1] as a consequence of their uncleanness when they defile the Tabernacle which is among them. This is the law for him who has a chronic discharge, who has an ejaculation by which he becomes unclean, and for her who is in menstrual infirmity and concerning anyone, male or female, who has a discharge and a man who lies with an unclean woman. [15:31–33]

---

[1] They will not die because of their uncleanness unless they participate in the religious rites while unclean.

The Day of Atonement: Yom Kippur

Introduction

125. The LORD spoke to Moses after the death of the two sons of Aaron when they approached the LORD and died. The LORD instructed Moses: Say to Aaron your brother that he is not to come **except on the Day of Atonement** into the Sanctuary behind the curtain, before the seat of Judgement[1] - which is on the Ark – so that he does not die,[2] for there I make my presence known in a cloud over the Seat of Judgement. [16:1–3]

126. How Aaron is to enter the inner-sanctum

This is how Aaron shall come into the Sanctuary – with a bull of the herd for a sin offering and a ram for a whole-offering. He shall put on the sacred linen tunic with linen-under garments on his body. He shall put a linen waistband around his waist and wear a linen head-dress – these are the sacred vestments. He shall bathe himself in water and dress himself with them. He shall take from the congregation of the Israelites two he-goats for a sin offering and one ram for a whole-offering. Aaron shall present a bull of the sin offering[3] which is for himself and make expiation for himself and his household. Then he shall take the two he-goats and place them before the LORD at the door of the Tent of Meeting. Aaron shall place lots upon the two goats – one lot **to designate the he-goat** for the LORD and the other for Azazel[4] into the

---

[1] When the text gives instructions on how it was to be crafted, it was translated as the 'cover plate' of the Ark. Now that it becomes the place where God sits between the two cherubs, it is translated as the Seat of Judgement. See **35** on p. 15.

[2] Does this suggest that the crime of Nadab and Abihu was an unauthorised visit into the Holy of Holies. The ancient rabbis believed that the two sons sought to usurp their father's authority, for it was only the High Priest who could appear before the LORD. Their deaths were a cautionary tale and the reason for restricting the High Priest's entry into the Holy of Holies only once a year – on the Day of Atonement.

[3] Aaron's own contribution, see earlier.

[4] An obscure Hebrew term. The Septuagint translates it as 'the one to be sent away'.

wilderness. Aaron shall present the goat which the lot marked for the LORD and offer it for a sin offering. But the goat which the lot marked for Azazel shall be kept alive before the LORD to make expiation over it to send it to Azazel in the wilderness. Aaron shall then present the bull of the sin offering which is for himself and for his household. He shall then slaughter the bull of the sin offering which is for himself; he shall take a fire pan full of glowing coals scooped from the Altar before the LORD and two handfuls of fine ground sweet incense and bring this behind the curtain. He shall place the incense upon the fire before the LORD so that a cloud of incense may cover the Seat of Judgement, which is upon the Testimony [the Two Tablets of the Ten Commandments] so that he does not die.[1] He shall take the blood of the bull and sprinkle it with his finger on the eastern side of the Seat of Judgement. He shall sprinkle the blood before the Seat of Judgement with his finger seven times. Then he shall slaughter the he-goat of the sin offering for the people and bring its blood behind the curtain and do with its blood as he did with the bull's blood – sprinkling it on the Seat of Judgement and before the Seat of Judgement. He shall make expiation for the Sanctuary because of the impurity of the Israelites and because of their transgressions – for all their sins; he shall do the same for the Tent of Meeting, which abides with them in the midst of their impurity. When he enters to make expiation in the Holy of Holies, nobody else shall be in the Tent of Meeting until he comes out. When he has made expiation for himself, for his household and for the entire community of Israel, he shall go out to the altar that is before the LORD and expiate it **for all his transgressions and those of his household and the Israelites**; he shall take some of the blood of the bull and of the goat and put it on all the horns of the altar; the remainder of the blood he shall sprinkle on it with his finger

---

[1] The cloud of incense prevents Aaron from seeing the LORD which would lead to his death because of the conviction that no one could see the face of the LORD and live.

seven times. Thus shall he purify it from the impurity of the Israelites and sanctify it. [16:1–19]

127. The rite of the scapegoat

When he has finished making expiation for the Sanctuary and the Tent of Meeting and the altar he shall bring near the live goat. Aaron shall lay both his hands on the head of the live goat and confess over it all the iniquities and transgressions of the Israelites – all their sins – and shall place them, **through the laying of hands,** upon the head of the goat; he shall send it off to the wilderness by a man standing ready. The goat shall carry the burden of all their sins into an inaccessible land and it shall be set free in the wilderness.[1] [16:20–22]

128. The continuation of the sacrificial rite

Aaron shall then go into the Tent of Meeting, take off his linen vestments, which he had put on when he went into the Sanctuary and shall leave them there. He shall bathe himself in a holy chamber, put on his vestments, come out and offer his whole-offering and the people's whole-offering and make expiation for himself and for the people. He shall turn the fat of the sin offering into smoke on the altar. [Also, he that had let the Azazel goat free shall wash his clothes and bathe himself and afterwards come back into the camp.] As for the bull of the sin offering and the goat of the sin offering whose blood was brought into the inner Sanctuary to make expiation – they shall be carried outside the camp. They shall burn with fire their hides, their flesh and their dung.[2] He who burned them shall wash his clothes, bathe himself in water and afterwards return to the camp. [16:21–28]

---

[1] Interestingly, the scapegoat was not killed but might have trouble fending for itself. Later custom was to throw it off a precipice, perhaps because the land was too greatly populated to enable the escort of the goat to an inaccessible place.

[2] Sin offerings of individuals could be eaten by the priests, but sin offerings of the High Priest or of the whole community could not ever be eaten.

129. An eternal statute

It shall be before you a law forever: on the tenth day of the seventh month, you shall humble[1] yourselves and do no manner of work, neither the native citizen, nor the alien who lives among you. Because on this day expiation shall be made for you to purify you from all your sins. You shall be pure before the LORD. It shall be a Sabbath of Sabbaths for you. You shall humble yourselves. It is a law for all times. The priest who has been anointed and ordained to serve as priest in his father's place shall make expiation and put on the linen vestments, even the sacred garments; he shall make expiation for the holy Sanctuary; he shall make expiation for the Tent of Meeting and for the altar and he shall make expiation for the priests and for the community. This shall be an eternal statute for you to make expiation[2] for the Israelites for all their sins once a year. And it was done as the LORD commanded Moses. [16:29–34]

130. Eating meat is forbidden except as part of a sacrificial offering

The LORD said to Moses: Tell Aaron, his sons and all the Israelites: This is what the LORD has commanded: If any Israelite slaughters an ox, lamb or goat, in or out of the camp, who has not presented it at the Tent of Meeting to offer it up as an offering to the LORD before the Tabernacle of the LORD, bloodguilt shall

---

[1] The Hebrew root *Ah'nah* has several meanings, all to do with being brought down, and afflicted. The word *anee*, meaning poor man, comes from the same root. It has always been assumed that it is a command to practise self-denial, i.e. no food, no washing, and no sex. Many translations render: 'you shall fast.' The definitive Old Testament Lexicon of Brown, Driver and Biggs assumes that this is the word's intention here, and the even more famous Gesenius Concordance concludes that, while there is no explicit command to fast in the Five Books of Moses, 'self-affliction' can only mean fasting.

[2] As the traditional translation for *K'pair* is atonement, not expiation, the most solemn day in the Jewish calendar is known as the Day of Atonement, in Hebrew, *Yom Kippur*.

be imputed to that man.[1] He has shed blood and that man shall be cut off[2] from his people. **This law is** so that the Israelites will bring the sacrifices which they would sacrifice in the open field to the LORD, to the entrance of the Tent of Meeting, to the priest, and sacrifice them up as sacrifices of peace offerings to the LORD. The priest shall sprinkle the blood on the altar of the LORD at the entrance of the Tent of Meeting and turn the fat into smoke as a pleasing fragrance to the LORD. They shall no longer offer their sacrifices to the satyrs[3] after whom they go astray. This shall be to them a law for all time, throughout the ages. You will say to them: Whosoever of the Israelites or of resident aliens offers up a whole-offering or sacrifice without bringing it to the entrance of the Tent of Meeting to sacrifice it to the LORD – that man shall be cut off from his people. [17:1–9]

131. Blood is not to be eaten
Whosoever of the Israelites or of the resident aliens consume blood of any kind – I will set my face against that person who consumes blood and will cut him off from his people. For the life of flesh is in the blood, and I have granted its use to you for

[1] Meat was a luxury so that a celebratory feast was normally the motive for eating it. It would have been common for the entrails to be offered up to the patron god or goddess. It could also be an occasion for boisterous and sexually illicit behaviour. The demand that meat should be eaten only by the central place of Israelite worship was intended to avoid these excesses and also to bring benefits to the priests. The deterrent was that, as blood was the life force which only belonged to God, he who shed blood without the sanction of God's priests was committing a great offence. This law was totally impractical as so few Israelites would be living near the centre of the sacrificial cult. The seer/prophet Samuel knew no such law as he offered sacrifices in different places.
[2] The consequences of being cut off are not known. It could have been ostracism from participation in the religious rites, or excommunication which would require the co-operation of the community, or that God would punish the offender in his own time.
[3] Modern translations of the Hebrew *s'eerim'* varies from satyrs to goat-demons or just demons. The worship of satyrs could have been imported to Canaan by the Philistines whose origin is believed to be Crete and who first invaded lower Egypt in the 12th century BCE. Sacrifices to the wild and playful satyrs could have been the occasion for sex orgies, but this is only a popular speculation based on ancient mythology.

making expiation for your lives on the altar; it is the blood as the source of life that achieves expiation. Therefore I said to the Israelites: None of your people or the resident aliens shall consume blood.[1] Whosoever of the Israelites or the resident aliens hunts down an animal or bird that is permitted to be eaten, he shall drain out its blood and cover it with earth. For the life of all flesh – its blood is its **source of** life. Therefore, I say to the Israelites: You shall not consume the blood of any flesh – for the life of all flesh is its blood. Anyone who consumes it shall be cut off. [17:10–13]

132. He who eats animals that have died or been torn by beasts

Any person, citizen or alien, who eats a dead animal or one who has been torn by beasts shall wash his clothes and bathe in water. He shall be unclean until evening and then will be clean. If he does not wash **his clothes** and body, he shall bear his guilt. [17:14–15]

Forbidden sexual relationships and Molech worship

Introduction

The LORD said to Moses: Instruct the Israelites **in my name**: I am the LORD your God. You shall not copy the practices of the land of Egypt in which you lived, nor those of the land of Canaan to which I am taking you, nor shall you follow their laws. You shall act according to my decrees and keep my laws faithfully; I am the LORD your God. Observe my laws and decrees – for by doing them a man finds life. I am the LORD. [18:1–5]

133. Forbidden sexual relationships

None of you shall approach anyone of his own flesh for illicit

---

[1] "Every living creature will be yours for food ... Only do not eat flesh while it has its life – its blood – in it. *Genesis 9:3,4 People's Bible* p. 18. LORD

sexual relations[1] I am the LORD. You shall not bring shame on your fathers by seducing your mother – she is your mother! You shall not lie with her. You shall not seduce your step-mother – it is to disgrace your father. You shall not seduce your sister, whether your father's daughter or your mother's daughter, whether she was born in the same house or elsewhere – you shall not seduce her. You shall not seduce your son's daughter or your daughter's daughter, for in shaming them you shame yourself. You will not seduce the daughter of your father's wife, who was born into your father's household – she is your **half**-sister – do not seduce her. You shall not seduce your father's sister – she is your own father's flesh **and blood.** You shall not seduce your mother's sister because she is your mother's flesh **and blood.** Do not bring shame on your father's brother by seducing his wife – she is your aunt. Do not seduce your daughter-in-law – she is your son's wife; do not bring shame upon her. Do not seduce your sister-in-law – to bring shame upon your brother. You shall not seduce a woman and her daughter, nor shall you marry her son's daughter or her daughter's daughter to reveal their shame. They are of your flesh **and blood** – it is depravity. You shall not marry your wife's sister to make her a rival wife by lying with her during her sister's lifetime.[2] You shall not approach to lie with a woman during her period of menstrual uncleanness. You shall not bed your neighbour's wife, to defile yourself with her.

134. Sacrifices to Molech, bestiality and homosexuality forbidden

You shall not sacrifice your children to Molech[3] , thus profaning the name of God: I am the LORD. You shall not lie with a man

---

[1] Literally, 'do not uncover the nakedness.' It is used both in the context of sexual intercourse and bringing shame upon a person. Some translate literally, 'intercourse', others 'carnal relations'. I vary the translation according to the context, i.e., seduce, shame, illicit relationships.

[2] This was the situation of Jacob who was married to two sisters, Rachel and Leah. It is ironic that eight of the twelve tribes of Israel are the descendants of two rival wives.

[3] A god of Phoenician origin worshipped by the Canaanites.

as you lie with a woman. It is detestable. Do not lie with any beast and defile yourself by doing so. Nor shall a woman stand before a beast to mate with it: it is a perversion. [18:6–23]

Concluding admonition

Do not defile yourself in any of these ways, for by doing these things the nations that I am driving out before you defiled themselves. Because the land is defiled, I will punish it for its iniquity so that the land will vomit out its inhabitants. You, however, shall keep my laws and decrees and not commit any of these detestable practices – neither the natives nor resident aliens; for those detestable practices were committed by the land's inhabitants before you which defiled the land. So let not the land vomit you out also, if you defile it, as it vomited out the nations that came before you. All who do these detestable things shall be cut off from their people.[1] You shall keep my warning against performing any of these detestable customs which were done before you. Do not be defiled by them. I am the LORD your God. [18:24–29]

Holiness and the imitation of God

135. Introduction and basic moral laws

The LORD spoke to Moses: instruct the entire community of Israelites, say to them **in my name**:

You shall be holy for I, the LORD your God, am holy. You shall each revere his mother and father.[2] You shall observe my Sabbaths.[3] I am the LORD your God. Do not turn to idols or make molten gods for yourselves: I am the LORD your God. When you offer a sacrifice of peace offering to the LORD, sacrifice it properly so that it may be accepted. On the day of the sacrifice, you shall eat it or on the day after, but what remains on the third day

---

[1] Here the term 'cut off,' means in most of these offences the death penalty.
[2] Parents fulfil the function of God in passing on their moral teachings.
[3] The Sabbath observance is *imitatio dei* because humans are to rest as God did from the labours of creation on the seventh day.

must be consumed by fire. It is offensive to eat it on the third day; it shall not be acceptable. Whoever eats it shall bear his guilt, for he has profaned what is sacred to the LORD; and that person shall be cut off from his people. [19:1–8]

136. Obligations to the poor

When you reap the harvest of your land, you shall not reap up to the edges of the field, or gather the gleanings of your harvest. You shall not strip your vineyard bare nor pick up the fallen grapes. You shall leave them for the poor and the stranger. I am the LORD your God. [19:9–10]

137. The obligation to be honest

You shall not steal. You shall not act deceitfully or falsely with one another. You shall not swear falsely in my name **to support your lying claim**, thus profaning the name of your God: I am the LORD. You shall not exploit nor rob your neighbour. You shall not keep your workers' wages overnight until morning, **but you shall pay him at the completion of his day's labour because he lives from hand to mouth.** [19:11–13]

138. Respecting the dignity of the disadvantaged

You shall not taunt the deaf by **hurling insults at him which he cannot hear** or put an obstacle before the blind. You shall be in fear of your God **who takes their side:** I am the LORD. [19:14]

139. Honesty in the administration of justice

You shall not pervert justice by favouring the poor or by showing deference to the powerful. You shall administer justice to your kinsmen with total integrity. [19:15]

140. Love your neighbour even if you 'hate' him

You shall not go up and down spreading mischief among your people. You shall not stand idly by when your neighbour's life is in jeopardy. I am the LORD. You shall not nurse hatred for your kinsfolk. You shall reprove **and warn** your neighbour **against any**

evil action so that you do not share in his guilt. You shall not take vengeance or bear any grudge against your fellow-countrymen, but you shall love your neighbour as yourself:[1] I am the LORD. [19:15–18]

Diverse Laws

141. Laws against 'unnatural' mixtures

You shall keep my laws. You shall not let your cattle breed with a different kind. You shall not sow your field with two kinds of seed; nor shall you put on clothes made of two different materials.[2] [19:19]

142. Punishment for lying with a betrothed female slave

Whoever beds down a woman slave who has not been redeemed or given her freedom, who is betrothed to a man – there shall be a penalty but they shall not be executed for adultery, because she was not a free woman.[3] **In addition**, he shall bring his guilt offering to the LORD to the entrance of the Tent of Meeting – **nothing less than** a ram for the guilt offering. The priest shall

---

[1] This passage has been woefully misunderstood, probably because of Jesus being quoted by Matthew [5:43–44]: "You have heard that it was said, 'You shall love your neighbour and hate your enemy, but I say, 'love your enemies'..." This is a distortion of the command which Jesus may be correcting and even expanding. From the preceding commandment to hate your kinsfolk, it is apparent that this applies to all your neighbours, whether or not you like them. What is significant is that there is the Hebrew preposition 'to' before 'your neighbour'. This suggests that the golden rule is not to love your neighbour as yourself, which would be unnatural, but to respect what appertains to your neighbour be it his dignity or property, i.e. love what is your neighbour's as much as what is your own. I was toying with changing the translation to reflect this, but have decided to bow to tradition and maintain my integrity by use of this footnote.

[2] The law is explicitly stated in *Deuteronomy 22:11* as wool and linen.

[3] This is an unusual case. Being betrothed or married makes a woman her husband's property. Adultery is a capital offence. Here, however, she is also her master's property. Leniency is therefore shown to both of them. Because she could not resist his advances, she is not executed and, as she is not executed, nor is he. The penalty may have been a fine paid to the woman's fiance.

make expiation for him with the ram of the guilt offering before the LORD for the transgression he has committed and it will be forgiven him. [19:20–22]

143. Diverse laws:
first fruits, divination, shaving, self-mutilation for the dead, harlotry,
keeping the Sabbath, raising the dead

- When you come into the land and you have planted all sorts of trees for produce, you shall consider the fruit as forbidden – for three years it shall be forbidden for you – not to be eaten. In the fourth year, all of their fruit shall be sacred for giving joyous thanks to the LORD. In the fifth year you shall eat its fruit that its yield to you will be increased: I am the LORD your God.
- You shall not eat anything with its blood.
- You shall not practise divination nor witchcraft.
- **In bereavement** do not clip the hair at the temples or trim the edges of your beard. Do not make gashes in your bodies for the dead or cut any markings on you. I am the LORD.
- Do not degrade your daughter by making her into a harlot, lest the land be prostituted and the land become full of depravity.
- You shall observe my Sabbaths and revere my Sanctuary: I am the LORD.
- Do not turn to ghosts and do not enquire of familiar spirits **by going to fortunetellers**, to be defiled by them: I am the LORD your God. [19:23–31]

144. Respect for the aged and the alien, and honest weights

- You shall rise up before the aged and defer to the old. Thus shall you revere your God: I am the LORD.
- When an alien dwells with you in your land, you shall not oppress him but you shall love him as yourself. The alien who resides with you shall be treated as one of your citizens, for **remember that** you were aliens in the land of Egypt: I am the LORD your God.

- You shall not falsify measures of length, weight or capacity. You shall have honest balances, honest weights, a true *ephah* and a true *hin*: I am the LORD your God who brought you out of the land of Egypt. You shall observe all my laws and decrees and do them: I am the LORD. [19:32–37]

145. Execution for sacrificing children to Molech

The LORD spoke to Moses: You shall admonish the Israelites: Whosoever of the Israelites or resident aliens in Israel that offers his children to Molech, he shall most certainly be executed. He shall be stoned by the people of the land. I will set my face against that man and cut him off from among his people because he has given a child of his to Molech to defile my holy place and to profane my holy name.[1] If the people of the land turn a blind eye to that man **who gives his offering to Molech and does not put him to death,** I will set my face **not only** against that man and his household to cut him off but **also** everyone from the community who has been disloyal with him to go astray after Molech **by not punishing him.** [20:1–6]

146. Punishment for those who turn to ghosts

The person who turns to ghosts and enquires of familiar spirits **by going to fortune tellers** – I will set my face against that person and will cut him off from among his people. [20:6]

147. Punishments for cursing one's parents and sexual immorality

Sanctify yourselves and be holy for I am the LORD your God. Observe my laws and do them: I am the LORD who sanctifies you.

---

[1] This verse 20:4 raises problems: 1) Why does God need to set his face against him, etc. if he is to be stoned? Possible answer: the act was committed secretly or the community have supported the sacrifice or have taken no action. The next verse suggests this. 2) How can this crime defile God's holy place and profane his holy name unless the perpetrators are claiming that the LORD as the supreme God over all gods has no objections to such worship of a local and inferior deity?

Everyone that curses his father or mother shall most certainly be put to death – for he has cursed his father or mother: he has brought his death upon himself. The man who commits adultery with a married woman, his neighbour's wife – they shall most certainly die – the adulterer and the adulteress. The man who lies with his step-mother – who has shamed his father – they shall both die. They have brought their deaths upon themselves. The man who lies with his daughter-in-law – they shall both surely die. They have acted perversely. They have brought their death upon themselves. A man who lies with men as he would with a woman; they have done a detestable thing. They shall die, they have brought their deaths upon themselves. If a man takes[1] a woman and her mother – it is a depraved act – they shall be executed by fire:[2] both he and them; so that there should be no depravity among you. If a man lies with an animal, he shall surely die and the animal shall be slaughtered. If a woman approaches an animal to have intercourse with it – they shall both die. They have brought these deaths upon themselves. A man who takes his half-sister, his father's daughter, or his mother's daughter and sees her nakedness and she sees his, it is a disgrace. They shall be excommunicated in the presence of the community. He has uncovered the nakedness of his sister, he shall suffer for his sin. If a man lies with a woman while she is menstruating – thus uncovering her nakedness; he has bared her fountain and her flow of blood; both of them shall be cut off from among their people. You shall not lie with your father's sister or your mother's sister for that is laying bare one's own flesh. They shall suffer for their sin. The man who lies with his uncle's wife, he has shamed his uncle; they shall suffer for their sin; they shall die childless. If a man takes his brother's wife, it

---

[1] Takes, usually in the case of 'taking a woman', means 'to make her his wife.' It is hard to understand how a person could marry against the law and custom of the community especially if he knows the nature of the punishment.

[2] Only in two instances is the execution specified as to be by burning, see **151** p. 81.

is a profanity. He has shamed his brother; they shall die childless. [20:7–21]

148. Concluding admonition

You shall observe all my laws and decrees and do them, so that the land to which I am bringing you to settle in does not vomit you out. You shall not walk in accordance to the laws of the nation that I am driving out before you. It is because they did these things that I detested them. Therefore, I said to you: You shall inherit their land for I am giving it to you as a possession – a land flowing with milk and honey. I am the LORD your God who has distinguished you from among the peoples. You shall therefore make a distinction between clean and unclean beasts and between unclean and clean birds and you not shall make yourselves repulsive through the eating of beasts or birds and whatever crawls upon the ground which I have determined is unclean for you. For you shall be holy to me because I am the LORD, I am holy, and I have distinguished you from among the nations to be mine. [20:22–26]

149. Punishment for those who raise the dead

A man or a woman who raises ghosts or spirits shall surely die. You shall stone them to death. They have brought their deaths upon themselves. [20:27]

Rules for priests and the Sanctuary

150. Restrictions for priests:
Touching the dead, forbidden marriages

The LORD said to Moses: So shall you instruct the priests, the sons of Aaron: None of them shall defile himself by contact with the dead among his kinsmen, except for those close to him – his mother, his father, his son, daughter and his brother; also for his sister who is a virgin and still close to him and has no husband – for her he may defile himself [but for a sister who is **not just engaged**, but married and no longer part of her family, he shall not make himself unclean; this would be to profane himself.][1] **In bereavement** they shall not shave their head, cut the side growths of their beards or gash their bodies. They shall be holy unto their God and not profane the name of their God for as their offering is the burnt offerings of the LORD, the food of their God – they must be holy. They shall not marry a woman defiled by prostitution or a divorced woman for they are holy to their God. You must guard their holiness because they offer up the food of their God. They shall be holy to you, because I the LORD your God, who sanctifies you, am holy. [21:1–8]

151. A priest's daughter who prostitutes herself
A priest's daughter who profanes herself through prostitution profanes her father – she shall be consumed in fire. [21:9]

152. The restrictions on the High Priest
The priest who is exalted above his fellows, **the High Priest**, over whose head the oil of anointment has been poured and who has been ordained to wear the vestments – shall not dishevel his hair, nor rend his clothes **while mourning.** He shall not have contact with any dead body – he shall not be defiled even for his father or mother. He shall not even leave the Sanctuary **by joining their funeral procession** nor profane the Sanctuary of his God for upon him rests the consecration of the anointing oil of his God: I am the LORD. He shall marry a woman who is still a virgin. A widow or a divorcee or a woman defiled by prostitution – he shall not marry any of these, but he shall only marry a virgin of his own kin. He shall not defile his descendants among his kin because I am the LORD who sanctifies him. [21:10–15]

---

[1] A woman once married became the possession of her husband, and was seen to have broken her filial ties to her prior family. The parenthetical phrase is the best translation I could invent from an obscure text.

153. A priest with physical defects

The LORD spoke to Moses: So must you instruct Aaron: No descendants of yours throughout the generations who has a defect shall offer up the food of his God. No one with any defect shall make an offering: a man who is blind or lame or who has a mutilated face or a disproportionate size limb; or a man with a broken leg or broken arm; or a hunchback or dwarf; or who has a growth in his eye or scabs or scurvy or crushed testes. No one of the descendants of Aaron the priest who has a defect shall come forward to sacrifice the fire offerings of the LORD. He has a defect. He shall not come forward to offer up the food of his God.[1] Nonetheless, he may partake of the most holy and less holy food of his God. But he shall not approach the curtain nor the altar because he has a defect. He shall not profane my holy places because I the LORD have sanctified them. So did Moses instruct Aaron and his sons and all the Israelites. [21:16–24]

154. Separation from holy food when impure

The LORD spoke to Moses: Instruct Aaron and his sons to keep apart in **their time of impurity** from the holy food of the Israelites which they have consecrated to me, so as not to profane my holy name: I am the LORD. Say to them: Throughout your generations, any one of your descendants who partakes in the holy donations which the Israelites have consecrated to the LORD while he is in a state of uncleanness, that person shall be cut off from before me: I am the LORD. None of Aaron's descendants who has a skin disease or has a bodily discharge shall partake of the holy food until he is clean. **This applies** to anyone who becomes unclean by contact with the dead or who has an ejaculation or who touches a creeping creature which renders him unclean, or by contact with a person who makes him unclean through whatever

---

[1] While the rejection of priests with defects to offer up sacrifices is unjust, we should remember that a sacrificial cult seeks to impress worshippers with a sense of God's majesty and power. In this primitive context, it would appear inappropriate for disabled or disfigured priests to be offering up food to God. It would also distract the worshipper from focussing attention on the divine rite.

source of his uncleanness. The person who has contact with any of these shall be unclean until evening and shall not eat the holy food until he has bathed himself in water. When the sun has set, he shall be clean and afterwards he shall partake in the holy offerings for that is his bread. He shall not defile himself by eating animals who die a natural death or those who have been mauled by wild beasts: I am the LORD. They shall keep my charge, lest they incur guilt and die because of it if they profane **the holy food:** I am the LORD who sanctifies them. [22:1–9]

155. Laity may not eat the holy food
No layman shall eat the holy food; no bound or hired servant of a priest may eat anything holy. But if a priest has acquired a slave by purchase he may eat of it just as the members born into his household may eat of his food. If a priest's daughter marries a layman, she shall not eat of the sacred offerings. But if the priest's daughter becomes a widow or divorced without child and she comes back to her father's house as in her youth she shall eat of her father's food, but no layman shall partake of it.[1] [22:10–13]

156. A layman who eats holy food
If a man unintentionally eats holy food, he shall return the food to the priest and **as a penalty** add on a fifth of its value. But, the priests shall not permit the Israelites to profane the holy food that they have dedicated to the LORD so that they bear the guilt of their transgression by eating their holy food: I am the LORD who sanctifies them. [22:14–16]

157. Sacrifices must be without blemish
The LORD spoke to Moses: Instruct Aaron and his sons and all the Israelites: Whosoever of the house of Israel or of the resident aliens in Israel approaches to present a whole-offering to the LORD, whether to fulfil his vow or as a free-will sacrifice, to be

[1] Once she had a child, it was the custom that her husband's family would maintain her.

acceptable it must be a male without blemish from cattle or sheep or goats. You shall not offer any animal with a blemish because it will not be accepted in your favour. When a man offers from the herd or the flock a peace offering to the LORD as fulfilment of a vow or as a free-will sacrifice, it must, to be acceptable, be totally unblemished – without any defects: anything blind, injured, mutilated, with a sore or scab or scurvy; you shall not offer such to the LORD. None such as these shall you give as offerings by fire on the altar to the LORD. You may, however, present as a free will offering an ox or a sheep with a limb disproportionately long or short, but for the fulfilment of a vow it cannot be accepted. You shall not offer any animal to the LORD whose testes are bruised, crushed, torn or cut. You shall not practise such **mutilations** in your land, nor shall you accept such **animals** even from a foreigner for offerings as food for your God – because they are mutilated, it is as if they were naturally blemished They shall not be accepted in your favour. [22:17–26]

158. Be humane when offering sacrifices
The LORD instructed Moses: when an ox or a sheep or a goat is born, it shall stay seven days with its mother. From the eighth day onward it shall be acceptable as an offering by fire to the LORD. But, no animal, whether cow or lamb, shall be slaughtered on the same day with its young. When you sacrifice an offering of thanksgiving to the LORD, sacrifice it wholeheartedly so that it may be accepted in your favour. On the same day it shall be eaten. Nothing from it shall remain until the morning: I am the LORD. [22:27–30]

Concluding charge
You shall keep my commandments to do them: I am the LORD. You shall not profane my holy name so that I may be sanctified among the Israelites: I am the LORD who sanctifies you, who brought you out of the land of Egypt to be your God: I am the LORD. [22:31–33]

The Festivals of the LORD

159. Introduction and the Sabbath
The LORD instructed Moses: Instruct the Israelites: These are the appointed festivals of the LORD that you shall proclaim as sacred occasions – my appointed festivals. On six days work may be done; but the seventh day is a Sabbath of complete rest, a sacred occasion on which you shall do no kind of work; it shall be a Sabbath to the LORD throughout your settlements. These are the appointed festivals of the LORD, the sacred occasions which you shall celebrate at the time appointed for them. [23:1–4]

160. The Passover
In the first month, on the fourteenth day of the month at twilight, there shall be a Passover offering to the LORD. On the fifteenth day of this month is the Festival of Unleavened Bread to the LORD. For seven days you shall eat unleavened bread. On the first day, you shall celebrate a sacred occasion. You shall do no work of any kind. Seven days you shall make offerings by fire to the LORD. The seventh day is a sacred occasion; you shall do no work of any kind. [23:5–8]

161. The counting of seven weeks
The LORD spoke to Moses: Instruct the Israelites: when you enter the land that I am giving you and reap its harvest, you shall bring the sheaf[1] of the first fruits of your harvest to the priest; he shall elevate the sheaf before the LORD for acceptance on your behalf; the priest shall elevate it on the day after the Sabbath. On the day you elevate the sheaf you shall offer an unblemished year-old lamb for a whole-offering to the LORD. The accompanying meal offering shall be two tenths of an ephah of fine flour mixed with oil – an offering to go up in flames to the LORD to make a pleasing fragrance. The accompanying libation shall be wine – a quarter of a *hin*. You shall not eat bread, parched

---

[1] In Hebrew, *omer*.

grain or fresh grain until that very day before making this offering to your God. This is an everlasting law throughout your generations in all your settlements. [23:9–14]

162. Pentecost – the Feast of Weeks

You shall count from the day after the Sabbath,[1] the day on which you give the sheaf for the offer of elevation, seven full weeks.[2] From the day after the Sabbath, you shall count fifty days and you shall offer a new meal offering to the LORD. You shall bring from your land two loaves for an elevation **offering**, each consisting of two tenths of an ephah. They shall be made with fine flour and shall be baked with leaven: these are first fruits for the LORD. You shall offer with the bread seven unblemished year-old lambs, one bull and two rams – a whole-offering to the LORD with their meal offering and their libations. When they go up in flames they shall make a pleasing fragrance to the LORD. You shall prepare one he-goat for the sin offering and two year-old lambs for the peace offering. The priest will elevate them with the bread of the first fruits as an offer of elevation before the LORD, together with the lambs. They shall be holy to the LORD **and set aside** for the priests. On that self-same day you shall proclaim a sacred occasion for yourselves. You shall not do any kind of work. It is an everlasting law in all your settlements throughout your generations. [23:15–22]

[1] The meaning of Sabbath – day of rest – in this context was a source for great debate between the Sadducees (the conservative party led by the priests) and the Pharisees (the party dominated by laymen who believed in an Oral Law given to Moses). This allowed the latter to change the Mosaic Law through creative interpretation. The Sadducees took the view that the counting of seven weeks should begin on the day following the Sabbath which fell during the seven days of Passover, which would mean that the fiftieth day – Pentecost – would always fall on a Sunday. The Pharisees interpreted 'Sabbath' to mean the day of rest, namely the first day of Passover, in which no work was permitted, which meant that Pentecost would occur during different days of the week. Interestingly, the Christians took the view of the Sadducees. Thus Christian Pentecost always falls on Sunday.
[2] The word for week is **Sabbath**, which indicates that the day of rest gave the structure to the seven-day period.

163. Part of the harvest belongs to the poor
When you reap the harvest of your land, you shall not reap the edges of your field, nor shall you collect the gleanings of your harvest. You shall leave them for the poor and the stranger: I am the LORD your God. [23:22]

164. A memorial for the blowing of trumpets[1]
The LORD spoke to Moses: Instruct the Israelites: In the seventh month, on the first day of the month, you shall have a day of rest, a day of remembrance by the blowing of trumpets – a sacred occasion. You shall not do any kind of work on that day and you shall offer up an offering of fire to the LORD. [23:23–26]

165. The Day of Expiation
The LORD instructed Moses: But on the tenth day of the seventh month is the Day of Expiation; it shall be a sacred occasion for you and you shall humble yourselves and bring an offering of fire to the LORD. On that self-same day, you shall not do any kind of work, for it is a day of expiation for you to make before the LORD your God. Any person who does not humble himself on that day shall be cut off from his people. Furthermore, any person who does any kind of work on that day – that life shall be destroyed from among his people. You shall do no kind of work. It is an everlasting law throughout your generations in all your settlements. It shall be for you a Sabbath of complete rest; you shall humble yourselves; from the evening of the ninth day until the evening **of the tenth day,** you shall keep your Sabbath.[2] [23:27–32]

166. The Feast of Booths [Tabernacles]
The LORD spoke to Moses: Instruct the Israelites: On the fifteenth

[1] More about this day which became known as the New Year in Jewish tradition, in *Numbers* 29. See *Numbers 10:1–10* in *Moses, Man of God* p. 180 for the use of trumpets throughout the year.
[2] Here Sabbath means a holy day, not just the seventh day, adding weight to the Pharasaic view that the first day of Passover could be considered as a Sabbath.

day of this self-same seventh month is the Feast of Booths – seven days for the LORD. The first day shall be a sacred occasion. You shall do no kind of work. For the seven days, you shall make offerings by fire to the LORD. On the eighth day, you shall observe a sacred occasion and bring an offering by fire to the LORD; it is a solemn gathering; you shall do no kind of work. These are the festivals of the LORD which you shall proclaim as sacred occasions to bring offerings by fire to the LORD – a whole-offering, and a meal offering, sacrifices and libations – on each day, that which is appropriate. These are in addition to that **which is to be offered** on the Sabbaths of the LORD, and in addition to your donations, the offerings to fulfil your vows, and all your free will offerings which you give to the LORD. But on the fifteenth day of the seventh month, when you have gathered in the produce of the land, you shall celebrate the festival of the LORD for seven days. The first day is a day of rest and the eighth day is a day of rest. You shall take for yourselves for the first day **of the festival** the fruit of a pleasant tree, branches of palm trees and branches of thick-leaved trees and willows of the brook;[1] you shall rejoice before the LORD your God for seven days. You shall celebrate it as a festival seven days each year. It is an everlasting law; you shall celebrate it on the seventh month. You shall dwell in booths[2] for seven days – all those born in Israel shall dwell in booths, so that your future generations may remember that I made the Israelites dwell in booths when I brought them out of the land of Egypt:[3] I am the LORD your God. So Moses

[1] To this very day, on the first day of Tabernacles, traditional Jewish men take a citron (the fruit of a pleasant tree), a palm branch to which are tied on one side myrtle branches (thick-leaved trees) and willow branches on the other side. During the synagogue morning service on the first day of Tabernacles, the citron is held in the left hand, the palm branch and accessories are held in the right hand touching the citron, and are pointed and shaken to the north, east, south and west, heavenward and to the ground. This ceremony takes place during the recitation of psalms of thanksgiving.

[2] Hence the name Tabernacles given to the festival.

[3] This is a strange explanation, as it is more likely that the Israelites dwelt in tents. Could it be that the environs of the Sanctuary became so crowded during this important harvest festival, that booths were needed to house all the

did instruct the Israelites in regard to the Festivals of the LORD. [23:33–44]

167. The Menorah and the Showbread
The LORD spoke to Moses: Instruct the Israelites: They shall bring to you pure olive oil prepared for the light to keep the lamps burning constantly. Aaron shall kindle it from evening to morning outside the curtain of the inner sanctum in the Tent of Meeting. It shall be an everlasting law throughout your generations. He shall see that the lamps on the gold Menorah are continually kept alight before the LORD. You shall also take fine flour with which you are to bake twelve loaves: one loaf shall be made with two tenths of an *ephah*. You shall place them in two rows – six in each row – on the pure **golden** table before the LORD. You shall put fine frankincense on each row so that it becomes the bread of remembrance **before the** LORD **for the Israelites,** even as the offerings made by fire to the LORD. He shall lay them out on every Sabbath day before the LORD – in perpetuity – as **a sign of** an everlasting covenant of the Israelites **with the** LORD. They shall belong to Aaron and his sons who shall eat them in the Sanctuary because it is the holiest of the offerings to Him – even of the offerings by fire to the LORD. It is an everlasting law. [24:1–9]

168. Stoning for blaspheming the name of the Lord
The son of an Israelite woman and an Egyptian man went out among the Israelites. The son of the Israelite woman quarrelled with an Israelite in the camp, **during which time** he blasphemed the Name. They brought him to Moses **for judgement.** The name of his mother was Shelomith the daughter of Dibri of the Danites. They locked him in a guard house until the LORD himself would declare **the punishment.** The LORD spoke to Moses: Bring out the man who blasphemed outside the camp, and let all those who

---

pilgrims? The Mosaic Law does not miss an opportunity to remind the Israelites of the fact that the LORD in all his power redeemed them from Egypt and therefore deserved their obedience and loyalty. It is for this reason that each of the nature festivals is given an historical foundation.

heard him **blaspheme** place their hands on his head and then let the entire community stone him. So shall you say to the Israelites: Whoever blasphemes his God shall bear the burden of his sin. He who thus pronounces the name of the LORD shall certainly be put to death; the entire community shall stone him – the alien as well as the native who blasphemes the name of the LORD shall be put to death. [24:10–16]

169. The law of reparations

When a man strikes a fatal blow against any human, he shall most certainly die. Should he kill an animal, he shall make reparations: a life for a life. If a man inflicts a disability on his fellow, so shall it be done to him: a wound for a wound, an eye for an eye, a tooth for a tooth; as he has inflicted a disability on a person, so shall it be done to him.[1] Whoever strikes down an animal shall make reparations but whoever kills a man must surely die. There shall be one and the same law for you – the alien will be treated no differently than the citizen because I am the LORD your God. So did Moses instruct the Israelites. They took the blasphemer outside the camp and stoned him.[2] So did the Israelites do as the LORD had commanded Moses. [24:17–23]

170. The Sabbatical year

The LORD spoke to Moses on Mount Sinai: Instruct the Israelites: When you enter the land which I am giving to you, the land shall have its rest – a Sabbath to the LORD. You shall sow your

[1] This appears to suggest that *lex talionis* was to be taken quite literally except for the fact that previously we are told that when a man kills an animal, he shall make reparations: "A life for a life." As it is obvious that the meaning is not to give the owner another slain beast, it must mean another animal of equal worth or exact monetary compensation. So did the ancient rabbis assume that to give a victim who was blinded the eye of his attacker could not have been the intention. What the victim was entitled to was the value of the loss of an eye or his sight. This is not revenge but justice. A human life, however, cannot be given a monetary value and, therefore, the killer must die.
[2] The sandwiching of the laws of reparation in the tale of blasphemy seems to indicate that only the death of the sinner can be an adequate reparation to God for his blasphemy.

field for six years and you shall prune your vineyard and gather
in its fruits for six years. But the seventh year shall be a Sabbath
of total rest for the land – a Sabbath to the LORD. You shall
neither sow your field nor prune your vineyard. That of your
harvest which grows of itself – you shall not reap; the grapes of
your undressed vine you shall not gather; it shall be a Sabbatical
year for the LORD. The land's Sabbath shall provide you with
food – for you, for your servant and your maid, for your hired
hand and for the resident alien, for your cattle and for the animals
who are in your land – all its yield will be for food. [25:1–7]

171. The Jubilee year

You shall count seven Sabbaths of years, seven times seven years.
The period **you are counting** for yourselves is seven Sabbaths of
seven years – forty-nine years. Then on the tenth day of the
seventh month, that is on the Day of Expiation, you shall blow
trumpets throughout the land to declare the fiftieth year sacred
and to proclaim liberty throughout the land to all the inhabitants.
It shall be a Jubilee[1] for you. Every man **who has sold his land
to pay his debts** shall return to his inherited possessions, and
every man **who has sold himself into slavery** shall return to his
family **a free man.** The fiftieth year is your Jubilee: You shall
neither sow nor reap that which grows of itself, nor gather the
grapes of the undressed vines. It is a Jubilee; it shall be holy[2] for
you. You shall eat the yield of the field **without collecting for
storage.** In this year of the Jubilee you shall allow every man to
return to his lot of land. If you sell anything to your fellow **as
land for tenancy** or if you buy something from your fellow, you
shall not deceive one another. According to the number of years

[1] Hebrew: *Yovel* which means ram's horn which was used as a trumpet. 'Y' in
Hebrew becomes 'J' in English, hence: Jubilee.
[2] That is, special, set aside. The land belongs to God and he looks after it and
its produce is for all to take. Every Israelite's land was given to him by God
when they entered the Promised Land at the time of Joshua. Thus, all contracts
which entitled the land to others were cancelled; so too as all humans are
God's servants, all Israelite slaves regain their freedom from human masters.

after the Jubilee **and the number of years until the next Jubilee**, and the number of years **remaining** of harvest shall you pay the price for purchase from your neighbour; and according to the number of years of harvests shall he set the price for you – an increase of price for more years and a decrease in price for less years; it is in relationship to the number of harvests that he is selling to you. You shall not wrong one another but you shall fear your God for I am the LORD your God. Therefore, obey my laws and accept my decrees; you will then dwell in security in the land. The land will yield its fruit and you shall eat until you are satisfied and dwell there in security. [25:8–19]

172. The Lord will provide before the Sabbatical year

If you think, 'What are we to eat in the seventh year as we are not sowing or harvesting the produce?' will I not command my blessing to descend upon you in the sixth year so that the earth yields enough produce for three years. You shall sow in the eighth year and eat of the stored produce until the ninth year when the harvest comes in: you shall eat of the produce, which has been stored.[1] [25:20–22]

173. The laws of redemption of land

The land shall not be sold freehold because it is I who own the land: You are only strangers and sojourners with me. In all the land which you possess, you shall ensure the redemption of land. If your kinsmen has become destitute and must sell some of his property, his closest relation shall redeem that which his kinsman has sold. If a man has no one **among his** kinsmen able to redeem it – if his fortunes take a turn for the better and he has enough to redeem it, then he should count the years during which the

[1] The lawgiver does not explain how the Israelites were to cope with a Jubilee following a Sabbatical, where they would need to have such a bumper crop in the forty-eighth year to provide for four years. We are told previously that God will cause the land in the Jubilee year to give a sufficient yield so that all the Israelites would be able to feed themselves hand to mouth without storing anything.

property had been sold, and return to the purchaser the difference between his profit from the crops of the field and the money he paid for it. He shall then repossess it. If, however, he does not have the means to repossess it, then that which has been sold shall remain with the purchaser until the Jubilee year. In the Jubilee year it shall be released and he shall return to his former possession. When a person sells a town house in a walled city, he may redeem it within a whole year after he sold it. His right of repossession extends for a full year. If the house is not redeemed within the year period, then the house in the walled city shall be a secure possession forever to him who purchased it, throughout his generations. It does not revert to its former owner in the Jubilee.[1] The houses in villages, however, which have no protective walls about them are considered as the country fields. They may be redeemed and then be released in the Jubilee year **and return to their original owner.**[2] The towns belonging to the Levites and the houses in the towns they possess, the Levites may redeem at any time. If a person purchases a house from the Levites, the house sold in the walled city shall become released in the Jubilee and return **to its original owner;** for the houses in the Levitical towns are their possessions among the Israelites. Furthermore, the fields of the pasture-lands surrounding their towns may never be sold, for it is their everlasting inheritance. [25:23–34]

174. The support of the poor

If your kinsman becomes impoverished and destitute, you shall support him: as a stranger and temporary resident shall he live with you.[3] Take no interest nor seek to make a profit from him but be in fear of your God so that your kinsmen may live **in**

---

[1] Is the reasoning here that this property is a luxury because it was not necessary for an income? In Biblical days homes were not purchased as investments for resale or rental income.

[2] This was due to the fact that the house was indispensable as living accommodation to the farmer who went out to work his field.

[3] This would indicate that strangers could expect hospitality from the prosperous citizens.

dignity with you. You shall not give him money for interest nor sell him his food for profit: I am the LORD your God who brought you up from the land of Egypt to grant you the land of Canaan in order to be your God. [25:35–38]

175. Laws for an Israelite tenured servant
If your kinsman becomes destitute and sells himself to you, you shall not make him serve you as a slave but as a hired servant or a temporary settler shall he be treated by you. He shall work for you until the Jubilee. Then he shall go out free from you, he and his children with him, and shall return to his own fold and to his paternal inheritance, because they are my servants whom I brought out of the land of Egypt; they shall not be sold as slaves. You shall not be a severe master, but shall act in fear of God. [25:39–43]

176. Foreign slaves are permitted
As for male and female slaves, whom you may own, it is from your neighbouring nations that you may purchase male and female slaves. Also, you may buy the children of the strangers who live among you as well as other members of their families who are with you who were born in your land; they may become your possessions. Of these you may take slaves who will remain yours forever, but as for your kinsmen, the Israelites, you shall not behave as severe masters, one over the other. [25:44–46]

177. Israelite slaves
Should an alien or temporary settler with you become very rich whereas a kinsman of yours **living** near him becomes poor, so that he sells himself to the alien or the temporary resident who lives among you, or, for that matter into the household of the alien's family – he may be redeemed after he is sold. One of his relations may redeem him – his uncle or his cousin – or any of the close kinsmen of his family may redeem him, or if he becomes rich, he may redeem himself. He shall reckon the price with him

who purchased him on the basis of the time from the year of his sale until the Jubilee year: the price of the sale shall be according to the number of years equal to the wages of a hire servant engaged by him **for those years.** If there are a large number of remaining years **to the Jubilee**, he may pay him back out of the money with which he was purchased, but if only a few years remain to the Jubilee year, he shall negotiate with him; on the basis of his years **with him**, shall he pay the price for his redemption. He shall be treated as a tenured servant all the years he is with him. He shall not be subjected to severe treatment before you **as he is an Israelite, one of your kinsmen.** If he cannot be redeemed in any of these ways, he shall go free in the Jubilee year, he and his children, for to me **alone** are the Israelites servants: they are my servants whom I brought out of the land of Egypt: I am the LORD your God. [25:47–54]

178. Worship the Lord alone

You shall make no idols, nor shall you set up a graven image or a pillar nor shall you put in any place in your land a figured statue to bow down to them, because I am the LORD your God. You shall observe my Sabbaths and have reverence for my Sanctuary: I am the LORD. [26;1–2][1]

179. Voluntary donations to the Sanctuary based on an individual's capital worth[2]

The LORD spoke to Moses: instruct the Israelites: When a man makes an extraordinary vow to make a donation to the treasury of the Sanctuary based on the value of the lives of his household, the assessment shall be made **according to this method:**

---

[1] Chapter 26:3–46 is a general exhortation and admonition very similar to those recorded in *Moses, Man of God.* As it does not contain any laws, it may be found in the appendix.

[2] The psychological motive for this voluntary poll tax might be anxiety for the continuation of his future prosperity. God needed to be placated to prevent the end of his good fortune. According to Biblical theology, God has personal control over each individual's destiny.

Male: age twenty to sixty: 50 shekels [of silver by the Sanctuary standard weight]
Female: age twenty to sixty: 30 shekels
Male: age five to twenty: 20 shekels
Female: age five to twenty: 10 shekels
Male: age one month to five years: 5 shekels
Female: age one month to five years: 3 shekels
Male: age sixty and older: 15 shekels
Female: age sixty and older: 10 shekels.

However, if he cannot afford this assessment, then he shall appear before the priest who shall assess him. According to the means of the person who made the vow, shall he be assessed.[1] [27:1–8]

180. Other donations to the Sanctuary

If a person **vows the donation of** a particular animal, any such that is appropriate to offer to the LORD he shall not alter or change it either for an animal of greater or lesser value, but if he does decide to change, both animals shall be holy **property.** If it be an unclean animal which cannot be offered as a sacrifice to the LORD, the animal shall be set before the priest who shall determine its value; however high or low its value, the value shall be as determined by the priest. If he decides that he would rather redeem it, he shall add a fifth of its value to the valuation. If a man shall dedicate his house as holy for the LORD, the priest shall assess its value according to its good or bad features; the value determined by the priest shall be valid. But, if he that dedicated it as holy would redeem his house, he shall add a fifth to its monetary value and it shall be his. If a man shall dedicate as holy for the LORD part of a field which he has inherited, the value shall be determined by an assessment of the yield of its produce based on the amount of seed sown: a *homer*[2] of barley seed shall be valued at fifty shekels. If he dedicates the field at the conclusion

---

[1] Even a man of modest means could be sufficiently grateful and pious to wish to guarantee or increase his future prosperity by making such a significant vow.
[2] Six bushels.

of the Jubilee year, then this is the means for assessing its value.
But, if he dedicates his field **some years** after the Jubilee, then the
priest shall assess the value in proportion to the number of years
until the Jubilee year and its assessment shall be so reduced.
Whenever the man who dedicated the field wishes to redeem it,
he shall add to its assessed value a fifth part of it, and it shall be
his. If he does not redeem the field, if he has sold the field to
another person, it shall not be capable of redemption; when the
field becomes released, it shall be the LORD's holy **property**, as a
dedicated field. It shall become the possession of the priest. If he
dedicates to the LORD a field which he has purchased – not a
field he inherited – then the priest shall assess for him its value
until the Jubilee year. Then he shall pay its price on the day that
it has been valued as a holy property of the **Lord's**. In the Jubilee
year, the field shall return to him from whom it was bought – to
him to whom the land belongs because it is his inheritance. All
the assessments shall be according to the standard of the Sanctuary shekel: twenty gerahs to the shekel. No one can dedicate the
first-born among animals, which already belongs to the LORD, be
it ox or sheep – it is already the LORD's. If it is **a clean animal
which is** unclean **because of a defect**, he shall pay its value according to your assessment of its value and add a fifth to it; or, if it
is not redeemed, it shall be sold according to its assessed value
and the money be given to the Sanctuary.[1] Of course, nothing
which has been irrevocably dedicated by a person to the LORD,
whether a slave or an animal or a field of his inheritance, shall
be sold or redeemed. Every prescribed object is most holy to the
LORD. [27:9–28]

181. A person doomed to die cannot be ransomed
No one who has been doomed to die **because of idolatry, blasphemy or for breaking the LORD's ban on captured property or
any crime subject to the death penalty,** shall be ransomed. He
must surely be put to death. [27:29]

[1] As it could not be used for a sacrifice.

182. The law of tithes

All the tithes[1] of the land, whether seed of the land or the fruit of trees, belongs to the LORD. They are dedicated to the LORD. If a man would redeem any part of his tithes, he must add on a fifth of its value. All the tithes of herds or flocks, whatever animals are counted by the shepherd's staff – a tenth of them shall be dedicated to the LORD. In making the selection, he shall not examine them to see whether they are a better or worse animal, nor **once it has been arbitrarily selected** shall he change it. If he should change it, then both it and the one for which it was changed shall be dedicated; it shall not be redeemed. These are the laws which the LORD commanded Moses for the Israelites on Mount Sinai. [27:30–34]

---

[1] The 10% levy on produce which went to the priests or the poor in different years.

NUMBERS

The descendants of Aaron

These are the descendants of Aaron and Moses at the time that the LORD spoke to Moses on Mount Sinai. These are the names of the sons of Aaron: Nadab, the first-born, Abihu, Eleazar and Ithamar. These are the names of the sons of Aaron, the very priests who were anointed, whom he ordained to serve in the priestly office. Now, Nadab and Abihu died in the presence of the LORD when they offered alien fire before the LORD in the wilderness of Sinai. They had no sons. Eleazar and Ithamar served in the priestly office under the supervision of Aaron their father.[1] [3:1–4]

183. The Levites are to serve Aaron and the priests

The LORD instructed Moses: summon the tribe of Levi. Make them stand before Aaron the priest and let them serve him. They shall obey him and serve the whole community before the Tent of Meeting to maintain the Tabernacle. They shall look after all the objects in the Tent of Meeting, to serve the Israelites by serving the needs of the Tabernacle. You shall assign the Levites to Aaron and his descendants. They, from among the Israelites, are to be totally assigned to him. You shall appoint Aaron and his sons, and they shall keep guard over their priesthood. The layman who seeks to usurp them shall die. [3:5–10]

184. The Levites replace the first-born

The LORD spoke to Moses: I have taken the Levites from among the Israelites in place of all the first-born that opens the womb

[1] Though the first verse states that this is the record of the descendants of Aaron and Moses, the descendants of the Lawgiver are not given. This could not have been lost on the early scribes and later biblical commentators. Whatever the rationalisation for this omission, I cannot help believing that a political motive is at work here to establish the sole authority of the descendants of Aaron as the LORD's priests and rulers of Israel. The only other possible explanation is that Moses, a 'mystical' figure, had no descendants who were known when this was written.

of the Israelites – **not the first-born but** the Levites shall be mine. **Of course**, all the first-born are mine because, on the day that I struck down all the first-born in the land of Egypt, I dedicated to myself all the first-born in Israel – man and animal.[1] They shall be mine. I am the LORD. [3:11–13]

Genealogy of the Levites

The LORD instructed Moses in the wilderness of Sinai: Number the sons of Levi according to their father's clans by families. Every male from a month old and over shall be counted. Moses counted them just as the LORD had instructed him. These are the names of the sons of Levi: Gershon, Kohath and Merari. These are the names of the sons of Gershon – by clan: Libni and Shimei; the sons of Kohath – by clan: Amram, Izhar, Hebron and Uzziel; the sons of Merari – by clan: Mahli and Mushi. These are the clans of the Levites named after their fathers. [3:14–20]

185. The number and responsibilities of the Gershonites

From Gershon are the clans of the Libnites and Shimeites – these are the clans of the Gershonites. According to their census, based on the numbering of all males from the age of one month and over – they amounted to 7,500. The Gershonite clans shall encamp on the western side of the Tabernacle. The chieftain of the clans of Gershon shall be Eliasaph ben Lael. The responsibilities of the Gershonites in the Tent of Meeting were the Tabernacle, the Tent itself, its covering, the screen for the entrance to the Tent of Meeting, the curtains of the court, the screen for the entrance of the court by the Tabernacle and round about the altar with its cords – all the service pertaining to these. [3:21–26]

---

[1] By saving the Israelite first-born during the tenth plague, the slaying of the first-born, he made them his possessions – his servants at his Sanctuary. He, however, decided to make the Levites the servants instead of them. The servants of the LORD are like ministers to the crown, the privileged and ruling class.

186. The number and responsibilities of the Kohathites

From Kohath are the clans of the Amramites, the Izharites, the Hebronites and the Uzzielites – these are the clans of the Kohathites. According to their census based on the number of all males from the age of one month and over – they amounted to 8,600 and were in charge of looking after the Sanctuary. The clans of the Kohathites shall encamp on the southern side of the Tabernacle. The chieftain of the clans of the Kohathites shall be Elizaphan ben Uzziel. Their responsibilities were the maintenance of the Ark, the table, the Menorah, the altars and the Santuary's utensils with which they, **the priests**, officiate, and the screen – all the service pertaining to these. [3:27–31]

187. Eleazar, the priest, in charge of the Levites

Eleazar, the son of Aaron the priest, shall be the head chieftain of all the chieftains of the Levites and be in charge of all those who were looking after the Sanctuary. [3:32]

188. The number and responsibilities of the Merarites

From Merari were the clans of the Mahlites and Mushites – these are the clans of Merari. Their census, based on the number of males from the age of one month and over – they amounted to 6,200. The chieftain of the clans of Merari shall be Zuriel ben Abihail. They shall encamp on the northern side of the Tabernacle. The designated responsibilities of the Merarites shall be the frames of the Tabernacle, its bars, its posts, its sockets, all its accessories – all the service pertaining to these; also the posts of the surrounding court, its sockets, its hooks and bands. [3:32–37]

The encampment of Moses and the descendants of Aaron

Moses[1] and Aaron and his sons, those who have responsibility for the Sanctuary as a duty on behalf of all the Israelites, shall

[1] I find it significant that the sons of Moses are not mentioned here. Were they not part of the 'royal' family? Was it because their mother was a Midianite woman? Moses's grandson is identified as an idolatnous priest. See *People's Bible, The Conquest of Canaan* p. 86–89.

encamp on the eastern side of the Tabernacle, at the front of the Tent of Meeting where the sun rises. Any layman who enters there shall be put to death. The census of the Levites made by Moses and Aaron by order of the LORD according to their clans – all the males from a month old and over – amounted to 22,000. [3:38–39]

189. The census of the Israelite first-born and redemption money

The LORD instructed Moses: count all the male first-born of the Israelites from one month and older and take down their names. You shall make the Levites mine – I am the LORD – in place of the Israelite first-borns, and the cattle of the Levites instead of all the firstlings of the Israelite cattle. Moses counted as the LORD had instructed him – all the first-born of the Israelites. All the Israelite male first-born tallied by their names from a month and older came to 22,273.[1] The LORD instructed Moses: take the Levites instead of all the first-born from the Israelites and the cattle belonging to the Levites instead of **the firstlings of** their cattle – the Levites shall be mine; I am the LORD. For the redemption of the 273 of the first-born of the Israelites which exceed the number of Levites, you shall pay five shekels for each according to the census – the standard weight of the Sanctuary. [The shekel is twenty *gerah*.][2] You shall give the money by which the extra numbers are redeemed to Aaron and his sons. Moses took the redemption money from them that exceeded the number that were redeemed by the Levites **on a one-to-one basis**. From the first-born of the Israelites he collected the money[3] – a 1,365 shekels Sanctuary standard weight. Moses gave the redemption-money to Aaron and his sons according to the LORD's word as the LORD had instructed Moses. [3:40–51]

---

[1] These would have been the first-born of their present generation, not fathers or grandfathers who were the first-born of their parents.

[2] A shekel's weight was ½oz.

[3] Did the last 273 to be counted have to each pay 5 shekels, or was the total sum divided by the 22,273? The verse seems to suggest the fairer method.

190. The work of the Kohathites

The LORD instructed Moses: Muster the males of the Kohathites by their clans of the Levites between the ages of thirty to fifty – the age when men go out to do battle – to minister in the Tent of Meeting. This is the work of the Kohathites in the Tent of Meeting in regard to the sacred things. When the camp is about to move on, Aaron and his sons shall go **into the Tent of Meeting** to remove the curtain of the screen and cover the Ark of the Testimony with it. This they shall in turn cover with fine leather and over that – a blue cloth. Then, they shall put its poles in place. Over the table for the showbread, they shall spread a blue cloth and put on it the dishes, the spoons, the bowls and ladles for pouring; the regular bread shall be on it **as well.** Over them all, they shall spread out a scarlet cloth upon which shall be fine leather covering; then they shall put its poles in place. They shall wrap up with a blue cloth the Menorah which gives light with its lamps, its tongs and trays and all its oil utensils with which it is serviced. They shall place it with all its utensils within a further covering of fine leather **which they will tie up** and connect to a pole **on which it will be carried.** They shall spread a blue cloth over the golden altar **of incense** and over it another covering of fine leather; then they shall put its poles into it **so that it may be carried.** They shall then take all the utensils of service with which they do service in the Sanctuary and wrap them up in a blue cloth and then in a fine leather covering and connect them to a pole **to be carried.**[1] They shall take away the ashes from the altar and cover them with a purple cloth; they shall put on it all its utensils with which they service it: its pans, flesh hooks, shovels and basins – all the altar's utensils; they shall then cover it all with fine leather and then put its poles into it.[2] Now, when Aaron and his sons have finished covering the sacred objects and all the sacred utensils as the camp is about to move on, only then shall

[1] The Ark, the showbread table and the incense altar all had rings on their sides to be carried by poles. The other sacred objects such as the Menorah and its accessories had to be tied up to a pole and carried that way.
[2] The main altar also had pole rings on its sides.

the Kohathites approach to carry them all. They must not touch the holy objects, lest they die. The bearing of those burdens from the Tent of Meeting is the responsibility of the Kohathites. [4:1–15]

191. Eleazar's supervisory role
Under the supervision of Eleazar, son of Aaron the priest, shall be the oil for the light, the sweet incense, the continual meal offering, the anointing oil, in fact all of the Tabernacle, and everything in it – the Sanctuary and all its sacred objects. [4:16]

192. The Kohathites must be protected
The LORD instructed Moses and Aaron: Do not cause the clans of the Kohathites to be cut off from the Levites **by showing disrespect for the sacred objects by touching them.** But act in this way, so that they may live and not die when they approach the most sacred objects. Aaron and his sons shall go in and assign to each and every one what he must do and what he must carry. But they, **the Kohathites,** must not go in to see the holy objects **uncovered** even for a moment, lest they die. [4:17–20]

193. The work of the Gershonites
The LORD instructed Moses: Muster up the males of the Gershonites, also according to their clans between the age of thirty and fifty – the age when men go out to battle – to work in the Tent of Meeting. This is the ministry of the Gershonite clans in serving and in the porterage: they shall carry the curtains of the Tabernacle, the Tent of Meeting, its covering and the leatherskin covering which is over it and the screen to the entrance of the Tent of Meeting; the hangings of the court and the screen to the entrance of the gate of the court which is near the Tabernacle and round about the altar and their cords and all their appurtenances and all that has to be done in regard to them. Under the instruction of Aaron and his sons shall be the service of the Gershonites, in whatever they have to carry and however else they serve – you shall charge them with their tasks of porterage.

This is the ministry of the clans of the Gershonites regarding the Tent of Meeting. They shall be under the supervision of Ithamar, the son of Aaron the priest. [4:21–28]

194. The work of the Merarites
You shall muster up the Merarites by their clans between the ages of thirty and fifty – the age when men go out to battle – to do work in the Tent of Meeting. This is their responsibility in regard to porterage – their service in the Tent of Meeting: the upright frames of the Tabernacle, its bars and posts and sockets; the posts throughout the court, their sockets, their pins and cords and accessories which they require. You shall clearly designate by name the items they need to carry. This is the ministry of the clans of the Merarites regarding the Tent of Meeting, under the supervision of Ithamar, the son of Aaron the priest. [4:29–33][1]

195. The cleansing of the camp
The LORD spoke to Moses: Instruct the Israelites to remove from the camp every sufferer from a virulent skin disease, everyone who has had an excretion and who has been polluted by contact with the dead. This applies to males and females – you shall send them outside the camp so that they do not defile their camp in whose midst I dwell. The Israelites did this and sent them outside the camp – as the LORD had instructed Moses, so did the Israelites. [5:1–4]

196. Restitution for wrongs done to others
The LORD spoke to Moses: Instruct the Israelites: When a man or woman commits any wrong to a human being which is a trespass against the LORD[2] – that person being found guilty shall confess the wrong he has committed: He shall make full restitution of that **property** which is the source of his guilt and add another

---

[1] 4:34–49 records the census of the clans of the Kohathites, the Gershonites and the Merarites and are to be found in the appendix.
[2] When a person is wronged, the LORD is wronged.

fifth of its value **as** a penalty. But if the **wronged** person has no kinsman[1] to whom restitution may be made, the restitution for that which was wrongfully taken shall be given to the LORD's representative – the priest; this in addition to the ram for expiation, by which expiation shall be made for him. Every offering of all that has been dedicated **to the** LORD by the Israelites presented to the priest shall be his, that is to say whatever sacred donation given to **a particular** priest shall be his **alone.** Whatever a person decides to give to a priest **of his choice** shall be his **alone.** [5:5–10]

197. The ritual for the suspected wife.[2]

In the case of any man whose wife may go astray, breaking faith with him in that a man beds her so that she becomes defiled – her husband having no knowledge, it being done clandestinely ... there being no witness, and she not having been caught in a compromising situation; if such a man in a passion of suspicion suspects his wife and **the reality is that she is guilty because** she has become defiled; or in a passion of suspicion suspects his wife and **the reality is that she is not guilty because** she has not become defiled, that man may take his wife to the priest bringing on her account this offering: a *tenth-ephah* of barley flour – no oil to be poured upon it, nor frankincense laid upon it for it is a suspicion offering, an evocatory offering, evocative of a crime. The priest then shall bring her forward, stationing her **in the dock** for the LORD's judgement **according to this procedure:** [5:11–16]

The priest is to take sacral water in an earthen vessel and taking **a few grammes** from the earth on the Tabernacle floor, shall put it into the water. In arraigning the woman before the LORD, the priest is to free the woman's hair **of any clasps,** place upon her palms the evocatory offering – the offering evocative of

---

[1] This is strange for one would think that every Israelite would have some near or distant relation.

[2] I am indebted to Herbert Chanan Brichto for his interpretive translations of this section. The student may wish to consult his monograph, *The Case of the Sotah and Biblical Law,* in the Hebrew Union College Annual (1975).

suspicion – while in the priest's hand is **held** the spell-inducing *marim*[1] water. The priest shall then solemnly charge the woman: "If **you have not committed adultery**: no man has bedded you other than your husband; if you have not strayed into **contracting** defilement – be immune to the effect from this spell-inducing *marim* water. But, see here, if you **have committed adultery**, have strayed from under your husband**'s authority**; if you have become defiled in that any man other than your husband has had sexual intercourse with you;" then shall the priest adjure the woman with the curse-charge; the priest shall say to the woman: "May the LORD make you **an example for** a curse and oath among your kin, as the LORD makes your pubis shrivelled and your belly swollen![2] **Yes**, when this spell-inducing water enters your vitals to swell belly and shrivel pubis!" And the woman is to say: "So be it, so be it." [5:17–22]

The priest is to put this curse into writing and blur it by **dipping it** into the *marim*-water; so that when he gives the woman the spell-inducing *marim*-water may enter her for *marim*.[3] The priest shall take from the woman's hand the suspicion-offering, brandish[4] the offering before the LORD and present it on the altar **as follows**: the priest shall scoop out of the meal offering a token-portion and turn it into smoke on the altar. Only then shall he give her to drink the water. [5:23–26]

When she has been administered the potion, it shall be **as follows**: If she **is guilty, that is** has become defiled, having broken faith with her husband, the spell-inducing water shall enter her for *marim* so that her belly will swell and her pubis shrivel, that woman thus becoming a curse, **an example** among her kin; but, if she **is innocent and** has not defiled herself, she shall be immune **and acquitted** and have issue. [5:27–28]

---

[1] *Marim* is normally translated as bitter but HCB argues for a "magical" content in the brew and so leaves it untranslated.

[2] Ibid. This is figurative. What is intended is 'not the physical atrophying of the procreative organs but a functional paralysis, that is to say, sterility.'

[3] Ibid. As a portent of whether or not she has committed the crime of adultery.

[4] I have always, as do others, translated the Hebrew *Hay-nif* as 'elevate.'

Such is the prescribed ritual for cases of suspicion when a woman contracted to her husband may go astray, contracting defilement; that is, when a man in a passion of suspicion suspects his wife, he is to arraign her before the LORD and the priest is to carry out with her this entire procedure. The man, **the putative adulterer who is unknown,** gets off scot-free,[1] though the woman suffers punishment for her crime. [5:29–31]

198. Laws for the Nazirite

The LORD said to Moses: instruct the Israelites: If a man or woman makes an exceptional vow – the vow of the Nazirite to consecrate himself to the LORD – he shall keep away from wine and liquor; he shall drink no vinegar of wine or liquor, nor shall he drink anything in which grapes have been soaked nor eat grapes, fresh or dried. Throughout the period of his vow as a Nazirite, he shall eat nothing that is made of the grapevine, from the seeds to the skin. Throughout the period of his vow as a Nazirite no razor shall touch his head – until the days in which he consecrated himself to the LORD have been completed, he shall be consecrated and shall let his hair grow long. Throughout the period of his being dedicated to the LORD he shall not go near a corpse. Even if his father, mother, brother or sister dies, he shall not defile himself **on their account** since his consecration to God was an obligation he took upon himself. Throughout his period of consecration, he is holy, **set aside,** to the LORD. If a person suddenly dies by his side and defiles his consecrated head **of hair,** he shall shave his head on the day he becomes clean – he shall shave it on the seventh day. On the eighth day, he shall bring two turtle-doves or two pigeons to the priest, at the entrance of the Tent of

---

[1] That is, no attempt is to be made to find him as there can be no proof that he was the adulterer. Furthermore, if the punishment was sterility, her crime would not be 'proved' until it was known that she could have no further children, in which case her husband could divorce her. What is interesting is that the prescribed ritual does not lead to capital execution, as is the law for adulterers. In this sense it was a safe ritual for a suspected wife. The jealous husband could humiliate his wife but only at the cost of sharing in her humiliation.

Meeting. The priest shall offer one for a sin offering and the other for a whole-offering and make expiation for him for the guilt that he incurred through the dead person. That same day he shall re-consecrate his head; he shall rededicate to the LORD his term as a Nazirite; he shall bring a yearling lamb for a guilt offering. The first period shall be void, since his consecrated head of hair had been defiled. [6:1–12]

199. The concluding ritual for the Nazirite

This is the prescribed ritual for the Nazirites on the day that his period of consecration has been completed. He shall be brought to the entrance of the Tent of Meeting; he will bring his offering to the LORD: one unblemished yearling male lamb for a whole-offering and one unblemished yearling ewe lamb for a sin offering and one unblemished ram for a peace offering and a basket of unleavened cakes of fine flour with oil mixed in and unleavened wafers covered with oil along with their meal offerings and libations.[1] The priest shall offer them to the LORD and present his sin and whole-offerings; he shall present the ram as a peace sacrifice to the LORD with the basket of unleavened cakes; the priest shall also perform its meal offerings and libations. The Nazirite shall shave his consecrated head of hair at the entrance to the Tent of Meeting and shall take the consecrated hair to place on the flames under the peace sacrifice. The priest shall take the shoulder of the boiled ram, one unleavened cake from the basket and one unleavened wafer, and place them into the hands of the Nazirite after he has shaved his consecrated head. The priest shall then elevate them as an offer of elevation before the LORD – this shall be the sacred donation to the priest in addition to the forequarter of the elevation offering and the thigh which is the donation **to the priest.** After that the Nazirite may drink wine. This is the prescribed ritual of the Nazirite because of the vow he has made.

---

[1] These offerings were very costly. This is theologically interesting as it imposes a penalty on a person who sacrifices personal pleasure and appearance – wine and hairdressing – in order to consecrate himself to God. It made it impossible for the poor to become Nazirites and discouraged the prosperous.

Such is the offering he must make to the LORD as a consequence of his Naziriteship, apart from anything else he can afford. He must carry out his vow in full according to the obligations inherent in his **vow of** consecration. [6:13–21]

200. The priestly benediction

The LORD said to Moses: Instruct Aaron and his sons: This is how you are to bless the Israelites. Say to them:

The LORD bless you and watch over you.

The LORD make his face to shine upon you and be gracious to you.[1]

The LORD grant you his favour and grant you peace.

So shall they invoke my name upon the Israelites and I will bless them.[2] [6:22–27]

201. Israelite donations to the Levites for transporting the Tabernacle, etc.

On the day that Moses completed setting up the Tabernacle, he anointed and consecrated it with all its furnishings, and anointed and consecrated the altar with all its utensils offered by the chieftains of Israel, the heads of their ancestral houses – the very same chieftains of the tribes who supervised the census **together with Moses**. They brought their donations before the LORD: six covered wagons and twelve oxen – a wagon from every two **tribal** chieftains and an ox for each one. They presented them before the Tabernacle. The LORD instructed Moses: Accept these from them for use in the service of the Tent of Meeting to give them to the Levites to implement their work obligations **of porterage**. So Moses took the wagons and the oxen and gave them to the Levites; he gave two wagons and four oxen to the Gershonites for their work;

---

[1] I have used the literal translation because of its poetry. Its meaning is: 'The LORD deal kindly and graciously with you.' [The New Jewish Publication Society Translation, 1985]

[2] It is important to take note of the fact that the priests do not bless the Israelites. They only ask God's blessing on them. Only God can bless or be the source of their blessings.

he gave four wagons and eight oxen to the Merarites for their work under the supervision of Ithamar ben Aaron the priest. He gave nothing to the Kohathites because the work of the Sanctuary was their responsibility – they carried it **with the staves** on their shoulders. [7:1–9]

202. Tribal donations for the dedication of the altar

This is what the chieftains offered as dedication donations for the altar when it was anointed. The LORD said to Moses: Each chieftain shall make his offering on the appointed day for the dedication of the altar. Nahshon ben Amminadab of the tribe of Judah made his offering on the first day;[1] on the second day Nethanel ben Zuar, the chieftain of Issachar made his offering; on the third day Eliab ben Helon, chieftain of the Zebulunites; on the fourth day Elizur ben Shedeur, chieftain of the Reubenites; on the fifth day Shelumiel ben Zurishaddai, chieftain of the Simeonites; on the sixth day Eliasaph ben Deuel, chieftain of the Gadites; on the seventh day Elishama ben Ammihud, chieftain of the Ephraimites; on the eighth day Gamaliel ben Pedahzur, chieftain of the Manassehites; on the ninth day Abidan ben Gideoni, chieftain of the Benjaminites; on the tenth day Ahiezer ben Ammishadai, chieftain of the Danites; on the eleventh day Pagiel ben Ochran, chieftain of the Asherites; on the twelfth day Abiaz ben Enan, chieftain of the Naphtalites. The offering **of each** was: one silver bowl weighing 130 shekels,[2] one silver basin weighing 70 shekels[3] by the Sanctuary **standard** weight, both filled with fine flour with oil mixed in for a meal offering, one gold ladle weighing 10 shekels full of incense; one bull from the herd, one ram, one yearling male lamb for a whole-offering; one male goat for a sin

[1] The donation is then described. The description of the identical donations made in subsequent days by each of the tribal chieftains follows. While the repetition may increase the sense of solemnity of each day's ceremony of dedication – to spare the reader the tedium, I have taken the liberty of abbreviating this section by eliminating the repetition.

[2] About 60 ounces.

[3] About 33 ounces.

offering; two oxen, five rams, five he-goats, five yearling male lambs for the sacrifice of the peace offerings. [7:12–83, summarised]

These were the dedication donations for the Altar when it was anointed by the chieftains of the Israelites: 12 silver bowls, 12 silver basins, 12 gold ladles; the silver weight of each bowl was 130 shekels. **The weight** of each basin **was** 70 **shekels.** Total silver of vessels: 2,400 Sanctuary shekels. The 12 golden ladles filled with incense – 10 Sanctuary shekels for each ladle – total gold weight of ladles, 120. Total of herd animals for whole-offerings, 12 bulls, 12 rams, 12 yearling lambs with the appropriate meal offerings; 12 goats for sin offerings. Total of herd animals for sacrifices of peace offerings: 24 bulls, 60 rams, 60 he-goats, 60 yearling lambs – that was the dedication offering for the Altar after its anointing. [7:84–88]

How the Lord spoke to Moses

When Moses went into the Tent of Meeting to speak to him, he heard the voice speaking to him from above the gold cover[1] on the Ark of Testimony, from between the two cherubim. There he spoke to him. [7:89]

203. Kindling the Menorah

The LORD spoke to Moses: Instruct Aaron with these words: When you prepare the lamps, let the seven lamps give light at the front of the Menorah. Aaron did so; he mounted the lamps at the front of the Menorah as the LORD had instructed Moses. Now this is how the Menorah was made: it was made of beaten gold, hammered from the base to the petals **of its branches**. According to the pattern that the LORD had shown Moses, so he had the Menorah made. [8:1–4]

---

[1] The 'mercy-seat', or place of atonement, or seat of judgement.

204. The dedication of the Levites

The LORD instructed Moses: Take the Levites from among the Israelites and purify them. This is how you shall purify them: sprinkle on them the water of purification; let them use a razor over their whole body; let them wash their clothes and so will they be purified. They shall take a bull from the herd together with its meal offering of fine flour mixed in with oil, as well as another bull of the herd for a sin offering. You shall make the Levites approach before the Tent of Meeting; you shall assemble the Israelite community. You shall make the Levites approach before the LORD; the Israelites shall lay their hands on the Levites[1] and Aaron shall dedicate the Levites as **though they were** an offer of elevation offered by the Israelites, to perform **on their behalf** the service of the LORD. The Levites shall then lay their hands on the heads of the bulls: one shall be offered to the LORD as a sin offering and the other as a whole-offering to make expiation for the Levites. Then stand the Levites before Aaron and his sons, giving them as an elevation offering to the LORD. So shall you separate the Levites from among the Israelites – the Levites shall be mine! [8:5–14]

205. The Levites are replacements for the first-born

Thereafter, the Levites will be able to serve in the Tent of Meeting, as you have purified them and dedicated them as an elevation offering. For they are wholly given to me from among the Israelites in replacement of all those who are the first to open the womb – the first-born of all the Israelites. I have taken them for myself, for all the first-born of the Israelites are mine – both man and beast. On the day that I struck down all the first-born in the land of Egypt, I consecrated them to be mine. So I am taking the Levites in place of all the first-born of the Israelites. I have furthermore given the Levites from among the Israelites as a gift to Aaron and his descendants to perform the service of the

[1] Just as a layman would place his hand on an animal sacrifice to identify himself with it as his gift to the LORD.

Israelites in the Tent of Meeting to make expiation for the Israelites, so that no plague may strike the Israelites for coming too close to the Sanctuary. [8:15–19]

So did Moses and Aaron and the entire community of Israelites act towards the Levites. The Israelites dealt with the Levites just as the LORD had instructed Moses. The Levites purified themselves of sin; they washed their clothes and Aaron offered them as a dedicated offering to the LORD. Aaron made expiation for them to purify them. Thereafter the Levites were able to go in to perform their service in the Tent of Meeting under Aaron and his sons. As the LORD had instructed Moses in regard to the Levites, so they did with them. [8:20–22]

206. Age qualification for Levitical labour
The LORD instructed Moses: as pertaining to the Levites: from the age of twenty-five years onwards they shall join the work force in the service of the Tent of Meeting. At the age of fifty, they shall retire from the work force to do no further service. They may assist their kinsmen in the Tent of Meeting by standing guard, but they shall do no work. So shall you deal with the Levites in regard to their duties. [8:23–26]

207. The first observance of Passover after the Exodus
The LORD spoke to Moses in the wilderness of Sinai in the first month of the second year of their coming out of Egypt, instructing him: let the Israelites observe the Passover at its designated time. On the fourteenth day of this month, twilight is the fixed time for performing it in accordance with all its rules and regulations. So Moses instructed the Israelites to perform the Passover. They prepared the paschal lamb in the first month on the fourteenth day at twilight in the wilderness of Sinai; just as the LORD had commanded Moses, so did the Israelites do. [9:1–5]

208. The Passover postponed
There were individuals who had become defiled by a dead human body and were not permitted to participate in the paschal sacrifice

on that day. That day they approached Moses and Aaron; these men complained to them, "Though we have become defiled through a dead human body, why should we be restricted from offering the LORD's offering at the designated time among the Israelites?" Moses replied, "Stay here until I hear the LORD's instruction concerning you." The LORD spoke to Moses: Instruct the Israelites: When any of you or of the generations that follow you are defiled because of touching a dead body, or are on a long journey and would offer a Passover sacrifice to the LORD – he shall offer it in the second month on the fourteenth day at twilight. They shall eat it with unleavened bread and bitter herbs. They shall leave nothing of it until morning; they shall not break a bone of it. According to all the rules of the Passover, they shall observe it. But that person who is ritually clean and is not travelling and does not bother to make Passover – that person shall be cut off from his people, because he did not offer up the LORD's offering at its designated time. That person shall bear the consequences of his sin. [9:6–13]

209. The resident alien may keep the Passover

If a resident alien among you would offer a paschal sacrifice to the LORD, he shall do so according to the rules and regulations of Passover. You shall have one law for the alien and the native-born alike.[1] [9:14]

210. Meal offerings and libations

The LORD spoke to Moses: Instruct the Israelites: When you enter the land I am giving to you to settle in, you will present offerings by fire to the LORD from the herd or from the flock, whether it be a whole-offering or sacrifice, in fulfilment of an exceptional vow or a freewill offering, or at your designated festivals to produce a pleasing fragrance to the LORD: Then shall he who makes an

[1] This is very significant as it indicates that the resident alien is allowed to integrate almost totally into the life of the native Israelites. Problems would appear only in regard to property rights.

offering to the LORD **also** bring a meal offering: a tenth of an *ephah* of fine flour with a quarter of *hin* of oil mixed in; and for the libation for each sheep, you shall offer a quarter of a *hin* of wine with the whole-offering or sacrifice. Or for a ram, you shall make for a meal offering two tenths of an *ephah* of fine flour with a third of a *hin* of oil mixed in; for the libation, you shall offer a third of a *hin* of wine of a pleasing fragrance to the Lord. When you prepare an animal from the herd for a whole-offering or sacrifice in fulfilment of an exceptional vow **such as the vow of the Nazirite** or peace offerings to the LORD, then shall you offer with the bull a meal offering of three tenths of an *ephah* of fine flour with half a *hin* of oil mixed in; for the libation you shall offer half a *hin* of wine, for an offering made by fire of a pleasing fragrance to the LORD. So shall it be done with each ox, or each ram or with any sheep or he-goat, as many as you offer, you shall do this with each one **in regard to meal offerings and libations**, as many as there are. Every native-born **Israelite** shall do this when making an offering by fire, a pleasing fragrance to the LORD. When a stranger lives with you or takes up residence with you throughout the ages and would present an offering by fire of pleasing fragrance to the LORD – as you do, shall he do. **In regard to the entire** community – there shall be one law for you and the resident alien, a perpetual law throughout your generations; as you are, so shall the alien be before the LORD: one law and judgement shall apply to you and the alien who lives with you.[1] [15:1–16]

---

[1] The desire and need to accommodate resident aliens does suggest that there were very many of them, who if not integrated into the community would have been a disruptive force. Were they the original inhabitants of the country? If this law is to be dated at the time of the Second Temple (500 BCE), they may have included the Samaritans, the descendants of the Israelites who lived in the Northern Kingdom, conquered by Sargon in 721 BCE, whose relationship with post-exilic Judaism was very tenuous, and so held in disdain by the Judeans who returned from Babylonia under the Edict of the Persian Emperors.

211. The contribution of the first bread

The LORD spoke to Moses: Instruct the Israelites: when you enter the land to which I am bringing you, and you eat of the bread coming from the land – you shall set some aside as a gift to the LORD from your first batch of dough, a loaf as a contribution. You shall set it aside as a gift just as you set aside a contribution from the threshing floor. You shall make a contribution to the LORD from the first batch of dough throughout all your generations. [15:17–21]

212. Offerings for unintentional sins of the community

If you unintentionally fail to observe any of the commandments which the LORD instructed to Moses – all that the LORD has commanded you through Moses – from the time that the LORD gave the commandment and throughout the generations: if this was done in error without the awareness of the community, the entire community shall present one bull from the herd as a whole-offering of pleasing fragrance to the LORD together with its appropriate meal offering and libation, as well as one he-goat for a sin offering. The priest shall make expiation for the entire community of Israelites; they shall be forgiven for it was done in error, and for their error they brought their offerings, an offering of fire to the LORD and a sin offering before the LORD. So the entire congregation of Israelites and the aliens who reside among them shall be forgiven, because the whole people shared in the error. [15:22–26]

213. Offerings for unintentional sins of the individual

If one individual sins unintentionally, he shall offer a yearling she-goat for a sin offering. The priest shall make expiation for the person who sinned in error before the LORD, making expiation for him so that he may be forgiven. You shall have one law for him who commits a sin in error, whether a native home-born or the alien who resides with you. [15:27–29]

214. Punishment for the knowing sinner
But the individual, be he a native home-born or a resident alien, who acts defiantly[1] – he scorns the LORD, and shall be cut off from among his people; because he despised the word of the LORD and broke his commandment; that person shall be utterly cut off. He is responsible for his sin. [15:30–31]

215. An example: A man who broke the Sabbath
While the Israelites were in the wilderness, they discovered a man gathering sticks on the Sabbath day. Those who found him gathering sticks brought him to Moses and Aaron and the **leaders of the** community. They placed him in custody because it was not clear what should be done to him. The LORD said to Moses: the man must certainly die; the whole community shall stone him outside the camp. So the whole community took him outside the camp and stoned him to death as the LORD had instructed Moses. [15:32–36]

216. The law of tassels on clothing
The LORD spoke to Moses: instruct the Israelites to make tassels on the corners of their clothing[2] throughout their generations. Let them attach a blue cord to the tassel at each corner. That shall be your tassel to look at and to remind you of all the LORD's commandments – to do them and not to follow the dictates of your own heart and eyes which lead you to unfaithfulness. Thus you will be reminded to do all my commandments and be holy **and be dedicated** to your God. I am the LORD your God who took you out of the land of Egypt to be your God: I am the LORD your God. [15:37–41]

217. The exclusive gift of the priesthood
The LORD said to Aaron:[3] You and your sons and your household shall bear any sins in connection to the Sanctuary; it is you and your sons who shall suffer for any sins pertaining to your

---

[1] Literally: high-handedly.
[2] This applied only to males whose outer garment took the shape of a four-cornered sheet to be wrapped around the wearer.
[3] A rare occasion in which the LORD addresses Aaron without Moses.

priesthood.[1] Your kinsmen also from the tribe of Levi, your ancestor, you shall employ to be your assistants, to serve you; but
you alone and your sons shall be in charge of the Tent of Testimony, **the Inner Sanctuary**. They shall obey your charges in
regard to the entire Tent **of Meeting**. But **even** they shall not
approach the vessels of the Sanctuary or the altar **to perform any
divine service**, so that they do not die, neither they nor you, for
you are **equally responsible for their trespasses**. They shall assist
you and be in charge of the Tent of Meeting for all the services
in the Tent, but a layman shall not assist you. You alone shall
keep charge of the Sanctuary and the altar that **God's** wrath no
longer descends upon the Israelites **as it did at the rebellion of
Korach, the Levite, and Dathan and Abiram, descendants of
Reuben, Jacob's first-born son, when they challenged the authority of Moses and Aaron**.[2] And I, it is I who has appointed your
kinsmen, the Levites, from among the Israelites: to you they are
dedicated by appointment of the LORD to serve in the Tent of
Meeting. You together with your sons shall keep close guard over
your priestly responsibilities in everything pertaining to the altar
and to what is behind the curtain, **in which place the Ark and
the Tablets of Testimonial rest**. I give you the responsibility of the
priesthood as a gift; the layman who encroaches shall be put to
death. [18:1–7]

218. The benefits of the Aaronite clan

The LORD spoke to Aaron: I, myself, have put you in charge over
all the contributions **from the house of Israel;** I have given all
donations sanctified by the Israelites to you and your descendants
as due to you forever. From the most sacred of dedicated objects

[1] What these sins are is clarified later in the text: the involvement of any
laymen, even Levites, in touching or sharing in the holy vessels or gift offerings
belonging to God, i.e., the priests alone, for which the penalty for the laymen is
death. It is an ironic turn of the tables – making it appear that the priests are
protecting the laity through their monopoly of priestly power.
[2] This rebellion, see *Numbers*, chapter 16, p.82 of *'Moses Man of God'*, *People's
Bible*, is justification for the exclusion of all but the descendants of Aaron from
the benefits and responsibilities of being the LORD's representatives on earth.

– these shall be yours from that which is not wholly consumed by fire **on the altar:** every one of their offerings, every one of their meal offerings, every one of their sin offerings and every one of their guilt offerings which they render to me, they are to be totally dedicated for you and your descendants to use. You shall eat them though they are the most sacred donations. Only males may eat of them. They are consecrated for your use. This too is yours: the contributions of their gift offerings – all the elevation offerings of the Israelites. I have given them to you, and to your male and female descendants as your due forever. Everyone that is ritually clean in your household may eat of them, the choicest of oils, the choicest of the vintage and cereals – the best of the yield – which they give to the LORD, I have given to you. The first fruits of everything in their land that they bring to the LORD shall be yours. Everyone of your household who is clean may eat them. Everything that has been dedicated to the LORD shall be yours. [18:8–14]

The first issue of the womb of all flesh, whether man or beast, shall be yours; but you shall have human first-borns redeemed, you shall also have the firstlings of unclean animals redeemed. Accept as their redemptive price, from the age of one month[1] and upwards, the monetary value of five *shekels* [sanctuary standard weights] which is twenty *gerahs.* But the firstlings of clean animals **which can be offered as sacrifices or consumed by the Israelites and priests** – cattle, sheep or goats may not be redeemed: they are dedicated **for the priests.**[2] You shall cast their blood against the altar, turn their fat into smoke as a fire offering to give a pleasing fragrance to the LORD; but their flesh shall be yours; it

---

[1] The redemptive price need not be paid for a child who dies before he is a month old. The first-born males of all the Israelites – those dedicated to the LORD – must have been the original priests. Ironically, once the Aaronite family were given or took the monopoly over the priesthood, they also, on the basis of the original custom that the first-born belonged to God, exacted the redemptive value of the first-born from all the Israelite tribes. This appears to me to be an unfair bonus.

[2] *Exodus* 34:19 f calls for the replacement of a donkey (the unclean animal) by a sheep.

Numbers

shall be yours just as is the breast of the elevation offering and the right thigh. [18:15–18]

All the sacred contributions that the Israelites have dedicated to the LORD, I have given to you and your sons and your daughters along with you, as your due forever. It shall be a covenant of salt – everlasting – before the LORD for you and your descendants. The LORD said to Aaron: You shall have, however, no territorial portion among them, **the Israelites**, no share will be yours among them. I am your share and your portion among the Israelites. [18:19–20]

219. The benefits of the Levites
To the Levites, I have given all the tithes in Israel as their portion as remuneration for the work they do in servicing the Tent of Meeting. The Israelites shall no longer trespass the Tent of Meeting to incur guilt leading to death. It is the Levites who will service the Tent of Meeting and it is they who will bear the iniquity[1] which may arise **from their work in the divine Sanctuary**. It is a law for all time throughout their generations, but they shall have no territorial share among the Israelites. But the tithes of the Israelites which they offer as a donation to the LORD, I have given to the Levites as their portion. For this reason I have said to them: they shall have no territorial share among the Israelites. [18:21–24]

[1] The suggestion is that because proximity to the divine is dangerous, this is a *quid pro quo*. The Israelites will not endanger themselves, and the Levites will receive tithes for accepting the risks of acting incorrectly in looking after the Sanctuary. This needs to be understood in connection with the words put into the mouths of the Israelites after the rebellion against Aaron is quashed by Moses (see *Numbers* 17:29; *Moses, Man of God* p. 93): They said to Moses, 'We are all dead men. We are utterly lost if everyone who comes near the Tabernacle dies.' The fear of God is instilled in the Israelites, so that they will be prepared to pay tithes to the Levites to be their delegates in serving in the LORD's Sanctuary. This is the justification given for clerical power.

220. The Levitical tithes to the priests

The LORD spoke to Moses: But so must you instruct the Levites: when you take from the Israelites the tithes I have given you from them as your portion, you too shall offer up as a contribution to the LORD, **that is to say, the priests,** a tithe of a tithe [one-tenth]. You should consider your contribution to the priests just as if it were grain from your own threshing floor or the flow from your wine vat. In this spirit, shall you also offer a contribution to the LORD from all your tithes, which you take from the Israelites – you shall bring from them a donation to the LORD to Aaron the priest. From all the donations given to you, you shall offer contributions to the LORD – the very best of them, the part that which is to be dedicated **for the Lord's use.** Therefore, say to them: When you contribute the best of it **to give to the Lord,** the remainder is to be reckoned by the Levites as the yield from their threshing floors and or the wine from their vats. You and your households may eat it anywhere, for it is your reward for your service in the Tent of Meeting. You shall incur no guilt because of it, once you have given the best of it **to the** LORD. You shall not profane the holy donations of the Israelites so that you do not die. [18:25–32]

221. The ashes of red heifer

The LORD instructed Moses and Aaron: This is the ritual law that the LORD has commanded: Tell the Israelites to bring me a perfect red heifer without any defect and who has never borne a yoke. You shall give it to Eleazar the priest; it shall be taken outside the camp and slaughtered before him. Eleazar the priest shall take of her blood with his finger and sprinkle it seven times towards the front of the Tent of Meeting. The heifer shall be burned in his sight – its hide, flesh, its blood shall be burned; even its dung shall be burned. The priest shall take cedar wood, hyssop and scarlet yarn and throw it into the fire consuming the heifer. The priest shall then wash his clothes, bathe himself in water and then come into the camp, the priest shall be unclean until the evening. He who executed the burning shall wash his clothes and bathe himself in water and be unclean until the evening. A man who is ritually clean shall gather up the ashes of the heifer and place them outside the camp in a ritually clean place; it shall be kept **to be used** for the water to remove impurity from the Israelite community. It is for the cleansing from sin. He who gathers up the ashes of the heifer shall wash his clothes and be unclean until evening. It is for the Israelites and the resident aliens an everlasting law. [19:1–10]

222. Water of purification for a person who touches a corpse

He who touches the corpse of any person shall be unclean for seven days; he shall purify himself on the third and on the seventh day so that he be cleansed; but if he does not purify himself on the third and seventh day, he shall not be cleansed. Whoever touches the corpse of any person and does not purify himself defiles the Tabernacle of the LORD; that person shall be cut off from Israel. Because the water of purification was not sprinkled on him, he shall be unclean; he remains in his impurity. [19:11–13]

223. For those who touch or who come into proximity with a corpse

This is the law: when a man dies in a tent, whoever enters the tent and whoever is already in the tent shall be unclean for seven days; every open vessel without a covering is unclean. Whoever in an open place touches one who has been killed by the sword, or a corpse, or a person's bone, or a grave shall be unclean for seven days. They shall take for the unclean some of the ashes from the burning **of the red heifer** for the purification from sin to which fresh water shall be added in a vessel. A ritually clean person shall take hyssop, dip it into the water and sprinkle it on the tent and all its vessels and upon the individuals who were there and on him who touched the bone, or the slain, or the corpse or the grave. The clean person shall sprinkle on the unclean on the third and seventh day; so on the seventh day he will be purified. He shall then wash his clothes, bathe himself in water and shall be cleansed by nightfall. But the person who has become unclean and does not purify himself, that person shall be cut off from the community because he has defiled the Sanctuary of the LORD – for the water of purification has not been sprinkled on him and he is, therefore, unclean. It shall be a perpetual rite for them. He who sprinkles the water of purification shall wash his clothes and be unclean until the evening. Whatever the unclean person touches becomes unclean, and any person who touches him shall be unclean until evening. [19:14–22]

224. Women may inherit: the laws of inheritance

The daughters of Zelophehad ben Hepher ben Gilead ben Machir ben Manasseh, of the clans of Manasseh, the son of Joseph, came forward. The names of the daughters were Mahlah, Noah, Hoglah, Milcah and Tirzah; they stood before Moses and Eleazar the priest and the chieftains and the whole assembly before the Tent of Meeting, and they said, "Our father died in the wilderness, but he was not one of the group who joined Korah's faction in rebelling against the LORD. He died for his own sins and he had no sons. Why should our father's name disappear from his clan just because he has no son? Give us a holding among our father's kinsmen." Moses brought their cause before the LORD. The LORD instructed Moses: The daughters of Zelophehad speak truly. You shall most certainly give them a holding among their father's kinsmen. You shall transfer to them their hereditary holding which would have been their father's **when the land is allotted.** You shall instruct the Israelites: If a man dies and has no son, you shall give the inheritance to his daughter. If he has no daughter, you shall give his inheritance to his brothers; if he has no brothers, you shall give his inheritance to his father's brothers. If his father had no brothers, you shall give his inheritance to his closest relative in his own clan, and he shall possess it. This shall be the legal ruling for the Israelites, as the LORD commanded Moses. [27:1–11]

Numbers

225. Public daily sacrifices
The LORD spoke to Moses: Instruct the Israelites: My offerings, my food as offerings by fire of pleasing fragrance to me – be careful to offer them to me at the appropriate times. Instruct them: These are the offerings by fire that you are to present to the LORD: As a perpetual daily whole-offering – two unblemished yearling lambs; you shall offer one lamb in the morning and the second lamb at twilight together with a meal offering of a tenth of an *ephah* of fine flour with a quarter of a *hin* of beaten oil mixed in – the perpetual whole-offering instituted at Mount Sinai – a fire offering to provide a pleasing fragrance to the LORD. Its libation shall be a quarter of a *hin* for each lamb, to be poured out in the sacred place as a libation of wine to the LORD. You shall offer the other lamb at twilight with the same meal offering and libation as in the morning – a fire offering to provide a pleasing fragrance to the LORD. [28:1–8]

226. Sacrifices for the Sabbath and on New Moons[1]
On the Sabbath day, **you shall offer** two unblemished yearling lambs with two tenths of an *ephah* of fine flour mixed in with oil for a meal offering and a libation. This is the whole-offering for every Sabbath; this is in addition to the regular whole-offering and its libation. On New Moons, you shall offer a whole-offering to the LORD of two bulls, one ram and seven unblemished yearling lambs; three-tenths of an *ephah* of fine flour mixed in with oil for a meal offering for each bull; and two-tenths of an *ephah* of fine flour for a meal offering mixed in with oil for the one ram; one-tenth of an *ephah* of fine flour mixed in with oil for a meal offering for each of the lambs – **all** for a whole-offering of pleasing fragrance to be a fire offering to the LORD. Their libations shall be half a *hin of wine* per bull, a third of a *hin* for the ram and a quarter of a *hin* for a lamb. That shall be the monthly whole-offering for each month of the year. There shall be one goat as a sin offering

---

[1] Literally: head of the month, i.e. the first day of the month.

to the LORD to be offered in addition to the regular burnt offering and its libation. [28:9–15]

227. The Passover sacrifice

In the first month on the fourteenth day of the month is a Passover to the LORD and on the fifteenth day of that month a festival; for seven days unleavened bread shall be eaten. The first day shall be a sacred occasion – no occupational work shall be done. You shall offer a fire offering, a whole-offering to the LORD: two bulls, one ram and seven yearling lambs – make certain that they are unblemished. As to their meal offerings: fine flour mixed in with oil – three-tenths **of a *hin*** to be offered with the bull, two-tenths with the ram and one-tenth for each of the seven lambs; also one goat for a sin offering to make expiation for you. These shall be offered in addition to the daily morning's whole-offering. So shall you make your daily offering of food for seven days, an offering by fire of pleasing fragrance to the LORD; they shall be offered in addition to the regular whole-offering with its libation. Also, the seventh day shall be a sacred occasion. You shall do no occupational work. [28:16–25]

228. Sacrifices for the Feast of Weeks [Pentecost] – Festival for the first fruits

On the day of the first fruits, when you offer an offering of new grain on your Feast of Weeks to the LORD, it shall be a sacred occasion for you. You shall do no occupational work. You shall offer a whole-offering to the LORD for a pleasing fragrance to the LORD: two bulls, one ram and seven yearling lambs. As to their meal offerings: fine flour mixed in with oil: three-tenths for each bull, two-tenths for the ram and one-tenth for each of the seven lambs; also a goat to make expiation for you. You shall present them – without blemish – with their libations in addition to the regular whole-offering and its meal offering.

Numbers

229. Sacrifices for the day of the blowing of trumpets[1]
The first day of the seventh month shall be for you a sacred occasion. You shall do no occupational work. It shall be for you a day for the blowing of trumpets. You shall present whole-offerings for a pleasing fragrance to the LORD: one bull, one ram, seven unblemished yearling lambs; their accompanying meal offerings – fine flour mixed in with oil: three-tenths **of a measure** for the bull, two-tenths for the ram and one-tenth for each of the seven lambs; one goat for a sin offering to make expiation for you. **These offerings are to be presented** in addition to the whole-offering of the New Moon with its accompanying meal offering and the regular whole-offering with its meal offering and their libations according to their prescribed rites, for a pleasing fragrance by fire offerings to the LORD. [29:1–6]

230. Sacrifices for the day of self-affliction[2]
The tenth day of the seventh month shall be for you a sacred occasion. You shall afflict[3] yourselves. You shall do no work. You shall offer a whole-offering to the LORD to give a pleasing fragrance: one young bull, one ram and seven yearling lambs – all must be without blemish. Their meal offerings shall be fine flour mixed in with oil: three-tenths of a measure for the bull, two-tenths for the ram and one-tenth for each of the seven lambs; one goat for a sin offering to make expiation for you, in addition to the sin offering of expiation, the regular whole-offering with its meal offering and their libations. [29:7–11]

231. Sacrifices for the festival of Tabernacles
The fifteenth day of the seventh month shall be for you a sacred occasion. You shall do no occupational work. You shall celebrate a festival for the LORD for seven days. You shall offer a whole-offering – an offering by fire – for a pleasing fragrance to the

[1] Celebrated as the Jewish New Year.
[2] Celebrated as the Jewish Day of Atonement.
[3] This has always been interpreted as forms of self-denial, particularly fasting.

LORD: thirteen bulls, two rams, fourteen yearling lambs – they shall be unblemished. Their meal offerings shall be fine flour mixed in with oil: three-tenths **of a measure** for each of the thirteen bulls, two-tenths for each of the two rams and one-tenth for each of the fourteen lambs; and one goat for the sin offering. **These are to be presented** in addition to the continual whole offering, its meal offering and libation. On the second day you shall offer twelve young bulls, etc.[1] On the third day – eleven bulls, etc. On the fourth day – ten bulls, etc. On the fifth day – nine bulls, etc. On the sixth day – eight bulls, etc. On the seventh day – seven bulls, etc. [29:12–34]

232. Sacrifices for the eighth day
On the eighth day you shall hold a solemn meeting. You shall do no occupational work, you shall offer a whole-offering – an offering of fire – for a pleasing fragrance to the LORD: one bull, one ram and seven unblemished yearling lambs. The meal offerings and libations for the bull, the ram and the lambs shall be according to their prescribed numbers; one goat for a sin offering; in addition to the regular whole-offering with its meal offering and libation. [29:35–38]

Summary of festival sacrifices
These shall you offer unto the LORD at the appointed festivals, in addition to your vows and voluntary offerings, whether they are whole-offerings, meal offerings, libations or peace offerings. So Moses spoke to the Israelites just as the LORD had commanded Moses. [29:39–30-1]

233. The irreversibility of vows
Moses spoke to the heads of the Israelite tribes: This is what the

---

[1] A repetition of 'the two rams, fourteen unblemished yearling lambs, their meal offerings and their libations for the bulls, the rams and for the lambs according to their prescribed numbers; and one goat for a sin offering; in addition to the continual whole-offering with its meal offering and their libations'. While the number of bulls diminish by one on each of the following days, the other sacrifices remain the same.

LORD has commanded: When a man makes a vow to the LORD or takes a self-restricting oath restricting his behaviour, he shall not break his word. He must carry out whatever he said. [30:2–3]

234. A woman's vow may be reversed

If a woman makes a vow to the LORD or takes a self-restricting oath regarding her behaviour while, because of her youth, she still lives in her father's house, and her father hears of her vow or the self-restricting oath and does not object, her vows shall be binding – every one of her self-restrictive vows shall be binding. But, if her father nullifies her **vow** when he hears of it, none of her vows or her self-restricting oaths shall be binding, and the LORD will forgive her because her father has forbidden her **from undertaking them.** If she should marry while her vow or her verbal undertaking which restricts her is being fulfilled by her, and her husband hears of it and does not object when he hears of it, then her vows and self-restricting oaths shall remain binding. But, if her husband nullifies her **vow** when he hears of it, he invalidates her vows and self-restricting undertakings, and the LORD will forgive her **for not fulfilling them.** Every vow of a widow or divorcee – everything by which she swore to restrict herself is binding upon her. If she makes a vow in her husband's house or takes a self-restricting oath in her husband's house, and her husband heard it and did not object or nullify her **vow**, all her vows shall be binding and all her restrictive oaths shall be binding. But if her husband made them null and void when he heard them, then whatever she said regarding her vows or self-restricting oaths shall not be binding, for her husband has nullified them, and the LORD will forgive her. Her husband may confirm or nullify any vow or self-restricting oath. But, if her husband makes no objection to her as the days pass, he thereby confirms all her vows and oaths which she has undertaken because he did not object at the time he heard of them. But if he declares them null and void **sometime** after he had heard them **without raising any objections,** then he shall bear her iniquity. These are the laws which the LORD commanded Moses on **these** matters relating between a man and his wife, between a father and his daughter when she is a young girl in her father's house. [30:4–17]

235. Purification rites for warriors who have killed or touched slain bodies[1] and their clothing

Whoever has killed anyone or touched anyone who was killed must encamp outside the **Israelite** camp for seven days, purify yourselves on the third and seventh day, your captives as well as yourselves. You shall purify the clothing and leather goods and that which is made of goats' hair and all wooden objects **that have come into contact with the dead.** [31:19–20]

236. Laws in regard to the purification of material objects

Eleazar the priest said to the warriors who had gone into battle **against Midian:** This is the prescribed law which the LORD commanded Moses: as for the gold, the silver, the copper, the iron, the tin and the lead, every utensil that comes into contact with fire,[2] you shall pass through fire to be purified. They still must be cleansed by the waters of purification; but those objects which do not usually come into contact with fire, you shall pass through the waters **of purification.** You shall wash your clothes on the seventh day and you shall be purified; after this you may enter the camp. [31:21–24]

237. Laws in regard to the spoils of war[3]

The LORD instructed Moses: Take a count of the spoils which were taken of both man and beast – you and Eleazar the priest and the heads of the clans are to do this. Divide the spoils equally into two parts: for those warriors who went into battle and for

[1] This follows the gruesome tale of the war against the Midianites as recorded in *Numbers* 30:1–18. These laws are introduced by a verse relating to the successful 'end of the battle'.

[2] This is the Talmudic view. Others say that this refers to everything which can survive fire.

[3] These laws are related in the text to the spoils of war from the Israelite victory over the Midianites. An example of the distribution of war booty is given in *Numbers 31:25–54*. See *Moses, Man of God*, p. 184.

all the community. Also, levy a tribute to the LORD from the warriors who engaged in combat: one life in five hundred – of persons, oxen, asses and sheep – shall be taken from their half-share and given to Eleazar the priest for a contribution to the LORD. But from the Israelites' half-share you shall take one in every fifty persons as well as oxen, asses and sheep – all of the animals – and give them to the Levites, who minister in the service of the LORD's Tabernacle. [31:25–30]

238. The Levitical towns
The LORD spoke to Moses in the plains of Moab by the Jordan at Jericho: Instruct the Israelites out of their holdings, to give towns to the Levites as well as pasture land around the towns. The towns shall be theirs and shall be for their cattle and beasts. The town pasture shall extend to a thousand cubits all around the town wall. You shall measure off two thousand cubits from the eastern, southern, western and northern limits of the town, with the town in the centre. Among the towns you give to the Levites shall be the six towns of refuge for the manslaughterer to flee to, to which you will add forty-two towns – in all forty-eight towns with their pasture. In doing this, take proportionally from the size of your tribe holdings, so that each tribe gives relative to the share it receives. [35:1–8]

239. The towns of refuge and the rights of the avenger
The LORD spoke to Moses: Instruct the Israelites: When you cross the Jordan into the land of Canaan, you shall provide for yourselves towns of refuge to which one who killed a person unintentionally may flee. The towns shall serve as a refuge from the avenger, so that the manslaughterer should not die unless he has stood trial before the community. In all you shall provide six towns – three beyond the Jordan and three in the land of Canaan. These six towns shall be for the Israelites and the resident aliens among them for refuge, for anyone who kills unintentionally to flee there. But anyone who strikes another with an iron object, which results in death, is a murderer and must be put to death;

this also applies if he struck him with a stone or wooden tool resulting in his death – he is a murderer and must be put to death. The blood-avenger[1] shall put the murderer to death when he meets him. But if he pushed him without malicious intent or unintentionally cast an object against him or unaware dropped on him a lethal stone object and the result was death, even though he was not his enemy and did not want to harm him – in such cases the authorities shall decide between the manslaughterer and the blood-avenger. The authorities shall protect the manslaughterer from the blood-avenger and restore him to the town of refuge to which he fled, where he shall remain until the death of the High Priest who was anointed with the sacred oil. But if the manslaughterer ever leaves the town of refuge's limits to which he fled, and the blood-avenger meets him outside its limits and kills the manslaughterer, there is no bloodguilt on his account. For he is obligated to remain inside the town of refuge until the High Priest's death; after his death, he may return **without anxiety** to his land holding. [35:9–28]

240. The death sentence for murders and ransom money

This shall be your legal procedure forever in your habitations: If anyone kills a person, the manslayer may be executed only on the evidence of witnesses. The testimony of one witness is not sufficient for a death sentence. You may not accept a ransom for the life of a murderer who is guilty of a capital crime; he must be put to death. Nor may you accept ransom to absolve a person's flight to a town of refuge to enable him to live on his holding before the death of the priest. You shall not pollute the land in which you live; for **innocent** blood pollutes the land, and the land can have no expiation for the blood shed on it except by the blood of the man who shed it. You shall not defile the land in which you live, and in which I rest my presence, for I the LORD dwell among the Israelite people. [35.29–34]

---

[1] Literally: redeemer.

241. Restrictions on the inheritance of daughters

The heads of families of the clans of Gilead ben Machir ben Manasseh, one of the Josephite tribes came forward and petitioned Moses, and the chieftains, tribal heads of the Israelites: The LORD commanded my lord to apportion shares of the land by lot to the Israelites; also my lord was commanded by the LORD to allot the share of our kinsman Zelophehad to his daughters. Now, if they marry men from another Israelite tribe, their share will be cut off from our ancestral portion and be added to the portion of the tribe to which they **and their children** shall belong – so shall it be that our ancestral portion will be less! Also, when the Jubilee shall occur for the Israelites, then their share will be added on to the tribe into which they marry, so will their share be cut off from the ancestral portion of our tribe. [36:1–4]

Moses commanded the Israelites at the LORD's instruction: The Joseph tribes speak truly. So this is what the LORD does command in regard to the daughters of Zelophehad: Let them marry whom they please, but only if they marry into a clan of their father's tribe. So no inheritance of the Israelites shall pass over from one tribe to another but the Israelites must each remain bound to the ancestral portion of his tribe. Every daughter among the Israelite tribes who inherits a share must marry someone from the clan of her ancestral tribe in order that the Israelites may hold on to the share allotted to their ancestors. Thus no inheritance shall pass over from one tribe to another, for the Israelite tribes shall remain bound to its own allotted portion. The daughters of Zelophehad did as the LORD had commanded Moses: Mahlah, Tirzah, Hoglah, Milcah and Noah, Zelophehad's daughters, were married to sons of their uncles, marrying into clans of the descendants of Manasseh ben Joseph; and so their share remained in the ancestral family of their tribe. [36:5–12]

Conclusion to the Laws in the Book of Numbers

These are the commandments and rules which the LORD commanded the Israelites, through Moses on the plains of Moab by Jordan near Jericho. [36:13]

DEUTERONOMY

242. The Ten Commandments

Face to face the LORD spoke to you on the mountain from
Amidst the fire. [I stood then between the LORD and you
To tell you the words of the LORD because you were
Frightened of the fire and did not ascend the mountain][1] ;

1. I am the LORD your God who brought you out of Egypt
   From a house of slaves.
   You shall have no other gods but me.

2. You shall not make yourself any sculpted image or
   Any physical representation of any body.
   In the heavens above,
   On the earth beneath or in the waters under the earth.
   You shall neither bow down to them nor worship them
   Because I, the LORD your God, am a jealous God
   Who remembers the sins of the fathers.
   Of them that hate me
   To the second, third and fourth generations.
   But who behaves kindly for a thousand generations
   To those who love me and keep my commandments.

3. Do not abuse the name of the LORD
   For he will not exonerate those who use his name
   For pernicious purposes, **but will punish them.**

4. *Observe* the Sabbath day to make it holy
   As the LORD your God has commanded you.
   During six days you may do all your tasks
   But the seventh day is a Sabbath to the LORD your God.
   You shall not work, you, nor your son nor your daughter
   Nor your male or female servant, *nor your ox,*
   Nor your donkey, nor any of your cattle,
   Nor the stranger within your gated walls

---

[1] In the description of the pronouncement of the Ten Commandments in
Exodus, God *does not allow* the Israelites to touch the mountain. For
comparative purposes of the two versions see p. 4. Italicised words indicate
differences with the *Exodus* version.

> *So that your male and female servants may rest as you do.*
> *You should remember that you were a slave in Egypt*
> *And that the* LORD *your God brought you out from there*
> *With a mighty hand and an outstretched arm.*
> *Therefore does the* LORD *your God command you*
> *To observe the Sabbath day.*[1]

5. Honour your father and mother
   As the LORD *your God commanded you*
   So that you may live long *and prosper*
   In the land which the LORD your God gives you.
6. You shall not murder.
7. You shall not commit adultery.
8. You shall not steal.
9. You shall not bear false witness against your neighbour.
10. You shall not covet your neighbour's wife,
    Nor desire your neighbour's house, his field,
    His male or female servant, his ox, his donkey
    Or anything that belongs to your neighbour. [5:4–18]

243. Destruction of the shrines of the native gods

These are the laws and judgements which you must be on guard to perform in the land which the LORD the God of your fathers is granting to you as your possession – throughout all the time you live on the earth. You shall utterly destroy all the shrines at which the nations you are dispossessing serve their gods – upon the lofty mountains and high places and under every majestic tree. You shall tear down their altars and shatter their pillars; you shall burn in fire their sacred poles; you shall strike down the engraved images of their gods; you shall obliterate their names from those places. [12:1–3]

---

[1] The reason given for the observance of the Sabbath is significantly different from the previous version. In *Exodus*, humanity is to rest because God, in whose image man was created, rested: *imitatio dei*. In *Deuteronomy*, it is the equality of all creatures in God's sight and therefore their equal rights to freedom and leisure. The two concepts from both versions express the basic foundations of a moral society. The salvation from Egypt is the basis of this version of the Ten Commandments.

244. The centralised worship of the Lord

You shall not behave in this manner to the LORD your God **to worship him on high places or under wide-spreading trees.** But you shall seek out and come only to the place which the LORD your God shall designate to put his name **and glory there** from among all the tribal lands to be his habitation. There, you shall bring your whole-offerings and your sacrifices and your tithes and your voluntary contributions, your votive and free will offerings and the firstlings of your herds and flocks. There, you and your family shall eat before the LORD your God and rejoice in how the LORD your God has blessed you in all your enterprises. You shall not behave at all as we do now here – every man doing what is right in his own eyes;[1] for you have not yet come in peace to your allotted portion which the LORD your God is granting you. But when you cross the Jordan to settle in the land which the LORD your God gives you to possess and he gives you rest from all the enemies around you so that you dwell in security, then shall you bring all that I am commanding you to the place which the LORD your God shall designate for the habitation of his name[2] – your whole-offerings and other sacrifices, your tithes and contributions and all the choice votive offerings which you have vowed to give to the LORD. You shall rejoice before the LORD your God – you, your sons and daughters, your male and female slaves and the Levites who live within your towns (who have no territorial portions among you). [12:4–12]

---

[1] This statement certainly contradicts the belief that these laws were given by Moses in the wilderness, for Moses is pictured as ruling autocratically, and that worship was centralised in the Tabernacle which was moved from place to place. The expression 'every man doing what is right in his own eyes' is what marks the behaviour of the Israelites after the death of Joshua and is the theological reason for the appointment of a king after the people's dissatisfaction with the rule of Samuel's sons. We must assume that the laws of centralised worship were written down at a far later date, perhaps even after the destruction of the Northern Kingdom of Israel in 721 BCE. Some would say, even after the Babylonian exile in 586 BCE.

[2] Presence.

245. The right to eat meat

Be on your guard not to offer up your whole-offerings in any
place that you might come upon – but only at the place which
the LORD shall designate among your tribal lands: there shall you
offer up your whole-offerings and there shall you do all that I
command you. But you may, as you wish, slaughter and eat
meat within your towns according to the blessings the LORD your
God has bestowed upon you. **As these are not sacrifices**, the
ritually unclean and clean alike may eat them, **animals** such as
the gazelle and the deer.[1] But you must not partake of the blood,
you shall pour it out on the ground as you do water. [12:13–16]

246. Foods forbidden outside the designated shrine

You may not eat in your towns the tithes of your grain, wine
and oil or of the firstlings of your herds and flocks or of any of
the votive offerings which you vow or of your free will offerings
and contributions. These you shall eat only before the LORD your
God in the place the LORD your God will choose: you, your son,
your daughter, your male and female slaves and the Levite who
lives in your towns – rejoicing before the LORD your God for **the
success of** all your enterprises. Be on guard not to neglect the
Levite for as long as you live in your land

247. Sheep and cattle may be eaten away from the central shrine.[2]

When the LORD enlarges your territory as he has promised you
and you think: I will eat some meat, for that is what you crave
– you may follow your craving and eat meat. **You shall do so at
the central shrine** but, if the place to which the LORD has designated to put his name is too great a distance from you, you may
slaughter any of the sheep or cattle which the LORD has given

[1] Gazelle and deer, while permitted food, were not used for sacrifices. The
suggestion here is that domesticated animals from herds and flocks could not
be eaten except at the central shrine, as in *Leviticus* 130, p. 70, but see **247**.
[2] This appears to be a reversal of the law in *Leviticus* 130 but may be a
modification.

you, as I have instructed you, to eat within your towns according to all the cravings of your heart. Just as you may eat gazelles and deer, so shall you partake of them. Both the ritually unclean and clean may eat of them. Only be certain not to partake of the blood, for the blood is the life, and you must not eat the life with the flesh. You shall not eat it but shall pour it out on the ground as if it were water. You shall not eat it so that you may prosper, and your descendants after you, because you have done what is right and pleasing to the LORD. [12:17–25]

248. Sacred items must be brought to the central shrine
But you shall take your sacred and votive donations to the place which the LORD has designated, where you shall offer your whole-offerings of flesh and blood on the altar of the LORD your God, and the blood of your sacrifices shall be poured out on the altar of the LORD your God, and **there** you may eat the flesh. Be careful to observe all these things which I command you so that you and your descendants after you may prosper forever because you will be doing what is right and proper in the sight of the LORD your God. [12:26–28]

249. Avoid the seduction of native practices
When the LORD your God shall cut down before you the nations whose land you are entering to possess, and you have dispossessed them and settled in their land – be on your guard lest you be enticed to follow them, even after they have been destroyed before you. Do not ask questions about their gods saying: 'How did these nations worship their gods?' and then saying, 'I will also do the same.' You shall not do the same to the LORD your God as they perform for their gods every abhorrent act that the LORD hates – for even their sons and daughters do they burn in fire for their gods. [12:29–31]

250. Death for the rebellious prophet
Be on guard to obey everything I command you. Do not add to it nor take away from it. Should there appear among you a

prophet or one who claims to have divinely inspired dreams;[1] and
he gives you a sign or a portent; if that sign or portent is fulfilled
on which basis he has said, '**If what I foretold comes true**, let us
follow other gods (whom you have not encountered) and let us
worship them,' you shall not listen to the word of that prophet
or that dreamer of dreams, for the LORD your God is testing you
through him to know whether you love the LORD your God with
all your heart and soul.[2] You shall follow the LORD your God;
him shall you revere and his commandments shall you obey and
to his voice shall you pay heed. You shall worship him and hold
fast to him! As to that prophet or that dreamer of dreams, he
shall be put to death for he incited rebellion against the LORD
your God who brought you out of the land of Egypt and redeemed
you from the houses of slaves – to draw you away from the way
that the LORD your God commanded you to follow. So will you
purge the evil in your midst. [13:1–7]

251. Rebels against God must be executed by their own families

If your brother – your mother's son – or your son or your daughter or the wife in whose bosom you rest, or your friend who is
as close to you as your own soul should in confidence entice you
by saying, 'Let us go and worship other gods whom neither you
nor your fathers have encountered – the gods of the neighbouring
peoples surrounding you, either near to you or distant, from one
end of the earth to the other: do not give assent or pay any
attention to him, nor pity him, nor show him compassion, nor
cover up for him. You shall surely kill him.[3] Your hand should
be the first to commence his execution with the rest of the people

[1] Literally, dreamer of dreams.
[2] Soul means life. According to this stricture, even miracles cannot be trusted
when they counter God's demands because they are his way of putting hiss
people to the test.
[3] I think we must assume that the culprits would first be brought to trial. The
force of this passage is the emphasis that the love of the LORD has priority even
over the loyalty to one's closest family and friends.

following your example. You shall stone him until he dies because he has tried to draw you away from the LORD your God who brought you out of the land of Egypt and out of the house of slaves. All of Israel will hear of this and be afraid and will not again contemplate the performance of such evil in your midst. [13:7–12]

252. The destruction of towns rebellious against God.[1]

If in one of your towns which the LORD has given you for settlement you hear that certain layabouts have incited the inhabitants of their town by saying: 'Let us go and worship other gods whom you never encountered,' you shall enquire and thoroughly investigate the matter. If it is undoubtedly true that if such an abhorrent thing took place in your midst, you shall most certainly put the inhabitants of that town to the sword, utterly destroying it and all that is in it together with the cattle – all shall be put to the sword. You shall collect all its spoil into the centre of the square and burn down the town with all its spoil as a holocaust to the LORD your God. It shall be an everlasting ruin; it shall never be rebuilt. Nothing of it which has been proscribed shall stick to your hand so that the LORD may restrain the ferocity of his anger and grant you compassion. He will show you mercy and increase you as he promised your ancestors but only if you heed the voice of the LORD your God to observe all his commandments which I command you this day to do what is right in the sight of the LORD your God. [13:13–19]

253. Laws peculiar to a chosen people:
no self-mutilation, dietary laws

You are children of the LORD your God: You shall not gash yourselves nor shave the forelocks of your head **in bereavement** for the dead. Because you are a holy people to the LORD your

[1] *Exodus 34:10–17; Numbers 33:50–52; Deuteronomy 7:1–5* which contains further strictures against the worship of foreign gods has not been included in *The Laws of Moses* but are in *Moses, Man of God* as they are among Moses's orations on the nature of the Covenant between God and Israel.

God. Only you did the LORD choose to be his special people out of all the peoples of the earth. You shall not eat any offensive thing. These are the animals you may eat: the ox, the sheep and the goat; the deer, the gazelle and the roebuck; the wild goat, the ibex, the antelope and the mountain sheep; and any animal that has proper hoofs with clefts through the hoofs and chews the cud – of such you may eat. These, however, who either chew the cud or have cloven hoofs you may not eat: the camel, the hare and the rock badger – because, while they chew the cud, they are not cleft-hoofed – they are unclean for you. The pig, while it has cloven hoofs, but does not chew the cud, is unclean for you. You shall not eat their meat nor touch their bodies. Of all that lives in the waters, these you may eat: you may eat anything that has fins or scales. But you may not eat anything which has no fins or scales – it is unclean for you. You may eat any clean bird. But these you may not eat: the eagle, the vulture and the osprey; the kite, the falcon and any kind of buzzard; every kind of crow; the ostrich, the night hawk, the sea gull and every kind of hawk; the little owl, the great owl and the ibis; the pelican, the buzzard, the cormorant, the stork and any kind of heron, the hoopoe and the bat. All winged insects are unclean for you. They may not be eaten. You may eat only clean winged creatures. You may not eat anything which dies a natural death. You may give it to the resident alien for him to eat; you may sell it to a foreigner. For you are a holy people to the LORD your God. You shall not boil a kid in its mother's milk.[1] [14:1–21]

254. Annual tithes

Make certain that you tithe all the yield of your annual produce which grows in your fields. You shall, before the LORD your God at the place he designates for the habitation of his name, partake

---

[1] This injunction is repeated here for the third time [*Exodus* 23:14 and 34:26]. Its contiguity to the passage emphasising the holiness of Israel indicates the importance ascribed to expressions of human sensitivity and compassion. Neither the kid nor its mother knows the source of the milk but the person eating it does!

of the tithe of your grain, your wine, your oil and the firstlings of your herds and flocks – to remind you always to revere the LORD your God. When the LORD your God blesses you **with a good yield**, if the distance is too great for you to carry it all, because the place where the LORD your God has designated to put his name there is too far away – you shall change it into money and take the purse of money and go to the place the LORD your God has designated. You shall use the money, however you please, to buy oxen, or sheep, or wine or liquor or what you yearn for – you shall eat there before the LORD your God, rejoicing with your household. You shall not neglect the Levite that has settled in your town because he has no territorial portion with you. [14:22–27]

255. Tithes for the Levites, the strangers, the orphan and widow

At the end of every three years you shall gather all the tithes of your yield on that year and place them somewhere within your town: and the Levite because he has no territorial portion with you, and the alien, and the orphan and the widow who are within your towns, shall come, partake and be satisfied. **Do this** so that the LORD your God may bless you in all your enterprises. [14:28–29]

256. The remission of debts

Every seventh year you shall remit all debts. This is the method of remission: every creditor shall remit any claim on his neighbour. He shall not exact it from his neighbour or kinsman because a remission from the LORD has been declared. You may exact it from a foreigner but whatever is due you from your kinsman you must remit. But there should be no poor among you **who need to go into debt,** for the LORD your God will most certainly bless you in the land which the LORD your God is granting you as a hereditary portion – but only if you fully obey the voice of the LORD your God to be on guard by performing all these commandments which I charge you with today. For the LORD your God will bless you as he promised you; you shall lend to many nations but you shall not borrow; you shall rule over many nations but they shall not rule over you. [15:1–6]

257. Treatment of the poor

If there should be a poor person amongst your kinsmen in one of the towns in your land which the LORD your God does grant to you, do not harden your heart, nor close your hand to your poor kinsman. You shall most certainly open up your hands to him and lend him sufficient for his required needs. Be careful not to have a mean thought in your heart thinking: The seventh year, the year of remission, is soon upon us – and you look with evil intent at your poor kinsman and you do not give him **what he needs**; for he will cry out about you to the LORD – and it will be reckoned as a sin for you. You shall certainly grant it to him and you shall not grieve at giving it to him because it is for this very reason that the LORD your God shall bless you in all your enterprises and in all your undertakings. For the poor, **because of your disobedience,**[1] shall never cease to be in the land. Therefore, I command you: Make certain to open your hand for the benefit of your kinsman, and the poor and destitute in your land. [15:7–11]

258. The freeing of a Hebrew slave

If your kinsman, a Hebrew man or woman, be sold to you and serves you for six years; in the seventh year you shall let him go free. When you release him, do not let him go empty-handed: you shall generously provide him from your flock, from your threshing floor and from your winepress. Just as the LORD your God has blessed you, so must you give to him **of your possessions.** Remember that you were a slave in the land of Egypt and the LORD your God redeemed you: therefore, I command you now to behave in this way. [15:12–15]

259. He who chooses to remain a slave

But, if he says to you, 'I will not leave you,' because he loves you

[1] My intervention is based on the admonition in the previous paragraph.

and your household, because he is happy with you, you shall take an awl and pierce a hole through his earlobe to touch the doorpost – so shall he become your slave forever. You shall act similarly to your female slave. Do not take it as a hardship when you let him go free from you, for he has given double the benefit you would have received from a hired labourer when he served you for six years – the LORD your God will bless you in all your enterprises **for treating him in this way.** [15:16–18]

260. The law of firstling males from the flocks
You shall dedicate as sacred all the male firstlings of your herd and flock to the LORD your God. You shall not work the firstlings of your oxen nor shear the wool of the firstlings of your flock. You shall eat[1] it before the LORD your God year by year in the place which the LORD shall designate – you and your household. If it has any blemish: lame or blind – any bad defect, you shall not sacrifice it to the LORD your God. You may eat it within your towns; both those who are ritually unclean or clean may eat it, just as they would the gazelle and deer. Only do not eat of its blood: you shall pour it on the ground like water. [15:19–23]

261. The paschal lamb may only be eaten at the sacred shrine on the Festival of Unleavened Bread
Observe the month of Abib and perform a paschal sacrifice before the LORD your God because during the month of *Abib*, the LORD your God brought you out of Egypt by night. You shall sacrifice the paschal offering to the LORD your God from your flocks and herds[2] in the place designated by the LORD for his presence[3] to dwell there. You shall not eat any leavened bread with it.

---

[1] The sacrifice of the firstlings is treated as a peace offering which is eaten by the donor and his family after the priest receives his due.
[2] This is strange as in *Exodus* 12:3f, it is clear that only a lamb is to be used for the paschal offering. II *Chronicles* 35:7f which describes the celebration of Passover writes of two offerings, the paschal lamb and the holy offerings which were oxen: the sacrifice offered on every festival.
[3] Literally: name.

For seven days you shall eat unleavened bread with it – the bread of affliction – because in great haste you left Egypt, so that you will remember the day of your departure from the land of Egypt all the days of your life. No kind of leaven shall be seen within all your borders for seven days, nor shall any of the meat which you have sacrificed in the evening of the first day be kept over night until the morning. You shall not be permitted to sacrifice the paschal offering within your towns which the LORD your God is giving to you, but only at the place which the LORD your God has chosen to place his presence – there you shall sacrifice the paschal offering in the evening, at the setting of the sun, at the time of your departure from Egypt. You shall roast it and eat it in the place which the LORD your God shall designate. In the morning you shall return to your homes.[1] For six days you shall eat unleavened bread; the seventh day shall be a sacred occasion to the LORD your God: You shall do no work! [16:1–8]

262. The Festival of Weeks [Pentecost]

You shall count seven weeks: from the time you begin to put the sickle to the standing grain you shall begin to count seven weeks. You shall observe the Festival of Weeks for the LORD your God with a tribute – a free will offering given by you in proportion to the blessings bestowed on you by the LORD your God. You shall rejoice before the LORD your God – you, your son, daughter, and your male and female slaves and the Levite within your town, and the alien, the orphan and the widow that are among you – in the place which the LORD your God shall designate for his

---

[1] This insistence that the paschal lamb could only be sacrificed at the sacred central shrine poses many questions. How was it possible for all the Israelites to go to the central shrine for the Passover, and what of those who did not go – did they not celebrate it? This suggests to me that the identification of the Spring Festival with the Exodus did not happen until the seventh century BCE, when it became a national festival to celebrate Israel's first redemption. Before then, it would have been observed locally as a nature festival celebrating the reawakening of earth and the lambing season.

presence to reside.[1] You shall remember that you were a slave in Egypt and observe all these laws.[2] [16:9–12]

263. The Festival of Booths
After the ingathering from your threshing and your winepress, you shall observe the Festival of Booths for seven days. You shall rejoice in your festival – you, your son, your daughter, and your male and female slaves and the Levite and the alien, the orphan and the widow within your towns. For seven days you shall hold a festival for the LORD your God in the place which the LORD shall designate, because the LORD your God will bless you in all your crops and undertakings; and you shall be altogether joyous. [16:13–15]

264. Summary of the three Pilgrim Festivals
Three times a year shall all the males[3] appear before the LORD your God in the place that he will designate. During the Festival of Unleavened Bread, the Festival of Weeks and the Festival of Booths; they shall not appear before the LORD empty-handed. Every man shall give according to his ability, in proportion to the blessings which the LORD your God has bestowed on you. [16:16–17]

265. You shall pursue justice
You shall appoint judges and magistrates for your tribes within all your towns which the LORD your God is giving you. They shall judge the people with true justice. You shall not pervert justice; you shall show no partiality according to the status of the individuals; you shall take no gift because a gift blinds even

---

[1] This would suggest that everyone throughout Israel would be required to present themselves before the LORD at the central shrine.
[2] On the basis that the command to observe all these laws is recorded here and that Pentecost takes place seven weeks after Passover, the Exodus, see *Leviticus* 161, 162, p. 85f, the rabbinic sages ruled that this festival also celebrated the time of the giving of the Torah.
[3] Here, the instruction is for the males alone. Previously, everyone was to rejoice before the LORD at the central shrine.

the eyes of the wise and overturns the cause of the righteous. Justice, justice shall you pursue so that you may live and occupy the land which the LORD your God is giving you. [16:18–20]

266. No sacred posts or pillars
You shall not set up a sacred post – any kind of wood beside the altar of the LORD your God which you shall erect; nor shall you erect a stone pillar which the LORD your God hates. [16:21–22]

267. No defective animals may be sacrificed
You shall not sacrifice to the LORD your God an ox or a sheep which has a defect of a serious nature, for that is abhorrent to the LORD your God. [17:1]

268. Death for transgressors of the Covenant
If there should be found among you, within one of your towns which the LORD your God is giving you, man or woman who does evil in the sight of the LORD your God by transgressing his Covenant; that is that they have gone to worship other gods and bowed to them or the sun or moon or any of the heavenly hosts which I have not permitted **you to worship.** When you are informed of this or it has come to your attention, you shall make diligent enquiries. If it be true and certain that such an abhorrent act was committed in Israel, you shall take that man or woman who committed this wicked act to your gates – that very man or woman – and stone them to death. [17:2–5]

269. The witnesses shall be the first to hurl the stones[1]
Only by the testimony of two or more[2] witnesses shall the condemned be put to death. One witness shall not be sufficient to execute a person. **Furthermore,** let the hands of the witnesses be the first against him to put him to death. Only afterwards shall

[1] The requirement of more than one witness and that they be the first to throw the stones of execution would make them realise the seriousness of their accusation and their responsibility for the infliction of the death sentence.
[2] Literally, 'three'.

the whole community join in; and you shall purge out the evil from among you. [17:6]

270. Judgements at the central shrine

If a matter **of judgement** occurs which is too difficult for you to judge, that is in reference to the nature of a killing, **manslaughter or murder**, or between two opposing civil claims or on matters of personal injuries – all of which have led to contention **among the elders** in your town – you shall promptly set forth to the place which the LORD your God shall designate. You shall go before the Levitical priests and to whoever is the judge at the time to submit your case; they shall tell you the proper judgement. You shall act according to the decision they render in the place that the LORD has designated. Be sure to do all that they instructed you. You shall act in accordance with the instructions they taught you and the judgement they rendered to you. You shall not deviate from the verdict they presented to you in any detail, to the right or to the left. The man who acts with contempt by not listening to the priest appointed to minister to the LORD your God or to the judge – that man shall die. You shall purge the evil out of Israel. All of the people will take heed and be afraid and cease ever to act with contempt **of the judgements of the presiding priest or judge.** [17:8–13]

271. The appointment of a king[1]

When you come to the land which the LORD is giving you to possess and to live there and say: I will set a king over me as do all the nations round about me. You shall only appoint a king over yourself whom the LORD your God shall choose; from among your kinsmen you shall appoint a king. You are not permitted to appoint over yourself a foreigner who is not one of your kinsmen. Moreover, he shall not keep many horses, nor send a levy of men

[1] These laws have to be read in the context of Samuel's sense of rejection when the Israelites demand a king and God comforts him by saying, "They have not rejected you but have rejected me from being king over them." See *The People's Bible, Samuel*, p.16.

to Egypt in order to acquire horses because the LORD has said to you: You must not go back that way again **after I have delivered you from that place.** He shall not have many wives, lest his heart go astray **after the gods they worship**, nor shall he amass an over-abundance of silver and gold.[1] When he is seated on his royal throne, he shall have a copy of this Torah[2] written for him on a scroll by the Levitical priests. It shall always be with him to be read by him so long as he lives, so that he may learn to revere the LORD his God to observe faithfully all the words of this Torah and all its laws. Thus he will not exalt himself above his kinsmen nor deviate from these commandments, either to the right or the left, so that he and his sons will reign long in Israel. [17:14–20]

272. The Lord is the only portion of the Levites
The Levitical priests, the whole tribe of Levi, shall have no territorial portion with **the other tribes of** Israel. They shall be sustained by the offerings of fire to the LORD which is their portion; they shall have no portion among their kinsmen. The LORD is their portion as he has promised them. This shall be the priests' due from the people; those who offer a sacrifice, whether an ox or a sheep, shall give the shoulder, the cheeks and the stomach to the priest. You shall **also** give him the first fruits of your new grain and wine and oil and the first shearing of your sheep. For the LORD your God has chosen him and his descendants out of all your tribes to stand and minister in the name of the LORD for all time. [18:1–5]

273. Levites who come to serve at the sacred shrine
If a Levite leaves any of the towns of Israel where he lives to come with longing to the place designated by the LORD **to be his house**, he may serve in the name of the LORD his God as do his

[1] Solomon seems to be the culprit who had many wives, horses and gold and silver. These admonitions must have been revealed long after the Mosaic period, probably after the fall of the monarchy.
[2] The Septuagint supposes this to be the book of *Deuteronomy* (perhaps that which was discovered in 622 BCE during Josiah's reign).

Levite kinsmen who stand before the LORD. They shall have equal sustenance **to those already in residence** in addition to the income he has from the sale of the possessions he inherited. [18:6-8]

274. Forbidden native practices

When you come into the land which the LORD your God is giving you, do not imitate the abhorrent practices of the nations **who live there.** There shall be none among you who puts his son or daughter through fire, or who is an augur, a soothsayer, a diviner, a sorcerer; one who casts spells or who brings up ghosts and familiar spirits or one who makes enquiries of the dead. Whoever does such a thing is detestable before the LORD. It is because of these abhorrent practices that the LORD your God is driving them out from before you. You shall be perfect with the LORD your God. For these nations you are about to dispossess do use soothsayers and augurs; but the LORD has not permitted you to do this. [18:9-14]

275. The divine appointment of prophets

From among your midst, your kinsmen, the LORD your God will raise up a prophet like me – you shall listen to him. This is what you asked of the LORD your God at Horeb on the day of the Assembly **for, on hearing the words of the Lord,** you said: "Let me not hear the voice of the LORD my God anymore, nor let me see this great fire anymore, lest I die."[1] The LORD said to me: "They have spoken correctly. I will raise up a prophet from among their kinsmen like you and I will put my words in his mouth and he will tell them all that I command him. The person who does not obey my words which he conveys in my name will have to answer to me." [18:15-19]

276. Death for the false prophet

"The prophet, however, who dares to utter in my name an oracle which I have not commanded him to say, or who speaks in the

---

[1] It is significant that the reason given for the gift of prophecy to the few is the fear that the ordinary person has of encountering the Deity.

name of other gods – that prophet shall die. But if you think, 'How shall I know that the oracle was not from the LORD?' If the prophet speaks in the name of the LORD and the oracle is not fulfilled, that is not an oracle from the LORD. The prophet has uttered it presumptuously; do not be in awe of him." [18:20–22]

Criminal Offences

277. Cities of refuge for the manslaughterer

When the LORD your God has cut down the nations whose land the LORD your God is giving you, and you have dispossessed them and are living in their towns and in their houses, you shall set aside for yourselves three towns within your land which the LORD is giving to you to possess. You shall indicate the route, dividing your land, which the LORD is giving you to possess, into three parts so that any manslaughterer may have a place to which he can flee.[1] These are the circumstances which define a person as a manslaughterer who may flee there and live: whoever kills a person unintentionally – someone whom he has not previously hated; an example: a man goes with his neighbour into a forest to cut wood, and as his hand swings the axe to cut down the tree, the axe-head flies off the handle and strikes his neighbour and he dies – he shall flee to one of these towns and live. Otherwise, if the distance **to the town of refuge** is too great, and the blood-avenger pursuing the manslaughterer in heated rage overtakes him and strikes him down dead, **this will not be justified** because he did not deserve death because he had never been his enemy. It is for this reason I command you: set aside three towns; and if the LORD your God expands your territory as he swore to your forefathers and gives to you all the land he promised to your forefathers – if you are intent in doing that which I now command you, to love the LORD your God and to walk in his ways all your days, add a further three towns to these three; so that innocent blood will not be shed for which you will be responsible in your

---

[1] The distance for his flight needs to be manageable.

land which the LORD your God is granting you as a possession.
[19:1–10]

278. Treatment of murderers
But should a man hate his neighbour and lie in wait for him and
stand over him and strike him down dead and flee to one of these
towns, the elders of his town shall send to fetch him from there.
They shall hand him over to the blood-avenger so that he is put
to death. You shall not pity him but you shall purge Israel of
innocent blood, so that you will prosper. [19:11–13]

279. Do not move a landmark
You shall not move your neighbour's landmark which was fixed
in earlier generations in the territorial portions that will be allotted
to you in the land that the LORD your God is giving you to possess.
[19:14]

280. False witnesses
One witness is insufficient to confirm the committal of any crime
of which a person may be guilty. The matter can only be proved
by the testimony of two or more witnesses. If a man comes forward
to give malicious testimony against another person as a false
witness, the two men who are in dispute shall appear before the
LORD – before the priests and the judges in authority. The judges
shall make thorough enquiries. If the witness is a false witness
and has testified falsely against his kinsman, you shall do to him
as he schemed to have done to his kinsman, so that you may
purge the evil among you: others will hear and be deterred and
will no longer do such evil things among you. You must show
no pity: a life for a life, an eye for an eye, a tooth for a tooth, a
hand for a hand, a foot for a foot. [19:15–21]

281. Setting out for battle:
Do not be afraid for the Lord is with you
When you set out for battle against your enemies, and see their
horses and chariots and forces larger than yours, do not be afraid

of them because the LORD your God is with you – he who brought you up from the land of Egypt. When you come close to do battle, the priest shall come forward and speak to the people: "Hear, O Israel, you are about to engage your enemies in battle. Let not your hearts be faint; do not be afraid, do not panic or quake before them, because the LORD your God goes with you, to fight for you against your enemies to bring you victory." [20:1–4]

282. Those who are excused from battle

The officers shall speak to the people: 'Is there anyone here who has built a new home and has not moved into it? Let him go and return to his house, lest he die in battle so that another man moves in? Is there anyone here who has planted a vineyard and has not partaken of its yield?[1] Let him go and return to his home lest he die in battle so that another man has the benefit of its yield. Is there anyone here who has betrothed a woman but has not taken her to be his wife? Let him go and return home, lest he die in battle so that another man takes her for his wife.[2] The officers shall go on to say: Is there anyone who is afraid and of a tender heart? Let him go and return home, so that the hearts of his kinsmen do not melt as his does.' When the officers have finished speaking to the people, then shall the commanders of the troop lead them from the front. [20:5–9]

283. The offer of peace to the enemy town

When you have approached the town you are engaging in battle, first offer it peace. If it agrees to a peaceful response and surrenders the town to you, let all its inhabitants become your vassals to serve you. But if it does not agree to a peaceful resolution, but would engage you in battle, you shall lay a siege upon it. The

---

[1] Literally: has not profaned it. He could not eat the first three years of the harvest. Only in the fourth year may he enjoy the grapes or wine.
[2] From what follows, these instructions seem to be based on the fear that these men could not focus on the battle because of their fear that death would unfairly deprive them of that which was due to them, leaving those who are alive to benefit from their deaths.

LORD your God will put it into your hands and you shall put every man to the sword; but you shall take as spoil the women, the children, the livestock and everything else in the town – all its spoil. You shall share in the spoils of your enemy which the LORD your God has given to you. So may you behave towards all the far-distant towns which are not of those nations **whom you are about to dispossess.**[1] [20:10–15]

284. Laws of war against the towns in Canaan

In regard to the towns of these peoples which the LORD your God is giving you as your inheritance, you shall not allow a soul to live. You shall proscribe them – the Hittites, the Amorites, the Canaanites, the Perizzites, the Hivites and the Jebusites, as the LORD your God commanded you. **You shall do this** so that they do not lead you to perform all their abhorrent practices which they observe for their gods – thus to sin against the LORD your God.[2] [20:16–18]

285. Do not destroy the trees around a besieged town

When in battle you lay siege against a town for a long time, you shall not destroy its trees by wielding an axe against them; you may eat their fruit, but you shall not cut them down – is the tree of the field deserving to be under your siege? But those trees which do not provide food, you may destroy by cutting them down to construct bulwarks against the town waging war on you until it falls. [20:19–20]

286. An unsolved murder

If a slain body be discovered in a field in the land which the LORD your God is giving you to possess, and the murderer cannot be

---

[1] This certainly indicated that wars of conquest were permitted. Was the freedom to leave the army applicable only to the wars of conquest and not to the obligatory campaigns against the nations of Canaan?

[2] Jewish and Christian believers who find this shocking have argued that, if these towns accepted the offer of peace and agreed to give up idolatrous practices, they could be allowed to live as a tributary people. The evidence from

identified, your elders and judges shall go out and measure the distances from the corpse to the nearest towns. The elders of the town nearest to the corpse shall take a heifer which has never worked nor drawn in a yoke. The elders of that town shall bring the heifer down to a wadi flowing with water which is not ploughed or sown; there in the wadi they shall break the heifer's neck. The priests, the sons of Levi, shall approach **the scene** for the LORD your God has chosen them to minister to him and to bless in the name of the LORD and to rule on every civil and criminal offence. All the elders of the town which was the nearest to the corpse shall wash their hands over the heifer whose neck was broken in the wadi; they shall make this declaration: Our hands have not shed this blood nor have our eyes seen it **done.** Absolve, LORD, your people Israel whom you have redeemed and do not let guilt from innocent blood remain among your people Israel. Let them be absolved of this blood. So shall you remove the guilt of shedding innocent blood from among you – by doing what is right in the sight of the LORD. [21:1–9]

287. Treatment of the captive woman

When you go out to engage in battle with your enemies, and the LORD your God has surrendered them into your hands and you take them away as captives, should you see among them a beautiful woman whom you desire so much that you take her as your wife; you shall bring her to your home. She shall shave off her hair and cut her nails.[1] She shall remove the clothes she wore as a captive; she shall stay in your house and mourn over her father and mother for a full month. After that, you shall go to her and be her husband and she shall be your wife. If, however, you take no delight in her, then you must let her go wherever she wishes. You shall certainly not sell her for money or treat her as mere merchandise, because you have demeaned her.[2]

---

the tale of the Gibeonites in *Joshua* does not support this rationalisation. See *Peoples' Bible – Conquest of Canaan*, p. 21f.

[1] Were these the signs of mourning over her past life?

[2] The call for sensitivity towards the captive woman is quite extraordinary.

288. Treatment of the first-born of an unfavoured wife

If a man has two wives, one loved and one hated,[1] and they have borne him children, both the loved and the hated; and his first-born was from the hated one. It shall be on the day that he allows his sons to inherit his possessions,[2] he shall not make the son of his loved one the first-born in preference to his first-born son – the son of the hated one. He shall acknowledge that the son of the hated one is his first-born by giving him a double portion of all he has, for he is the first fruits of his strength – the right of the first-born is his. [21:10–17]

289. The treatment of the rebellious son

When a man has a rebellious son who refuses to obey his father or his mother, though they chasten him often, he persists in his disobedience, they shall take hold of him and drag him to the town elders where they sit by the gates. They shall say to the town elders, "This, our son, is rebellious; he will not obey us. He lives riotously and is totally debauched." All the men of the town shall stone him to death; so shall you purge the evil from among you. All the Israelites will learn of this and be deterred.[3] [21:18–21]

[1] The black and white situation is interesting. It seems to parallel the story of Jacob and his wives Leah and Rachel. Leah's first-born, Reuben, is deprived of his birthright on the basis that he seduced his father's concubine, and Joseph, Rachel's first-born, receives two portions of the inheritance, as his sons Ephraim and Menasseh both have tribes, while Jacob's other sons only have one tribe. Jacob, therefore, broke this law.

[2] This may indicate that men divided the inheritance while they were still alive and then lived off their sons' estate. Alternatively, it could relate to the time he announces his will.

[3] This seems to be a very savage law. But the right of parents to slay their children which was accepted in ancient law is limited here by the need to bring him to the elders of the town. They might not wish to humiliate themselves by doing so, and the elders might discourage them. The parents cannot take the law into their own hands. The rabbinic Oral Law, in fact, negated capital punishment. The ancient rabbinic sages maintained that the law of the Rebellious Son was never carried out. These sages named as wicked the Sanhedrin which executed one man in seven years. The great Martyr, Rabbi Akiba, said it was wicked if it did this even once during its tenure. This is an indication that the Written Law was in fact subservient to later rulings which were claimed to be the Oral Laws given to Moses and handed down

290. The criminal must be buried on the same day
When a man commits a sin culpable of the death penalty and he is put to death – if he is hanging from a tree, his body shall not remain there throughout the night but shall be buried on the same day, because he who is hanged is accursed by God; you shall not defile the land which the LORD your God gave you as your inheritance.[1] [21:22–23]

291. Restoring lost property
Should you see the ox or sheep of your kinsman going astray do not ignore it; you must return it to your kinsman. If your kinsman does not live near you or if you do not know the owner, you shall take it to your home and keep it until your kinsman comes looking for it; you shall return it to him. You shall do the same for his donkey or a piece of clothing or anything lost by your kinsman, which you have found. You must not turn a blind eye to your kinsman's lost property. [22:1–3]

292. Assisting to lift fallen beasts
Should you see your kinsman's donkey or his ox fallen down on a public path, do not ignore him. You must certainly help him to lift them up. [22:4]

293. Law against transvestism
A woman shall not wear men's clothing nor a man woman's clothing. Whoever does this is abhorrent to the LORD your God. [22:5]

---

through the generations. The method for achieving leniency was the demand that two witnesses not only saw the crime but warned the sinner of the legal consequences; i.e., the punishment to be suffered for committing the capital offence.

[1] It was a disgrace not to be buried immediately and even the criminal is spared exposure to shame. Also, an unburied body could mean that its 'spirit' could not rest.

294. Sparing the mother-bird

Should you find a bird's nest on a path or in any tree or anywhere on the ground with fledglings or eggs, and the mother is sitting over the fledglings or on the eggs, you must not take the mother with the young. You shall let the mother go, though you may take the fledglings for yourself. **Do this** so that you may prosper and live to an old age. [22:6–7]

295. Parapets to house roofs

When you build a new house,[1] you shall make a parapet for your roof, so that you do not bring the guilt of innocent blood on your household, should a person fall off it. [22:8]

296. No mixing of seeds

You shall not sow your vineyard with two kinds of seeds lest the entire yield be proscribed[2] – both the seed which you have sown and the produce of the vineyard. [22:9]

297. No yoking of different beasts together

You shall not plough with an ox and a donkey under the same yoke. [22:10]

298. No mingling of clothing materials

You shall not wear mingled clothing that is a combination of wool and linen.[3] [22:11]

299. Tassels for four-cornered garments.[4]

You shall make tassels for the four corners of the garment with which you cover yourself. [22:12]

---

[1] Houses in Eastern countries had flat roofs which were used for sleeping, eating, etc.

[2] Literally: consecrated, which meant set aside, i.e. not to be used, because it was considered an unnatural practice.

[3] This is a prohibition for which the ancient sages had no explanation, but had to be obeyed because it came from God.

[4] See *Numbers* 15:37–41 for the rationale of this instruction.

300. False charges against a bride

Should a man take a wife and have intercourse with her and hate her, so that he accuse her of shameless behaviour which disgraces her reputation: he says, "I took this woman; when I came to her, I found no signs of her virginity." The father and mother of the girl shall bring proof of her virginity to the Town Elders who sit by the gates. The girl's father shall say to the elders: "I gave my daughter to this man to wife and he hates her, and now he is accusing her of shameless behaviour by saying that he has not found in my daughter the signs of virginity, and yet here is proof of my daughter's virginity." They shall spread the cloth before the Town Elders; the Town Elders shall summon the man and chastise him. They shall fine him a hundred silver shekels and give them to the girl's father because he disgraced the reputation of an Israelite virgin; she shall remain his wife and he will never be able to divorce her.[1] [22:13–19]

301. The guilty bride

But if it was the truth and there was no proof of her virginity, they shall take the girl to the door of her father's house and the townsfolk shall stone her to death because she has acted shamelessly in Israel by playing the harlot in her father's house. So shall you purge the evil from among you.[2] [22:20–21]

302. Adultery of the married or betrothed woman

If a man is found lying with a married woman, both of them shall die – the man that lay with the woman as well as the woman – so shall you purge yourself of the evil in Israel. If the girl was a virgin betrothed to a man, and another man comes upon her in town and lies with her, you shall bring them both to the town gates and stone them to death – the girl because she

---

[1] This seems by modern standards to be unfair on the wife, but in ancient days the situation of a divorce was very difficult.

[2] Modern post-biblical Judaism rejects the execution by capital punishment for any sexual offences.

did not cry out in protest for she was in the town **and could have been heard** and the man because he humbled his fellow's wife.[1] Thus you shall purge the evil from among you. However, should a man find a betrothed girl in the field and rape her, then only the man must die; do nothing to the girl: she has not committed a sin worthy of death. Her situation was no different than that of a man against another who stood up to kill him. **He is only the victim.** This case is exactly the same **for the girl.** For he had come across her in the fields; the betrothed girl had cried out but there was none to help her. [22:22–27]

303. The rape or seduction[2] of a virgin

If a man finds an unbetrothed virgin, grasps her to himself and lies with her and they are found – the man who has lain with her shall give her father fifty silver shekels. She shall become his wife because he has humbled her; he may never divorce her.[3] [22:28]

304. Marriage with a stepmother forbidden

No man shall marry his father's wife **after his father's death** to claim that which his father possessed.[4] [23:1]

305. The man with crushed testes

No man whose testes are crushed or whose member is cut off shall enter into the congregation of the LORD.[5] [23:2]

---

[1] A betrothed woman was legally considered to be a wife.

[2] The Hebrew does not make it clear whether she was forced.

[3] As uncivilised as this law may appear to the modern age, it did protect the woman's status. Consider today the domestic killings of daughters in some Muslim countries because they have disgraced the family through their seduction, even rape.

[4] Literally: shall not uncover his father's garment.

[5] This would mean that he could not marry an Israelite woman. Is this because he could not father children and satisfy his wife?

306. The *mamzer*[1] shall not enter into the congregation of the Lord

The *mamzer* shall not enter into the congregation of the LORD even up to the tenth generation – none of his children shall enter into the congregation of the LORD. [23:3]

307. Ammonites and Moabites

No Ammonite or Moabite shall enter into the congregation of the LORD[2] even to the tenth generation – none of their children may enter into the congregation of the LORD forever. This is because they gave you no bread or water on your journey when you came out of the land of Egypt; also because they employed Balaam ben Beor from Pethor of Aram-naharaim to curse you. But the LORD your God did not want to listen to Balaam. The LORD your God turned the curse into a blessing for you because the LORD your God loves you. Do not seek their welfare or prosperity so long as you live. [23:4–7]

308. Do not abhor an Edomite

You shall not abhor an Edomite, for he is your kinsman. You shall not abhor an Egyptian, because you were a stranger in his land. The children of the third generation that are born to them may enter the congregation of the LORD.[3] [23:8–9]

[1] *Mamzer* is usually translated as 'bastard' which refers to a child born to a single woman. A *mamzer* is a child of an adulterous or incestuous relationship. The child of an unmarried woman suffers no disadvantages in Jewish law. The origin of this 'offensive' law is the desire to deter such relationships and also the belief that the individual lived on in one's children and, therefore, the punishment passed through the generations. A *mamzer*, however, could, marry a foreigner or an alien. Progressive Judaism has nullified this category, but Orthodox Judaism has not, though the more enlightened are always seeking loopholes to avoid the law's severity.

[2] The impact was that no Moabite or Ammonite who was a resident alien in Israel could marry into the Jewish people and participate in their rituals. Ruth, the Moabite woman who married Boaz, the ancestor of King David, was an anomaly, which led the ancient rabbinic sages to say that this prohibition only applied to the males of these nations.

[3] This would mean that the Edomite who was a resident alien could marry into the Israelite community, but only the grandchild of an Egyptian living in Israel would be permitted to do so.

309. Ritual cleanness in the camps of war

When you go out as a company against your enemy, you shall avoid any contamination. If there be among you someone who is rendered ritually unclean because of a nocturnal emission, he shall leave the camp and not return to it; towards evening, he shall wash himself in water and, when the sun sets, he may come within the camp. There shall be for you an area outside the camp where you may relieve yourself. Among your weapons, you shall have a pike, so that when you squat to relieve yourself, you may dig with it and then cover up your excrement. **Do this** because the LORD your God walks about in your camp to deliver you by surrendering your enemies to you; therefore, the camp must be holy, so that he sees no unclean thing among you and turns back from you. [23:10–15]

310. Fugitive slaves

Do not hand over to his master a slave who has fled to you from his master. He shall live with you, among you in any place he chooses within your towns because it is to his liking. You shall not oppress him.[1] [23:16–17]

311. Cult prostitution

No Israelite woman shall be a cult prostitute nor shall any Israelite man be a cult prostitute. [23:18]

312. Desecrated earnings

You shall not bring the fee of a whore or the wages of a male prostitute[2] into the house of the LORD your God to fulfil any vow because both of these **occupations** are abhorrent to the LORD your God. [23:19]

---

[1] A quite extraordinary law, when one considers the previous instructions to return lost property. A distinction is made in regard to human property. The law assumes that the run-away slave was fleeing from persecution, and, therefore, could not be handed back. Even if the law was instituted as late as the 5th century BCE, it is an advance on the slave laws even of the 18th century.
[2] Literally: dog.

313. Interest forbidden on loans to kinsmen
You shall not charge interest to your kinsman, whether in money or food or in anything else that can be paid as interest, but you may charge interest to a foreigner but not to your kinsman – you shall not charge interest. **Do this** so that the LORD your God may bless you in all your enterprises in the land which you are going to possess. [23:20–21]

314. Fulfilment of vows
When you make a vow to the LORD your God, you shall not delay in fulfilling it, for the LORD your God will certainly require it from you, and you would have incurred guilt **if you did not pay it.** If you refrain from making a vow, it will not involve you in any guilt, but that which has left your lips, you must observe, do and fulfil just as you have vowed to the LORD your God – a voluntary offering which you have promised with your mouth. [23:22–24]

315. Eating your neighbour's produce
When you enter your neighbour's vineyard you may eat as many grapes as you please until you are satisfied, but you shall not put any into your vessel. When you enter your neighbour's field of standing grain, you may pluck the ears with your hand, but you shall not put a sickle to your neighbour's grain.[1] [23:25–26]

316. Divorce laws
If a man marries a woman and possesses her and she does not please him because he discovers something shameless about her, he may write her a bill of divorcement, give it to her and send her out of his house. When she leaves his home she may become another man's wife. If her second husband dislikes her, writes her a bill of divorcement, gives it to her and sends her off, or if

---

[1] This is an extraordinary liberty. The rabbinic sages thought it only applied to day labourers. Were there such a licence to all neighbours, the vineyards and fields could be picked clean.

he dies, her first husband who sent her off may not marry her
again after she has been forbidden to him because such behaviour
would be abhorrent before the LORD. Let not the land which
the LORD your God is giving you as an inheritance be full of
sin. [24:1–4]

317. Obligations to a new wife
A man who marries a new wife shall not enter the army nor shall
he be given any business responsibility. He shall be unoccupied for
one year. He shall be free of obligations for one year to give
happiness to the woman he has married. [24:5]

318. The tools of trade cannot be taken as security
No man shall take the lower or upper millstone as security, for
to do this is the same as taking his life as security, **for a man's
livelihood is his life.** [24:6]

319. Kidnapping
If a man steals the life of his kinsman from among the Israelites
and treats him as a slave or sells him that thief shall be executed.
You shall purge out evil from among you. [24:27]

320. Observance of laws regarding virulent skin diseases
Be very much on guard against virulent skin diseases to observe
to the letter what the Levitical priests instruct you to do. Do that
which I commanded them. Recall what the LORD your God did
to Miriam on the way when you left Egypt. [24:8–9]

321. The redemption of security
When you make any kind of loan to your neighbour, you may
not enter into his house to collect your security. You shall stand
outside and the man to whom you have given a loan shall bring
out the security to you. If he is a poor man, **and he has given
you his cloak as security**, you shall not go to sleep in possession
of that security, but you shall restore it to him when the sun
sets so that he may sleep in his cloak and bless you **for your**

Deuteronomy

consideration; and it shall be to your credit before the Lord your God. [24:10–13]

322. Treatment of day labourers
You shall not exploit a hired labourer who is poor and destitute, whether he is of your kinsmen or the aliens that have settled in the towns of your country. Daily you shall pay him his wages. The sun shall not set before you do this because he is poor and sets his heart upon it **for without it he can buy no food. Do this** so that he does not cry out against you to the Lord, and it be accounted as sinfulness on your part. [24:14–15]

323. A person dies for their own sins
Fathers shall not be put to death for **the guilt of** the children, nor shall children be put to death for **the guilt of** the fathers. Every person shall be put to death only for his own sin. [24:16]

324. Treatment of the vulnerable
You shall not pervert justice for the stranger, or the fatherless, or take a widow's cloak as security. Remember that you were slaves in Egypt, and the Lord your God redeemed you from there. It is for this reason that I command you to behave in this way. [24:17–18]

325. Food for the vulnerable
When you reap your harvest and have overlooked a sheaf in the field, you shall not return to retrieve it; it shall be for the stranger, for the fatherless and for the widow, so that in response the Lord your God may bless you in all your undertakings. When you shake your olive tree **to bring down the olives,** you shall not do it again and again. That will be for the stranger, for the fatherless and for the widow. When you gather the grapes of your vineyard, you shall not pick it over again **to find the grapes you overlooked.** They shall be for the stranger, the fatherless and the widow, for you shall remember that you were a slave in the land of Egypt. It is for this reason I command you to behave in this way. [24:19–22]

326. The punishment of forty stripes

When there is a conflict between people and they go to the court, the judges are to render their judgement – they shall confirm those who are righteous and denounce those who are wicked. If the wicked man is culpable of being lashed, the judge shall make him lie down and be struck in his presence, the number being commensurate with his wrongdoing. But he shall not exceed forty stripes, for if it be more and be exceeded by many more stripes, your kinsmen will become utterly contemptuous of you.[1] [25:1–3]

327. Do not muzzle the ox

You shall not muzzle an ox when it is threshing. [25:4]

328. The Levirate[2] marriage. [Hebrew: *Yibum*]

When two brothers are living together[3] and one dies without a son, the widow shall not go and marry someone outside the family. Her husband's brother shall have intercourse with her and take her as a wife, and perform the duty of the brother's husband with her. Her first-born shall inherit the name of his dead brother **and his property**, so that his name should not disappear from Israel. [25:5–6]

329. Refusing to perform the duty of the Levirate marriage

If a man does not want to take his sister-in-law, then she shall go up to the gate where the elders sit and say: My husband's brother refuses to establish a name for his brother in Israel; he will not perform with me the duty of a Levir. The Town Elders will summon him to persuade him. But if he stands unmoved and says: I do not want to take her, his sister-in-law will approach him, strip the sandal from his foot, spit in his face and declare: So shall be done to the man who will not build up his brother's

---

[1] The excess of lashes would lead to such cries of pain, the begging for their end, that the sinner will lose his human dignity.

[2] *Levir* – Latin for husband's brother.

[3] The rabbinic sages understood this to mean that they were contemporaries.

house. He shall be known in Israel as: The house of him with the stripped sandal.[1] [25:7–10]

330. Punishment for seizing a man's genitals

If two men are in a fight, and the wife of one of them intervenes to save her husband from the attack of the one who is striking him, puts out her hand and takes hold of his genitals, you shall cut off her hand; show no pity![2] [25:11–12]

331. Crooked weights and measures

You shall not carry in your bag alternative weights, larger and smaller, using them **to charge more and pay less;** nor shall you have in your house alternative measures, larger and smaller, **using them to charge more for what you are selling and to pay less for what you are buying.** You shall have totally honest weights and you shall have totally honest measures, so that you may live long on the land which the LORD your God is giving to you. For all who behave in such a manner, all those who behave wickedly, are abhorrent to the LORD your God. [25:13–16]

332. Remember Amalek, to wipe him out

Remember what Amalek did to you on the way when you left Egypt, how he fell on you on the road, striking the feeble ones lagging behind, when you were tired and weary – because he had no fear of God. When the LORD your God gives you rest from all the enemies round about you in the land which the LORD your God is giving to you to possess – you shall blot out the memory of Amalek from under the skies; you shall not forget! [25:16–19]

---

[1] This ceremony is called *'Halitzah'*, literally: 'the stripping'. The ancient sages abolished the Levirate marriage, but still required the enactment of the procedure which turned out to be unfair on the brother-in-law who has to undergo the embarrassment, but more so on the woman who cannot remarry unless her brother-in-law is prepared to go through with it. Unscrupulous men have been known to blackmail their sisters-in-law before doing it. Progressive Judaism has abolished the practice.
[2] This is the only case of mutilation as a punishment in the Laws of Moses. The rabbinic sages converted this into a heavy fine.

333. The proclamation of the Israelites

When you enter the land which the LORD your God is giving you as your inheritance, and you possess and settle in it, you shall take the first yield of the first fruit of the ground, which you shall harvest from the land that the LORD your God is giving you. You shall place them in a basket and go to the place which the LORD your God has designated to establish his name. You shall go to the priest in charge at that time and speak in this fashion: "I solemnly proclaim on this day to the LORD your God that I have come into the land which the LORD vowed to our fathers to give us." The priest shall take the basket from you and place it before the LORD your God. You shall then profess before the LORD your God, "My father was a fugitive Aramean. He went down to Egypt in very few numbers and settled there; he became a great nation – powerful because of its vast numbers. The Egyptians made our lives a misery and oppressed us; they imposed hard labour on us. We cried out to the LORD, the God of our fathers. The LORD heard our voices. He saw our affliction, our labour and our oppression. The LORD took us out of Egypt with a mighty hand and an outstretched arm and with an awesome power with signs and wonders. He brought us to this place and gave us this land, a land flowing with milk and honey. And now – see, I have brought the first yield of the fruit of the ground which you, LORD have given me." You shall put it down before the LORD your God and bow down low before the LORD your God. You shall rejoice in all the good bounty that the LORD your God has given you and your family – you, the Levite and the alien who resides among you. [26:1–11]

334. The tithing for the poor in the third year

When you have set aside a full tenth of all your yield in the third year – the year of the tithe – and you have given it to the Levite, the alien, to the fatherless and the widow, so that they may eat and be satisfied within your towns, you shall declare before the LORD your God: "I have removed the consecrated produce from my house and have given it to the Levite, to the alien, to the fatherless and to the widow just as you have commanded me. I have not transgressed any of your commandments nor have I overlooked them. I have not eaten any of it while in mourning, nor have I removed any of it while I was ritually unclean, nor have I given any part of it to the dead,[1] but I have obeyed the voice of the LORD my God and done just as you have commanded me. Look down now from your holy dwelling, from heaven, and bless your people Israel and the soil you have given us, as you swore to our fathers – a land flowing with milk and honey. [26:12–15]

335. Rules following the crossing of the Jordan

Moses and the elders of Israel commanded the people: Keep all the commandments which I now command you: when you cross the Jordan into the land which the LORD your God is giving to you, you shall set up large rocks; coat them with plaster and write on them all the words of this Torah. **Do this** when you have crossed over so that you may enter the land which the LORD your God is giving you – a land flowing with milk and honey – as the LORD, the God of your fathers, promised you. On crossing the Jordan, after setting up these rocks coated with plaster which I command you this day on Mount Ebal, you shall build an altar to the LORD your God, an altar of stones. Do not use any iron tool on them; you shall construct an altar to the LORD your God of unhewn stones; you shall offer whole-offerings on it to the LORD your God. You shall sacrifice peace offerings and eat **of them** there; you shall rejoice before the LORD your God. On the rocks you shall write the words of this Torah; engrave them carefully **so that they may be understood.** [27:1–8]

Moses and the Levitical priests spoke to all the Israelites: Hush and hear, O Israel! On this day you have become the people of the LORD your God. Therefore, you shall hear the voice of the

---

[1] Does this refer to the custom as practised in Egypt in placing food for the dead in the tomb, or is it for a sacrifice to propitiate the dead, or, according to rabbinic tradition, for the provision of a coffin, or a meal in the house of mourning?

LORD your God and do all his commandments and laws which I command you on this day. Moses charged the people on that same day: When you have crossed over the Jordan, these shall stand on Mount Gerizim to bless the people,[1] **the elders of the tribes of** Simeon, Levi and Judah, Issachar, Joseph and Benjamin. These shall stand on Mount Ebal for the damnations: Reuben, Gad and Asher, Zebulun, Dan and Naphtali. [27:9–13]

336. Damnations[2] on those who commit grievous offences

The Levites shall say to all the Israelites, declaring in a loud voice:

- Damned be the man that makes a sculpted or molten image, offensive to the LORD – the work of an artisan – which is set up secretly. All the people shall respond: So be it.[3]
- Damned be the one who insults his father or mother. And all the people shall say: So be it.
- Damned be he who moves his neighbour's land mark **to steal his property.** All the people shall say: So be it.
- Damned be the man who leads the blind astray. All the people shall say: So be it.
- Damned be he who deprives the stranger, the fatherless, the widow of her rights. All the people shall say: So be it.
- Damned be he who lies with his stepmother, **even after his father's death,** for he has removed his father's bed cover[4] , **and has desecrated his memory.** All the people shall say: So be it.
- Damned be he who has sexual intercourse with any beast. All the people shall say: So be it.
- Damned be he who lies with his sister, his stepsister of his father or mother. All the people shall say: So be it.

---

[1] The blessings do not follow in the same pattern as do the damnations.
General blessings for Israel's obedience are in Moses's discourse to be found in *Moses, Prophet of God*, chapter 28.
[2] The common translation of *arure* is cursed or accursed. I preferred 'damned' because it comes closer to its desired effect as a deterrent: to be damned is both to be assigned to eternal perdition and to be condemned in this world.
[3] The Hebrew is 'Amen'.
[4] A son cannot treat his stepmother as his inheritance to do with as he pleases.

- Damned be he who lies with his mother-in-law. All the people shall say: So be it.
- Damned be he who strikes down his fellow countryman in secret. All the people shall say: So be it.
- Damned be he that takes a bribe to shed innocent blood.[1] All the people shall say: So be it.
- Damned be he that does not establish the words of the Torah to observe them. All the people shall say: So be it. [27:14–26]

Summary
These are the words of the covenant which the LORD commanded Moses to make with the Israelites in the land of Moab, beside the covenant which he made with them in Horeb. [28:69]

337. The reading of the Torah
Moses wrote this Torah and gave it to the priests, sons of the Levites, who carried the Ark of the Covenant of the LORD, and to all the elders of Israel. Moses commanded them: Every seventh year, in the year of release,[2] during the Festival of Booths, when all Israel is to appear before the LORD at the place he will designate, you shall read this Torah in the hearing of all the Israelites. Assemble the people – the men, women, children and the aliens living in your towns – so that they may hear and so learn to revere the LORD your God to observe and perform all the words of this Torah – and that their children also who have not known may hear and learn to revere the LORD your God, so long as you live in the land that you are about to cross the Jordan to possess. [31:9–13]

---

[1] It is not clear from the text whether the damned is he who accepts payment to kill an innocent person or takes a bribe to have an innocent person condemned to death or both. I am indebted to the *New Revised Standard Version* for this translation which allows both possibilities.
[2] When the land is given a sabbatical rest.

Appendix to Exodus

Chapter 35:4 to the conclusion of Exodus *is a description of the implementation of the* LORD*'s commands to Moses regarding the building and manufacture of all the needs of the priestly office to serve him. The place where the corresponding instructions can be found are in brackets at the end of the passages. Where the material is virtually identical, only the references are given*

35:4–9 · Voluntary donations for the Sanctuary

Moses spoke to the whole community of Israel: This is what the LORD has commanded: Offer from among yourselves gifts for the LORD; each as his heart prompts him, let him bring it as a gift to the LORD: gold, silver and copper; blue, purple and crimson yarns; fine linen and goat's hair, ram's skins dyed red, fine leather and acacia wood; oil for the lamp, spices for the anointing oil and for the fragrant incense; onyx and other gems to be set in the and Breastpiece.

35:10–19 · The work to be done

Let every skilled person among you come forward to make all that the LORD has commanded: The Tabernacle and its Tent, its covering, its loops, it sheets, its bars, its posts and sockets; the Ark, its staves, the plate-cover of the Ark and the screening curtain; the table, its staves and utensils and the showbread; the Menorah which will give light, its utensils, its lamps and oil for burning; the altar for incense, its staves, the anointing oil and the fragrant incense, and the screen for the entrance to the Tabernacle; the altar of burnt offering with its copper grating, its staves and all its utensils; the laver and its stand; the curtains of the court of the Tabernacle, their posts and sockets and the screen for the court entrance, the pegs for the Tabernacle, the pegs for the Court and their cords; the elaborately designed vestments for Aaron the priest and his sons' vestments for their priestly office.

35:20–29 · The response of the community

The whole community took their leave of Moses. Every man who was inspired and everyone of a generous spirit brought gifts to the LORD for the building of the Tent of Meeting and all that was required for its servicing and for the sacred vestments. They came, both men and women, all who had a generous heart. They brought brooches, earrings, signet rings and necklaces – all jewels made of gold – all lifting up their offerings of gold before the LORD. Everyone who possessed blue, purple and scarlet yarns, fine linen, goats' hair, rams' skins dyed red and fine leather, brought them; everyone who would make gifts of silver and copper brought them as contributions to the LORD; everyone who possessed acacia wood for any work of the **divine** service brought it. All the talented women spun with their hands and brought that which they had spun: the blue and purple and scarlet – the fine linen. And all the skilful women who were inspired spun the goats' hair. The chieftains bought lapus lazuli and other gems for setting, for the and Breastpiece; also spices and oil, for lighting **the Menorah** and for anointing and for fragrant incense. So did the Israelites – every man and woman – whose hearts were moved to bring anything as a gift to the LORD for the work which the LORD had commanded to be made, through Moses.

35:30–36 · **The appointment of Bezalel and Oholiab**, see 31:1–6

36:1–7 · **The people bring too much**
Bezalel and Oholiab and every talented person to whom the LORD has granted the skill and knowledge to execute the work connected with the service of the Sanctuary shall carry out all that the LORD has commanded. **Therefore,** Moses summoned Bezalel and Oholiab and every person with skills to whom the LORD had imparted talents – everyone whose heart was moved to volunteer to do the work. They took from before Moses all the gifts, which the Israelites had brought for the building of the Sanctuary they kept bringing their donations every morning. All the skilled people involved in the building of the Sanctuary, left what they were doing to speak to Moses, "The people are bringing much more than is needed for the work that the LORD has commanded to be made." Moses gave

an order which was relayed through the camp by proclamation: No person, man or woman should make any more efforts to bring gifts for the Sanctuary. So the people stopped bringing, for what they had already brought was more than enough to do all the work.

36:8–19 · Making of the hangings for the Tabernacle, see 26:1–11; 14

36: 20–34 · Building of the framework for the Tabernacle, see 26:15–20

36:35–38 · Making of the curtain screen, see 26:31–34; 36–38

37:1–9 · Making of the Ark, see 25:10–15; 17–20

37:10–16 · Making of the Table, see 25:23–29

37:17–24 · Making of the Menorah, see 25:31–39

37:25–28 · Making the Incense altar, see 30:1–5

37:29 · Preparing the anointing oil and incense spices
He, Bezalel, made the sacred anointing oil and the pure incense of fragrant spices according to the art of the perfumer.

38:1–7 · Making the burnt-offering altar, see 27:1–8

38:8 · Making the Laver
He, **Bezalel**, out of the mirrors of the women who waited to render service at the gateway to the Tent of Meeting, made a copper laver with a copper stand,[1] see 30:18–21

38:9–20 · Building the Court of the Tabernacle, see 27:9–19

38:21–31 · Amounts of metals used
These are the records of the Tabernacle – the Tabernacle of Testimony, which was audited by order of Moses for the Levitical

---

[1] From the Hebrew text, the role of the women is obscure.

service under the supervision of Ithamar ben Aaron the priest. Bezalel ben Uri ben Hur of the tribe of Judah made all that the LORD commanded Moses. Assisting him was Oholiab ben Ahisamach of the tribe of Dan, an engraver, an ingenious craftsman, an embroiderer in blue, purple and scarlet yarns and fine linen. The gold that was used in all the works of the Sanctuary, the gold brought as gifts, amounted to 29 talents[1] and 730 shekels according to the standard set by the Sanctuary. The silver received from the community added up to a 100 talents and 1,175 shekels according to the standard set by the Sanctuary: it was a beka per head – one half shekel according to the standard set by the Sanctuary – from all those men twenty years old and upward who were counted; they were 603,550 men.[2] The 100 talents of silver were for the casting of the sockets of the Sanctuary and the curtain screen; 100 sockets to the 100 talents – a talent per socket. Of the 1,775 shekels, he made hooks for the posts, overlay for their tops and the bands around them. The gifts of copper amounted to 70 talents and 2,400 shekels. With them he made the sockets for the gateway to the Tent of Meeting, the copper altar and its grating and all the altar's utensils; also the sockets of the court round about and the gateway to the court; all the pegs of the Tabernacle and all the pegs of the court around and about.

39:1 · Making the sacral vestments

From the blue, purple and scarlet yarns, they made the service vestments for officiating in the Sanctuary. They made all the sacral vestments for Aaron as the LORD had instructed Moses.

39:2, 4–7 · Making the Ephod, see 28:6–12
39:3 · They hammered out sheets of gold and cut threads to be

---

[1] Josephus writes that a talent weighed 100 pounds.
[2] The silver collected was not the voluntary offering but the poll tax referred to in *Exodus* 30:11–16.

worked into the designs among the blue, purple and scarlet yarns
and fine linen.

39:8–21 · Making the Breastpiece, see 28:15–28
39:22–26 · Making the robe of the Ephod, see 28:31–34
39:27–29 · Making the tunics and head-dress, see 28:39–42
39:30–31 · Making the gold medallion for the head-dress, see
28:36–37

39:32–43 · The work is completed
So was completed all the work of the Tabernacle of the Tent of
Meeting. The Israelites did as the LORD had instructed Moses. So
did they do. They then brought the Tabernacle to Moses, the
structural parts of the Tent and its furnishings: its clasps, its
frames, its bars, its posts and its sockets; the covering of rams'
skins dyed red and the covering of fire leathers and the curtain
for the screen; the Ark of the Testimony and its staves and the
plate cover **of the Ark**; the table and all its utensils and the
showbread, the pure Menorah and its lamps – lamps in proper
order – and all its utensils and the oil for the light; the golden
altar, the anointing oil and the fragrant incense and the screen
for the entrance to the Tent; the copper altar and its copper
grating, its poles and all its utensils, the laver and its stand, the
curtains of the court **of the Tabernacle**, their posts and sockets
and the screen for the court gateway, their cords and pegs and
all the utensils for the service of the Tabernacle, for the Tent of
Meeting; the elaborately designed vestments for sacral services,
the sacred vestments for Aaron the priest and his sons' vestments
for the priestly office – just as the LORD had instructed Moses, so
had the Israelites done all the work. Moses saw that they had
performed all the work just as the LORD had instructed **Moses**.
Moses blessed **and congratulated them.**[1]

---

[1] Jewish tradition finds this blessing in Psalm 90: *A prayer of Moses*, which
includes: "Establish the work of our hands upon. Yea, establish the work of our
hands." [v.17]

40:1–19 · Instructions regarding the erection of the Sanctuary
The LORD instructed Moses: On the first day of the first month,[1]
you will erect the Tabernacle of the Tent of Meeting. In it you
will put the Ark of Testimony; you will screen off the Ark by the
curtain; bring in the table and place in order the things that go
on it; bring in the Menorah and kindle its lamps. Place the golden
altar for incense in front of the Ark of Testimony. Then put up
the screen for the gateway to the Tabernacle. Place the altar for
the burnt offering before the gateway of the Tabernacle of the
Tent of Meeting. Place the laver between the Tent of Meeting and
the altar and put water into it. Set up the court round about and
put in place the screen for the gateway to the court. Take the
anointing oil, anoint the Tabernacle and all that is in it – sanctify
it and all its furnishings and it will be holy. Anoint the altar of
burnt offerings and all its utensils – sanctify the altar and the
altar will become most holy. Anoint the laver and its stand to
sanctify it. Then bring Aaron and his sons to the gateway of the
Tent of Meeting and wash them with water. Dress Aaron in the
holy vestments; anoint him and sanctify him that he may serve
me in the priestly office. Bring his sons and dress them in tunics
– anoint them as you anointed their father that they may serve
me in the priestly office. Their anointing shall entitle them to an
eternal priesthood throughout their generations. So did Moses, in
all that the LORD instructed Moses, so did he do.

40:17–33 · The erection of the Sanctuary
So, in the first month in the second year – on the first day of
that month – the Tabernacle was established. Moses erected the
Tabernacle and laid its sockets, set up its frames, put up its bars
and erected its posts. He spread the Tent over the Tabernacle,
placing the covering of the Tent on top of it as the LORD had
instructed Moses. He took and placed the Testimonial – **the two**

[1] Later in this passage, we are told that this is at the beginning of the second
year after the Exodus, which is quite an extraordinary achievement for so short
a period of time.

tablets of stone – in the Ark; he fixed the staves to the Ark and placed the plate covering[1] on top of the Ark. He carried the Ark into the Tabernacle and set up the screen of curtain and screened off the Ark of Testimony, as the LORD had instructed Moses. He put the table in the Tent of Meeting on the north side of the Tabernacle outside the curtain-screen. He placed the bread in its proper place on it before the LORD, as the LORD had instructed Moses. He placed the Menorah in the Tent of Meeting opposite the table, on the south side of the Tabernacle; he kindled the lamps before the LORD, as the LORD had instructed Moses. He placed the golden altar in the Tent of Meeting in front of the screen and burnt on it an incense of fragrant spices, as the LORD had commanded Moses. He put up the screen of the entrance to the Tabernacle. He erected the altar of burnt offering at the entrance of the Tabernacle of the Tent of Meeting. He offered upon it the burnt offering and the meal offering, as the LORD had instructed Moses.[2] He placed the laver between the Tent of Meeting and the altar and put water into it for washing. Moses and Aaron and his sons would wash their hands and feet from it: When they went into the Tent of Meeting and when they approached the altar, they washed, as the LORD had instructed Moses. He erected the court around the Tabernacle and the altar and put up the screen for the gateway of the court. Moses finished the work.

---

[1] I remind the reader that the Ark's plate covering was made of gold, with two cherubim coming out of it. Between the wings of the cherubim, the LORD rendered judgement. For this reason it was called the Mercy-seat.

[2] It is significant that Moses is performing the priestly tasks. The Torah appears to be indicating that Moses is God's servant *par excellence*, a man, the model of a man close to God who is never to appear again, but that the practical tasks of priestly service and government are to go to Aaron and his sons, rather than to Moses's progeny. The mystery is that in the book of *Judges* we are informed that Moses's grandson becomes an idolatrous priest to the tribe of Dan.

Appendix to Leviticus

EXHORTATION AND ADMONITION · Chapter 26

Rewards for obedience

If you follow my laws and keep my commandments to do them,
Then will I provide the rain due in their seasons;
The land will yield generous crops:
The trees of the orchards will yield their fruit.

You will have so much threshing to do so that
By the time of its completion it will be time
To cut the vines **for their grapes**;
By the time the vintage has been completed,
It will be time to sow again.

You shall eat your food until you are fully satisfied
And you shall live securely in your land.
I will grant peace to the land.
When you lie down, none shall give you cause for anxiety.

I will put an end to wild beasts in the land
Nor shall the sword of war pass through your land.
You shall pursue your enemies
And they shall fall before your swords. Five of you will pursue a
    hundred
And a hundred of you shall pursue ten thousand.
Your enemies will be put to the sword before you.

I will show you favour and make you fruitful
And cause you to increase and fulfil my covenant with you.
You shall eat from what you have stored a long time ago.
You shall bring out the old **before the new**
Because your harvests are so abundant.

I will set my abiding presence in your midst.
I will not reject you.
I will walk among you.

Appendix to Leviticus

I will be your God and you will be my people.
I am the Lord your God
Who brought you out of the land of Egypt
So that you should not be slaves.
I have broken the bars of your yoke to make you stand tall.

The wages of disobedience

But if you will not listen to me and will not observe
All these commandments;
If you reject my laws and despise my decrees so that you
Do not obey all my commandments but break my covenant,

I will do this to you in turn:
I will overwhelm you with chaos – consumption and fever
Will cause your eyes to fail and your souls to pine away.
You shall sow your seed in vain,
For your enemies will eat of its harvest.

I will set my face against you and
Your enemies shall strike you down.
They that hate you shall rule over you;
In your anxiety you shall flee when no one is pursuing you.

And if, after these terrors, you still do not listen to me,
I will punish you more – sevenfold – for your sins.
I will bring down your arrogance of power.
I will turn your sky to iron – **no rain will come through** –
Your earth to copper, **so that nothing will grow out of it.**
You shall waste your energy for nothing,
For your land shall not yield her harvest
Nor will the trees of the land yield their fruit.

And if you still do not follow me and do not listen to me,
I will punish you with sevenfold more diseases
To match your sins.
I will send wild beasts against you
Who will ravage your children and destroy your cattle
And decimate you; your roads will be desolate.

If this does not make you change your ways to return to me,
But you continue to take opposite paths from me,
Then I will oppose you; I will strike you down, yes I will,
Seven times more for your sins.

I will bring the sword of war against you,
Shall exact retribution for your breaking the covenant.
You will huddle together in your towns,
But I will spread disease among you.
You shall be handed over to your enemy.

I will deprive you of flour for bread;
So that ten women will only need one oven
To bake bread for their families.
There will be so little bread
That it will be distributed in measured weights.
While you may eat, it will not satisfy your hunger.

And if, in spite of this, you will not listen to me
But still persist in your contrariness,
I will turn against you with unbridled fury.
I will punish you sevenfold for your sins.

You shall be compelled to eat the flesh of your sons,
Even the flesh of your daughters.
I will destroy your **altars on the** high places
And cut down your images for the sun-god,
And cast your corpses on the shattered ruins of your idols.

By my life, I will detest you.
I will make your cities into a wasteland
And make your sanctuaries desolate.
I will ignore **your petitions which you send up with**
The pleasing fragrance of your incense **offerings.**

I will make the land desolate; your enemies who move in
Will be astonished by the scale of it.
I will scatter you among the nations **of the earth**.
I will draw out the sword of war against you;

Your land shall be desolate and your cities shall be ruins.
Then the land will enjoy its sabbatical years
For as long as it is a desolation while
You are living **in exile** in the land of your enemies.
Then shall the land be able to rest and have
The benefits of her sabbatical years.
For as long as it is in ruins it shall have the rest,
The rest you did not give her during the sabbatical years,
As I commanded you to do, when you were living there.

To the survivors among you in enemy-land,
I will send anxious hearts;
The sound of a driven leaf will **appear to** chase them,
They shall flee as one runs away from a threatening sword
Though no one is pursuing them.
In their panic, they shall fall down **from fatigue**
Even when no one is pursuing them.
They shall stumble over each other.
You shall not have the strength to stand
In the face of your enemies.
You shall perish among the nations
And the land of your exile will eat you up.
The survivors will pine away because of their iniquity
In the lands of their enemies.
Because of the iniquities of their fathers ,
They will sigh mournfully just as they did.

God's forgiveness

They shall confess their iniquity
And the iniquity of their fathers
In their transgressions against me;
And also that they rebelled against me

So I turned against them
To bring them into the land of their enemies;
But, if their uncircumcised hearts would be humbled and
They would accept that they had been punished for their sins,

I will remember my covenant with Jacob;
Also my covenant with Isaac and
Also my covenant with Abraham will I remember.
And I will remember the land.

The Land will be forsaken of them.
She shall enjoy her Sabbaths
While she lies desolate without them.
They shall accept the punishment for their iniquity
Because they know they rejected my decrees,
And their very lives hated my laws

For all that, when they are in the land of their enemies
I will not reject them, nor hate them
To destroy them completely and to break
My covenant with them for I am the LORD their God.
For their sakes I will remember
The covenant of their founders
Whom I brought up out of the land of Egypt
In view of the nations to be their God:
I am the LORD.

These are the laws and decrees and instructions, which the LORD established between himself and the Israelites on Mount Sinai through the hand of Moses. [26:14–46]

Translator's note: Logically, as an oration of Moses, this should appear in Moses, Man of God. *However, the argument for keeping the entire book of* Leviticus *as an integral work made it sensible to place it in the appendix of* Leviticus.

Appendix to Numbers

Census of Levitical clans· [4:34–49]

Moses, Aaron and the chieftains of the community listed the Kohathites by the clans of their ancestral houses; from the age of thirty years up to fifty, all who were to do service in carrying out work in the Tent of Meeting. Those that were listed according to their clans were 2,750. This was the enrolment of the Kohathite clans – all who served in the Tent of Meeting, whom Moses and Aaron recorded at the command of the LORD through Moses. Those that were listed of the Gershonites by their clans of their ancestral houses, from the age of thirty years up to fifty, all who were to do service in carrying out work in the Tent of Meeting. Those that were listed by the clans of their ancestral houses were 2,630. This was the enrolment according to their clans of the Gershonites – all who served in the Tent of Meeting whom Moses and Aaron recorded at the command of the LORD through Moses. Those that were listed of the Merarites by the clans of their ancestral houses, from the age of thirty years up to fifty, all who were to do service in carrying out work in the Tent of Meeting. Those that were listed according to their clans were 3,200. This was the enrolment according to their clans of the Merarites whom Moses and Aaron recorded at the command of the LORD through Moses. All those that were listed of the Levites whom Moses and Aaron and the chieftains of Israel recorded by the clans of their ancestral houses, from the age of thirty years up to fifty, all who were to do service and porterage in the Tent of Meeting – those that were recorded amounted to 8,580. All were given their duties in their service and porterage at the LORD's command through Moses. Each one was recorded as the LORD had instructed Moses.